THE
INTERCESSOR'S
DEVOTIONAL

OTHER BOOKS BY JENNIFER LECLAIRE

The Prophet's Devotional

The Making of a Watchman

The End Times Watchman

101 Tactics for Spiritual Warfare

The Next Great Move of God

Mornings with the Holy Spirit

Victory Decrees

Walking in Your Prophetic Destiny

JENNIFER LECLAIRE

THE
INTERCESSOR'S
DEVOTIONAL

365 DAILY INVITATIONS
TO ACTIVATE AND ACCELERATE
YOUR PRAYER LIFE

AWAKENING MEDIA, INC.

P.O. Box 30563, Ft. Lauderdale, FL 33303

Awakening Your Spirit

This book and all other Awakening Media and Jennifer LeClaire books are available at www.jenniferleclaire.org and online book sellers.

Cover design by: Jeffrey Mardis

For more information on foreign distributors, message jenniferleclaire.org/contact. Reach us on the Internet: www.jenniferleclaire.org

ISBN: 978-1-949465-12-9

For Worldwide Distribution, Printed in the U.S.A.

DEDICATION

The Intercessor's Devotional is dedicated to modern-day intercessors who pray without ceasing, despite the personal costs, despite the weariness, and despite the opposition—and to my Awakening Prayer Hubs leaders around the world (www.awakeningprayerhubs.com). I applaud each and every one of you for your dogged determination to stand in the gap and make up the hedge, to pursue the character of Christ the Intercessor, and to raise up others to pray always in every place. You are history makers, moving the Hand that moves the world. You are overcomers who help others overcome. And rest assured, eternal rewards await you.

CONTENTS

INTRODUCTION

In 2012, God told me to make prayer my life's work. I had no idea what He meant. No, not really. Actually, I had no idea at all! Making prayer my life's work sounded like a monumental undertaking. And I wasn't much of an intercessor.

That same year, in response to this heavenly directive, I launched Awakening House of Prayer. But I had little fruit to show for my consistent efforts. It was harder than I thought—much harder. I didn't have any real training in prayer or intercession. I was praying alone most of the time. And the prayer was often dry. Very dry. My first effort to make prayer my life's work was by far the most difficult endeavor I ever attempted. I was tempted to quit many times, but by the grace of God I remained faithful.

Around that time, a seasoned intercessor told me emphatically, "God wants you to lay down your life in intercession." It was sort of like God saying, "Make prayer your life's work." You might call it a confirmation, but somehow her words seemed more serious. Task-driven work was more familiar to me than the notion of laying my life down in prayer hours a day. I couldn't wrap my mind around it.

Indeed, I didn't see it—and I didn't have time for it. I was the editor of *Charisma* magazine working on heavy deadlines. I was a single mother who was very involved in the church and missions. However, slowly the Holy Spirit started opening my eyes to intercession. And I didn't even realize it was happening.

At the recommendation of my publisher, I started a 6 a.m. prayer call in January 2014. It was supposed to be a ten-day introduction to my *Morning with the Holy Spirit* devotional. I was nervous. I didn't like it. I didn't want to do it after the first day. I could barely pray the whole thirty minutes. I struggled. It sweat. I was stretched far beyond my comfort zone. I had to recruit other intercessors who would take on ten-minute slots just to keep it going.

To my surprise, after the first ten days, people were urging me to continue. The broadcast has been going on five days a week since then. Today, the *Mornings with the Holy Spirit* prayer broadcast runs an hour a day five days a week—and it's just me and the Holy Spirit doing the heavy lifting.

Through that journey, I found the intercessor in me. But that was just the birthing of the intercessor. Some years later I had an encounter with the Holy Spirit about my high calling—interceding for nations and souls and raising up others to do so. I remember when I finally saw it. Cindy Jacobs was a big part of it, as was Dick Eastman. Eastman is Chief Prayer Office at Every Home for Christ, which has seen millions of souls saved through prayer and evangelism.

One day, I suddenly had an "aha" moment. I could see the high calling. Of course, all hell broke loose against me immediately after the revelation. It was harder than ever to find time to pray. Every distraction and demonized person seemed to be standing in the way. I was (and as of the time of this writing) still am getting hit on many sides at once. But I am determined to make prayer my life's work come hell or highwater, as my grandmother used to say. Maybe you can relate. Maybe prayer is your life's work, too.

Like Awakening House of Prayer and Awakening Prayer Hubs (small cells of intercessors in dozens of nations around the world) this devotional was birthed as part of my life's work. I pray it encourages, inspires and challenges you to engage in prevailing prayer. I pray you'll join Awakening Prayer Hubs so we can stand together for revival in the nations.

JANUARY

"If you abide in Me, and My words abide in you, you will ask what you desire, and it shall be done for you" (John 15:7).

What Is Prayer, Really?

"Let my prayer be set before You as incense, the lifting up of my hands as the evening sacrifice" (Psalm 141:2).

If you ask ten people what prayer is, you might get ten different answers. Yes, essentially, prayer is talking to God. But it's so, so much more than that. A quick look at how some seasoned intercessors from days gone by defined prayer is more than a little eye opening.

S.D. Gordon, a prolific author and minister in the 18th and 19th centuries, had a deep understanding that: "Prayer is repeating the victor's name (Jesus) into the ears of Satan and insisting on his retreat." Prayer, then, is a weapon against dark forces that dare to intrude upon God's will in the earth.

St. Augustine of Hippo, a fourth century theologian, had a different take. He said, "Whether we realize it or not, prayer is the encounter of God's thirst with ours. God thirsts that we may thirst for Him." What a thought! Teresa of Avila, a 16 Century, a Spanish mystic, religious reformer, author and theologian, offered, "Prayer is nothing else than being on terms of friendship with God." A beautiful sentiment, indeed!

Charles Spurgeon, a 19th Century Englishman known as the prince of preachers, put it this way: "True prayer is neither a mere mental exercise nor a vocal performance. It is far deeper than that. It is a spiritual transaction with the creator of Heaven and Earth." Meanwhile, the late evangelist Billy Graham opined, "Prayer is spiritual communication between man and God, a two-way relationship in which man should not only talk to God but also listen to Him."

Finally, Andrew Murray, a late South African pastor, teacher and author, offered insight into prayer and answered prayer: "Prayer is reaching out after the unseen; fasting is letting go of all that is seen and temporal. Answered prayer is the interchange of love between the Father and His child."

What is my definition of prayer? Prayer is a gift that extends an invitation to access natural and spiritual help, plead for divine intervention in affairs of mankind, and drive the enemy out of our midst, in the name of Jesus.

— *Prayer* —

Father, in the name of Jesus, would You help me understand the dimensions and purposes of prayer, which are more vast than I can comprehend with my finite mind? Would You share with me Your definition of prayer? Let a revelation of prayer power inspire me to pray more and more.

Mercy Me!

"Yet now, if You will forgive their sin—but if not, I pray, blot me out of Your book which You have written" (Exodus 32:33).

Moses displayed the heart of an intercessor—and the heart of God. Moses goes down in Bible history as the meekest man on the face of the earth. But he was also a man of mercy. While Moses was up on Mount Sinai talking to God and receiving the 10 Commandments written by the very finger of God, the Israelites were back in the camp making a new god—a golden calf.

Shockingly, it was Moses' brother Aaron who helped coordinate the mass idolatry. Aaron instructed the people to bring him their golden earrings. He used fire to meld them into an idol. The Israelites had the audacity to declare this was the god that delivered them out of Egypt. Adding insult to injury, Aaron built an altar before the golden calf and proclaimed a feast the next day. The Israelites brought burnt offerings and peace offerings and celebrated.

Of course, God saw it all, and said to Moses "I have seen this people, and indeed it is a stiff-necked people! Now therefore, let Me alone, that My wrath may burn hot against them and I may consume them. And I will make of you a great nation" (Exodus 32:9-10).

Moses had his own challenges with the Israelites, and could have easily agreed with the Lord to do away with the idolatrous people and start over. Instead, he pled for mercy. Moses cried, "Oh, these people have committed a great sin, and have made for themselves a god of gold! Yet now, if You will forgive their sin— but if not, I pray, blot me out of Your book which You have written" (Ex. 32:31-32).

The result? God did not wipe out the Israelites, but only held accountable those who committed the sin. Moses' selfless intercession from a heart of mercy saved many Israelite lives. Intercessors would do well to cultivate a heart of mercy toward those who are sinning against God. Intercessors, we are not the judge. Jesus is the Judge. God is not willing that any should perish, but that all should come to repentance (see 2 Pet. 3:9). Standing in the gap for sinners, even "Christian sinners" is an expectation of the intercessor.

— *Prayer* —

Father, in the name of Jesus, help me stand in the place of intercession even when I am tempted to stand in the place of judge. Sculpt in me a heart of mercy, like Yours, so that through my acts of intercession I can help preserve the lives of those who are recklessly defying You.

Miriam's Malicious Murmuring

"Now Miriam and Aaron spoke against Moses because of the Cushite woman whom he had married (for he had married a Cushite woman)..." (Numbers 12:1).

Miriam was a prophetess but she didn't always use her mouth to prophesy the song of the Lord. No, she used her anointed mouth to murmur to Aaron about her little brother Moses. Apparently, Aaron joined in but God ultimately held Miriam responsible. That tells me she was likely either the one who initiated it or the one who wouldn't let it go.

Miriam fell prey to a murmuring spirit—and the Lord heard it. (Of course, the Lord hears everything!) I believe the murmuring spirit that was in the camp—the Israelites were notorious for murmuring against Moses—caught Miriam's ear. In other words, she gave ear to the murmuring spirit and eventually agreed with it. She may have even had common ground to begin with! That's why it's so important we don't give ear to the murmuring spirit—or any other spirit—ever! Miriam ultimately bowed to the murmuring spirit, which is highly contagious. She should have known better.

Moses wasn't just the God-ordained leader of the Israelites; this was Miriam's own brother whose life she helped save by placing him in a basket in the Nile River to avoid Pharoah's murderous decree. She knew God providentially rescued him and raised him up, and now she was complaining against him. It doesn't make sense, right? When things don't make natural sense, there's usually an evil spirit in the mix somewhere.

It's been said our murmuring is the devil's music. The devil loves it when we murmur because it opens us up to attack. Indeed, allowing murmuring to take over your tongue is a dangerous sin. James, the apostle of practical faith, warns us, "Do not grumble against one another, brethren, lest you be condemned. Behold, the Judge is standing at the door!" (James 5:9)

Look what happened to Miriam in Numbers 12:9-16: "And the anger of the Lord was kindled against Miriam and Aaron, and He departed. But when the cloud had withdrawn from over the tent, behold, Miriam was leprous, as white as snow. And Aaron turned and looked at Miriam, and behold, she was leprous." If you have fallen to murmuring repent. If there's murmuring in your prayer group, address it swiftly.

— *Prayer* —

Father, in the name of Jesus, I repent for engaging with the murmuring spirit, either by spewing criticism or giving ear to it. Help me discern the spirit behind my words before I speak—and the spirit behind the words of others speaking to me.

The E.M. Bounds Prayer Anointing

"But know that the Lod has set apart for Himself him who is godly; The Lord will hear when I call to Him" (Psalm 4:3).

"What the Church needs today is not more machinery or better, not new organizations or more and novel methods, but men whom the Holy Ghost can use—men of prayer, men mighty in prayer. The Holy Ghost does not flow through methods, but through men. He does not come on machinery, but on men. He does not anoint plans, but men—men of prayer."

These were the words of E.M. Bounds. Bounds was a Methodist pastor in the Civil War era. Serving as a Chaplain with the Confederacy, he spent a year and a half in federal prison after Union Troops arrested him. Doubtless through prayer, he was later released in a prisoner swap.

Bounds started writing what are now classic books on prayer at the age of 58. He also engaged deeply in intercessory prayer, praying from 4 a.m. until 7 a.m. every day before he set out to write his books. Inspired by John Wesley, he started pastoring at the age of 24.

In the foreword to *Necessity of Prayer*, Claude Chilton, Jr. wrote, "Edward McKendree Bounds did not merely pray well that he might write well about prayer. He prayed because the needs of the world were upon him. He prayed, for long years, upon subjects which the easy-going Christian rarely gives a thought, and for objects which men of less thought and faith are always ready to call impossible.

"From his solitary prayer-vigils, year by year, there arose teaching equaled by few men in modern Christian history. He wrote transcendently about prayer, because he was himself, transcendent in its practice. As breathing is a physical reality to us so prayer was a reality for Bounds. He took the command, 'Pray without ceasing' almost as literally as animate nature takes the law of the reflex nervous system, which controls our breathing."

Bounds left a legacy with his writings that should inspire every intercessor. Through his books, this deep thinker and revelator continues to disciple countless intercessors over a century after he went on to glory.

— *Prayer* —

Father, in the name of Jesus, would You help me understand the deep truths about prayer that Bounds taught? I want to catch the spirit of prayer that rested upon him. I want to be a person of prayer.

Never, Never Stop Praying

"Rejoice always; pray without ceasing" (1 Thessalonians 5:16).

Paul issued an edict for believers: pray without ceasing. Some translations say, "pray continually" or "never stop praying" or "be unceasing and persistent in prayer." If Paul had said this once, it would have been enough. But he echoes this mandate in Romans 12:12, "rejoicing in hope, patient in tribulation, continuing steadfastly in prayer."

That's two witnesses, but yet there is still a third. In Ephesians 6:18, Paul admonishes us to "Pray in the Spirit at all times and on every occasion. Stay alert and be persistent in your prayers for all believers everywhere." Paul said he prayed in tongues, which is one aspect of praying in the spirit, more than anyone (see 1 Cor. 14:18).

Maybe Paul heard the words of Jesus, who offered a parable to His disciples "that men always ought to pray and not lose heart" (Luke 18:1). This is the intercessor's mission, but how do we execute it? How do we literally pray without ceasing with the hectic pace of life? How do we obey this four-fold command, which first came from Christ and was echoed by Paul as led by the Spirit?

Clearly, we can't live in our prayer closet. We have responsibilities, and God knows that well. Praying without ceasing is taking a prayerful attitude toward life. Praying without ceasing is being willing to respond to the call of Jesus, the Chief Intercessor, at any moment—day or night.

Praying without ceasing means being spiritually alert to our natural and spiritual surroundings and serving as a prayer solutionist concerning problems we discern throughout the day. Praying without ceasing means prayer is our response—our knee-jerk reaction—when situations arise that are not in line with God's Word.

Practically speaking, though, praying without ceasing means praying with frequency. It means praying often. It means not giving up until we see the answer to prayer or sense it's done in the spirit. Praying without ceasing is the intercessor's mandate, and it's possible. It's a mindset and a heart posture that's ready to pounce in prayer.

— *Prayer* —

Father, in the name of Jesus, would You help me to pray without ceasing? Help me remember when a need arises to run to the throne of grace boldly to deliver my petition humbly to the King. Teach me how to walk with a heart bent toward prayer as a primary solution.

Guarding the Gates

"And he set the gatekeepers at the gates of the house of the Lord, so that no one who was in any way unclean should enter" (2 Chronicles 23:19).

A gatekeeper is one who guards the gate or one who controls access. An intercessor is one who intercedes—one who stands between the enemy and God's people to forbid access, or between God and His people to plead for them.

God is raising up gatekeeper intercessors in this era that have a keen sense of what should be allowed into a territory and what should be completely shut out. They are, in a very real sense, guarding the spiritual gates. They are making up a wall, so to speak, forbidding access to unauthorized intruders and demonic forces.

Gatekeepers, then, are experts at using the keys to the Kingdom Jesus described in Matthew 18:18 (AMPC) "Truly I tell you, whatever you forbid and declare to be improper and unlawful on earth must be what is already forbidden in heaven, and whatever you permit and declare proper and lawful on earth must be what is already permitted in heaven."

Mature gatekeeper intercessors understand the laws of the Kingdom and discern what God wants in and out; what He forbids and what He allows. We see gatekeepers in everyday life all the time.

When you go to the movies, for example, there's a gatekeeper. The attendant makes sure you have your ticket before you are allowed access to the theater. When you go to the grocery store, there's a gatekeeper. The clerk makes sure you pay for your groceries before you take them home.

When you call a business to talk to an attorney or professional, they have a gatekeeper called a secretary that decides if you get access to them. They are standing between you and the person you are trying to get to. When I was editor of *Charisma* magazine, I was a gatekeeper. I decided what stories got into the magazine and what stories didn't.

Ask the Lord to give you the gatekeeper revelation, and an understanding of what should be allowed and forbidden in your life, your church and your region. Then use the keys of the Kingdom expertly as you stand in the gap.

— *Prayer* —

Father, in the name of Jesus, would You give me a revelation of the gatekeeper?
Raise me up as one who sees what heaven forbids and allows. Help me discern
enemies disguised as friends. Make me bold and brave to stand between intruders
and the gate You've called me to keep.

JANUARY 7

Wrestling With Public Prayer Fears

"For God has not given us a spirit of fear, but of power and of love and of a sound mind"
(2 Timothy 1:17).

I still remember fear striking my heart every Friday night. Corporate intercession before service was mandatory for leaders in the church, and I dreaded every minute of it.

The woman of God who led prayer was a powerhouse in the spirit. Anointed, God-glorifying, devil-busting prayers emanated from this woman like glory emanates from Jesus. She had a certain cadence, a rhythm. It was almost as if she were singing her prayers—only she wasn't. In any case, I know it was music to our heavenly Father's ears.

I knew when they were about to call upon me for prayer. So I did what any intimidated intercessor would do: I slipped out of the sanctuary and hid in the bathroom until service started. Yes, really! I was too scared to pray—much less prophesy. I struggled to pray in public. There was a roadblock. Actually, it was a soul block.

Ultimately, this is a fear issue. There are many types of fears and phobias. If you're typically not fearful in most situations, the fear of man is likely at the root of your public prayerlessness. You may be comparing yourself to others and decide inwardly that you are not as equipped or as powerful. You may be concerned about people judging you as inadequate in intercession. I assure you, most believers are not critiquing your public prayer. Ask the Lord to deliver you from the fear of man, which brings a snare (see Prov. 29:25).

Ultimately, there's nothing more powerful in your life than your own will. Even God won't usurp the human will. The devil can't stop you from praying. You can consciously choose to "do it afraid." You can make a determined decision to take my advice and implement it. You can break through this blockage, this hindrance, this frustration by the power of your will.

— *Prayer* —

Father, in the name of Jesus, help me overcome every fear, anxiety and insecurity associated with public prayer. Help me stop comparing myself to other intercessors. Give them boldness and courage to release powerful prayers in Your name and for Your glory.

Rub Up Against Jesus

"Then he poured some of the anointing oil on Aaron's head, anointing him and making him holy for his work" (Leviticus 8:12, NLT).

If you feel weary, it's a sign you need a fresh prayer anointing. Simply put, the anointing is God's power. The anointing is a manifestation of God's presence on you to perform His will. Jesus told us in Acts 1:8, "You shall receive power when the Holy Spirit has come upon you."

Intercessors, we need this power. We need this anointing. And it's not a "one and done" anointing. At times, we need a fresh anointing of the Holy Spirit to stand and withstand in the evil day. After all, intercession can be hard work even though you are anointed and graced for the work. Intercession can take a toll on the physical body and open us up to all sorts of enemy attacks.

Intercessors, God wants to anoint you afresh. He wants to pour out a spirit of prayer upon you so you can continue contending for His purposes in the earth. He wants to consecrate you for His use. All of this comes with a fresh anointing.

"We are to be continually filled with God's Spirit so that we can be used by God mightily in these days to fulfill His will in our lives," wrote Kenneth E. Hagin in his classic book, *A Fresh Anointing*. "God has made an abundant provision for His people to be filled up at all times with His Spirit, regardless of outward circumstances, so we can live unto His glory!"

You can receive this fresh anointing by crying out to God for it. You can also receive a fresh anointing from close fellowship with God. When the Pharisees saw Peter and John's courage and understood they were ordinary men, they concluded the disciples had been with Jesus (see Acts 4:13). The more time we spend with Jesus, the more the anointing will "rub off on us." If you want the anointing of Christ the Intercessor, spend more time with Him—and ask Him.

— Prayer —

Father, in the name of Jesus, will You give me a fresh anointing for prayer? Will You consecrate me anew for Your Kingdom work? Will You pour out a spirit of prayer over my heart? Will You empower me to serve Your people through my anointed intercession?

JANUARY 9

Multiplying Your Firepower

"Five of you shall chase a hundred, and a hundred of you shall put ten thousand to flight" (Leviticus 26:8).

Corporate prayer—or praying together with a group of people—is foundational to the intercessor's success. Although we spend long hours effectively praying in our secret place, we must resist the temptation to altogether shun corporate prayer events.

There's far more firepower in unified corporate prayer. You've probably heard it said one can put a thousand to flight and two can put 10,000 to flight. This is a revelation that needs to seep deep into our soul.

Deuteronomy 32:30 tells us, "How should one chase a thousand, and two put ten thousand to flight, unless their Rock had sold them, and the Lord had given them up?" God is a God of multiplication and when we gather in corporate prayer, our combined anointings are explosive.

Again, we see the multiplication effect of corporate prayer in Leviticus 26:8, "Five of you shall chase a hundred, and a hundred of you shall put ten thousand to flight, and your enemies shall fall before you by the sword." I'm no math expert, but this synergy is motive enough for me to join with the right company in intercession.

Remember the 120 disciples in the Upper Room? Before an outbreak of the Holy Spirit, what were they doing? They were in unified corporate prayer. Then again, recall when Peter was put in prison. Acts 12:5 tells us, "constant prayer was offered to God for him by the church." This wasn't just constant prayer, it was constant unified prayer. Many believers were gathered in clusters, including at the house of Mark's mother Mary, praying (see Acts 12:12). The result: an angel came to Peter's rescue and he showed up at Mary's house a free man.

If you don't have a large group of intercessors, don't fret. Corporate prayer doesn't always take large numbers. Jesus said, "If two of you agree on earth about anything they ask, it will be done for them by My Father who is in heaven. For where two or three are assembled in My name, there I am in their midst" (Matt. 18:19-20).

— Prayer —

Father, in the name of Jesus, would You give me a deep revelation of the power of corporate prayer? Let the examples You've offered in Your Word inspire me to gather with those of like precious faith to partner in prayer for Your purposes. Please, multiply my prayer power.

Entering Apostolic Intercession

"Truly the signs of an apostle were accomplished among you with all perseverance, in signs and wonders and mighty deeds" (2 Corinthians 12:12).

Apostolic intercession has a different sound than other types of intercession—and a different target. Words associated with the apostolic in Scripture give you a hint as to the nature of apostolic intercession.

Doing a search through the New Testament, we see words like impart, confirm, activate, father, pioneer, messenger, and ambassador. We see words like strengthen, plan, ordain and architect. We see words like reform, govern, structure and administrate. And we see words like demand, build, foundation, sent-one, and warrior.

Apostolic intercessors are governing intercessors, which is different than governmental intercessors. Apostolic intercessors blaze trails with their pioneering prayers in a territory. Indeed, apostolic intercessors release strategic intercession over territories and people groups. Apostolic intercessors are Kingdom-minded, high-level, hard-core warriors that advance the church in their appointed region.

Apostolic intercessors have a father's (or mother's) heart. That means apostolic intercessors work with the Holy Spirit to raise up other intercessors with a strong foundation in intimacy with God, the Word and prophetic unctions. Apostolic intercessors are intercessors for other intercessors. Apostolic intercessors impart their anointings, gifts, and knowledge to those they raise up.

Paul the apostle was an apostolic intercessor. You can discern the flavor of an apostolic intercessor in action by the apostolic prayers he prayed for both territories and people.

Paul prayed for the revelation of Jesus' beauty and the Bride's destiny unto transforming our heart (see Eph. 1:17-19); for the release of supernatural strength in the heart unto experiencing God's emotions (see Eph. 3:16-19); for God's love to abound in our heart resulting in discernment and righteousness (see Phil 1:9-11); and to know God's will, to be fruitful in ministry, and strengthened by intimacy with God (see Col. 1:9-12).

— Prayer —

Father, in the name of Jesus, would You give me an anointing for apostolic prayer? Would You raise me up as an apostolic leader in intercession so I can labor to pioneer Your plans and purposes in the earth? And would you help me raise up others to do so?

The Daniel Nash Prayer Anointing

"Devote yourselves to prayer, keeping alert in it with an attitude of thanksgiving"
(Colossians 4:2, NASB).

Daniel Nash held prayer keys to revival in America's Second Great Awakening. You might not recognize his name on earth, but all of heaven and hell knows who he is. He served faithfully as the personal intercessor to Charles Finney. Finney, of course, goes down in Christian history as the most famed revivalist in the awakening.

Nash went ahead to the cities where Finney would preach at his revival meetings. As the story goes, he was known to stay in his room for days at a time, interceding. Weeping and groaning could be heard coming from his room. Daniel Kolenda of Christ for All Nations reports that Nash would not quit making intercession until he felt that the spiritual atmosphere had been prepared for Finney's arrival.

Another record tells: "On one occasion when I got to town to start a revival a lady contacted me who ran a boarding house. She said, 'Brother Finney, do you know a Father Nash? He and two other men have been at my boarding house for the last three days, but they haven't eaten a bite of food. I opened the door and peeped in at them because I could hear them groaning, and I saw them down on their faces. They have been this way for three days, lying prostrate on the floor and groaning. I thought something awful must have happened to them. I was afraid to go in and I didn't know what to do. Would you please come see about them?' 'No, it isn't necessary,' Finney replied. 'They just have a spirit of travail in prayer.'"

Hundreds of thousands of people were saved through Finney's Gospel preaching, but many didn't realize the preaching was undergirded through powerful intercession. After Nash died, Finney's revivals started to die out with him. Here's a fascinating point: Four months after Nash passed away, Finney stopped preaching revival meetings to pastor a church.

— Prayer —

Father, in the name of Jesus, give me a steadfast spirit so I can devote myself to interceding for a leader who has a call to see souls saved, bodies healed and miracles worked. Give me a Daniel Nash anointing and help me keep my mind on things above.

Yielding to 'Stegnamos' Prayer

"My little children, for whom I labor in birth again until Christ is formed in you"
(Galatians 4:19).

Travailing prayer is prevailing prayer. Too many churches today are not only shutting out the intercessors, they are also quenching travail. We need to let God be God even if it makes "religious" people uncomfortable. And we need to teach about aspects of prayer like travail. Young intercessors need to understand these spiritual dynamics so they are not afraid when they see or experience these manifestations of Holy Spirit-inspired prayer.

Paul discusses the spiritual practice in Romans 8:26-29: "Likewise, the Spirit helps us in our weaknesses, for we do not know what to pray for as we ought, but the Spirit Himself intercedes for us with groanings too deep for words. He who searches the hearts knows what the mind of the Spirit is, because He intercedes for the saints according to the will of God."

These "groanings too deep for words" are one manifestation of travailing prayer. The Greek word for "groanings" in that Scripture is "stenagmos," which simply means a groaning or a sigh. *Merriam-Webster* defines "travail" as "a painful or difficult work or effort." *Webster's Revised Unabridged Dictionary* goes a little deeper, defining travail as "labor with pain; severe toil or exertion" and "to suffer the pangs of childbirth; to be in labor." Again, if you've ever entered into travail, you can relate.

Many times before travailing prayer comes upon you, you'll feel grieved, heavy or otherwise burdened. Less experienced intercessors may believe they are under spiritual attack—and sometimes they are—but sometimes it's the Holy Spirit moving on your spirit to engage in travail with Him. That can be heavy!

Notice I say "with Him." Again, you can't stir up travail in your soul or your flesh. It is Spirit-inspired. The important thing to know is that when you sense this coming on you, you need to yield to the Holy Spirit to birth His purposes—or to wage war against what is standing in the way of His will.

— *Prayer* —

Father, in the name of Jesus, I am willing to be used in travail. I know I can't stir this up in my emotions, but I can grow more in tune with Your emotions. Inspire my heart to travail for Your purposes in the earth. I will serve You.

Deconstructing Prayer Biases

"For there is no partiality with God" (Romans 2:11).

I like vanilla ice cream better than chocolate. I like Adidas better than Nike. I like filet mignon better than escargo. I have biases. But those biases don't affect my intercession. Other biases may. Not all biases are bad. Most are harmless. But some are evil. Many can influence your intercessory prayer in an ungodly way.

Bias is "a particular tendency, trend, inclination, feeling, or opinion, especially one that is preconceived or unreasoned; unreasonably hostile feelings or opinions about a social group; prejudice," according to Dictionary.com.

Studies show most biases are completely unconscious. Our brains are wired to find and respond to recognizable patterns, which turn into stereotypes. Catch that. Your bias is unconscious. You don't readily discern the bias or you would reject it. Your bias is like that piece of lettuce stuck on your teeth that you can't see but everyone else can.

It's scary to think I could be making intercession through a biased lens and not know it. The overall problem is biases cloud our perspective and if we are not aware of our biases we make intercession out of our perspective instead of God's perspective.

Jesus said you are responsible for every idle word you speak. So don't you think we're responsible for biased intercession? Or refusing to pray for someone due to our biases? We need to confront biases as the bullies they are. Our biases want to a voice that's louder than God's.

God is not partial to anything but the truth. His bias, if you could call it that, is truth. James 1:2 warns, "My brethren, do not hold the faith of our Lord Jesus Christ, the Lord of glory, with partiality." It's not up to us who we want to pray for or how we pray. We must follow the Holy Spirit's leadership in the realm of intercession. Ask God to expose and root out your biases.

— *Prayer* —

Father, in the name of Jesus, I don't want to make biased intercession or favor certain issues or people because of my own prejudice. I want to be led by You in all my ways. Would You show me my biases so I can repent? Would You root out of me the biases that sully my intercession?

Knowing the Ways of God

"Teach me Your way, O Lord; I will walk in Your truth; Unite my heart to fear Your name"
(Psalm 86:11).

The most insightful intercessors understand the ways of God, which requires study and first-hand experience with His Spirit. God wants us to know His ways—His ways of seeing things and doing things. He wants us to be intimately acquainted with what moves His heart.

Since God's ways are higher than our ways, we need to pray for a revelation of His ways. We don't want to assume or presume how He moves or what touches His heart. We want to know with certainty what He likes and doesn't like. When we pray for a revelation of God's ways, we stand as more strategic intercessors.

David frequently petitioned God to understand His ways. In Psalm 25:4, he cries, "Show me your ways, O Lord; Teach me Your paths." Again in Psalm 27:11 he pleads, "Teach me Your way, O Lord, and lead me in a smooth path, because of my enemies." And again in Psalm 86:11 he petitions, "Teach me Your way, O Lord; I will walk in Your truth; Unite my heart to fear Your name."

Consider Moses, the consummate intercessor. He cried out in Exodus 33:13, "Now therefore, I pray, if I have found grace in Your sight, show me now Your way, that I may know You and that I may find grace in Your sight." When we pray for insight into His way of seeing things and doing things, He will answer. Psalm 103:7 proves it, "He made known His ways to Moses, His acts to the children of Israel."

We need to press into God's ways in prayer because, as Proverbs 14:12 says, "There is a way that seems right to a man, but its end is the way of death." Sometimes we think we are praying the right way, but our prayers don't produce life. Put another way, we don't want to waste our time with dead end prayers.

— *Prayer* —

Father, in the name of Jesus, would You teach me Your ways? Would You help me understand Your higher ways so I can pray more effectively? I want to understand Your ways of seeing things and doing things.

JANUARY 15

Standing in the Office of the Intercessor

"And God has appointed these in the church: first apostles, second prophets, third teachers, after that miracles, then gifts of healings, helps, administrations, varieties of tongues"
(1 Corinthians 12:28).

When we think of offices, we think of the five-fold gifts of apostles, prophets, evangelists, pastors and teachers, who equip us for the work of the ministry (see Eph. 4:11). But many believe intercessors also hold an office. While technically all Christians are supposed to make intercession, there are some who are clearly and specifically gifted for intercession. In this way, there is an office of intercessor.

I first learned this from the late C. Peter Wagner, who wrote about it in his excellent book *Prayer Shield*. He explained his understanding of "office" as a public recognition that a believer has a specific spiritual gift used regularly in ministry.

"Conferring an office takes several different forms, anywhere from the public ordination service of a person who will subsequently use the title 'Reverend' and receive certain privileges from the denomination and the Internal Revenue Service, to the naming of a person to be a fifth grade Sunday School teacher," he wrote. "Sometimes the person in the office is reimbursed, sometimes the service is voluntary. Either way it has an official recognition."

Wagner made a strong suggestion in his book, with which I agree: churches should take steps to establish the office of the intercessor and give public recognition to members who have the gift of intercession.

"We do it for those with gift of pastor, evangelist, and teacher. We do it with the gift of mercy (such as minister of visitation), the gift of service (such as deacon or deaconess), the gift of exhortation (such as minister of counseling) and many more," he wrote. "I think we should add intercessor to the list."

Even if your church doesn't take this stance, know that you are standing in an office and that office is important to your church. You don't need a title or an ordination from man when the Chief Intercessor Himself has called you into the office.

— Prayer —

Father, in the name of Jesus, would You help me to not get hung up on offices or titles, while at the same time accepting the responsibility of the office You've assigned me? Help me fully occupy the office of the intercessor and execute my duties in holy fear.

Interceding Through Impossibilities

"With God all things are possible" (Matthew 19:26).

I was falsely accused of a crime I didn't commit and the district attorney wanted to send me to prison for ten years. My defense attorney tried to talk me into taking a plea deal, but I was innocent. My praying grandma made intercession on my behalf in what looked like an impossible situation. God swiftly delivered me and vindicated me.

Prayer brings God's solutions to seemingly impossible problems. Put another way, we can pray through and even pray away impossibilities.

Jeremiah faced some difficult situations in his ministry, but this interceding prophet proclaimed with great confidence: "Ah, Lord God! Behold, You have made the heavens and the earth by Your great power and outstretched arm. There is nothing too hard for You" (Jer. 32:17).

Let that really sink in. No matter what you are up against in the spirit, it's not too hard for God. Jesus said all things are possible to the one who believes (see Mark 9:23). Jesus said, "Until now you have asked nothing in My name. Ask, and you will receive, that your joy may be full" (John 16:24).

Jesus said, "For assuredly, I say to you, if you have faith as a mustard seed, you will say to this mountain, 'Move from here to there,' and it will move; and nothing will be impossible for you" (Mat. 17:20). That word nothing in the Greek means what it says: nothing.

Again, let that sink in. There are times when it's not God's will to see a thing happen, but if it's God's will prayer can pull it out of the heavenly realm and into the natural realm. In the middle of his pain, Job declared, "I know that You can do everything, and that no purpose of Yours can be withheld from You" (Job 42:2).

Don't let what looks like impossibilities stop you from praying. Stand on God's Word and pray until you see the promise.

— *Prayer* —

Father, in the name of Jesus, when I'm facing impossibilities help me remember nothing is too hard for You, that nothing is impossible with You, that You can do everything, and that no purpose of Yours can be withheld from You. I want to glorify You.

Your Intercessory Prayer Posture

"My son, give me your heart, and let your eyes observe my ways" (Proverbs 23:26).

What's your posture in prayer? We see so many prayer postures throughout the Word of God. Some wonder what position they should take while making intercession.

We see Abraham fell on his face and prayed (see Gen. 17:3). That's called laying prostrate before the Lord. Another time we see Abraham bowing in prayer (see Gen. 24:52). Moses prayed with his hands outstretched (see Ex. 9:27–29.)

King Solomon knelt in prayer (see 1 Kings 8:54). Jesus prayed looking up into heaven (see Mark 6:41; John 11:41; 17:1.) Paul suggested warfare prayer should be done standing (see Eph. 6:12-18). Of course, we can sit before the Lord in prayer. We are seated with Christ at the right hand of the Father (see Eph. 1:15–23; Eph. 2:4–7.)

I'm not saying these postures are insignificant, but physical posture in prayer doesn't matter nearly as much as our heart posture. Jesus reveals this in Luke 18:10-14:

"Two men went up to the temple to pray, one a Pharisee and the other a tax collector. The Pharisee stood and prayed thus with himself, 'God, I thank You that I am not like other men—extortioners, unjust, adulterers, or even as this tax collector. I fast twice a week; I give tithes of all that I possess.'

"And the tax collector, standing afar off, would not so much as raise his eyes to heaven, but beat his breast, saying, 'God, be merciful to me a sinner!' I tell you, this man went down to his house justified rather than the other; for everyone who exalts himself will be humbled, and he who humbles himself will be exalted."

— Prayer —

Father, in the name of Jesus, would You help me keep my heart posture right as I
boldly approach the throne of grace? Would You help me walk in humility as I
make intercession so You will hear and answer my prayers?

Discerning Anti-Intercession Demons

"But let him ask in faith, with no doubting, for he who doubts is like a wave of the sea driven and tossed by the wind" (James 1:6).

Doubt is one of the intercessor's many enemies. Doubt can be so subtle you don't immediately discern it—and if you don't discern doubt it can be deadly to your prayer life. Doubt means "to be uncertain about something or to believe that something may not be true or is unlikely." Clearly, doubt and faith don't mix. We need to learn to discern doubt as the devil it is!

James, the apostle of practical faith, explained it this way: "If any of you lacks wisdom, let him ask of God, who gives to all liberally and without reproach, and it will be given to him. But let him ask in faith, with no doubting, for he who doubts is like a wave of the sea driven and tossed by the wind. For let not that man suppose that he will receive anything from the Lord" (James 1:5-7).

You could change the word "wisdom" in that verse to just about anything and it would still hold true. If any of you lacks peace, joy, favor, finances, healing, ask in faith with no doubting. Doubt opens the door to demonic interference. Simply stated, you will not receive a prayer answer when your heart is full of doubt.

So how do you discern doubt in your heart? If you aren't sure God will do what He said He will do, that's doubt. If you hesitate to pray over a matter, doubt may be in the way. If you believe one minute but not the next, doubt is speaking to you. If you don't feel qualified to tackle an issue in prayer, doubt is ministering to you.

Doubt is a deadly weapon the enemy uses against intercessors to steal, kill and destroy the would-be fruit of this critical ministry. You have to root out doubt at the first sign of its presence. Resist doubt out loud—then pray all the louder and watch God move.

— Prayer —

Father, in the name of Jesus, help me discern the voice of doubt speaking to my soul. Help me see this devil for what it is—an enemy that seeks to make me a double-minded intercessor. I break the powers of doubt over my mind!

Entering Into Enjoyable Prayer

"Even them I will bring to My holy mountain, and make them joyful in My house of prayer" (Isaiah 56:7).

As a young Christian, I never enjoyed prayer. It was drudgery—and I was scared to pray publicly. Prayer was at the same time scary and boring. It seemed dry and rote many days. It was hard to think of much to pray for. And I wasn't sure how effective it was despite James' argument that the effective fervent prayer of a righteous person makes tremendous power available (see James 5:16).

Mike Bickle not only taught me new ways to study the Bible; he also taught me how to make prayer more enjoyable—and more effective. IHOP has sixteen values of enjoyable prayer, and employing just a few of these in your prayer life can make all the difference. I am not going to recite his list here, but I thought I'd point out a couple.

First, is the necessity of combining worship with intercession. I realize old-school intercessors often lay prostrate on the floor with only the sound of travail to accompany them, but praying with worship music can set the stage for intimacy and fuels your passion to pray.

Second is praying in the Spirit and spontaneous singing. Praying in the Spirit has long been part and parcel of my prayer life because I need to build myself up in my most holy faith (see Jude 20). Plus, I don't know how to pray as I ought (see Rom. 8:26). But spontaneous singing also makes prayer enjoyable. Paul said he would sing with the Spirit and his understanding (see 1 Cor. 14:14-15).

Third, God-centered spiritual warfare. I came out of spiritual warfare camps that were too extreme. But spiritual warfare is nevertheless vital. Putting God in the center means we are agreeing with God and His Word rather than hyper-focusing on talking to the devil. There are times to address the devil, and we certainly bind and loose, but agreeing with and declaring God's promises is more fruitful and enjoyable than screaming at the devil.

— *Prayer* —

Father, in the name of Jesus, make me joyful in the house of prayer. Would You make me sensitive to Your joy when I pray and stand in intercession? Help me press through all restraints as I co-labor with Christ the Intercessor to pray heaven's will to earth.

Avoiding Jezebel's Intercessors

"Now it happened, when Joram saw Jehu, that he said, 'Is it peace, Jehu?' So he answered, 'What peace, as long as the harlotries of your mother Jezebel and her witchcraft are so many?'"
(2 Kings 9:22)

Jezebel loves intercession, but not because she wants prayer answers—because she wants to control, manipulate and overthrow true intercession. Jezebel is a false intercessor, and you need to learn to discern this spirit in operation because, sooner or later, it will manifest in your midst. (Check out the *Discerning Jezebel's Intercessors* course at www.schoolofthespirit.tv.)

The revelation of Jezebel's intercessors came to me when I was teaching at my School of Prophecy. Under the unction of the Holy Spirit I said, "There are those who espouse themselves to be intercessors but they are nothing more than gossipers. They never pray about a thing. They just want the information. They are Jezebels in disguise.

"Jezebel is an information-seeking spirit. They are not seeking the information so they can pray and see God intervene. They are seeking information to prey–p r e y–on your hurts and wounds. All intercessors are not pure-hearted or true. Some of them have false agendas."

Think about it. It only makes sense. We see a lot of warnings in the Bible about false gifts… and intercession is a gift. We see warnings about false prophets, and all prophets are intercessors. And you can't read a single book in the New Testament that doesn't warn about deception or falsity.

Keep in mind though, usually Jezebel's intercessors started out as sold-out, on-fire prayer warriors. But something happened. They got hurt somehow. Perhaps they were wounded by friendly fire. Or they made an inner vow in a moment of vulnerability and attracted Jezebel as their protector. Jezebel loves to collect intercessors like trophies because she hates to see the will of God come to pass.

Beyond discerning Jezebel's intercessors and dealing with them in a godly manner, we must also look for the witch in us. Any intercessor can fall prey to the attack of this spirit. Any intercessor can flow in a Jezebel spirit. And any intercessor can repent and get back on track.

— *Prayer* —

Father, in the name of Jesus, would You give me discernment to see the false operations of Jezebel's intercessors? Help me see them and confront them so they don't hinder prayer. And help me, Lord, not to fall prey to the influence of this nefarious spirit.

Stepping Into the Simplicity of Prayer

"And when you pray, do not use vain repetitions as the heathen do. For they think that they will be heard for their many words" (Matthew 6:7).

While many intercessors will spend long hours in prayer, there are times when it's not possible to lay on our faces prostrate before the Lord all day long crying out for His will. Don't let the enemy deceive you. You don't have to pray long eloquent prayers to be effective. There's power in simple prayer.

It's the heart filled with faith, not the long prayers with many words, that spur God to action. Remember when Jesus taught His disciples to pray? He gave them what we call *The Lord's Prayer* in Matthew 6:9-13. That prayer covers a lot of ground and it's only sixty-six words. Look at its simplicity:

"Our Father in heaven, hallowed be Your name. Your kingdom come. Your will be done on earth as it is in heaven. Give us this day our daily bread. And forgive us our debts, as we forgive our debtors. And do not lead us into temptation, but deliver us from the evil one. For Yours is the kingdom and the power and the glory forever. Amen."

Jesus always got His prayers answered. Of course, this is not the only example of simple prayer. When Jesus called Peter to walk on the water, he succeeded until he took his eyes of Christ. Then he began to sink. Probably without thinking, Peter prayed a simple three-word prayer: "Lord, save me" (Matt. 14:30). Jesus immediately answered him.

Remember the ten lepers in Luke 17:13? Their prayer was, "Master, have mercy on us" (Luke 17:13). How did Jesus respond? He cleansed them. When Jesus asked Bartimaeus what he wanted, the blind man offered a simple prayer: "Rabboni, that I may receive my sight" (Mark 10:51). There is power in simplicity.

— Prayer —

Father, in the name of Jesus, would You help me never to fall into the trap of praying long prayers for long the sake of praying long prayers? I want to step into prayer action in an instant, no matter where I am or what I am doing. Give me the revelation of simple prayer.

The Rise of Remnant Intercessors

"So too at the present time there is a remnant, chosen by grace" (Romans 11:5, ESV).

I heard the Lord say, "I'm looking for some intercessors who will put the Kingdom over their own comfort, who bear the marks of an intercessor in their body; who will keep on praying for God's will no matter what it costs."

I call these remnant intercessors. See, there are intercessors and then there are remnant intercessors. Remnant intercessors are a different breed. Remnant intercessors have a different spirit like Joshua and Caleb who clearly saw the giants in the land but saw an even greater God with a great and precious promise.

Who or what is the remnant? You may not be familiar with the term remnant, so let me define it for you. The remnant is the church within the church. The remnant is a small number of people among a large crowd. It's a group of survivors with boldness to do and say what the Lord wants done and said despite the personal cost. The remnant is not called the remnant for nothing.

Remnant intercessors aren't usually famous during their lifetime. But when you look back in history you see how critical their work was. Listen, remnant intercessor, the church may not appreciate you but God appreciates you. The work you are doing is critical.

Some intercessors' prayer closets are dusty and filled with cobwebs because their visits are few and far between. The prayer closet of the remnant looks like a war room. There are often tears on the floor.

There's a steep price on the level of intercession that shifts the destinies of people and nations. It's more than you can pay in your flesh but it will cost you some sweat and tears. It's more than you can pay in your soul but you'll agonize in prayer. Remnant intercessors don't just pray through, they pray beyond until the breakthrough is in their hands.

— *Prayer* —

Father, in the name of Jesus, I want to be counted among the remnant. I want to
be an intercessor who stands apart in Your eyes, even if no one on earth
recognizes my name or my work in the prayer closet and in the war room. I choose
to sell out to Your plans and purposes through prayer.

JANUARY 23

Enlarging Your Prayer Territory

"Oh, that You would bless me indeed, and enlarge my territory, that Your hand would be with me, and that You would keep me from evil, that I may not cause pain!"
(1 Chronicles 4:10)

When I started out in intercession, I wanted to pray for America. After all, America is home to over 300 million people. America sends out missionaries. America is a beacon of light among nations. And I live here. I asked the Lord to give me a prayer burden for America—and He said no.

That didn't make any sense to me. Why wouldn't He give me a prayer burden for America? Well, because that wasn't my prayer territory at the time. I wasn't ready to take on the principalities and powers brewing over the United States at my young age. I wasn't experienced enough in prayer to carry that burden.

The Lord, instead, gave me Antigua and Barbados. These were tiny specs on the map—so small I could barely see them. Looking back, I realize that the Lord increases our prayer territory little by little. We usually don't start off praying for pivotal nations. We gain experience in the small things.

Our faith must increase before our territory increases.

Still, if you have a heart to go beyond where you are in intercession—if you have a heart to pray for large people groups, the various mountains of society, or nations—you can release the prayer of Jabez. The Amplified translation puts it this way:

"Jabez cried out to the God of Israel, saying, 'Oh that You would indeed bless me and enlarge my border [property], and that Your hand would be with me, and You would keep me from evil so that it does not hurt me!' And God granted his request."

As you pray this prayer, know that God is preparing you for the prayer territory He's assigned to your future self. He might not grant your request immediately but as you show yourself faithful to make intercession, He will eventually enlarge your territory and bless you indeed with prayer answers.

— *Prayer* —

Father, in the name of Jesus, increase my faith to pray for the territory You have given me now and prepare me for the territory You have in mind to assign me in the future. Enlarge my territory and let Your hand be with me as I stand in the gap.

When God Tells You to Stop Praying

"Pray no more for these people, Jeremiah. Do not weep or pray for them, for I will not listen to them when they cry out to me in distress" (Jeremiah 11:4, NLT).

There are three reasons to stop making intercession. The first reason is when you discern a breakthrough in your spirit. You know that it's done. You know the answer is coming and you are free to move on to the next assignment. The second reason when you see the prayer answer. You don't have to pray for what you already have.

The third reason, however, is almost startling at first glance. The third reason is when God tells you to stop praying. See, Jeremiah was a prophet but he was also an intercessor. (All prophets are intercessors but not all intercessors are prophets.) Barring a breakthrough in your spirit or a prayer answer, it can be difficult to let go of a person or issue you've been laboring over in intercession for days, weeks, months or even years.

But twice in Scripture, God told Jeremiah to stop praying for people. We see this in Jeremiah 7:16-18 reads, "Therefore do not pray for this people, nor lift up a cry or prayer for them, nor make intercession to Me; for I will not hear you. Do you not see what they do in the cities of Judah and in the streets of Jerusalem? The children gather wood, the fathers kindle the fire, and the women knead dough, to make cakes for the queen of heaven; and they pour out drink offerings to other gods, that they may provoke Me to anger."

God gave the Israelites over to their idolatry. Then again, we see God halt the prophet's prayer in Jeremiah 11:14 for the same reason: "So do not pray for this people, or lift up a cry or prayer for them; for I will not hear them in the time that they cry out to Me because of their trouble." Although this can be startling and uncomfortable, if the Lord tells you to stop praying you may as well stop. He's not going to answer intercession He told you not to release.

— *Prayer* —

Father, in the name of Jesus, would You make me more sensitive to Your Spirit? I want to discern the breakthroughs. I want to see the prayer answers. But I do not want to pray in vain. I do not want to waste my intercession on a lost cause. Help me discern Your leadership.

Activating Audacious Intercession

"I will not let You go unless You bless me!" (Genesis 32:26)

What is audacious intercession? Another way to say it is intrepidly daring prayer. It's intercession that's marked with resolute fearlessness, fortitude, and endurance.

Audacious intercession is the kind of intercession Abraham entered when he contended with God for the righteous living in Sodom and Gomorrah. Audacious prayer marked Moses' petition to Jehovah to "show me Your glory" (see Ex. 33:18). Audacious prayer is wrestling with God and declaring, "I will not let You go unless You bless me!" (Gen. 32:26).

Yes, all these men of God had the audacity to persevere in prayer until Jehovah answered them. But audacious prayer is more than persevering prayer. Audacious prayer is courageous prayer. It's risky prayer. It's prayer that puts its mustard seed faith out on the line hoping for a positive response.

Audacious intercession is prayer that defies natural circumstances and asks God for a miraculous intervention, supernatural deliverance, and uncommon provision. The audacious intercessor is undaunted by what is happening in the natural realm because he sees behind the veil and understands Who's really in control. Abraham knew he was pushing and pressing, but He also understood God's mercy and compassion when he prayed over Sodom and Gomorrah. Listen in to his audacious prayer and let it inspire you. We find the tail end of his intercession in Genesis 18:30-32:

"Then he said, 'Let not the Lord be angry, and I will speak: Suppose thirty should be found there?' So He said, 'I will not do it if I find thirty there.' And he said, "Indeed now, I have taken it upon myself to speak to the Lord: Suppose twenty should be found there?' So He said, 'I will not destroy it for the sake of twenty.' Then he said, 'Let not the Lord be angry, and I will speak but once more: Suppose ten should be found there?' And He said, 'I will not destroy it for the sake of ten.'"

Is your intercession audacious?

— *Prayer* —

Father, in the name of Jesus, make me into an audacious intercessor who is willing
to press beyond the world's limits into Your limitless goodness. Give me an
understanding of Your will and the perseverance to pray without ceasing until You
release the blessing.

Combatting Prayer Overwhelm

"As I thought of you I moaned, 'God, where are you?' I'm overwhelmed with despair as I wait for your help to arrive" (Psalm 77:3).

Every intercessor deals with overwhelm at one point or another. Sometimes the needs seem too great and the prayer army too small. Sometimes the enemy is hitting from all sides. When that happens, know this: You may be dealing with spiritual warfare. You may be dealing with the spirit of overwhelm.

Merriam Webster's dictionary defines "overwhelm" as: "to affect (someone) very strongly; to cause (someone) to have too many things to deal with; to defeat (someone or something) completely. Overwhelm also means "upset, overthrow; to cover over completely, submerge; to overcome by superior force or numbers; to overpower in thought or feeling."

The first step in battling overwhelm is to recognize it and acknowledge the situation in which you find yourself. Denying feelings of overwhelm won't help you conquer your flesh or the devil. Once you've acknowledged the reality of an overwhelmed heart, you can work with the Holy Spirit to get to the root of your feelings.

What is causing this overwhelm, really? Is the enemy blowing things out of proportion? Is the situation as bad as it looks, really? Or is this pressure purely demonic? Put your circumstances—and your emotions—into perspective. Is there anything you can do right now in the natural to relieve some of the burdens you feel?

Get your mind off the overwhelming circumstances and onto the Word of God. Pray for grace, strength and whatever else you need from your heavenly Father in the moment. Remind yourself of His promises. There are a few I like to keep in mind when overwhelm tries to wreak havoc on my soul: "The Lord is my strength and my shield; My heart trusted in Him, and I am helped; Therefore my heart greatly rejoices, and with my song I will praise Him" (Psalm 28:7). "I can do all things through Christ who strengthens me" (Phil 4:13). "Be still, and know that I am God" (Psalm 46:10).

— *Prayer* —

Father, in the name of Jesus, would You help me discern the voice of overwhelm before it drowns my faith and hinders my intercession? Would You remind me to wait on You to strengthen me and refresh me when I feel overwhelmed by my prayer responsibilities?

Living On the Prayer Wall

"Set your mind on things above, not on things on the earth" (Colossians 3:2).

Intercessors who live on the wall have a perspective that can only be attained by living on the wall. Put another way, some intercessors only see the wall the enemy has erected. Other intercessors try to peek over the wall to see what God is doing.

But intercessors who live on the wall can see further out into the spirit, gain God's view into the situation, and tap into a divine prayer strategy to see His will come to pass.

Rahab lived on the wall. No doubt, she prayed on the wall. And when the walls of Jericho came crashing down God's wall of protection preserved Rahab and her family. Her act of intercession paved the way for God's will and actually paved the way for the Messiah, who was birthed through her family line (see Matt. 4:1-6).

Rahab had a different perspective than the Canaanites in the Promised Land. She had prophetic insight from her place on the wall. She helped the Israelites because, as she said in Joshua 2:9-11:

"I know that the Lord has given you the land, that the terror of you has fallen on us, and that all the inhabitants of the land are fainthearted because of you. For we have heard how the Lord dried up the water of the Red Sea for you when you came out of Egypt, and what you did to the two kings of the Amorites who were on the other side of the Jordan, Sihon and Og, whom you utterly destroyed. And as soon as we heard these things, our hearts melted; neither did there remain any more courage in anyone because of you, for the Lord your God, He is God in heaven above and on earth beneath."

Intercessors who live on the wall see things differently. They have a revelation that God's ways are higher than our ways (see Is. 55:8-9). They discern between friend and foe. And they accomplish the will of the Lord through prayer.

— *Prayer* —

Father, in the name of Jesus, help me gain Your perspective before I release my intercession so I can pray with the right mindset. Help me not to be moved by the circumstances but to be moved by Your Spirit dwelling in me.

Praying the News

"Take heed, watch and pray; for you do not know when the time is" (Mark 13:33).

Before I was a Christian, I was a journalist. Before I was in full-time ministry, I was a journalist. As such, I wrote news articles all day, every day. Indeed, I wrote for major media outlets covering political elections, economic crises, sports and more. Eventually, I became the first-ever female editor of *Charisma* magazine. That's when I started praying the news.

What do I mean by praying the news? Well, every morning after I spend several hours in prayer and Bible study, I read the news headlines. I don't dive deep into most stories. Rather, I scan the headlines to see generally what's going on in the world. This helps me stay abreast of crises, trends, and the general goings on in the nations. I only spend about twenty minutes a day doing this. It's not a major time investment but it's part of watching.

Some will say, "Well, the news is fake." Some of it is, but if there is a hurricane coming or an assassination attempt or a famine somewhere, it's not typically fake. Some will say, "Smith Wigglesworth never let a newspaper in his house." I get it, but I'm not Wigglesworth. My calling as an intercessor is different than his calling as an apostle of faith who raised the dead. And, again, I am just scanning the headlines most of the time.

We can use the news as a tool to inform our effective intercession. We can use the news as a way to watch and pray without ceasing. When I scan news headlines, the Holy Spirit will illuminate what He wants me to pray for. Not every news event in the world is part of my prayer assignment that day, but oftentimes something stands out and that's when I intercede.

Intercessor, we can't put it all on the Holy Spirit to tell us everything going on in the world. Jesus told us to watch and pray. One way we can do that is by looking at the news, and then waiting on Him for our assignment.

— *Prayer* —

Father, in the name of Jesus, would You stir me to stay aware of current events so I can watch and pray with accuracy? Lord, there are so many needs in the world. I know I can't possibly pray for them all. Help me discern my daily prayer assignment through the news.

Are There Holes in Your Prayer Mantle?

"Jesus said, 'Therefore I say to you, do not worry about your life...'" (Matthew 6:25).

What is worry? The definition is really telling. According to *Merriam-Webster's* dictionary, it means: "choke, strangle, to harass by tearing, biting, or snapping especially at the throat, to shake or pull at with the teeth, to touch or disturb something repeatedly."

Worry also means, "to change the position of or adjust by repeated pushing or hauling, to assail with rough or aggressive attack or treatment, torment, to subject to persistent or nagging attention or effort, to afflict with mental distress or agitation, to make anxious."

You can see how the enemy will use worry to choke out your prayer life. In Matthew 6:25-32, Jesus said, "Therefore I say to you, do not worry about your life, what you will eat or what you will drink; nor about your body, what you will put on. Is not life more than food and the body more than clothing? Look at the birds of the air, for they neither sow nor reap nor gather into barns; yet your heavenly Father feeds them. Are you not of more value than they? Which of you by worrying can add one cubit to his stature?"

Later in the discourse, Jesus described them as having little faith. You don't need great faith to see prayer answers. You just need mustard seed faith. But that faith needs to be pure faith, not mixed with worry.

Consider what Jesus said. Your heavenly Father knows everything you need. We should never worry about provision, prodigals, healing or anything else. Worry wears holes in your prayer mantle. Worry works against your faith. You can't walk in worry and walk by faith at the same time. When the voice of worry comes, bind it up and cast it down. Cast your worry on Jesus because He cares for you passionately (see 1 Pet. 5:7).

— *Prayer* —

Father, in the name of Jesus, would You help me discern the voice of worry seeking to derail my intercession? I don't want to pray from a place of worry. I want to pray from a place of confidence in the God who supplies all my needs— and all my prayer answers.

The Samuel Prayer Anointing

"Moreover, as for me, far be it from me that I should sin against the Lord in ceasing to pray for you; but I will teach you the good and the right way" (1 Samuel 12:23).

Samuel was a prophet and God didn't let any of his words fall to the ground (see 1 Sam. 3:19). But have you ever considered this? None of his prayers fell to the ground either. God heard Samuel's prayers. Just as all of Israel from Dan to Beersheba knew Samuel was a prophet, all of Israel also knew he was an intercessor who got results.

Samuel had a heritage of prayer. He was the product of a praying mother, Hannah, who cried out to the Lord in her barrenness. I imagine Hannah continued on as a praying woman, modeling to young Samuel the power of prayer before she sent him to live with Eli the priest in fulfillment of her vow to the Lord.

Over and over again, we see Samuel in intercession. Twenty years after the men of Kirjath Jearim took the ark of the Lord, the Israelites lamented. Samuel prophesied a word of victory followed by repentance and gathered Israel to Mizpah, where he promised, "I will pray to the Lord for you" (1 Sam. 7:5).

Later, when the Israelites demanded a king like the surrounding nations, Samuel prayed to the Lord (see 1 Sam. 8:6). When the Israelites finally realized they made a mistake asking for a human king, they again turned to Samuel the intercessor and cried, "Pray for your servants to the Lord your God, that we may not die; for we have added to all our sins the evil of asking a king for ourselves" (1 Sam. 12:19).

Samuel considered failing to make intercession a sin against the Lord (see 1 Sam. 12:23). The Samuel anointing for intercession is an anointing that provides leadership through prayer. It is an anointing that sees the sin of the people but also sees it as a sin not to pray for a sinful people.

— *Prayer* —

Father, in the name of Jesus, would You grace me with the Samuel anointing for intercession? Give me a compassion for people who are going the wrong way and a grace to continue praying for them until they see the truth.

JANUARY 31

Triggering Dynamite Prayers

"For the word of God is living and powerful, and sharper than any two-edged sword, piercing even to the division of soul and spirit, and of joints and marrow, and is a discerner of the thoughts and intents of the heart" (Hebrews 4:12).

The Word of God gives your prayers life and power. The Word of God makes your prayers sharp and piercing. Heaven and earth will pass away, but God's Word will never pass away (see Matt. 24:35). God's Word is the truth that defies the enemy's lies.

Part of the science of intercession, if you will, is praying the Word. We can pray out of our mind, emotions, or intellect and may get some results. But when we pray the Word of God He is faithful to watch over that Word to perform it (see Jer. 1:12). His Word does not return void—it accomplishes what we send it to do (see Is. 55:11).

An intercessor who doesn't pray the Word is a like a demolition company that doesn't use dynamite. They may tear down the building one brick at a time but it will take much longer to get results. Releasing the Word of God into your intercession is like adding gunpowder to your prayers.

If you work the Word into your intercession, then the Word will work to bring prayer results. Of course, you have to use the right Word for the right occasion. Just as a surgeon uses the right scalpel to cut out a cancer or a golfer uses the right club to get the best results on the greens, the intercessor must know what Word to apply to what situation.

That means the intercessor must be a student of the Word. Paul told Timothy, "Be diligent to present yourself approved to God, a worker who does not need to be ashamed, rightly dividing the word of truth" (2 Tim. 2:15). An intercessor who cannot rightly divide the word of truth is not completely prepared to combat the enemy's lies.

Choose to give yourself over the Word. Meditate on the Word day and night and be careful to do all it says and you will be prosperous and successful in your intercession (see Josh. 1:18).

— *Prayer* —

Father, in the name of Jesus, make me a lover of Your Word. Help me get the Word in my heart and let it renew my mind so it flows out of my mouth when I pray. I want to wield the Sword of the Spirit accurately.

FEBRUARY

"I desire therefore that the men pray everywhere, lifting up holy hands, without wrath and doubting" (1 Timothy 2:8).

FEBRUARY 1

Finding Prayer Inspiration

"And let us consider one another in order to stir up love and good works" (Hebrews 10:24).

If we're honest, we'll admit we don't always feel "inspired" to pray. While there are times when we feel the burden of the Lord, the grace of God and an anointing to make intercession, sometimes this supernatural inspiration seems to allude us.

So what do you do when you don't feel particularly inspired? Well, you can choose to pray in the spirit until you feel inspired. As I share in my book *Tongues of Fire*, when we pray in the spirit many things can happen simultaneously. We can press past our flesh, tap into the prophetic, and more. We can choose to pray in tongues whenever we want.

Reading news headlines inspires me to pray. When I see the issues going on in my city or in the world, suddenly I feel a sense of urgency to make intercession. Likewise, reading classic books on prayer inspires me to pray. When I see the depths of the prayer lives of people like Edward Bauman and Andrew Murray, it spurs me to intercede.

I love to read quotes on prayer. The wisdom from men and women from past generations offers me quick inspiration. Here are few: George Herbert, a Welsh poet, orator and priest of the Church of England, once said, "Prayer should be the key of the day and the lock of the night." An anonymous author wrote, "If you only pray when you're in trouble, you're in trouble." E.M. Bounds, the author of many books on prayer, said, "Prayers outlive the lives of those who uttered them; outlive a generation, outlive an age, outlive a world."

A prayer list may inspire you or may not. Praying corporately may inspire you to pray. Listening to a prayer broadcast (like my *Mornings with the Holy Spirit*) can inspire you to pray along. Reading the Word of God can inspire you to pray. If you can't find any inspiration, do it for Jesus' sake. When you pray, He'll join you.

— *Prayer* —

Father, in the name of Jesus, would You inspire my heart to pray even in the driest seasons of my prayer life? Would You help me find the inspiration I need to keep pressing into intercession so the enemy doesn't take advantage?

A Blueprint for Answered Intercession

"Behold, how good and how pleasant it is for brethren to dwell together in unity!"
(Psalm 133:1)

I heard the Lord say, "I am uniting different streams of intercessors to release My power, My fire, My glory and an awakening among you. This awakening must first happen among the prayer warriors, the watchmen on the wall, the travailing saints, and the other streams of intercessors before we will see it manifest widely in the body.

"My intercessors need to get on the same page, not always with the minute details of theology but with the big picture in My heart to see transforming revival ... I am calling you to model true unity in intercession. I am calling you to walk in love despite your differences. I am calling you to rise up and pray together to see My will come to pass as it is in heaven.

"I am calling you to be part of a great army of intercessors that understands the power of blessing and refuses to curse. I am calling you to step into My Kingdom order in prayer, to submit your revelations one to another with an open spirit, to stand together in the midst of the warfare that resists you as You seek My strategies.

"I am calling you to network together, to band together, to run together and to experience Me together. I am creating intimacy among the intercessors, interpersonal relationships where your hearts are knit together in love.

"There will no longer be competition and jealousy and power struggles among you when you lay your heart bear before Me and commit to My greater cause. Is there not a cause? Keep the cause in mind and decide even now that My plans and purposes are greater than cultural, ethnic, racial and denominational lines. Stand in unity and you will see the blessing of prayer answers."

— Prayer —

Father, in the name of Jesus, help me get on the same page with Your agenda for intercession in the earth. Make me willing to connect with intercessors who don't sound like me. Help me find prayer warriors of like precious faith to walk with, pray with, and war with.

The Intercessor's Intercessor

"Greater love has no one than this, than to lay down one's life for his friends" (John 15:3).

I'm grateful for the intercessors in my life. There are several who are so in tune with what is going on in the spirit realm that they (seemingly) randomly reach out and let me know, "You've been on my heart. I'm praying." This happens with no conversation, and even if we haven't spoken in a long while. And it's uncanny. Every time I get that text, it's right on time.

Maybe you've heard it said, "She's an intercessor to intercessors." Have you ever wondered what that meant? The one who is an intercessor to intercessors is greatly gifted with a mantle of prayer and a spirit of compassion that gives them a heart to pray for other intercessors, especially those who are younger in the Lord or who are on the front lines of battle.

Being an intercessor to intercessors is a calling in and of itself. Intercessors who are called to cover other intercessors have a responsibility to stand in the gap at even the most inconvenient times. They are, essentially, laying down their life in intercession for the sake of the intercessory prayer movement itself. Think about that.

I've said many times every serious intercessor needs a backup intercessor, someone who can sense when they need prayer without them speaking a word. I believe every serious intercessor needs an intercessor because no one understands the plight or mission of an intercessor like another mature intercessor. Intercessors need prayer.

So how do you pray for intercessors? Well, as the Holy Spirit leads, of course. Generally speaking, though, you pray for their protection. You pray God would root them and ground them in love and give them revelation to release effective prayers that drive results. You release the blessing of the Lord over their lives. You pray in tongues. These are but a few ways to get you started. There's a blessing in being an intercessor to intercessors.

— Prayer —

Father, in the name of Jesus, if You are calling me to be an intercessor to intercessors I am willing. Give me a compassion and an unction to pray for the intercessors who need it the most. Give me the grace to lay down my life for You—and Your friends.

The Corrie Ten Boom Prayer Anointing

"But if you do not forgive men their trespasses, neither will your Father forgive your trespasses"
(Matthew 6:15).

When Christians stop praying, the devils shout for joy. So said Corrie ten Boom, whose family helped Jews escape the horrors of the Nazi-driven Holocaust during World War II. Reports suggest the family saved about eight hundred Jews from fiery furnaces by hiding them in a secret room.

"We never know how God will answer our prayers, but we can expect that He will get us involved in His plan for the answer," Corrie once said. "If we are true intercessors, we must be ready to take part in God's work on behalf of the people for whom we pray."

The devout Christian family's rescue mission came to a screeching halt when a fellow Dutch citizen betrayed them to the Nazis. The entire family, who considered the Jews "God's ancient people" was put in prison in the Netherlands near Amsterdam. Corrie and her sister were sent to the notorious Ravensbrück concentration camp in Germany.

Twelve days after her sister died there, Corrie was miraculously released. Obviously, this was an answer to prayer. She once said, "What wings are to a bird, and sails to a ship, so is prayer to the soul." She saw prayer as a steering wheel where many other see it as a spare tire—used in case of emergency. She understood that a Christian on her knees is powerful.

With these revelations Corrie went on to start a worldwide ministry that spanned to more than 60 nations to offer rehab centers for survivors of Nazi concentration camps. Along the way, she learned the power of prayer and intercession. She once said, "When you want to work for God start a committee. When you want to work with God start a prayer group."

Perhaps most of all, Corrie had to learn forgiveness, which is a prerequisite for prayer. If we don't forgive, God won't even hear our prayers. She opined, "Forgiveness is an act of the will, and the will can function regardless of the temperature of the heart."

— *Prayer* —

Father, in the name of Jesus, teach me how to walk in sacrificial intercession like Corrie ten Boom. Would You help me to keep short accounts with people and with You? Teach me the power of forgiveness and help me walk in it continually.

Finding Immunity From Fear

"Fear not, for I am with you; Be not dismayed, for I am your God. I will strengthen you, yes, I will help you, I will uphold you with My righteous right hand" (Isaiah 41:10).

When we walked into the prayer meeting I sensed it was going to be an all-out war, I looked for fearless soldiers to run to the battle line with me. Long story short, we engaged the enemy over our territory. Prophetically, we identified strongholds in our region and took authority over them in the name of Jesus. We stood on God's Word. We worshipped the King. But some of the intercessors weren't ready for what happened next: demonic retaliation.

The enemy got to one of the intercessors. Ironically, she had propped herself up as the most experienced of us all. She often boasted about her experience in sending the devil packing, and she was bold in prayer. But this experience struck fear in her heart. She began to criticize the prayer meetings—even though it was extremely rare that we entered into that level of warfare. She began to question the leadership. And she never came back to the group. In a way, the enemy gained a victory. He took her out with a little bout of dizziness.

Fearful intercessors are ineffective intercessors. If you are too scared of the enemy to follow the Lord into battle, you are walking in a measure of defeat rather than the Christ-won victory. They say dogs can smell fear on you. Well, so can the enemy. Enter every battle from a position of victory, understanding your authority in Christ. And when the battle is over, plead the blood of Jesus over yourself, bind spirits of retaliation and walk in freedom rather than fear.

Yes, sometimes the devil hits you back. But God is in control. Don't give up because the devil retaliates. Seek more revelation that "the Lord is a warrior" (see Ex. 15:3) and "the battle is the Lord's" (see 2 Chron. 20:15-17). Seek more revelation about your authority in Christ (see Luke 10:19). And get equipped practically with training on how to use the weapons of your warfare more accurately.

— *Prayer* —

Father, in the name of Jesus, Your Word tells me the righteous are bold as a lion. I declare I am bold. I declare I am fearless. I declare I am strong in the Lord and the power of His might. I shall not fear. I shall stand in the faith of God in prayer.

Adopting a Nehemiah Mindset

"O Lord, I pray, please let Your ear be attentive to the prayer of Your servant, and to the prayer of Your servants who desire to fear Your name; and let Your servant prosper this day, I pray, and grant him mercy in the sight of this man" (Nehemiah 1:11).

When you think of Nehemiah, you probably think of an apostolic grace—a builder's anointing. But Nehemiah was a man of prayer before he was a builder of walls. I heard the Lord say:

"I am calling on intercessors to rise in the spirit of Nehemiah and rebuild the hedge of protection around America. I am calling on those who will refuse to come down from the wall, who will discern the enemy's strategies and refute them, and who will complete the work I've called them to start.

"I am seeking governmental intercessors to rally other prayer warriors to get in step with what I am trying to rebuild—and restore what the enemy has destroyed and stolen. Rise up now and pray. Rise up now and stand in the gap. Rise up now to make up the hedge. I am looking for those who are willing so that My plans may be accomplished in this nation."

What is a Nehemiah anointing in prayer? Nehemiah intercessors won't come down from the wall, despite the mockery, the false accusations, the misunderstandings, or even the works of weariness. The Nehemiah mindset confronts injustice. The Nehemiah anointing is not afraid of the fight. The Nehemiah mindset isn't afraid to labor long in prayer until the job is done. The Nehemiah mindset has a passion for the prayer assignment that unlocks grace and anointing.

When you tap into the Nehemiah mindset and anointing, you will find the grace to withstand natural opposition, false prophets and other enemy assignments that thwart the rebuilding. Although the Nehemiah intercessor's job is never really done and the warfare is real, the reward is great. Who will rise up and rebuild the walls in prayer in their nation? Will you?

— *Prayer* —

Father, in the name of Jesus, would You help me cultivate a Nehemiah mindset in my intercessory prayer ministry? Help me to be selfless in my intercession, laying my life down for Your cause and inspiring others to join the campaign.

The Intercessor's 'Aha' Moments

"But God has revealed them to us through His Spirit. For the Spirit searches all things, yes, the deep things of God" (1 Corinthians 2:10).

If you want more revelation, make more intercession. Let me say that again. If you want more revelation, make more intercession. Intercession and revelation often go hand in hand. God is a rewarder of those who diligently seek Him (see Heb. 11:6). For the intercessor, sometimes that reward is revelation.

Put another way, revelation often comes through intercessory prayer sessions. The Holy Spirit is the spirit of prayer. When we lean into Him in our intercession, our prayers can bring forth the prophetic intelligence, wisdom and revelation we need to better partner with His heart.

There's absolutely nothing wrong with a prayer list. Prayers lists can help us stay on track. But often there's something else, something more, on the Holy Spirit's heart. People may tell you how they need you to pray, but remember flesh and blood didn't reveal the revelation of Christ to Peter. The Spirit of God did (see Matt. 16:17). The same Spirit of God will reveal how you can best pray for people, places and things.

You don't have to be a seasoned intercessor—someone who has stood in the gap for decades on end—to receive revelation through intercession. You don't even have to consider yourself prophetic. Praying the Word of God can bring you into revelation in your intercession. Psalm 119:130 (HCSB) tells us, "The revelation of Your words brings light and gives understanding to the inexperienced."

The Holy Spirit is the one who searches the deep things of God (see 1 Cor. 2:10). When you yield to the Holy Spirit in prayer—when you let Him help you pray—He can reveal those deep things to you for the purpose of prevailing intercession. When you set out to pray, ask the Holy Spirit to help you. Ask Him to inform your intercession. Ask Him to help you yield to Him in prayer. You'll love the results.

— *Prayer* —

Father, in the name of Jesus, I yield to You in my intercession. Would You help me to pick up on Your thoughts, Your plans, Your purposes and Your emotions as I intercede? Would You give me revelation that helps me be an effective fervent intercessor?

The Rejected Intercessor

"If the world hates you, you know that it hated Me before it hated you" (John 15:18).

Intercessors are often rejected. Intercessors can be other-worldly, so to speak, and typically do not fit in with the lukewarm Christian mold. They are passionate about prayer and may spend significant times in prayer at the expense of what others want from them.

Often, pastors don't understand the intercessor—or are intimidated by the prayer warrior. Some pastors find intercession messy and don't understand its inherent value is worth the mess. Others are concerned the intercessor will see their secret sin. Still others won't make a place for prayer in the church, leaving the intercessor to walk alone.

The enemy wants intercessors to feel rejected and unappreciated so they will grow weary in well doing and throw in the prayer towel. Rejection works to steal, kill and destroy (see John 10:10). If the rejection you've suffered is not processed through God's love, you can open yourself up to the voice of rejection and ultimately the spirit of rejection.

If you don't move to heal that wound that allowed rejection in, rejection will set you up for a life of pain. Too many intercessors are walking in deep-seated rejection and God wants to bring deliverance. But even when He delivers you, you have to walk it out. You have to get the revelation that God loves you because you will be rejected again.

The unfortunate truth is, you will be rejected—sometimes even by the ones for whom you are laboring in travail. You will be misunderstood. You will be shunned at times as an "odd bird." But don't let the voice of rejection become louder than God's voice, as that will hinder your intercession.

Reject the voice of rejection. Christ, the Intercessor, is not rejecting you. He's celebrating your work in His name and the Father is answering your prayers. Why else would the enemy work overtime to get you to stop?

— Prayer —

Father, in the name of Jesus, deliver me from any and all rejection. I want to be free to stand in the gap without reservation, without concern about what people think about me, and with absolute freedom. I need to hear Your voice clearly. Deliver me, Lord.

Thanking Your Way to the Prayer Breakthrough

"Enter into His gates with thanksgiving ... " (Psalm 100:4).

Ephesians 5:20 exhorts us to "give thanks always for all things to God the Father in the name of our Lord Jesus Christ." 1 Thessalonians 5:18 tells us, "In everything give thanks, for this is the will of God in Christ Jesus concerning you."

Psalm 50:14 says, "Sacrifice a thank offering to God, and pay your vows to the Most High." Psalm 136:1 urges, "Give thanks to the Lord, for he is good, for his steadfast love endures forever." Colossians 3:15 says, "And let the peace of Christ rule in your hearts, to which indeed you were called in one body. And be thankful."

Have you ever wondered why the Bible has so much to say about gratitude? It's not because God has a big ego and wants you to be a "thank you" bot. Gratitude is as much for our sake as it is for the One to Whom we express it. Think about what gratitude really is. Gratitude is being thankful but it's more than being thankful. Gratitude is showing appreciation and returning the kindness.

The psalmists said, "Enter into His gates with thanksgiving." What if we took some time to express our thanks to God for who He is and what He has already done before we ask Him to do one more thing? I believe our gratitude would build our faith to pray all the more. I believe gratitude causes the Lord's ears to perk up.

How do I know? Because Scripture records an incident in which Jesus cleansed ten lepers. He basically rescued them from a lonely life of banishment, as lepers were considered the outcasts of society. They all cried out for mercy. They all received mercy. But Luke 17:15 records what happened next: "And one of them, when he saw that he was healed, returned, and with a loud voice glorified God, and fell down on his face at His feet, giving Him thanks." Only one gave thanks. Let that be you.

— Prayer —

Father, in the name of Jesus, help me remember to always thank You for who You are and what You've done in my life. If You never did another thing, I would be forever grateful. Inspire me to maintain an attitude of gratitude.

Praising Your Way Into His Presence

"Go into his courts with praise" (Psalm 100:4, NLT).

Ruth Ward Heflin used to say, "Praise until the worship comes. Worship until the glory comes. Then stand in the glory."

Over and over again in the Psalms, we find David praising the Lord. Over and over again in the chronicles of his exploits, we find him winning huge battles and progressing further into his destiny despite enemy traps.

David understood when he praised his way into God's presence, he was entering the shelter of the Most High, his Rock, his fortress, his deliverer, his protector from the arrows that fly by day and the terror by night and the pestilence and destruction (see Psalm 91).

Every intercessor needs to enter His courts with praise. It's a key that opens a door to prayer answers through recognition of who He is, not just what He can do. *The Passion Translation* of Psalm 100:4 puts it this way: "You can pass through his open gates with the password of praise." Let that sink in. Think of praise as a password to the promises. We praise in faith when the winds are against us, and our praise leads us into faith to ask and keep on asking until we see the answer.

If discouragement has gripped your heart and you can't find the words with which to praise Him, turn to the psalms. Psalm 150:1-6 is a good place to start. It reads:

"Praise the Lord! Praise God in his sanctuary; praise him in his mighty heaven! Praise him for his mighty works; praise his unequaled greatness! Praise him with a blast of the ram's horn; praise him with the lyre and harp! Praise him with the tambourine and dancing; praise him with strings and flutes! Praise him with a clash of cymbals; praise him with loud clanging cymbals. Let everything that breathes sing praises to the Lord! Praise the Lord!"

— *Prayer* —

Father, in the name of Jesus, I praise You. I praise You for the work of the cross. I praise You for Your faithfulness. I praise You for Your mercy and Your grace. I declare I will use the password of praise all my days.

Praying Mountaintop Prayers

"And when He had sent the multitudes away, He went up on the mountain by Himself to pray. Now when evening came, He was alone there" (Matthew 14:23).

Although I choose to live in a South Florida city near beaches, where palm trees pepper the local roads and the sun shines most of the year, I love the mountains. More specifically, I love to pray in the mountains. Apparently, Jesus did, too.

Over and over in Scripture we see Jesus praying on the mountain. Beyond Matthew's account, Mark records this habit: "And when He had sent them away, He departed to the mountain to pray" (Mark 6:46). Luke records this habit: "Now it came to pass in those days that He went out to the mountain to pray, and continued all night in prayer to God."

At times, Jesus even took His disciples to the mountains to pray. Luke 9:28 tells us, "Now it came to pass, about eight days after these sayings, that He took Peter, John, and James and went up on the mountain to pray." This was what we call the Mount of Transfiguration. You know what happened next. Moses and Elijah appeared and spoke to Jesus about the crucifixion.

What is it about praying in the mountains? Why did Jesus pray mountaintop prayers? I believe it was, in part, because the mountains are quiet. I love to go to Moravian Falls, for example, because it's so quiet you can hear the leaves on the trees blow in the slight wind. And that's about all you can hear. Well, I take that back. You can hear the voice of God.

When you are in a spiritual valley, you need to find your proverbial mountain and pray mountaintop prayers. When you can't hear God's voice in the midst of the chaos all around you, you need to find your mountain and listen for His whisper. You may not be able to escape to a literal mountain, but you can find your mountaintop.

Maybe your mountaintop is a local nature park early in the morning before children start running around playing. Maybe your mountaintop is a hotel room you rent for a day to be in solitude. Maybe your mountaintop is your car on long drive down windy scenic roads. Find your mountain.

— *Prayer* —

Father, in the name of Jesus, would You help me find my victory mountain? When the mountains of life threaten to overwhelm me, would You lead me to a quiet place where I can gain Your perspective and release my prayers of faith that moves those mountains?

Discerning Your Inner Circle Intercessors

"Now it came to pass, about eight days after these sayings, that He took Peter, John, and James and went up on the mountain to pray" (Luke 9:28).

I'm all for praying in secret in your prayer closet. That is one of the most thrilling types of intercession because it's you and the Holy Spirit. But every intercessor needs a small core team of intercessors with whom to pray.

You're not always called to pray alone. Sometimes you just need more firepower. And sometimes you need to fellowship with intercessors of like-precious faith. C. Peter Wagner spoke about three circles of intercessors in his book, *Prayer Shield: How to Intercede for Pastors and Christian Leaders.*

There are some intercessors with whom you will have a casual relationship. They may attend your church or be part of a prayer network to which you belong. You may join prayer calls with intercessors you never meet. You enjoy that synergy but they are at arm's length in some respect.

You may also find fellowship with intercessors in your city. You may develop friendly relationships with them, pick their brains about prayer strategies, or encourage them when they post something profound on social media. God may put them on your heart or put you on their heart from time to time—and you may have brief conversations randomly.

But then there are what I call the inner circle intercessors. These are close relationships you develop with intercessors over time. These are the intercessors you go to when you have a personal prayer need that's private but immediate. These are the intercessors you really trust to pray for you in times of need.

Inner circle intercessors are the prayer warriors who understand what the Lord is doing through you and in you. They support that in prayer. These are intercessors who also see what the enemy is planning against you and war for you. These are people you share intimately with.

So how do you find them? You don't, really. The Lord assigns them to you and you to them. But, like everything else in an intercessor's life, you can pray them in. God knows it's not good for you to stand alone in your prayer closet. He wants to give you intercessor friends who get you and stand for you.

— *Prayer* —

Father, in the name of Jesus, would You lead me and guide me by Your Holy Spirit to the inner circle intercessors You've assigned to my life? Would You help me to be intentional about building relationships with other intercessors so I discern the ones to draw closer?

FEBRUARY 13

Praying In Supernatural Wealth Transfers

"'The silver is Mine, and the gold is Mine,' says the Lord of hosts" (Haggai 2:8).

Some people have the gift of giving. Some people have a gift to pray in the giving. Meet financial intercessor, who can stand in the gap and tear down assignments against wealth creation.

The financial intercessor has a deep revelation of God as Jehovah Jireh. They understand the silver is God's. The gold is God's. The cattle on a thousand hills is God's (see Psalm 50:10). Financial intercessors have a revelation that riches come from God (see 1 Chron. 9:12). They have a revelation that the blessing of the Lord makes one rich, and He adds no sorrow to it (see Prov. 10:22).

The financial intercessor has a keen sense of discernment to expose enemy blockages. They have a Jeremiah-like anointing to root out, pull down, destroy and throw down resistance to the provision God is pouring out (see. Jer. 1:10). And they have wisdom on how to build and plant with the seed God has given to the sower.

The financial intercessor breaks through the powers sabotaging the power to create wealth to establish God's covenant in the earth (see Deut. 8:18). The financial intercessor targets hindering spirits and spirits of delay that are clogging up the pipelines of provision. The financial intercessor can sometimes see the hidden treasures and riches stored in secret places (see Is. 45:3).

The financial intercessor may receive sowing strategies from the Lord that bring short- and long-term returns on the investment. They have a revelation that God will in fact supply every need according to His riches in glory in Christ Jesus and prophetic insight on how to lift up specific needs at specific times, prioritizing the urgent (see Phil. 4:19).

The financial intercessor doesn't have to beg for bread but prays the Word, decrees the Word, proclaims the Word and prophesies against the resistance to the Word until the provision manifests. The financial intercessor, then is, priceless.

— *Prayer* —

Father, in the name of Jesus, would You give me prayer strategies for provision for those to whom You've called me to pray? You own it all, and You're a generous God. Help me break through the resistance to Your financial flow.

Intercessors of Love

"And now abide faith, hope, love, these three; but the greatest of these is love"
(1 Corinthians 13:13).

God is love and love motivates all true intercession. Love will motivate you to pray without ceasing when your flesh is wrestling against the spirit of prayer upon you. If love is not motivating your intercession you will surely grow weary. You will surely faint in the day of adversity. Paul the apostle wrote these poignant words in 1 Corinthians 13:1-8:

"Though I speak with the tongues of men and of angels, but have not love, I have become sounding brass or a clanging cymbal. And though I have the gift of prophecy, and understand all mysteries and all knowledge, and though I have all faith, so that I could remove mountains, but have not love, I am nothing. And though I bestow all my goods to feed the poor, and though I give my body to be burned, but have not love, it profits me nothing.

"Love suffers long and is kind; love does not envy; love does not parade itself, is not puffed up; does not behave rudely, does not seek its own, is not provoked, thinks no evil; does not rejoice in iniquity, but rejoices in the truth; bears all things, believes all things, hopes all things, endures all things. Love never fails."

Intercession motivated by love never fails. When God, who is love, motivates your prayer it simply cannot fail. It cannot return void. Love watches over the prayer and delivers the answer. Intercessors need a baptism not just of the Holy Spirit and fire but a baptism in the spirit of love. It takes the love of God to continue hammering away at hard cases.

In his book, *The Ministry of Intercession*, Andrew Murray wrote these words that should prick the heart of every true intercessor: "The attempt to pray constantly for ourselves must be a failure; it is in intercession for others that our faith and love and perseverance will be aroused, and that power of the Spirit be found which can fit us for saving men."

— *Prayer* —

Father, in the name of Jesus, reduce me to love. Encounter me with Your great love. Fill me with love to overflowing. May love—agape love—continually motivate my intercession so I can have the confidence that Your love will make a way out of no way.

The John Hyde Prayer Anointing

"Continuing steadfastly in prayer" (Romans 12:12).

He goes down in Christian missionary history with the nickname "Praying John." John Hyde was an American missionary who preached in the Punjab of India. Serving the Lord in the 1800s and early 1900s, he was also known as an Apostle of Prayer. His primary focus was praying for a Jesus awakening in India.

As history tells it, praying John went days and days without eating or sleeping for the sake of fasting and prayer. Even though he was partially deaf in the natural, he had no problem hearing the Holy Spirit's call to see souls saved in the Asian nation where Hinduism was rampant. And when he prayed, he expected results.

He once said, "On the day of prayer, God gave me a new experience. I seemed to be away above our conflict here in the Punjab and I saw God's great battle in all India, and then away out beyond in China, Japan, and Africa. I saw how we had been thinking in narrow circles of our own countries and in our own denominations, and how God was now rapidly joining force to force and line to line, and all was beginning to be one great struggle."

His heart's cry was, "Give me souls, O God, or I die." What a commitment to souls and to the ministry of prayer! Indeed, praying John did pass away doing the work of the ministry. His heart moved over from the left side of his chest to the right side. The doctors were baffled and told him if he didn't start resting more he would not live another six months.

Defying the doctor's orders, he continued praying. Praying John lived for another two years and, before he went on to glory, he witnessed what he was waiting for: a wave of revival swept through the Punjab as well as the rest of India. Souls were saved. He got the souls and he went home to the Lord. Ask for the John Hyde prayer anointing.

— *Prayer* —

Father, in the name of Jesus, I want to give my life to prayer. I want to continue steadfastly in prayer for souls, for new believers, and for the final harvest. Would You give me an anointing to pray selflessly like John Hyde?

When Angels Deliver Prayer Answers

"Yes, while I was speaking in prayer, the man Gabriel, whom I had seen in the vision at the beginning, being caused to fly swiftly, reached me about the time of the evening offering" (Daniel 9:21).

Daniel the prophet was as much an intercessor as any other we see in the pages of the Bible. He had a habit of praying three times a day. One day, he set his face toward God to make requests by prayer and supplications, with fasting, sackcloth and ashes. He entered into repentance for Israel.

Daniel's beautiful, heartfelt prayer got heaven's attention and God sent an angel in what goes down in Bible history as a dramatic prayer encounter. We read it in Daniel 9:20-23:

"Now while I was speaking, praying, and confessing my sin and the sin of my people Israel, and presenting my supplication before the Lord my God for the holy mountain of my God, yes, while I was speaking in prayer, the man Gabriel, whom I had seen in the vision at the beginning, being caused to fly swiftly, reached me about the time of the evening offering.

"And he informed me, and talked with me, and said, 'O Daniel, I have now come forth to give you skill to understand. At the beginning of your supplications the command went out, and I have come to tell you, for you are greatly beloved; therefore consider the matter, and understand the vision." Gabriel, a messenger angel, proceeded to explain the vision.

Angelic encounters are possible in realms of prayer. But notice what activated this encounter. It wasn't Daniel's eloquence. It was Daniel's willingness to repent on behalf of a hard-hearted people who were in bondage to the Babylonian system. He didn't think more highly of himself than he ought, but rather humbled himself before God in repentance for Israel as if he alone were responsible for the condition of this people group.

Some intercessors fall into the trap of seeking angelic encounters, but this is a mistake. Satan can appear as an angel of light and the encounter-seeking intercessor can end up deceived, and propagating deception. Daniel, by contrast, was simply seeking the Lord with a contrite heart that got heaven's attention—and God sent an angel.

— *Prayer* —

Father, in the name of Jesus, forgive me for putting encounters above Your Word. Help me to seek Your face in prayer and trust You to send angelic messengers if and when they serve Your purposes in my intercession.

Pray Just Like Elijah

"Elijah was a man with a nature like ours, and he prayed earnestly that it would not rain; and it did not rain on the land for three years and six months" (James 5:17).

Catch that. Elijah was a person just like you. He had faults just like you. He got discouraged just like you. He wanted to quit sometimes, just like you. Still, he was a powerful prophet and intercessor. You can pray with the same power as Elijah.

First, Elijah exercised his power to stop the rain. He told Ahab, "As the Lord God of Israel lives, before whom I stand, there shall not be dew nor rain these years, except at my word" (1 Kings 17:1). That would have been presumptuous, except the Lord put those words in the prophet's mouth. Just as Elijah decreed it, there was no rain. The result was a massive drought that eventually caused a famine.

For three and a half years, Israel saw no rain. But one day, after defeating the false prophets at Mt. Carmel, Elijah prophesied rain was coming. He heard the sound of the abundance of rain in the spirit. That sound caused him to drop to his knees to pray without ceasing until he saw the prophesied end to the drought that plagued Israel.

Elijah prayed with faith in what God said He would do, even though he couldn't see it. We read in 1 Kings 18:42-43, "And Elijah went up to the top of Carmel; then he bowed down on the ground, and put his face between his knees, and said to his servant, 'Go up now, look toward the sea.' So he went up and looked, and said, 'There is nothing.'" And seven times he said, 'Go again.'"

Elijah was so confident in the prophetic word that he was not willing to abandon the cause. He had a word from the Lord. And that's why it's so critical that intercessors have the word of the Lord. Once God speaks, there's faith to pray through even when nothing seems to be changing. There's faith to pray through unto the breakthrough.

— *Prayer* —

Father, in the name of Jesus, help me not look at my own weaknesses as an intercessor but to listen for the sure word of the Lord. Help me hear what Your plans are so I can get into prayer agreement with what You've spoken.

Releasing 'Nevertheless' Faith

"Nevertheless, the Lord raised up judges who delivered them out of the hand of those who plundered them" (Judges 2:16).

Nevertheless. It's a powerful word every intercessor must utter at some point. Nevertheless faith is something every intercessor needs to cultivate because circumstances often seem to defy your best-laid prayers.

Nevertheless means "in spite of." There are times when you need to pray long and pray strong in spite of your weariness. There are times when you'll have to keep releasing decrees in spite of the unbelief in the hearts of those around you. There are times when you'll have to keep prophesying to the dry bones in spite of the stillness.

Peter released "nevertheless faith" in Luke 5. He was fishing all night when Jesus appeared on the scene with a prophetic instruction about where to find the fish. Jesus' advice was contrary to the fisherman's natural wisdom. "But Simon answered and said to Him, 'Master, we have toiled all night and caught nothing; nevertheless at Your word I will let down the net'" (Luke 5:5). Peter's nevertheless faith brought in a net-breaking blessing.

David stood in "nevertheless faith" during trouble, saying, "Blessed be the Lord, for He has shown me His marvelous kindness in a strong city! For I said in my haste, 'I am cut off from before Your eyes'; Nevertheless You heard the voice of my supplications when I cried out to You" (Ps.31:21-24). Sometimes it looks like God's not moving, but "nevertheless faith" keeps waiting on the Lord.

Nehemiah demonstrated "nevertheless faith" as he set out to rebuild the wall around Jerusalem: "Now it happened, when Sanballat, Tobiah, the Arabs, the Ammonites, and the Ashdodites heard that the walls of Jerusalem were being restored and the gaps were beginning to be closed, that they became very angry, and all of them conspired together to come and attack Jerusalem and create confusion. Nevertheless we made our prayer to our God, and because of them we set a watch against them day and night" (Neh. 4:7-9).

— Prayer —

Father, would You help me build myself up in "nevertheless faith" so I can stand strong when the winds are contrary, when the blessing seems delayed and when the warfare seems too strong for me? Help me stand in faith that nevertheless, You will deliver me.

Dividing Between Soul and Spirit Burdens

"Bear one another's burdens, and so fulfill the law of Christ" (Galatians 6:2).

E.M. Bounds, a 19th Century Methodist author who wrote nine important books on prayer, understood intercessory prayer burdens. And he understood how to recognize them. Do you? It's important for every intercessor to learn this realm of Holy Spirit prayer prompting.

Sometimes God places someone on your heart and you pray. That type of prayer burden is not difficult to recognize. For example, Sally comes to mind and you yield to the Holy Spirit's prompting to pray for her. You don't understand it at the time. Later you find out she was facing a major battle on the home front that same day. Your prayers gave her strength. You fell satisfied knowing you were used of God to be a prayer solutionist.

But it's not always that clear. Many times there's a spiritual weight that comes with a prayer burden. You may feel a heaviness of heart, a restless mind, a spirit of mourning, or depressed emotions that seem to come out of nowhere.

If we don't discern the call to pray, if we are going through our own trial and tribulation, or if we are not as sensitive to the Holy Spirit as we should be, we will think it's us. When we mistake the prayer burden as an emotional burden we focus on ourselves rather than pressing into intercession. We suffer needlessly in our own souls rather than helping another soul in need.

Here's my point: When you feel heavy-hearted, when you feel depressed, when you feel oppressed, when you feel out of sorts, don't get into your carnal mind about it. Even if it is your own personal problem, that's not going to solve it. Pray in the Spirit. He is willing to help you with your infirmities and He wants to pray through you to help the infirmities of others. E.M. Bounds offered: "Desire burdens the chariot of prayer, and faith drives its wheels."

— *Prayer* —

Father, in the name of Jesus, would You help me discern prayer burdens? Would You help me divide my soul from my spirit so I can respond quickly to Your call to pray? Please, make me more sensitive to Your Spirit.

Praying the Apostolic Prayers

"Grace and peace be multiplied to you in the knowledge of God and of Jesus our Lord, as His divine power has given to us all things that pertain to life ..." (2 Peter 1:2-3).

You don't have to be the least bit apostolic to pray the apostolic prayers found in the Bible. Kenneth E. Hagin taught me the value of praying these prayers many years ago, and it's become a staple of my prayer life. If you'll adopt these prayers, you'll find yourself growing in many dimensions.

The apostolic prayers are prayers Jesus and the apostles prayed—and they are recorded in Scripture. Nineteen of the twenty-seven New Testament books contain apostolic prayers. Many were penned by the apostle Paul. While I'm sure the apostles prayed many things, there is deep value in coming into agreement with the apostolic prayers for ourselves and others.

The apostolic prayers include prayers for boldness with signs and wonders (see Acts 4:24-31); prayers for Israel to be saved (see Rom. 10:1); prayers for the church to be unified (see Rom. 10:1); prayers to be filled with the Spirit (see Rom. 15:13). But let me share with you one of my favorites that help strengthen the inner life of the intercessor. It comes from Ephesians 3:14-21:

"For this reason I bow my knees to the Father of our Lord Jesus Christ, from whom the whole family in heaven and earth is named, that He would grant you, according to the riches of His glory, to be strengthened with might through His Spirit in the inner man, that Christ may dwell in your hearts through faith; that you, being rooted and grounded in love, may be able to comprehend with all the saints what is the width and length and depth and height—to know the love of Christ which passes knowledge; that you may be filled with all the fullness of God. Now to Him who is able to do exceedingly abundantly above all that we ask or think, according to the power that works in us, to Him be glory in the church by Christ Jesus to all generations, forever and ever. Amen."

— Prayer —

Father, in the name of Jesus, help me make the apostolic prayers part of my prayer habit as I intercede for the church and pray for myself. Help me see the value in using these wise prayers as a guide in my prayer ministry.

Put on Christ the Intercessor

"The spirit indeed is willing, but the flesh is weak" (Matthew 26:41).

We underestimate the power of the flesh and its ability to hinder our intercession. Our spirit is always willing to pray, and the Holy Spirit is always ready to help in the effort. But our flesh wars against the desires of the Spirit.

In Matthew 26:41, Jesus said to watch and pray. He also said the Spirit is willing but the flesh is weak. Again, your spirit man wants to pray. Your flesh wants to lay in bed and sleep, stuff its face full of ice cream, or whine and complain about something. Your spirit man wants to leap into intercession and work with the Holy Spirit to bring the will of God into the earth. Who will win out?

In Galatians 5:16, the Apostle Paul said, "Let the Holy Spirit guide your lives. Then you won't be doing what your sinful nature craves." That's wisdom. What does your sinful nature crave? Anything that gratifies it at the time. And prophetic intercession doesn't gratify the flesh. The carnal mind is enmity against God (see Rom. 8:7).

Jesus said, "It is the spirit that quickeneth; the flesh profiteth nothing" (John 6:63, KJV). And in Romans 8, Paul said, "For they that are after the flesh do mind the things of the flesh; but they that are after the Spirit the things of the Spirit. So then they that are in the flesh cannot please God. But ye are not in the flesh, but in the Spirit, if so be that the Spirit of God dwell in you."

So what are we to do? "Put ye on the Lord Jesus Christ, and make not provision for the flesh, to fulfill the lusts thereof" (Rom. 13:14, KJV). "For he that soweth to his flesh shall of the flesh reap corruption; but he that soweth to the Spirit shall of the Spirit reap life everlasting" (Gal. 6:8). The bottom line? Walk after the Spirit and you won't fulfill the lusts of the flesh.

— *Prayer* —

Father, in the name of Jesus, help me crucify my flesh. Strengthen me in my inner man so I can overcome the power of the flesh that wants to destroy my prayer life. Teach me to overcome the lusts of the flesh so I can serve You well in intercession.

Letting Compassion Mark Your Intercession

"Therefore, as the elect of God, holy and beloved, put on tender mercies, kindness, humility, meekness, longsuffering; bearing with one another, and forgiving one another, if anyone has a complaint against another" (Colossians 3:12-13).

Christ the Intercessor is full of compassion. In fact, every time in Scripture Christ was moved with divine compassion miracles happened. Compassion defined is a sympathetic consciousness of someone else's distress, along with a desire to help.

We see Christ move with compassion throughout the Gospels. Read Mark 6:34, "And Jesus, when He came out, saw a great multitude and was moved with compassion for them, because they were like sheep not having a shepherd. So He began to teach them many things." And again in Matthew 14:14, "And when Jesus went out He saw a great multitude; and He was moved with compassion for them, and healed their sick."

Seasoned intercessors can discern the compassion of the spirit of Christ within them, urging them to pray. We see Christ's compassionate prayer in the story of the Widow of Nain in Luke 9:11-15:

"Now it happened, the day after, that He went into a city called Nain; and many of His disciples went with Him, and a large crowd. And when He came near the gate of the city, behold, a dead man was being carried out, the only son of his mother; and she was a widow. And a large crowd from the city was with her.

"When the Lord saw her, He had compassion on her and said to her, 'Do not weep.' Then He came and touched the open coffin, and those who carried him stood still. And He said, 'Young man, I say to you, arise.' So he who was dead sat up and began to speak. And He presented him to his mother."

Let Christ's compassion move you to intercession.

— Prayer —

Father, in the name of Jesus, make me a compassionate intercessor. I want to pray for what moves Your heart. Help me sense when the Spirit of Christ in me is moved with compassion so I can lend my voice to His mission.

FEBRUARY 23

Beware of Interceding With Soulish Compassion

"For the word of God is living and powerful, and sharper than any two-edged sword, piercing even to the division of soul and spirit, and of joints and marrow, and is a discerner of the thoughts and intents of the heart" (Hebrews 4:12).

We've learned about Christ's compassion but there's another type of compassion that can actually work against Christ's purpose in someone's life. It's called soulish compassion. Intercessor, you need to learn to discern between Christ's compassion and soulish compassion so you can fully cooperate with God.

It's not always easy, especially if you have the gift of mercy. I've made the mistake of falling into soulish compassion more than once before I learned this lesson. The last time was the last time—and it had to do with someone operating in a wrong spirit playing on my kindness. See, some people will play on your good heart. Some people will take advantage of your compassion.

Compassion that comes from Christ is unelicited. The Holy Spirit highlights someone to you and you feel Christ's compassion for them. Romans 5:5 puts it this way: "Now hope does not disappoint, because the love of God has been poured out in our hearts by the Holy Spirit who was given to us."

Soulish compassion can come because people are pulling on your heart strings. Let me give you an example. I see commercials all the time asking for money to donate to this, that and the other cause. Obviously, I can't possibly donate to every organization, even though their campaign pulls on my heart strings. I have to wait until the Lord instructs my heart to give.

Know this: Your soulish compassion can cloud spiritual discernment. If it's a small thing, it won't make much difference but you can't take on a prayer assignment that's life-altering based on soulish compassion or you will wear yourself out and may even be getting in God's way. God may be trying to teach someone something and you're being a crutch for them—or they may need to press in for themselves for the sake of their relationship with Him.

— *Prayer* —

Father, in the name of Jesus, would You teach me to discern between Your compassion and soulish compassion that can lead my intercession astray? I don't want to get in Your way. Help me divide between soul and spirit.

Raising Up Your Timothy

"And the things that you have heard from me among many witnesses, commit these to faithful men who will be able to teach others also" (2 Timothy 2:2).

Paul the apostle was an equipper. He was a multiplier. And Paul wanted those he poured himself into to reproduce themselves. Intercessor, it's not enough for you to pray with power. You need to pour what you know into up-and-coming intercessors.

Younger intercessors need a portion of the spirit of prayer that's on you. They need the wisdom that you've gained in your prayer closest. Paul poured his life out as a drink offering. He reproduced reproducers who reproduce reproducers. You need to look for your Timothy.

What's a Timothy? A Timothy is someone you raise up. A Timothy is someone you trust to impart some of your anointing to. A Timothy is someone you can send on your behalf on a prayer mission when you are occupied with another assignment.

Paul said in Philippians 2:19-20 (AMPC): "But I hope and trust in the Lord Jesus soon to send Timothy to you, so that I may also be encouraged and cheered by learning news of you. For I have no one like him [no one of so kindred a spirit] who will be so genuinely interested in your welfare and devoted to your interests."

Raising up a Timothy is biblical. The AMPC version of 2 Timothy 2: tells us, "And the [instructions] which you have heard from me along with many witnesses, transmit and entrust [as a deposit] to reliable and faithful men who will be competent and qualified to teach others also."

So how do you choose a Timothy or Timothys? Look for those who are faithful. Look for those who are pursuing the anointing on your life. Look for those who are active in the prayer campaigns you organize. Look for those asking how they can serve the vision. But let them earn your trust. Give them small assignments to see if they will be faithful over a little before you make them ruler over much. Ask God to show you your Timothy.

— *Prayer* —

Father, in the name of Jesus, would You show me who You want me to raise up?
Show me who is ready for the next step. Bring me Timothys I can impart to, share
wisdom with, and train for the assignments on Your heart.

Clean Hands, Pure Heart

"Who may ascend into the hill of the Lord? Or who may stand in His holy place? He who has clean hands and a pure heart, who has not lifted up his soul to an idol, nor sworn deceitfully" (Psalm 24:23-24).

Effective intercession demands ascension. But ascension demands clean hands and a pure heart. If we are going to approach the throne of grace boldly, we need to ascend from the flesh and into the spirit. We have to go through a gate to the get to the throne room and only the righteous can enter (see Ps. 118:20).

While we are the righteousness of God in Christ Jesus, it's difficult to ascend to the holy hill in authority when we have common ground with the enemy. In order so stand in the holy place and petition God to show mercy on a person, a city or a nation, we must be free from the sin over which we're pleading in prayer for mercy.

Abraham could not have effectively interceded for Sodom and Gomorrah if he had lust is his heart. Moses could not have effectively interceded for the Israelites if he had idolatry in his heart. Paul could not have prayed effectively for the churches he planted and interceded for their growth in godly living if he wasn't living a godly life.

If we are asking God to pardon a person, a city or a nation for a sin we must first ask Him to cleanse us from the transgression in question. If we are going to pray against racism, we need to be sure we don't have any hint of racism in our hearts. If we do, we must ask God to purge us. If we are going to pray against greed in a leader's heart, we need to make sure we aren't committing the same sin.

Look at the priests in the Old Testament. The priest always offered atonement for himself before he dared to intercede for the nation. We don't have to be perfect to intercede. Our atonement is in the blood of Jesus. He cleanses our hands by washing us with the water of the Word. He purifies our hearts.

— *Prayer* —

Father, in the name of Jesus, help me to search my heart for common ground with the enemy so my authority is not diluted by secret sin. If I have hidden sin in my heart, show me so that I can repent in Your presence and find refreshing for my weary soul.

Building Mega Prayer Stamina

"Then He came to the disciples and found them sleeping, and said to Peter, 'What! Could you not watch with Me one hour?'" (Matthew 26:40)

Prayer stamina comes easier for some than others. What do I mean by prayer stamina? Prayer stamina is the physical and mental capacity to sustain intercession for long periods of time. Prayer stamina applies not only to the length of a prayer session (such as one hour). Prayer stamina also relates to prolonged seasons of intercession for a particular need.

Prayer stamina is critical to seeing breakthroughs. The writer of Hebrews put it this way: "For you have need of endurance, so that after you have done the will of God, you may receive the promise" (Heb. 10:36). And again, "And we desire that each one of you show the same diligence to the full assurance of hope until the end, that you do not become sluggish, but imitate those who through faith and patience inherit the promises" (Heb. 6:11-12).

When Jesus was in the Garden of Gethsemane, He knew He was about to get arrested, tried, flogged and crucified. He asked Peter, James and John to watch and pray with Him. When He came back to check in, He found them all asleep. He said, "What! Could you not watch with Me one hour?" (Matt. 26:40).

I'm sure it was disappointing to see how little prayer stamina the disciples had after He taught them to pray and walked with them for over three years. Jesus went off to pray again and twice more He checked on His disciples, only to find them asleep. This signals that walking with Jesus and seeing His miracles alone doesn't produce prayer stamina. Prayer stamina must be intentionally developed.

So, then, how does one tap into prayer stamina? The ways are too long to list here but let me give you some thoughts. First, ask God for the grace to intercede. The anointing is for other people, but the grace is to empower you to walk in that prayer anointing. Remember, apart from Christ you can do nothing.

— *Prayer* —

Father, in the name of Jesus, would You help me develop prayer stamina? I don't want to faint before I see the harvest of prayer answers. Give me an enduring spirit so I can pray without ceasing until the answer comes.

Gaining Intercession Momentum

"Now when He had taken the scroll, the four living creatures and the twenty-four elders fell down before the Lamb, each having a harp, and golden bowls full of incense, which are the prayers of the saints" (Revelation 5:8).

Momentum is the intercessor's friend—and you know when you've tapped into it. Everything goes higher and flows more freely.

Momentum is the strength of force of something has when it's moving. When you have momentum, your prayer life grows stronger and faster more quickly. Momentum defies logic, and it becomes a supernatural intercessory prayer boost the enemy finds harder to stop.

You can't always see momentum. Naysayers point to the houses of prayer all over the world—some of them are filling the bowls 24/7—and insist there is no discernible change for all their effort. Others point to prayer movements that fill stadiums and insist we've done all we can do to fulfill 2 Chronicles 7:14. But prayer momentum is undeniable to the intercessor's heart even if it's not discernible to the world's eyes.

We can't merely look at the results in the natural to gauge our impact in the spirit. As more saints intercede in alignment with the heart of the Father, the prayer movement becomes like a proverbial snowball rolling down a hill—eventually the bowls of prayer will tip over (see Rev. 5:8). We'll see the reality of the momentum we've always known was there. The results will eventually become visible if we remain faithful to believe God's Word doesn't return to Him void (see Isa 55:11).

Let us not become weary or faint in praying for God's will. We will reap a harvest from our faithful prayers if we do not give up (see Gal. 6:9). And reaping a harvest of prayer results can sure light a fire in the heart of an intercessor who wants to see God's Kingdom manifest—and who wants to see spiritual awakening and transforming revival. As that fire spreads, so does God's will across the earth. We can see transformation in the nations.

— *Prayer* —

Father, in the name of Jesus, help me tap into intercession momentum. Help me discern it by the Spirit. Help me not to grow weary because I don't see the answer, but to stand in the reality of Your momentum.

When Power Intercessors Emerge

"And my speech and my preaching were not with persuasive words of human wisdom, but in demonstration of the Spirit and of power..." (1 Corinthians 2:4).

You've heard of power evangelists—and you know that intercession paves the way for successful propagation of the Gospel. Look for the rise of power intercessors in this hour. These are intercessors who understand the power that raised Christ from the dead dwells in them. These are intercessors who take authority over every obstacle to God's will in the earth.

When we earnestly desire spiritual gifts as Paul said, we'll see signs and wonders following us. God is stirring the hearts of intercessors to tap into the power gifts of the Spirit to see transformed lives and even transformed cities. Know this: Power is for those who press into God's heart of compassion to see souls saved, healed and delivered.

I heard the Lord say: "I am calling forth a new breed of intercessors who have in past seasons been hidden in prayer closets, petitioning behind the scenes, declaring behind closed doors, and proclaiming in the secret places.

"These nameless, faceless power intercessors will emerge on the scene to change the scene with displays of the gifts of My Spirit. They will move in My dunamis power because they have been willing to bear My burdens and labor to relieve the suffering of those battling wicked attacks of the enemy and people under his nefarious influence. I am calling forth this new breed, which is not really a new breed at all. I am calling forth the power intercessors who see, hear, say, pray and operate in a dimension of My glory that will bring solutions to the suffering."

This is quite a Word. Are you a power intercessor? Do you want to be? If this stirs your heart, begin to press into the power of God to remove everything that hinders you from operating in signs and wonders.

— Prayer —

Father, in the name of Jesus, I want to move in Your power in prayer but also in Your power for signs, wonders and miracles. I want to demonstrate the power of prayer with signs following. Would You use me as a power intercessor?

FEBRUARY 29

Living As a Living Sacrifice

"I beseech you therefore, brethren, by the mercies of God, that you present your bodies a living sacrifice, holy, acceptable to God, which is your reasonable service. And do not be conformed to this world, but be transformed by the renewing of your mind, that you may prove what is that good and acceptable and perfect will of God" (Romans 12:1-2).

Reese Howells once said words that marked me forever. Listen carefully and let the Holy Spirit mark you with these deep words of wisdom:

"Unless your death to self is real, you will not prevail to deliver others. There is death involved in intercession. But the focus is never just death. The Spirit of God is gaining ground all the time. You will gain tremendous power over the enemy."

Meditate on that for a moment. While some intercessors fall into the trap of gossip and seem to have an anointing to share people's personal business with the rest of the church, the self-sacrificial intercessor understands selflessness is a weapon in their arsenal against which no opposition cannot stand.

Revelation 12:11 (AMP): "And they overcame and conquered him because of the blood of the Lamb and because of the word of their testimony, for they did not love their life and renounce their faith even when faced with death." That's self-sacrifice.

What does the self-sacrificing intercessor look like in action? The self-sacrificing intercessor dies daily (see 1 Cor. 15:31). The self-sacrificing intercessor picks up his cross and follows Jesus wherever He leads them (see Luke 9:23). The self-sacrificing intercessor prays for other people more than they pray for themselves, trusting God will raise up others to pray for them in a time of need.

Paul may as well have been describing the self-sacrificing intercessor when he wrote Galatians 2:20-21, "I have been crucified with Christ; it is no longer I who live, but Christ lives in me; and the life which I now live in the flesh I live by faith in the Son of God, who loved me and gave Himself for me. I do not set aside the grace of God; for if righteousness comes through the law, then Christ died in vain."

— *Prayer* —

Father, in the name of Jesus, I want to live as a living sacrifice. I want to discern Your will perfectly so I can pray prayers You will hear and answer. I want to serve Your Kingdom purposes above all. Make me a living sacrifice.

MARCH

"Now this is the confidence that we have in Him, that if we ask anything according to His will, He hears us. And if we know that He hears us, whatever we ask, we know that we have the petitions that we have asked of Him" (1 John 5:14-15).

MARCH 1

Mind Your Gap

"So I sought for a man among them who would make a wall, and stand in the gap before Me on behalf of the land, that I should not destroy it; but I found no one" (Ezekiel 22:30).

There's never been a more critical time to stand in the gap. What does that really mean? Standing in the gap is a selfless posture, a Christ-like posture. Standing in the gap is making a defense against an enemy attack. Standing in the gap is exposing oneself to enemy fire in order to protect something or someone else.

That may sound somewhat daunting, but when you understand the plan and will of God it's exhilarating.

When you stand in the gap God assigns you, you are standing in His will and nothing by any means shall harm you. When you stand in the gap God assigns you, God is fighting for you and with you and you cannot lose. When you stand in the gap God assigns you, you are surrounded with favor like a shield (see Ps. 5:12). He is your rear guard (see Is. 52:12).

As I've said many times, God is not a one-issue God. There are many issues on God's heart, and He will place certain issues on our hearts at certain times. He will call us to stand in the gap—a specific gap. Indeed, I believe God is always looking for someone to stand in the gap, just like He did in Ezekiel's day.

"I looked for someone who might rebuild the wall of righteousness that guards the land. I searched for someone to stand in the gap in the wall so I wouldn't have to destroy the land, but I found no one" (Ez. 22:30).

If you are an intercessor, there's a gap for you to stand in. When you find that gap, you'll be the most effective in your intercessory prayer efforts. Remember, though, that although God may give you specific assignments for specific seasons, He's not a one-issue God. As intercessors, it's easy enough to fall into that trap and miss His leading into other gaps in which He needs you to stand, sometimes even only temporarily.

— *Prayer* —

Father, in the name of Jesus, would You give help me deny myself and stand like Christ in intercession? Would You help me find the gap to stand in where I can be most effective? Would teach me to guard the land?

Day and Night Intercessors

"I thank God, whom I serve with a pure conscience, as my forefathers did, as without ceasing I remember you in my prayers night and day..." (2 Timothy 1:3).

Day and night. Night and day. These are themes that run through the Bible—from Genesis to Revelation—and they are awakening the praying church to new realms of intercession.

Fellowshipping with God through prayer and worship is what we were created for. It's just that simple. Yet how easy it is to stray from this reality when the spirit of the world is tugging on your sleeve with trouble, with persecution, with the worries of this life, or the deceitfulness of riches.

When I explored Scripture, I found this running "night and day" and "day and night" theme I mentioned earlier. God's Word does not return to Him void, but it shall accomplish what He pleases and it shall prosper in the thing for which He sent it (see Is. 55:11). When we pray out His Word day and night, it will make an impact on the earth. It has to.

Jesus made us a promise around prayer in the Parable of the Unjust Judge: "Shall God not avenge His own elect who cry out day and night to Him, though He bears long with them? I tell you that He will avenge them speedily ..." (Luke 18:7-8). No matter what the enemy has stolen from you—no matter what injustice God has called you to confront—day and night prayer is a means to invite God's righteous rule into the situation.

Anna, an elderly prophetess, was one of the first to recognize the Messiah in the flesh. The Bible says she "did not depart from the temple, but served God with fastings and prayers night and day" (Luke 2:37). We know that Paul prayed day and night for the Thessalonians (see 1 Thess. 3:9-11) and for his spiritual son Timothy (see 2 Tim. 1:3). Intercession for God's will upon the earth is a night and day work because our enemy never sleeps. Let the fire on the altar never go out.

— Prayer —

Father, in the name of Jesus, would You help me embrace the principle of day and night prayer? Just as Joshua meditated on the Word day and night, would You give me the grace to pray day and night, night and day?

MARCH 3

The One Prayer Every Intercessor Should Pray

"Do not be wise in your own eyes" (Proverbs 3:7).

I pray for many things every day. I pray for my family, my friends, my ministry, my nation—and, of course, myself. I pray for protection. I pray for a deeper revelation of God's love. I pray for the fruit of the Spirit—and more.

But there's one thing I've been praying for more and more lately—and I am convinced that if we would pray more for this one thing we would make better use of our time, live happier lives, and ultimately see more answers to our prayers.

What is this one thing I've been praying for more and more lately? Wisdom. I believe if we pray more for spiritual wisdom—even if it means praying less for natural needs—we'll receive more wisdom and our natural needs will be more than met.

We could all take a hint from Solomon. You know the story. The Lord appealed to Solomon in a dream and made this invitation: "Ask! What shall I give you?" Can you imagine the Lord coming to you in a dream and making such an invitation? What would you ask God for if you could ask and assuredly receive anything?

It seems Solomon had enough wisdom to ask for the principal thing: wisdom. Solomon replied to God's invitation with these words: "Give to Your servant an understanding heart to judge Your people, that I may discern between good and evil. For who is able to judge this great people of Yours?" (1 Kings 3:9).

That made God happy. The ear of the wise seeks knowledge (see Prov. 18:15). The wise man listens to advice (see Prov. 12:15). A man's wisdom makes his face shine (see Eccl. 8:1). By wisdom your house is built (see Prov. 24:3). Wise ones are cautious and turn away from evil (see Prov. 14:16). The words of the wise win him favor (see Eccl. 10:12). Wisdom will keep and guard you if you love it (see Prov. 4:6-7).

— *Prayer* —

Father, in the name of Jesus, would You give me wisdom? Give me wisdom on what to say and how to pray. Give me wisdom on how to plead and how to intercede. Give me wisdom on how to move and live and have my being in You. And with wisdom give me understanding.

Operating as an Undercover Intercessor

"After this, Nun's son Joshua sent two men from the Acacia groves as undercover scouts. He told them, 'Go and look over the land. Pay special attention to Jericho.' So they went out, came to the house of a prostitute named Rahab, and lodged there" (Joshua 2:1, ISV).

Undercover intercessors are rare birds. They go on assignments seeking to make an impact many will see without knowing who made the sacrifice to call it forth. They put themselves in harm's way for the greater good without any thought of personal glory. They are hidden agents of God on assignment to usher in His will.

Regarding those He's called to be underground, undercover intercessors, I heard the Lord say: "I can trust you in these next-level assignments. I will lead you into battle. I will lead you into victory. Don't take on those things I've not called you to, but do take on the things I'm prompting you to take on. Do follow My lead because I will take you into deep places of intercession. I will take you into that deep, deep place, where you will see things you've longed to see. You will see things you've never seen before... things you've heard people have experienced—those realms of glory, those realms of victory in warfare.

"There are realms of intercession and there are realms of travail you will walk in. You will walk in the confidence of Christ with this mantle of boldness that I am giving to you. If you will walk in it—if you will walk in this confidence—I can use you. I can cause you to rise up and tackle things that have come against your family and even your city."

I see an underground project of intercessors. At the right time they are going to surface like a groundhog. These intercessors are rooting down before they begin to rise up in different cities. These intercessors are not concerned about who goes to what church. They are about the Kingdom. Are you one of them?

— *Prayer* —

Father, in the name of Jesus, make me an undercover intercessor. I want to spy out the land and pray out the giants. I want to go on underground missions in the spirit, covert operations in the nations. Teach me to be an undercover intercessor.

Engaging in 'Bakah' Intercession

"Now while Ezra was praying, and while he was confessing, weeping, and bowing down before the house of God, a very large assembly of men, women, and children gathered to him from Israel; for the people wept very bitterly" (Ezra 10:1).

This is an intense scene from the Book of Ezra. Notice how the priest was praying and the praying led to weeping. Ezra was mourning over the unfaithfulness of the Israelite exiles. But Ezra was not the only weeping intercessor. Nehemiah was also known to weep.

The word weeping in the Ezra 10:1 comes from the Hebrew word *bakah*, which means to weep, bewail, cry or shed tears, according to *The KJV Old Testament Greek Lexicon*. It means to weep in grief or humiliation, to weep bitterly, and to lament. And it's intense.

When Nehemiah learned the Jews who had survived Babylonian captivity were in great distress and reproach, and the wall of Jerusalem was broken down, and its gates burned with fire, Nehemiah sat down and wept and mourned for many days. He fasted and prayed to God (see Neh. 1:1-4).

Nehemiah also entered into *bakah*. It's a painful weeping. It's the kind of weeping David's mighty men entered into when they came back to Ziklag and found their wives and children were kidnapped and the city was burned to the ground. 1 Samuel 30:4 says the wept until they had no more power to weep. That's *bakah*. Again, it's intense.

Jeremiah wasn't called the weeping prophet for nothing. Fourteen times between the book of Jeremiah and Lamentations, which he also wrote under the inspiration of the Holy Spirit, we see weeping. Jeremiah wrote: "Oh, that my head were waters, and my eyes a fountain of tears, that I might weep day and night for the slain of the daughter of my people!" (Jer. 9:1).

Weeping intercessors feel the heart of God at such a deep level that they are moved to tears. I believe Jesus felt the heart of the Father when He wept over Lazarus (see John 10:35) because the Pharisees were so hard hearted. He wept over Jerusalem because of what was coming (see Luke 19:1). Don't fear weeping.

— *Prayer* —

Father, in the name of Jesus, would You help me embrace the weeping when it comes? I don't want to quench Your Spirit. I want to feel Your emotions. Help me understand and navigate the bakah dimension of prayer.

The Intercessor's Vindication

"Vindicate me, O Lord, for I have walked in my integrity, and I have trusted in the Lord without wavering" (Psalm 26:1, NASB).

Intercessors are largely misunderstood. They may be falsely accused of being busy bodies when they are simply seeking information so they can pray more effectively. They may be underappreciated for the labor of love that they continually pour out. They may be largely overlooked in the grand scheme of any ministry.

Intercessors, God will vindicate you but you need to know Him as your vindicator. Instead of getting bitter at the injustices you've suffered in the church, the misunderstandings from pastors, and even the envy of other intercessors, learn to trust God as your vindicator and pray on. Bitterness will affect your intercessory prayer flow

So how do you get to know God as your vindicator? As I write in my book, *Vindicated*, one way is just to get to know God better in a general sense. When you grow in the grace and knowledge of our Lord and Saviour Jesus Christ, you will more clearly see Him as vindicator (see 2 Peter 3:18). If you seek Him as the vindicator you will find this aspect of His character.

Unfortunately, one of the best ways to get to know God as vindicator is to suffer injustice for which you need vindication. There's nothing like practical, firsthand experience with the vindication of God to help you see Him and know Him as Vindicator.

David experienced God as Vindicator over and over again. In Psalm 62:5-7, David said this: "I depend on God alone; I put my hope in him. He alone protects and saves me; he is my defender, and I shall never be defeated. My salvation and honor depend on God; he is my strong protector; he is my shelter" (GNT).

Pray for the one who wronged you like you'd pray for the person you love most in the world. Forgive them for wronging you. Bless them who persecuted you. Keep doing this and soon you will see promotion, favor and open doors of opportunity in your ministry of intercession.

— Prayer —

Father, in the name of Jesus, I depend on You alone as my vindicator. Would You give me a revelation of You as vindicator despite what the enemy is doing or has done in my life? Would You help me wait on You?

MARCH 7

Escaping Prayer Heresies

"But there were also false prophets among the people, even as there will be false teachers among you, who will secretly bring in destructive heresies, even denying the Lord who bought them, and bring on themselves swift destruction" (2 Peter 2:1).

I saw a false prophet on social media saying something beyond atrocious. Indeed, it was a full-blown heresy. This false prophet said we need a mediator between God and man—and he wasn't talking about Jesus. He was talking about himself. Praying to Mary, the mother of Jesus, or to Peter or Paul is also a prayer heresy. We don't need any other mediator than Jesus.

These are a couple of the many prayer heresies I've seen. What is a heresy? According to *The Seer's Dictionary*, heresy is a doctrine or message contrary to the divine will of God as expressed in Scripture; destructive doctrines that lead people away from Christ; 2 Peter 2:1 reads, "But there were also false prophets among the people, even as there will be false teachers among you, who will secretly bring in destructive heresies, even denying the Lord who bought them, and bring on themselves swift destruction."

Some say the Sinner's Prayer or contemplative prayer or sozo prayer is heretical. Many people have opinions about what heresy is. While we can be too quick to call something a heresy that is not heresy—there are plenty of heresy hunters out there condemning Bible-believing, Spirit-led people to hell because they don't believe in the work of the Holy Spirit today—there is true prayer heresy of which we need to beware.

Beyond praying to Peter or Mary, some pray to St. Anthony of Padua. Ironically, he's called "The Hammer of Heretics." Some believe if you are going to take your salvation seriously, you need St. Anthony's help. That might not be tempting for you, but what about praying to angels. Angels can deliver prayer answers, like we saw in Daniel 9. But we don't pray to angels. Nor do we command angels. Jesus is the Captain of the Hosts. Not all prayer heresies are so obvious, but make no mistake: prayer heresies are rising.

— *Prayer* —

Father, in the name of Jesus, help me discern prayer heresies—whether obvious or subtle—so I can avoid them. Jesus, it is only in Your name that I pray. It's by Your righteousness alone I approach God's throne of grace.

Spontaneous Prayer Surprises

"Rejoicing in hope; patient in tribulation; continuing instant in prayer" (Romans 12:12).

I love to be spontaneous. Unfortunately, the older I've gotten the more scheduled my life has become so I am not as spontaneous as I once was. That said, I try to be open to the Holy Spirit and what He may want to do in any given moment. I am still spontaneous in prayer.

I define spontaneous prayer this way: intercession that arises from a Holy Spirit impulse. Spontaneous prayer is prayer that is unplanned, unscheduled, and uncoordinated—except by the Spirit of Christ, the Intercessor, who lives within you. Spontaneous prayer is when the Holy Spirit moves upon you suddenly—seemingly out of nowhere and often at a less than convenient time—to stop and pray for someone in front of you or to enter your prayer closet for a secret place session with Him.

Of course, spontaneous prayers can also be eruptions of praise or thanksgiving. Spontaneous prayers can also be sudden cries for help. Spontaneous prayers can come forth as spiritual warfare or praying in tongues. (Check out my book, *Tongues of Fire*, for 101 benefits of praying in tongues.) The serious intercessor must stand ready to follow the Holy Spirit anywhere and everywhere—including into spontaneous prayer.

Beyond the leadership of the Holy Spirit, spontaneous prayers are often in response to something we see or hear in the natural that compels us to pray. Take Nehemiah for example. When he heard the walls of Jerusalem were broken down and the captives who came back from Babylon were in distress, he entered into spontaneous prayer:

"So it was, when I heard these words, that I sat down and wept, and mourned for many days; I was fasting and praying before the God of heaven. And I said: 'I pray, Lord God of heaven, O great and awesome God, You who keep Your covenant and mercy with those who love You and observe Your commandments…'"

— Prayer —

Father, in the name of Jesus, help me enter into realms of spontaneous prayer. Help me follow Your leadership. Make me aware of the people and situations around me and move my heart when You want me to be instant in prayer.

Scheduling God on Your Calendar

"And they heard the sound of the Lord God walking in the garden in the cool of the day, and Adam and his wife hid themselves from the presence of the Lord God among the trees of the garden" (Genesis 3:8).

While spontaneous prayer is a thrilling must for the sold-out intercessor, so is making an appointment with God in prayer. There are times when God will spontaneously interrupt your regular schedule because He wants to co-labor with you in intercession. But that's not typically a daily occurrence.

I've learned over the years if we want to stay instant in prayer, we need to set a prayer time. We need to make an appointment with the God who bows down His ear to hear us in prayer. It seems to me Jesus had an appointment with the Father. He arose early in the morning to pray. And David cried out, "Early will I seek you" (Ps. 63:1).

You might be thinking, "Great, I'm not a morning person." There is no law about when you can meet God. He's available any time. But the spiritually disciplined intercessor will find that time. The serious intercessor will make their prayer closet a priority. They will take the time to meet with God over matters of His heart.

Adam and Eve had an appointment with God every day. Your appointment with God is the most divine appointment you can make. And you can make it every day—at any time and multiple times throughout the day. This is in line with Matthew 6:33, "But seek first the kingdom of God and His righteousness, and all these things shall be added to you."

Moses had appointments with God at the Tent of Meeting. A pilar of cloud descended and stood at the door and the Lord talked with Moses. Exodus 33:11 tells us, "So the Lord spoke to Moses face to face, as a man speaks to his friend. And he would return to the camp, but his servant Joshua the son of Nun, a young man, did not depart from the tabernacle."

I often wonder if Moses had a standing appointment with God, too. If we don't make an appointment with God to pray, chances are something else will distract our hearts from this mandate.

— *Prayer* —

Father, in the name of Jesus, would You remind me to put You first place on my calendar? There are many tasks I must complete in a day, but help me seek first Your Kingdom so that I can find the strength, grace and wisdom I need to intercede and keep on interceding.

The Value of an Intercessory Prayer List

"Praying always with all prayer and supplication in the Spirit, being watchful to this end with all perseverance and supplication for all the saints..." (Ephesians 6:18).

Beyond your appointment with God, prayer lists can be a helpful tool in the intercessor's toolbox. By no means am I suggesting you should stick to a prayer list throughout your intercession session. Prayer lists can be limiting if we don't include the Holy Spirit. However, prayer lists can help us get out of the gate. Prayer lists can help us remember to pray for things that we might otherwise forget.

D.A. Carson, president of the Gospel Coalition, once said, "All of us would be wiser if we would resolve never to put people down, except on our prayer lists." What wise words! We should do more praying about people's problems than talking about them. When we are tempted to judge someone in their struggle, that's a sign to put them on our prayer list instead.

Creating a prayer list can fuel our prayer time. Even if you don't end up using the list every time, it comes in handy when you don't feel inspired. Prayer lists can be helpful when you need to ask and keep on asking. Some issues require you to pray repeatedly. Prayer lists can prime the pump of persistence by reminding you of a need that could slip your mind on an especially busy day.

Time and time again, Paul the apostle told the people to whom he penned letters that he was remembering them in his prayers. He told Philemon, "I thank my God, making mention of you always in my prayers..." (Phil. 1:4). Paul told Timothy, "I thank my God, making mention of you always in my prayers..." (2 Tim. 1:3). And Paul told the church at Ephesus he did "not cease to give thanks for you, making mention of you in my prayers."

I don't know if Paul had a prayer list written out on paper or not. But he had a prayer list written on his heart. And before he said much else to those who followed his ministry, he wanted them to know that they were on his prayer list.

— Prayer —

Father, in the name of Jesus, lead me and guide me as I write a prayer list. Help me keep my prayer list current. Help me to use it as a jumping off point, then lead me by Your Spirit down the prayer paths You have ordained.

MARCH 11

Dealing in Desperate Faith

"I rise before the dawning of the morning, and cry for help; I hope in Your word" (Psalm 119:147).

Scripture tells us to fight the good fight of faith. One of the main ways we do this is through prayer—and sometimes desperate prayer mixed with desperate faith. There comes a time in every intercessor's prayer journey that desperation hits the heart.

One definition of desperate is "having lost hope," according to *Merriam-Webster*'s dictionary. The desperation that sits right on the edge of hopelessness is part and parcel of the desperate faith. The desperate faith that captures God's attention arises when we've lost hope in our own ability to see the prayer answer we need.

Desperate faith comes when we reach the end of ourselves—when we've prayed without ceasing and don't feel like we can utter one more petition. Desperate faith manifests when we realize nothing outside of God's miracle-working power will bring a breakthrough.

As I write in my book *Breaking the Miracle Barrier*, "Desperate faith, then, is not hopeless faith because faith is the substance of things hoped for and the evidence of things not seen (see Heb. 11:1). Desperate faith is faith placed in the right Person—on the Everlasting God. But desperate faith often expresses itself with desperate measures."

We can locate the measure of faith in our heart by what comes out of our mouth. If we are upset, doubting, and fearful, we are not in desperate faith. We may be desperate, all right, but desperation alone doesn't move God.

"Desperate faith—the type of faith undaunted by obstacles, opposition and odds—undergirds the sound of now," I wrote in *Breaking the Miracle Barrier*. "Desperate faith doesn't give up in the face of a challenge to seeing the promise, but is supercharged with even more determination to see God's will come to pass. Desperate faith is persistent faith, then, but not all persistent faith is desperate faith. Desperate faith has nothing left to lose except the promise—and refuses to lose at any cost."

— *Prayer* —

Father, in the name of Jesus, would You help me understand the value of desperation so that when the enemy releases hopelessness at my soul I can choose to refocus on You and release a faith-filled cry that touches Your heart? Teach me to persevere in hope.

When God is Silent

"Do not be silent to me, lest, if You are silent to me, I become like those who go down to the pit"
(Psalm 28:1).

Doubtless, you have heard it said—and said rightly—that prayer is a conversation with God. So what are we to make of it when God is silent?

I don't like when God is silent. I don't pray without expecting a response. Once I was trying to make a decision about a project that I no longer enjoyed. I didn't feel grace on it. I was almost to the point of resentment. I felt trapped. I knew I couldn't shut it down but I didn't want to continue the exercise of beating my head against a wall.

Finally, after a season of silence and after pledging to the Lord that I would do His will if I just knew what it was, He said one thing, "Stop kicking against the pricks." Those are the same words Jesus told Pre-Paul Saul when he thought he was doing the will of God but was actually unknowingly resisting God's will (see Acts 26:14).

In my case, God had been silent waiting for me to see what should have been obvious. He finally spoke as I studied the Word. I was looking at the project as a thorn in my side. I was focusing on pricks, but I didn't know I was kicking against them. I had to repent.

When God is silent, read the Word. Paul told Timothy: "All Scripture is given by inspiration of God, and is profitable for doctrine, for reproof, for correction, for instruction in righteousness, that the man of God may be complete, thoroughly equipped for every good work" (2 Tim. 3:16-17).

Even if God doesn't speak to your specific situation through the Word, you are still posturing your ear to hear and God is a rewarder of those who diligently seek Him. When God is silent, try to remember the last thing He told you—and obey it.

— *Prayer* —

Father, in the name of Jesus, would You help me press through the silent seasons, remembering Your last instruction and trusting You will still lead me? Help me obey Your written Word in the times when I can't hear Your spoken Word. Your Scripture speaks volumes to my heart.

A Pre-Prayer Answer?

"It shall come to pass that before they call, I will answer; And while they are still speaking, I will hear" (Isaiah 65:24).

While God may be silent at times—and sometimes for reasons we can't understand—He consistently emphasizes that He will answer us. Sometimes, He answers us before we even pray. He's an omniscient God who loves us so much that sometimes He tells us what we need to know before we ask.

The *Contemporary English Version* of Isaiah 65:24 puts it plainly: "I will answer their prayers before they finish praying." The *New Living Translation* says, "I will answer them before they even call to me. While they are still talking about their needs, I will go ahead and answer their prayers!"

Many times there's a waiting period between the crying out and the answer delivery. We need to get our faith higher and understand the sovereignty of God. God knows what we need before we do. That's why Jesus said, "Do not worry, saying, 'What shall we eat?' or 'What shall we drink?' or 'What shall we wear?' For after all these things the Gentiles seek. For your heavenly Father knows that you need all these things" (Matt. 6:31-32).

In His all-knowing, God can offer the wisdom we need to succeed before we cry out. He already knows we're going to cry out for wisdom. He knows we might wait until we're in a predicament before we ask, so He pre-empts our ask with an answer. He knows what we need before we need it. He knows what we are going to pray before we pray it. He even helps us pray the right prayers so we can get the right answers.

Barnes' Notes on the Bible offers: "How ready is He to anticipate our needs! How watchful is He of our necessities; and how rich His benevolence in providing for us! Even the most faithful and prayerful of His people receive numerous favors and comforts at His hand for which they have not directly asked Him."

— *Prayer* —

Father, in the name of Jesus, thank You for knowing me so intimately, for loving me so completely and caring about my needs so thoroughly. Help me build faith that You, when necessary, will answer me before I even call out to You. That's how good You really are.

The Necessity of Holy Fear

"The fear of the Lord is the beginning of knowledge..." (Proverbs 1:7).

Wise intercessors cultivate the spirit of the fear of the Lord in their lives. That's because we know the Lord is our strength, our Intercessor, our defense. He's our everything. We reverence Him as the Bridegroom, King and Judge.

While some fear the Lord in a wrong way, the seasoned intercessor understands the benefits of intimacy and the necessity of reverence. One simply cannot do without the other. We don't want to risk getting so "familiar" with the Lord as Abba that we don't esteem Him as the Almighty in deference and devotion.

One of the keys to successful intercession is walking in the fear of the Lord. Before I move on, let's define the fear of the Lord by looking at some Greek and Hebrew words. One definition of the Hebrew word *yare* means "to fear, to respect, to reverence." The Greek word *phobos* can be translated "reverential fear." *Vine's Complete Expository Dictionary* defines it as "not a mere 'fear' of His power and righteous retribution, but a wholesome dread of displeasing Him." That's intense!

The fear of the Lord is to hate evil (see Prov. 8:13). The fear of the Lord is the beginning of wisdom (see Prov. 9:10). The fear of the Lord is the beginning of knowledge (see Prov. 1:7). The secret of the Lord is with those who fear Him (see Ps. 25:14). There is no want for them who fear Him (see Ps. 34:9). In the fear of the Lord, there is strong confidence and a fountain of life (see Prov. 14:26-27). By the fear of the Lord are riches, honor and life (see Prov. 22:4).

I could go on and on about Scriptures that talk about the benefits of cultivating the fear of the Lord in your heart, but I'll stop there. Ask the Holy Spirit to help you cultivate the spirit of the fear of the Lord in your heart.

— *Prayer* —

Father, in the name of Jesus, would You give me the spirit of the fear of the Lord Isaiah mentions? Would You help me cultivate an honor and respect for Your thoughts, Your ways and Your Person? You are the all-powerful God.

MARCH 15

When Intercession is Risky

"If I perish, I perish" (Esther 4:16).

Intercession can be risky business. Although we never see an example of Esther's prayers in the Bible like we do Daniel's or Jeremiah's, we know she fasted when Haman was working behind the scenes to destroy the Jews. If she was fasting, I figure she had to be praying. Though we do not read her prayers, we do see her intercession.

You know the story. When the Jewish people heard King Ahasuerus issued a decree that their people should be destroyed, they entered into mourning. When the news got back to Queen Esther through her uncle Mordecai about Haman's plot, she was deeply distressed. Mordecai wanted her to approach the king and she was reluctant. That's when Mordecai admonished her:

"Do not think in your heart that you will escape in the king's palace any more than all the other Jews. For if you remain completely silent at this time, relief and deliverance will arise for the Jews from another place, but you and your father's house will perish. Yet who knows whether you have come to the kingdom for such a time as this?" (Esther 4:12-13).

Esther got the revelation and responded rightly, "If I perish, I perish" (Esther 4:16).

Esther's heart posture should be the heart posture of every intercessor on assignment for the King of kings. Like Esther, when we pray what He tells us or leads us to pray, we will find favor not only in His sight but in the sight of people involved that can serve as agents to bring God's will to pass in the earth.

In the Book of Esther, we see the queen approach the throne. The king graciously asked for her petition, promising her up to half the kingdom. Haman's conspiracy to extinguish the Jewish race was exposed and ultimately failed. Indeed, Haman was hung on the gallows that he erected for Mordecai.

— *Prayer* —

Father, in the name of Jesus, would You give me the courage to step out in risky faith? Would You help me get my mind off what I might lose and what the Kingdom might gain? I choose to lose my life in You so I can find it.

Don't Let Delay Derail Your Prayers

"For the vision is yet for an appointed time; But at the end it will speak, and it will not lie. Though it tarries, wait for it; Because it will surely come, it will not tarry" (Habakkuk 2:3).

We all like God to answer us before we call, but that's not the usual way of intercession. Many times, there are delays. We know Daniel waited 21 days for an angel to show up with his prayer answer. Abraham waited twenty-five years—yes, twenty-five years—for the promised son Isaac. The Israelites waited 40 years to enter the Promised Land of Canaan.

Delays occur for many reasons. Double-mindedness can delay the answer. Disobedience can delay the answer. Demon powers can delay the answer. But God's will stands. He's constantly working all things together for our good, according to Romans 8:28. He's constantly ordering our steps (and reordering our steps when need be). I believe He also orders and reorders our prayer at times.

A delay is not a denial. Peter tells us the Lord is not slow to fulfill His promise (see 2 Pet. 3:9). It may seem slow to us but God is an on-time God. There is an opportune time and we must patiently pray while we wait for it. We must resist the fainting spirit that comes to steal our harvest. Your prayer releases power. Certain situations demand more power than other situations, so you need to be persistent in prayer.

Think about Jesus' promise of the Holy Spirit. The disciples waited forty days for the wind to rush in and the fire to rest upon them. It seemed like a delay in the promise, but it was a call to perseverance. The disciples continued praying on one accord until the appointed time and then everything changed. God's promises are worth the wait.

Jesus is returning again. He asked, "However, when the Son of Man comes, will He find [persistence in] faith on the earth?" (Luke 18:8, AMP). Some answers come speedily. There are miraculous interventions. But delay is not a denial. He is working. Keep praying.

— *Prayer* —

Father, in the name of Jesus, help me not to grow weary in well doing. Help me to keep in mind that a delay is not a denial. Help me continue standing in faith until I see the manifestation of the promise, no matter how long it takes.

MARCH 17

Binding Up the Intercessor's Wounds

"He heals the brokenhearted and binds up their wounds" (Psalm 147:3).

Many years ago, a close intercessor friend of mine went through a significant trial. She was trying to preserve her land—an inheritance from her parents—but she fell on hard financial times. The intercessors she raised up were supportive at first, but the deeper she fell into financial distress the more they questioned her reasoning.

See, she was living in a house that was in disrepair. She didn't have the means to fix it, and the conditions there grew worse and worse until the property was almost unliveable. No one could convince her to move off the land. She was like Shammah in the pea field (see 2 Sam. 23:11).

Soon, things grew worse. She needed back-to-back major surgeries. The intercessors she faithfully raised up abandoned her all at once. They decided she brought all this on herself and, instead of praying her through like she had prayed them through many crises, they scattered. She was seriously hurt and wounded.

Maybe you've never had people abandon you in a time of need or betray your heart. Maybe your hurt and wound came at the hand of someone you love passing away and you just can't bring yourself to pray to the Lord who allowed it. Maybe it's a divorce or a prodigal child causing the pain in your emotions. God wants to heal you.

Likewise, intercessors may be wounded doing the work of the ministry. Intercessors are often misunderstood, often rejected, often undervalued and unappreciated. Sometimes, pastors and leaders crush the spirit of the intercessor. Here's the point: intercessors are not immune to hurts and wounds.

Remember Psalm 34:18, "The Lord is near to those who have a broken heart, and saves such as have a contrite spirit." God will surely heal your heart. Let Him.

— *Prayer* —

Father, in the name of Jesus, would You heal me of every hurt and wound? I don't want to allow this pain to fester and infect my prayer life. Restore my soul. Restore the joy of my salvation. Help me through this trial.

On the Wrong Edge

"But he himself went a day's journey into the wilderness, and came and sat down under a broom tree. And he prayed that he might die, and said, 'It is enough! Now, Lord, take my life, for I am no better than my fathers!'" (1 Kings 19:4)

Intercessors can get burned out. Burnout is "feelings of energy depletion or exhaustion; increased mental distance from one's job, or feelings of negativism or cynicism related to one's job; and reduced professional efficacy," according to the World Health Organization. Most serious intercessors face these feelings at one point or another in their prayer careers.

Moses was on the edge of burnout in the wilderness. Thank God for mentors like Jethro, his father-in-law, who warned him: "'What is this thing that you are doing for the people? Why do you alone sit, and all the people stand before you from morning until evening? ...The thing that you do is not good. Both you and these people who are with you will surely wear yourselves out. For this thing is too much for you; you are not able to perform it by yourself'" (Ex. 18:13-14; 117-18).

There are clear signs of intercessory burnout. In the early onset of burnout, you may just feel tired all the time. You feel physically and emotionally exhausted in prayer. You may forget what to pray for. You may not be able to focus on the intercessory tasks at hand, which makes everything more stressful. You may even have physical issues like chest pain, shortness of breath, headaches, stomach issues, dizziness and fainting.

With burnout, you may get double-minded or pessimistic. You may be frustrated that the prayer answer hasn't come. You may start losing your enjoyment in prayer. In the early stages, you may not feel like going to corporate prayer. In the latter stages, you may be annoyed or angry when people ask you to pray for one more thing. These are just a few of many signs, some are more subtle. I teach this in-depth in School of Prayer at *www.schoolofthespirit.tv.*

— *Prayer* —

Father, in the name of Jesus, would You please help me recognize the first fruits of burnout so that I don't continue to push past Your grace on my life? Would bring me a Jethro to help me see what I can't see as I serve You?

MARCH 19

Conquering Intercessory Burnout

"Come to Me, all you who labor and are heavy laden, and I will give you rest. Take My yoke upon you and learn from Me, for I am gentle and lowly in heart, and you will find rest for your souls. For My yoke is easy and My burden is light" (Matthew 11:28-30).

Intercessory prayer burnout is not unusual. Why does it happen? There are many reasons. Perhaps you didn't take time out for self-care—to enjoy life beyond the prayer closet. Perhaps you didn't learn to set boundaries and took on anybody and everybody's prayer requests, yet nobody is praying for you.

Want more reasons? Perhaps you neglected your own devotional time with the Lord for the sake of interceding for others. Perhaps you've put in long hours and even overnight sessions in prayer a little too often. Maybe you fasted without a directive from the Holy Spirit.

No matter how you got to the point of burnout, you don't want to stay there. So, then, how do you move out of burnout? Start by looking within. What is driving you? The Holy Spirit will not lead you into burnout. You may need to reprioritize your prayer appointments with His help rather than letting people drive your intercession agendas. You may need to learn to say no.

Next, look for ways you've moved beyond His grace. If you don't feel grace to pray for something, take that as a sign it may not be your assignment (or that the resistance is intense!). Consider this: Could some of your time in prayer be better spent raising up other intercessors who can help carry the prayer load? Or who can join with you to send ten thousand to flight?

Maybe you need a sabbatical from intercession for a short season. Even a few days break from incessant intercession can bring refreshing. If you are burnt out, it's a "come to Jesus" moment where He wants you to rest in Him. He wants you to believe that He is answering the prayers you've already prayed so you can stop and breathe and get filled with the Holy Spirit again.

Discover with the help of the Holy Spirit your prayer passion and try to stay in that lane. The prayer needs never cease and although we're called to pray without ceasing, sometimes we do need to just be still and know that He is God. Remember, the life of an intercessor is not a sprint. It's a marathon.

— *Prayer* —

Father, in the name of Jesus, help me remember to set my prayer priorities with the Holy Spirit and never apart from Him. Would You fill me once again to overflowing with Your life-giving Spirit? Please, refresh and restore me.

The David Livingstone Prayer Anointing

"And He who sent Me is with Me. The Father has not left Me alone, for I always do those things that please Him" (John 8:29).

"Death alone will put a stop to my efforts." Those were the determined words of David Livingstone, a missionary to Africa who died on his knees praying. Read that again. Livingstone died on his knees in the heart of Africa praying for souls.

A pioneering Scottish missionary, Livingstone lived in the 1800s. He sailed to Cape Town in 1840, and eventually traveled seven hundred miles to Kuruman ministering to the Backwain tribe of the Bechuanas. The explorer for Christ went throughout Africa preaching the Gospel, but prayer was the foundation of his success in what many called the "Dark Continent" and the "White Man's Graveyard."

Christianity Today relates, "Livingstone pushed his men beyond human endurance. When they reached a 30-foot waterfall, he waved his hand, as if to wish it away, and said, 'That's not supposed to be there.' His wife, who had just given birth to her sixth child, died in 1862 beside the river, only one of several lives claimed on the voyage. Two years later, the British government, which had no interest in 'forcing steamers up cataracts,' recalled Livingstone and his mission party."

Ultimately, Livingstone never gave up. He walked over 29,000 miles through Africa. One of his prayers was: "Send me anywhere, only go with me. Lay any burden on me, only sustain me. Sever any ties but the tie that binds me to Your service and to Your heart." Once while praying in Zambia, he cried, "Lord, on this land where I rest my bended knees, let it become a mighty Christian nation, a beacon of hope to the African continent and a light to the rest of the world."

His gravestone dons these words from his heart: "All I can say in my solitude is, May Heaven's rich blessing come down on every one—American, English, Turk—who will help to heal this open sore of the world." And, again, when his dead body was found he was perched on his knees, having cried out for souls in Africa to his last breath.

— *Prayer* —

Father, in the name of Jesus, send me anywhere in intercession. Give me the grit of Livingstone as he cried out for the salvation of souls in dark nations. Give me a passion to stand in the gap for those who do not know You.

Fully Invested

"But Jesus said to him, 'No one, having put his hand to the plow, and looking back, is fit for the kingdom of God'" (Luke 9:62).

Seasoned intercessors get to a place in prayer where they feel a personal responsibility for the breakthrough. Responsibility leads to a greater spiritual authority because you are fully invested. You'll keep your hand to the plow.

"The intercessor must become responsible for the prayer that the Holy Spirit gives them," Reese Howells says. "They must 'pray through' until the prayer is answered. They cannot walk away from the prayer—it is their responsibility and it is the Holy Spirit who intercedes through the willing servant."

The seasoned intercessor sees prayer as an obligation, not an option. You take on a duty in allegiance with what's on the Holy Spirit's heart. The prayer burden is not heavy, but light because you are co-laboring with the Spirit of Christ in prayer. He is helping you bear someone else's burdens.

When you take on the responsibility of intercession you won't stop no matter how much the enemy works to wear you out. You'll realize the grace of God is sufficient, reject the spirit of weariness and receive Holy Spirit empowerment to complete the mission.

When you take on the responsibility of intercession, it doesn't matter how busy you get. You'll make time for prayer because you know it's up to you to carry the ball across the finish line. When you take on the responsibility of intercession, it doesn't matter how much retaliation you get because you'll have a revelation that greater is He who is in you than he who is in the world (see 1 John 4:4).

When you take on the responsibility of intercession, you won't stop pushing and pressing because you know the prayer assignment is your baby and you must birth the answer. You will have a determination not to abort no matter what. You will stand and withstand in the evil day and when you've done all you can do, you'll stand.

— Prayer —

Father, in the name of Jesus, help me take on the prayer responsibilities you've assigned to me, nothing more and nothing less. Help me find the prayer plow You've ordained for me and keep my hand to that plow at all costs. I am fully invested in Your will.

Mantled With Influence

"Let your light so shine before men, that they may see your good works and glorify your Father in heaven" (Matthew 5:16).

Intercessors, you have favor in heaven and hell is afraid of you. You have influence and your influence will grow as you press into the Holy Spirit, who is the spirit of prayer. You are positioned for impact.

I heard the Lord say, "I am calling forth the intercessory influencers to make a mark in the spirit realm that the enemy can't ignore. He will bow at the sound of your voices in the name of Christ. I am calling forth intercessory influencers who will decree My Word in the atmosphere so angels can rise up and use it as a sword to fight and execute My plans in the earth.

"I am calling forth intercessory influencers who will set aside childish things and the distractions of this age to hear My heart and pray My Word. As they press into deeper dimensions of prayer, they will see an increase in influence, increase in favor and an increase in wisdom. Intercession is not for the faint of heart, but it moves My heart to action. Intercessors, stand on your watch, pray and receive My mantle of influence."

A mantle of influence. That's quite a word! What kind of influence? *Merriam-Webster's* dictionary defines influence as, "the power to change or affect someone or something: the power to cause changes without directly forcing them to happen; the emanation of spiritual or moral force; to have an effect on the condition or development of."

Intercessors, don't forget you have clout. You carry a spiritual force that changes things. His name is Holy Spirit. Through your prayers, you are pressuring the kingdom of darkness to bow down to the Christ in you. Through your heart's cry, you are taking the land for Jesus!

— *Prayer* —

Father, in the name of Jesus, would You help me understand the influence You've given me? I want to be salt and light. I want to release Your will into a situation. Would You give me even more influence?

Missing the Prayer Mark

"You ask and do not receive, because you ask amiss, that you may spend it on your pleasures"
(James 4:3).

James says we can pray amiss. *The New Living Translation* puts it this way: "And even when you ask, you don't get it because your motives are all wrong—you want only what will give you pleasure."

Intercessor, your motive makes a difference. Some intercessors are motivated by fame, but all serious intercessors are motivated by love. Some intercessors are motivated by money, but all serious intercessors are motivated by God's urging to pay the price for prayer answers.

In Matthew 6:2, Jesus said, "Therefore, when you do a charitable deed, do not sound a trumpet before you as the hypocrites do in the synagogues and in the streets, that they may have glory from men. Assuredly, I say to you, they have their reward." The same truth applies to anything you do for the purpose of gaining the favor or recognition of man. True intercessors are not looking for any recognition. The prayer answers are their reward.

I'd rather have influence in the spirit than influence in the natural—but you can have both. The two are not mutually exclusive. God has rewarded me with influence in the natural. Over 1 million people a month listen to my prayer broadcasts. But that influence didn't come through striving. That influence came through being obedient to make intercession.

When your motive is right, God can trust you with greater influence. When you are willing to minister without the reward of man—the applause of man, the financial gifts from man, the favor of man—God can give you favor and influence in the spirit and in the earth that endures. When you make intercession, you are acting like Christ, who is sitting at the right hand of the Father even now continually making intercession for us.

When you strive to make your name great, you have earth's temporary rewards. When you make prayer your life's work, you get heaven's eternal rewards.

— *Prayer* —

Father, in the name of Jesus, I don't want to pray amiss. Help me keep my motives right. Help me keep my heart pure. Help me keep my hands clean. I want to pray Your will and Your will only.

Beware Carnal Prayer Polluters

"Don't spread gossip and rumors" (Leviticus 19:16, The Message).

Gossip is a device of the devil and, as Paul the apostle said, we must not be ignorant to the devil's devices (see 2 Cor. 2:11). With that, beware gossiping intercessors. I assure you, their gossip in not on assignment of God.

It's important to understand what the Bible says about gossiping and meddling. Consider the strong language the Bible uses: "Don't spread gossip and rumors" (Lev. 19:16, Message). And again, "And the women also who serve the church should be dignified, faithful in all things, having their thoughts set on truth, and not known as those who gossip" (1 Tim. 3:11).

Need more? "A twisted person spreads rumors; a whispering gossip ruins good friendships" (Prov. 16:28, TPT). And again, "That you also aspire to lead a quiet life, to mind your own business, and to work with your own hands, as we commanded you…" (1 Thess. 4:11)

Even if it's just a work of the flesh and not a spirit of gossip, you can be sure the enemy is inspiring the work of gossipers and meddlers. In order to take authority over the attack, you first need to forgive the evildoer. Harboring unforgiveness in your heart just opens the door wide to more enemy attacks.

Next, confront the spirit of gossip that has targeted you. Bind the spirit of gossip, in the name of Jesus. Ask the Lord to forgive those who are gossiping about you, and return good for their evil (see 1 Pet. 3:9). Moving in the opposite spirit sets you up for God's vindication in your life.

Take pity on gossipers because, remember, they are typically insecure people who want attention. Hurting people hurt people. Realize they must not be happy people and that their gossip grieves the Holy Spirit, which affects their relationship with Him. Proverbs 12:13 (Message) tells us: "The gossip of bad people gets them in trouble…"

— Prayer —

Father, in the name of Jesus, deliver me from the temptation to share what I know with others, compromising the privacy of those who trust me with their heart. Help me disconnect from gossipers who try to drag me into drama.

Exposing Intercessory Temptations

"Not by might nor by power, but by My Spirit,' says the Lord of hosts" (Zechariah 4:6).

Intercessors, God uses you as an agent to work extraordinary miracles through your fervent prayer Indeed, many souls are saved because of the persevering intercessor. Many bodies are healed. Minds are delivered from demonic oppression. Marriages are saved. People prosper and see all manner of breakthrough through the ministry of intercession. Glory!

But every intercessor faces a dangerous temptation at some point along the road of their prayer journey. Many especially effective intercessors face this temptation more than once. Here's how it happens:

God may assign you to pray without ceasing for someone's situation. Maybe it's a healing. Maybe it's a financial issue. Someone shares with you a critical need—or God shows you the pressing need in your prayer closet— and you fall to your knees in serious intercession for them as if it was for yourself.

Then, days, months or even years later the answer comes and the one for whom you have been praying comes to you with a rush of excitement. They got the breakthrough for which you've been praying, sometimes with specific details over which you interceded. The temptation comes to tell them, "Yes, I was praying for you." The temptation comes to take the credit for the breakthrough because of your prayer labor for them.

Beloved, this is a mistake that grieves the Lord. This is spiritual pride and it's dangerous. Spiritual pride is perhaps the worst kind of pride. It's the pride that got Satan cast out of heaven. J. Oswald Sanders, a British writer and Anglican theologian, once said, "For pride is spiritual cancer: it eats up the very possibility of love, or contentment, or even common sense.

God wants to use you as His war club—His weapon for battle (see Jer. 51:20). But we must remember we are tools in the hand of the Potter. It's not by might or by power, but by His Spirit that breakthrough comes (see Zech. 4:6). He is the breaker.

— Prayer —

Father, in the name of Jesus, help me be mindful not to take credit for the prayer answers, or even for the unction to pray. Remind me that apart from You I can do nothing. I depend completely upon Your generous Spirit to pray Your will.

Issuing Heaven-Rending Intercession

"Oh, that You would rend the heavens! That You would come down! That the mountains might shake at Your presence" (Isaiah 64:1).

Rend the heavens is formal language. *The New Living Translation* says, "Burst from the heavens..." *The New American Standard* is more violent, "Tear open the heavens..." *The Contemporary English Version* puts it this way, "Rip the heavens apart!"

Let your imagination run free with this. What if God were to burst from the heavens and visit us? What kind of intercession would it take to rend the heavens? What kind of prayer would compel God to not just look down from the heavens but to tear the invisible veil and visit us with revival, display His power, and break through every opposition and obstacle in our lives?

What kind of petition would motivate our awesome God to manifest Himself to us in this way? What kind of supplication would move Him to hear our prayers and respond in grace and avenge us of our adversaries, causing demon powers to tremble at His feet?

I believe prayer that rends the heavens is prayer of deep desire—a desire that goes beyond our natural mind and comes from the depths of our spirit in agreement with the Holy Spirit. I believe it is a prayer of confession that acknowledges we are powerless without His might and a soul willing to adjust her will to His will.

I believe prayer that rends the heavens is prayer that won't stop until it sees an answer. I believe it is intercession in faith. God delights in the prayers of the righteous. It's not the prayer of the beggar but the prayer the old who go to the throne of grace adamantly crying out to the only One who has the answer. I believe it is prayer with a motive to see God's glory cover the earth as the waters cover the sea. Isaiah's prayer was answered. If we pray in that same spirit, so will ours be.

— *Prayer* —

Father, in the name of Jesus, give me a spirit of intercession that is inexhaustible in pressing past the earth realm and the second heaven into Your throne room.
Teach me how to pray in line with Your Spirit's desire.

Your Prayers Make God Smile

"The sacrifice of the wicked is an abomination to the Lord, but the prayer of the upright is His delight" (Proverbs 15:8).

Your prayers delight God. *The Message* translation says, "He delights in genuine prayers." *The Passion Translation* puts it this way: "Every prayer of the righteous is pleasing to his heart." And *The Voice* tells us, "The prayers of those who do right are a pleasure to Him."

When you really get this revelation, it will inspire you to pray without ceasing. Think about it for a minute: God loves to hear you pray. The word "delight" means joy. Your intercession brings God joy because it's a sacrifice for His Kingdom. It means a "a high degree of gratification or pleasure." Imagine that. God receives pleasure from Your intercession because you are obeying His command to pray.

You are the righteousness of God in Christ Jesus (see 2 Cor. 5:21). That makes you upright—or in right standing with God. One of the reasons why we enter into repentance—asking God to forgive our sins and cleanse us from all unrighteousness—before we enter into intercession is so He can delight in our prayers. Sin separates us from fellowship with God and hinders our prayer life. When we repent, we stay upright and can confidently pray in faith.

Charles H. Spurgeon, known as the prince of preachers in the 19th century, once wrote, "If our prayer is God's delight, let us not stint Him in that which gives Him pleasure. He does not consider the grammar of it, nor the metaphysics of it, nor the rhetoric of it; in all these men might despise it. He, as a Father, takes pleasure in the lispings of His own babes, the stammerings of His newborn sons and daughters. Should we not delight in prayer since the Lord delights in it? Let us make errands to the throne. The Lord finds us enough reasons for prayer, and we ought to thank Him that it is so."

— *Prayer* —

Father, in the name of Jesus, help me to seek first Your Kingdom and Your righteousness in all my ways and for all my days. Help me stay upright so I can pray in faith and make intercession that delights Your heart.

The Dietrich Bonhoeffer Prayer Anointing

"Greater love has no one than this, than to lay down one's life for his friends"
(John 15:13).

He goes down in history as a modern-day martyr at the hands of Nazi Germany. Dietrich Bonhoeffer lived in Germany, the "Cradle of Reformation." He was disgusted with the work of Adolph Hitler in his nation and grieved over how little Christians did to stand against his agenda.

Bonhoeffer laid his life down for the cause of Christ in Germany, doing everything he could to preserve the nation's biblical roots amid Nazi propaganda attacks to undermine the faith. He was accused of conspiring to assassinate Hitler and arrested for being part of Operation 7, which worked to transport Jewish people across Germany's border to Switzerland. He died by hanging in a Nazi extermination camp.

Many may not think of Bonhoeffer as an intercessor in the same way as Reese Howells, who also stood against the Nazis in prayer. But he was just as much as intercessor. He understood the power of intercession.

"A Christian fellowship lives and exists by the intercession of its members for one another, or it collapses," he once said. "I can no longer condemn or hate a brother for whom I pray, no matter how much trouble he causes me. His face, that hitherto may have been strange and intolerable to me, is transformed in intercession into the countenance of a brother for whom Christ died, the face of a forgiven sinner.

"That is a blessed discovery for the Christian who is beginning to offer intercessory prayer for others. As far as we are concerned, there is no dislike, no personal tension, no disunity or strife that cannot be overcome by intercessory prayer. Intercessory prayer is the purifying bath into which the individual and the community must enter every day."

The Dietrich Bonhoeffer prayer anointing is an anointing that is willing to lay its life down for the cause of Christ against evil powers waging war on a generation. This is an anointing intercessors sorely need in this hour.

— *Prayer* —

Father, in the name of Jesus, help me lay my life down in prayer for a generation the enemy is hell bent on destroying. Help me stand against demonic ideologies that are deceiving the masses and separating them from You. Give me a prayer anointing like Bonhoeffer carried.

MARCH 29

Developing Healthy Prayer Habits

"For God sees everything you do and his eyes are wide open as he observes every single habit you have" (Proverbs 5:21-22, The Passion).

Our habits in this lifetime are affect our eternal rewards. Let that sink in. Ultimately, our habits on earth ripple through all eternity. That's the power of a habit.

Let's define habit: A habit is an acquired mode of behavior that has become nearly or completely involuntary. A habit forms by frequent repetition.

Prayer habits can sustain you when you are not feeling motivated. Prayer habits can turn you into the intercessor you really want to be. British Poet Frederick Langbridge once said: "We are our own potters; for our habits make us, and we make our habits."

If you want to rise early in the morning to pray like Jesus did, for example, you need to go to bed early enough the night before to rise and shine. One of my prayer habits is to thank the Lord when I get out of bed and then start praying in the Spirit. Another prayer habit is using my shower time to pray prayers of protection. Another prayer habit is to use a prayer list for mundane prayer I may forget about.

Smith Wigglesworth never let an hour go by when he wasn't in the Word of God. You could install a habit that you pray for a few minutes every hour. That, practically speaking, is probably going to require setting an alarm so you don't forget, at least at first. Another prayer habit might be setting aside a special place to pray or praying three times a day like Daniel.

A strategic prayer habit to install is waiting upon the Lord. Remember, prayer is a conversation not a monologue where you talk, talk and talk some more. God wants to speak back to you. He wants to inform your prayer. He wants to tell you what to pray for, at times. You may not always hear something immediately, but we should at least give Him the space to speak. What are your prayer habits?

— *Prayer* —

Father, in the name of Jesus, please help me establish healthy prayer habits in my life so I can be as effective and efficient as possible in my assignment. Show me the prayer habits You want me to install in my life.

Breaking Bad Prayer Habits

"I can do all things through Christ who strengthens me" (Philippians 4:13).

Maybe you know what your bad prayer habits are. Or maybe you are blind to them. Spend some time with the Holy Spirit asking Him about your prayer habits. This is important because bad habits deceive us but Jesus said the truth sets us free.

Maybe your bad prayer habit is talking, talking, talking but never stopping to listen for God's instruction. Maybe it's self-centered, self-focused prayers that leave no time to intercede for others. Maybe you allow yourself to be distracted with cell phones or random thoughts during prayer.

When you see bad prayer habits in your life, you're going to want to do a purge—but you can't change everything at once. You'll end up overwhelmed. feel powerless and give up. Mark Twain once said, "A habit cannot be tossed out the window; it must be coaxed down the stairs a step at a time."

Start with your why. Why do you want to break this bad prayer habit? What is your motivation? List at least three compelling reasons why you need to break the bad prayer habit. You can also ask yourself, "What's at stake if I don't break this bad prayer habit?" That can be convicting for sure. But don't stop there. What does breakthrough look like when you conquer this bad prayer habit? How does this positively change your prayer life?

It's work. But remember a bad prayer habit almost never disappears miraculously. It's an undo-it-yourself project.

Thankfully, God will give you the grace but you'll have to put in the work. No one can overcome your bad prayer habit for you. And it's uncomfortable. When things get tough, remember your motivation.

Noah's motivation was the get the ark built before the flood came. Jesus' motivation was to do the will of His father. Paul's motivation was to live for Christ. Don't just keep the "why" in your head. Journal it so when you need some motivation you can go back and read it.

— *Prayer* —

Father, in the name of Jesus, please help me see my bad prayer habits so that I can confess them and find freedom from them. Help me, Lord, to overcome every bad prayer habit that stands in the way of me and the breakthrough.

Praying to the Lord of the Harvest

"The harvest truly is plentiful, but the laborers are few. Therefore pray the Lord of the harvest to send out laborers into His harvest" (Matthew 9:37-38).

Praying to the Lord of the harvest is a command of Christ. I'm quite sure Christ Himself prayed for the harvest of souls for whom He would give His life. Christ was the consummate intercessor. When He walked the earth He had a burden for souls—and He still does. We should, too.

We might not always feel "led" to pray to the Lord of the harvest, but we don't need to feel led to obey Scripture. By contrast, there may be certain situations or seasons when we will feel especially led to pray to the Lord of the harvest. Either way, we need to pray. In Matthew 9:35-38, we see Jesus doing what Jesus does:

"Then Jesus went about all the cities and villages, teaching in their synagogues, preaching the gospel of the kingdom, and healing every sickness and every disease among the people.

"But when He saw the multitudes, He was moved with compassion for them, because they were weary and scattered, like sheep having no shepherd. Then He said to His disciples, 'The harvest truly is plentiful, but the laborers are few. Therefore pray the Lord of the harvest to send out laborers into His harvest'."

There's never a wrong time to pray to the Lord of the harvest. Jesus said in John 4:34-36: "Jesus said to them, 'My food is to do the will of Him who sent Me, and to finish His work. Do you not say, There are still four months and then comes the harvest'? Behold, I say to you, lift up your eyes and look at the fields, for they are already white for harvest! And he who reaps receives wages, and gathers fruit for eternal life, that both he who sows and he who reaps may rejoice together.'"

Pray to the Lord of the harvest. When you do, you'll feel the joy of the Lord. Remember, there is joy in heaven when a sinner gets saved.

— *Prayer* —

Father, in the name of Jesus, help me remember to consistently pray for laborers to enter the harvest fields with the good news of Your Gospel. Grace me stand in intercession with those who preach salvation.

APRIL

"If My people who are called by My name will humble themselves, and pray and seek My face, and turn from their wicked ways, then I will hear from heaven, and will forgive their sin and heal their land" (2 Chronicles 7:14).

APRIL 1

Avoiding Foolish Intercession

"Neither filthiness, nor foolish talking, nor coarse jesting, which are not fitting, but rather giving of thanks" (Ephesians 1:4).

Have you ever entered foolish intercession? You may have without knowing it. The Bible has plenty to say about fools and foolishness. Foolishness relates to a loss of composure. Foolishness marks an emotional or immature intercessor. We don't want to be foolish in our intercession.

What does foolish intercession look like? Proverbs 29:11 gives us one clue, "A fool vents all his feelings, but a wise man holds them back." If we're not careful, we'll pray out of our feelings instead of His feelings. We'll pray out of our soul instead of His Spirit. If we're not careful, we'll pray foolish prayers that do nothing more than air our "people grievances" to God. Wisdom holds back opinions in intercession and seeks to pray His will. Foolish intercession lacks good sense, judgment or discretion.

Foolish intercession is thoughtless intercession. Foolish intercession defies both common and biblical sense. Foolish intercession is marked by our will, wants and desires instead of the desires of His heart. Foolish intercession relies on poor judgment about who to pray with and who not to pray with over critical issues.

Foolish intercession is laced with pride rather than sincere humility. Foolish intercession is a form of corrupt communication—and Paul warned us not to let any corrupt communication come out of our months, but only words that are edifying and minister grace to people who hear them (see Eph. 4:29). Foolish intercession can be rooted in bitterness and defile a prayer meeting (see Heb. 12:15).

Foolish intercession may release the power of death over a situation instead of the spirit of life. Foolish intercession continues after God has said to stop. Foolish intercession engages the enemy without the leadership of the Holy Spirit. Foolish intercession is marked by competition in a prayer meeting over who is the most eloquent. Ask the Lord to help you avoid these and all other manifestations of foolish intercession.

— *Prayer* —

Father, in the name of Jesus, I don't want to be a foolish intercessor. Help me check my heart at the door of my prayer closet before I engage in foolish thoughts, words, and prayers. Help me develop wisdom in intercession.

Bold As a Lion

"Now, Lord, look on their threats, and grant to Your servants that with all boldness they may speak Your word..." (Acts 4:29).

I used to be extremely timid in intercession (and every other area of life). For years, on the advice of a mentor, I prayed fervently for boldness. Eventually, I found myself bold—extremely bold.

Do you want more boldness? Ask the Lord to give you boldness, but be sure to also cultivate faithfulness to His agenda. The Lord showed me the intercessors who have been faithful—who have been pressing, pushing back darkness, and decreeing and declaring what He says—are receiving a new mantle of boldness.

I'm talking about boldness in the spirit, not a rude demeanor. Bold means fearless before danger. It's a daring spirit. Cloaked with boldness, faithful intercessors are going into new territories in the spirit to take on special assignments that few will dare to touch.

God is giving intercessors new boldness to tackle issues in society like abortion, perversion—things that have come to infiltrate the church and things that have come at our youth. There is a boldness to come against those things that have come to wreck our marriages, and things that have come to pollute the Gospel message.

I heard the Lord say: "That mantle of boldness is coming upon you. Those things you were not sure about in past seasons, the things you didn't know if you should step into, I'm going to show you. I'm going to show you how to step. I'm going to show you how to press. I'm going to teach your hands to war and your fingers to battle at a new level. I'm giving intercessors new strategies for this season. I'm giving intercessors new tactics in this season, even new weapons in this season. The righteous are as bold as a lion."

I hear a boldness coming from the intercessors. I hear a roar coming from the intercessors, and the gates of hell shall not prevail against the church. I see new assignments coming for the intercessors with this mantle of boldness.

— Prayer —

Father, in the name of Jesus, would You give me boldness in the spirit? Break off any timidity that hinders my prayer life. Help me shake off the fear of man and other fearful intimidating voices that cause me to shrink back in prayer.

APRIL 3

Organizing Your Prayer Closet

"But thou, when thou prayest, enter into thy closet, and when thou hast shut thy door, pray to thy Father which is in secret; and thy Father which seeth in secret shall reward thee openly" (Matthew 6:6, KJV).

I have large walk-in closets with built in drawers. Despite all the organizational functions meant to help me keep clothes and shoes straight, my closet still gets messy from time to time. Every few months, I take the time to reorganize my closet. I do this for my own sake, of course, since nobody but me and God sees the inside of my closet.

At times, we must do the same with our prayer closet. In case you wonder where that term "prayer closet" came from, it's old school language from the *King James Version* of the Bible. Although the *War Room* movie certainly took a literal interpretation, you don't have to pray in a closet.

The New Living Translation puts it this way, "But when you pray, go away by yourself, shut the door behind you, and pray to your Father in private." *The Berean Study Bible* calls it an "inner room." *Holman* calls it a "private room." Other translations call it an inner chamber. The idea is, it's a private place where you go to pray. Nobody knows what goes on in that closet but you and God.

But, at times, we need to organize—or reorganize—our prayer closet. You may pray in your bedroom or a den. If it's cluttered up in the natural, it can be distracting to your soul. By the same token, you may need to equip your prayer closet. You should always make sure you have a Bible in your prayer closet, as well as a pad and pen.

I recommend removing all electronic devices from your prayer closet because, if you haven't yet noticed, when you go into your prayer closet with a smartphone it dumbs down your prayers. In other words, people start texting, calling, social media alerts pop up and so on. Even if you put it on mute, the vibration can disturb and distract you from your time with God. Do you need to reorganize your prayer closet?

— *Prayer* —

Father, in the name of Jesus, help me to declutter my prayer closet so I can focus completely on my petitions to You and Your instructions to me. Help me to equip my prayer closet with the tools I need to be more effective.

The Power of Proximity

"Every place that the sole of your foot will tread upon I have given you, as I said to Moses"
(Joshua 1:3).

I love my prayer closet. I tread on serpents and scorpions in the spirit and nothing by any means harms me. But I have also learned the value of taking back what the enemy stole through treading in the natural while praying in the spirit.

Some call this prayer walking. Others deem it a prayer march. I like to call it praying with proximity or on-site intercession. On-site intercession is targeting a specific area to walk around and pray. Perhaps the Lord has called you to shut down an abortion clinic or to guard the gates of the city. There's nothing like going on-site to get the job done.

God told Joshua, "Every place that the sole of your foot will tread upon I have given you, as I said to Moses" (Josh. 1:3). As the Scripture suggests, God made the same promise to Moses in Deuteronomy 11:24.

Joshua had to put his foot on the ground in warfare to take the land. He had to invade to dispossess the former occupants and take control of the land. Joshua's assignment required proximity. If you want the land, sometimes you have to put your feet on the ground and contend.

On-site intercession gives you a greater connection to the city, which helps you love the city and hate the demons attacking the city. If you are going to be effective in praying for your city long-term, you need to feel connected to your city. Drive around until you hear the cry of your city. When you drive around, you see the prostitutes, the homeless, the lost souls.

Ask the Lord to give you a strategy for praying with proximity in your city. This should not be a random event but a leading of the Holy Spirit to tread on a territory with your boots of peace and pray without ceasing with a team of intercessors treading to bring God's will to a city.

— *Prayer* —

Father, in the name of Jesus, would You help me grasp the power of on-site intercession? Give me a territory and a cause and I will walk around in intercession until we take the land. I want to hear the cry of my city.

APRIL 5

Entering Prophetic Prayer Realms

"And the Holy Spirit helps us in our weakness. For example, we don't know what God wants us to pray for" (Romans 8:26, NLT).

Prophetic intercession may be a foreign concept to some. But even if you haven't heard of prophetic intercession, it's quite possible that you've entered into it.

There are many definitions of prophetic intercession, I suppose, but the bottom line is this: it's intercession informed by prophetic intelligence from the Holy Spirit. Prophetic intercession is prayer infused by the presence and power of the Holy Spirit. Prophetic intercession is beyond our natural minds because we're in the spirit.

As I wrote in my book, *Waging Prophetic Warfare*, prophetic intercession is both an art and a science. And you can't put prophetic intercession in a box. Prophetic intercession is not one size fits all, but the foundation is Spirit-inspired prayer and sometimes even prophetic acts that help us to pray in line with God's perfect will. It's one more way the Holy Spirit helps us in our weakness when we don't know how to pray as we ought, or when we don't even know that we don't know how to pray as we ought (see Rom. 8:26).

"When I say that prophetic intercession is an art, I mean that it is a skill that sharpens with experience or observation. Prophetic intercession is both taught and caught," I wrote in *Waging Prophetic Warfare*. "Like anything, you master it by doing it. You can't decide to enter prophetic intercession. The Spirit of God must lead you into it. That's where the science, which is essentially the operation of laws, comes in."

So how do you enter into prophetic intercession? You do so at the invitation of the Holy Spirit. You do so by acknowledging Him in your prayer set. You do so by understanding that, many times, we do not know how to pray as we ought—but He does. You do so by refusing to lean on your own understanding—what you see with your natural eyes or hear with your natural ears alone. Holy Spirit is omniscient.

— *Prayer* —

Father, in the name of Jesus, would You make me more prophetic as an intercessor? Would You teach me not to lean on what I know in the natural only, but pray through what Your Spirit knows so I can be effective in prayer?

Praying the Great and Precious Promises

"God is not a man, that He should lie, nor a son of man, that He should repent. Has He said, and will He not do? Or has He spoken, and will He not make it good?"
(Numbers 23:19)

There are over seven thousand promises in Scripture. And all of them are yes and amen. A quick examination about what Scripture says about Scripture promises is itself will encourage every faithful intercessor.

Peter said God has "given to us exceedingly great and precious promises" (2 Pet. 1:4). Peter also assured us, "The Lord is not slack concerning His promise, as some count slackness," (2 Pet. 3:9). That's good news to the preserving intercessor that is meeting with delay after delay.

God's promises never fail because His promises are His Word and His Word never fails. "Deep in your hearts you know that every promise of the Lord your God has come true. Not a single one has failed!" (Josh. 23:14, NLT) God has put His Word above His name! (see Ps. 138:2).

In 1 Kings 8:56, we are reminded of the unfailing promises yet again: "Blessed be the Lord, who has given rest to His people Israel, according to all that He promised. There has not failed one word of all His good promise, which He promised through His servant Moses."

Paul wrote, "For all the promises of God in Him are Yes, and in Him Amen, to the glory of God through us" (see 2 Cor. 1:20). And he was "fully convinced that what He had promised He was also able to perform" (see Rom. 4:21). Finally, the writer of Hebrews put it this way: "Let us hold fast the confession of our hope without wavering, for He who promised is faithful" (see Heb. 10:23).

When you pray the promises, you can rest assured that He is watching over that Word to perform it (see Jer.1:12). God is not a man that He should lie (see Num. 23:19). Even if we are not faithful, He remains faithful for He cannot deny Himself (see 2 Tim. 2:13).

— *Prayer* —

Father, in the name of Jesus, help me to stand on, decree, declare, confess and pray Your promises. Your Word is true and Your name is powerful. If You made the promise, You will keep it. You are the promise keeper.

APRIL 7

Throwing Jezebel Down

"Then he said, 'Throw [Jezebel] down.' So they threw her down, and some of her blood spattered on the wall and on the horses; and he trampled her underfoot" (2 Kings 9:33, AMP).

Intercessors, it's time to throw Jezebel off the wall. But you can't throw Jezebel off the wall if you don't dwell on the wall. Intercessors who live on the wall of intercession—those watch and pray day and night, night and day—gain a position of authority to throw Jezebel down.

You can't dwell on the wall until you build the wall. God is looking for intercessors who will make a wall, stand on it, and actually dwell on it to prevent Jezebel from gaining further inroads of destruction in families, churches and cities.

God is emphasizing Ezekiel 22:30 (NLT) in this hour: "So I sought for a man among them who would make a wall, and stand in the gap before Me on behalf of the land, that I should not destroy it; but I found no one."

When Joshua sent two spies into Jericho, the spies entered Rahab's house. When the king found out about it, he sent men to her house to take the Israelites captive. Instead of handing them over, she made a wall of intercession. Rahab told the king's men the Hebrews had escaped—then helped them escape.

Consider this act of intercession in Joshua 2, understanding that one definition of intercession is "interpose." Interpose means to intervene or to put a barrier or obstacle between or in the way of, according to *Dictionary.com*.

"Then she let them down by a rope through the window, for her house was on the city wall; she dwelt on the wall. And she said to them, 'Get to the mountain, lest the pursuers meet you. Hide there three days, until the pursuers have returned. Afterward you may go your way'" (Josh. 2:15-16).

Since she lived on the wall, she could interrupt the enemy's plans. When you live on the wall of intercession, you are positioned rightly to throw Jezebel down.

— Prayer —

Father, in the name of Jesus, help me build my wall of intercession and live there. Help me take my place on the wall so I can see every spiritual enemy, including Jezebel, and throw them down.

APRIL 8

End Times Intercessory Assignments

"Therefore you also be ready, for the Son of Man is coming at an hour you do not expect"
(Matthew 24:44).

There were end times intercessors long before we entered the end times, but God is rapidly calling intercessors who may have been assigned to other prayer tasks to also intercede concerning end times events.

An end times intercessor is an intercessor who God entrusts with revelation that informs their prayer about end times sign events and trends—either to stand against the enemy's timing, pray for the church, or pray in what God is doing, even if it seems contrary to those who don't understand His Word and what is on His heart.

End times intercessors pray, at times, for the church with the heart of the Bridegroom. What does that mean? End times intercessors pray through Scriptures in the Book of Revelation. End times intercessors pray for the persecuted church to endure. End times intercessors pray for the lukewarm church to heat up. End times intercessors pray for the compromising church to overcome Jezebel.

End times intercessors pray, at times, with the delegated authority of the King of kings against the enemy's plans. What does that mean? End times intercessors pray against the enemy changing times and laws. End times intercessors pray against the spirit of deception in the end times. They pray against offense and other enemy plots rising.

End times intercessors pray, at times, prayers that agree with God's end times plan. What does that mean? End times intercessors pray for the Gospel to be preached to all nations so the end can come. What does that mean? When they hear the first trumpet sound, they will pray for the next of the seven trumpets to sound. They discern the times and agree with what God is doing in those times.

I wrote much more about *The End Times Watchman*, which includes a heavy emphasis on intercession. Is God raising you up as an end times intercessor?

— Prayer —

Father, in the name of Jesus, would You prepare me for the end times? Help me understand the importance of end times intercession so I can stand on the wall. Teach me to watch and pray with an end times bent.

Discerning the Prayer Breakthrough

"The one who breaks open will come up before them; They will break out, pass through the gate, and go out by it; Their king will pass before them, with the Lord at their head" (Micah 2:13).

Many intercessors stop praying just shy of the breakthrough. Others keep praying for the same issue after they've already attained the breakthrough because they don't discern that they have broken through in the spirit. Either way, savvy intercessors do not stop short or keep pressing in prayer past the point of breakthrough. Rather, they discern the prayer breakthrough.

Let's tackle both sides of this breakthrough equation. Just because you see the first fruits of a prayer answer doesn't mean it's time to stop praying. We don't want a halfway breakthrough. We don't want to stop short of the overwhelming triumph God has planned or settle for less than His absolute best. We want to see total victory, in Jesus' name.

By the same token, if we keep fighting and clawing in prayer for a breakthrough that we've attained in the spirit—even though we haven't seen its natural manifestation—we are wasting prayer power on a done deal. We are missing the opportunity to pray into the next urgent issue. Since we can only pray so many hours a day, it's important that we discern the breakthrough.

So, then, how do we discern when we've broken through? There are many ways and means to discern a breakthrough. But the first rule is to remember we walk by faith and not by sight (see 2 Cor. 5:7). It can look like there's no breakthrough when there is and it can look like there's a breakthrough where there is not.

You discern the breakthrough in your spirit. Your mind may be saying one thing, but your spirit will bear witness through a joy unspeakable full of glory or through a peace that passes all understanding. If you stay still before the Lord and quiet your soul, you'll know when to keep pressing and when to move to another Holy Ghost agenda.

— *Prayer* —

Father, in the name of Jesus, make me more sensitive to Your heart. I want to discern the breakthrough—or lack of breakthrough—in my prayer assignments. I want to be effective. Teach me to discern the breakthrough.

Praying In the Spirit

"But you, beloved, build yourselves up in your most holy faith. Pray in the Holy Spirit"
(Jude 20).

When we pray in the Sprit, we're accelerating our spiritual growth. If there is fear in our hearts, for example, the Holy Spirit works to drive out that fear so we can become spiritual giants on the battlefield.

Sometimes unbeknownst to us the Holy Spirit is dealing with issues in our lives that open the door for the enemy. He may be purging our hearts of doubt, unbelief, selfishness, pride, and other hooks the enemy can use.

At the same time, when we pray in the Spirit, we're more likely to get God's perspective on the battlefield because, like an edifice, we're rising higher and higher in the spirit. Just as David ran to the battle line with a prophetic strategy that took out Goliath, we can expect to push back darkness when we pray in the Spirit. When we pray in the Spirit, we're making spiritual progress against our enemies whether we can see it or not.

Paul explains: "For he who speaks in an unknown tongue does not speak to men, but to God. For no one understands him, although in the spirit, he speaks mysteries" (1 Cor. 14:2). What are those mysteries? They are often unknown, unless they manifest themselves in the natural. See, the devil can't understand what you are praying in tongues and you usually can't either. God may reveal to you what you are praying for, but many times He will let it remain a mystery until the appointed time.

I can say all that with confidence because, just as you probably have, I've read—and memorized—Romans 8:26–27. In case you need a reminder, it says this: "Likewise, the Spirit helps us in our weaknesses, for we do not know what to pray for as we ought, but the Spirit Himself intercedes for us with groanings too deep for words. He who searches the hearts knows what the mind of the Spirit is, because He intercedes for the saints according to the will of God."

— *Prayer* —

Father, in the name of Jesus, would You fill me with Your Spirit to overflowing?
Help me develop the discipline to pray in the Spirit at all times. Help me press past
my flesh and into the supernatural realm of prayer.

When Your Pastor Is Against Intercession

"Devote yourselves to prayer" (Colossians 4:2).

A precious and confused saint once asked me this heart-breaking question: "Can you please give us clarity? I hear pastors say God did not call intercessors and that you can't find intercessors in the Bible. He said only Jesus can intercede. Thank you." God help us!

Of course, there are plenty of Scriptures to refute such a nonsensical claim. For starters, in 1 Timothy 2:1-3 Paul instructed his spiritual son to "make supplications, prayers, intercessions, and thanksgivings for everyone." I might also point to Acts 12:5, when the church "prayed to God without ceasing" for Peter when he was in prison. Or what about James 5:14 where Christ's half-brother instructed the sick to "call for the elders of the church, and let them pray over him, anointing him with oil in the name of the Lord."

Why on earth would a pastor—or anyone—try to convince their members to abandon the call to intercession? Technically, we're all called to intercession, though I believe some people have a stronger ministry mantle and anointing to intercede.

Abraham was an intercessor (see Gen. 18; 19). Moses was an intercessor (see Ex. 32:1-14; Ps. 106:23). Samuel was an intercessor (see 1 Sam. 7:3; 1 Sam.12:24). Hezekiah, Paul, Stephen, Amos, Solomon, Anna the prophetess, Ezra, Elijah, Daniel and Nehemiah all entered into strong intercession. Although intercessors are called to do more than occupy a prayer closet, believers are certainly called to intercede.

So what is the root of all this? Why would pastors say such a thing? It could be a lack of knowledge (see Hos. 4:6). It could be flat-out deception. It could be a controlling spirit. It could be a very real fear the intercessors will gain prophetic insight into the hidden sin in their lives. It could be wrong teaching on the topic. It could be bad experiences with immature intercessors who overstepped their boundaries. Intercessor, pray on. If your pastor is against intercession, it may be time to find a praying church.

— Prayer —

Father, in the name of Jesus, help me not to get caught up in a silly debate over whether God calls intercessors. Help me, rather, to intercede for those who try to shut prayer down. Help me to be part of the solution to prayerlessness. Help me stay steady in prayer.

A Three-Pronged Prayer Strategy

"Keep on asking and it will be given you; keep on seeking and you will find; keep on knocking [reverently] and [the door] will be opened to you. For everyone who keeps on asking receives; and he who keeps on seeking finds; and to him who keeps on knocking, [the door] will be opened"
(Matthew 7:7-8, AMPC).

This is a promise from God. So long as what you desire is His will—and His Word is His will—you can be assured if you keep on asking, keep on seeking and keep on knocking, you will eventually see God's will come to pass. Let me expound on these three principles.

Ask. Although God knows what we need before we ask Him, He usually won't provide our needs until we ask because He wants relationship with us. So ask, and keep asking, until you feel a release in your spirit—and then thank Him until you see His will manifest.

Seek. It's not always enough just to ask. More often than not, you also have to seek. In other words, add some works to your faith. If you've asked Him for a new job, seek a new job. If you've asked Him for reconciliation in a relationship, seek reconciliation. If you've asked Him for healing, seek healing. Don't sit back and wait for an angel to do all the work. Faith without works is dead (see James 2:26). (Be led by the Spirit, of course. You can't bulldoze your way through the doorway to God's promises.)

Knock. Once you see God's promise in clear view, knock and keep on knocking until the promised door is open. Let's say you've asked Him for a new job. You're seeking a new job and you know in your spirit (or even hope in your heart) that it's a perfect match. Start knocking. God opens doors that no one can shut (see Rev. 3:8), but often you have to knock.

Can you see it? There is a time to pray once, hand it over to God, and trust Him to answer. But there is also a principle of persistent faith where you ask and keep on asking, seek and keep on seeking, and knock and keep on knocking until you receive the promise. How do you know the difference? The easy answer is to be led by the Spirit.

— *Prayer* —

Father, in the name of Jesus, give me a deeper revelation of this three-pronged strategy for breakthrough prayer answers. Help me not to grow weary in asking, seeking and knocking so I can reap a harvest of prayer answers. Give me a diligent spirit that refuses to back down from Your promises.

The Intercessor's Legacy

"One generation shall praise Your works to another, and shall declare Your mighty acts" (Psalm 145:4).

Intercessors leave a legacy in the chronicles of heaven even if no one on earth knows their name. We think of Daniel, Abraham and Anna in Scripture. We think of John Wesley, Ruth Ward Heflin and Reese Howells in more modern times. But don't discount your own intercessory prayer legacy.

What is a legacy? Your legacy is your contribution to the generations that pray after you. Your legacy is your mark on the realm of intercessory prayer. Your legacy is the impact you leave after you graduate to heaven. It connects your past and present to the future.

Psalm 145:4 puts it this way, "One generation shall praise Your works to another, and shall declare Your mighty acts." Even if no one on earth knows your name, the great cloud of witnesses is cheering you on. Remember that when you feel weary.

Paul told Timothy, "And the things that you have heard from me among many witnesses, commit these to faithful men who will be able to teach others also" (2 Tim. 2:2). One way you leave a legacy is by pouring out your life as a drink offering for the next generation. It's not about how many social media followers you have. It's about your commitment to the disciples He has given you to steward.

Paul said things to his disciples like: "The things which you learned and received and heard and saw in me, these do, and the God of peace will be with you" (Phil. 4:9). And again, "Brethren, join in following my example, and note those who so walk, as you have us for a pattern" (Phil. 3:17).

It's about modeling the way. Peter said to be an example to the flock (see 1 Pet. 5:3). Jesus said, "For I have given you an example, that you should do as I have done to you" (John 13:15). And Paul said, "Therefore I urge you, imitate me" (1 Cor. 4:16). And again, "Imitate me, just as I also imitate Christ" (1 Cor. 11:1). Intercessors worth imitating leave a legacy. Be one of them.

— *Prayer* —

Father, in the name of Jesus, would You help me press into Your heart, learn, grow and teach others the way of intercession? I want to leave a spiritual inheritance. I want to leave a prayer legacy.

Unleashing Intercessory Force

"The effective, fervent prayer of a righteous man avails much" (James 5:16).

If I am going to make intercession, I want it to be effective. Who has time to waste with ineffectual prayer? Effective, fervent prayer is powerful and accomplishes God's will. With every prayer we release, we should set out to be effective. We should pay attention to what works and what doesn't work—what's effective and what's ineffective——in any prayer campaign.

Let's look at James 5:16 in several verses so you can be thoroughly convinced how important it is to be effective. *The Amplified Classic* puts it this way, "The earnest (heartfelt, continued) prayer of a righteous man makes tremendous power available [dynamic in its working]. Elijah was a human being with a nature such as we have [with feelings, affections, and a constitution like ours]; and he prayed earnestly for it not to rain, and no rain fell on the earth for three years and six months. And [then] he prayed again and the heavens supplied rain and the land produced its crops [as usual]."

That says a lot! Effective means "producing a decided, decisive, or desired effect." Effective prayer knows where the bullseye is and how to hit it. Effective prayer is released through an intercessor who is ready for service or action; who is equipped for the good work of petitioning, decreeing, declaring and travail.

The Berean Study Bible reads, "The prayer of a righteous man has great power to prevail." Effective prayer is prevailing prayer. It's prayer that doesn't pull back until it breaks through. *The Holman Christian Standard Bible* tells us, "The urgent request of a righteous person is very powerful in its effect." Effective prayer is urgent prayer. It's prayer that seizes the moment, not just the day. *The World English Bible* says, "The insistent prayer of a righteous person is powerfully effective." Effective prayer insists on God's will in every situation.

— Prayer —

Father, in the name of Jesus, I want to be effective so give me fervency, insistency, determination, grit, urgency and anything else I need in order to bring Your will to pass on earth as it is in heaven. Make me an effective intercessor who releases tremendous prayer power.

The John Wesley Prayer Anointing

"Come, my people, enter your chambers, and shut your doors behind you" (Isaiah 26:20).

I've been in John Wesley's house more than once. John Wesley, an English cleric, theologian and evangelist from the 18th Century, is the founder of the Methodist church. Wesley's house in England has been preserved and you can walk through it. When you do, you feel the presence of God.

Both times I went to his house, I spent time in his prayer closet. He had a small room in which he knelt in prayer for hours at a time. You can still see the indentations his knees made on the wood from long hours of prayer.

Wesley spent two hours every morning in his prayer closet, a room that became known as "The Powerhouse of Methodism." What was he doing on his knees? He once said, "Bear up the hands that hang down, by faith and prayer; support the tottering knees. Have you any days of fasting and prayer? Storm the throne of grace and persevere therein, and mercy will come down."

Wesley understood all too well that prayer is where the action is. But he wasn't just a man who sought intimacy with the Lord in prayer. He was a man who understood the value of corporate prayer and the fruit of the corporate prayer anointing. He once said:

"About three in the morning as we were continuing instant in prayer, the power of God came mightily upon us, insomuch that many cried out for exceeding joy, and many fell to the ground. As soon as we recovered a little from the awe and amazement at the presence of His Majesty, we broke out with one voice, 'We praise Thee, O God, we acknowledge Thee to be the Lord.'"

It was Wesley who said God does nothing except in response to believing prayer. We need that John Wesley anointing to pray for hours on end, in the secret place, and to pray without ceasing in the open until we see God's will done and His Kingdom come on earth as it is in heaven.

— Prayer —

Father, in the name of Jesus, would You give me the John Wesley anointing for prayer? Help me to be so committed to intercession and intimacy that I think nothing of spending hours a day on my knees in loving adoration, expecting You to move.

APRIL 16

Yielding to God's Perfect Will

"My son, give me your heart, and let your eyes observe my ways" (Proverbs 23:6).

If we ask amiss, we will not get a prayer answer. What is asking amiss? Asking amiss is translated as "asking with wrong motives" in some versions of the Bible. Other times it's translates as "ask wrongly" or even "ask wickedly."

When our will is surrendered to God's will, we will not ask amiss. But there is a danger called self-will that can subtly creep in. When we want something desperately (even if it's not for ourselves) the enemy can more easily tempt us to enter intercession without first discerning the Lord's will.

Let's be honest, sometimes we've prayed for what we want without first understanding what God wants. God won't always answer self-willed prayers. He's not obligated to fulfill your every wish. He's not a genie in a bottle—and we should be glad He's not. We should be grateful we don't get everything we ask for. Father knows best.

The good news is when we surrender to His will we will see more prayer answers. Of course, when we know His will it's at least a little easier to surrender. John the beloved said:

"Now this is the confidence that we have in Him, that if we ask anything according to His will, He hears us. And if we know that He hears us, whatever we ask, we know that we have the petitions that we have asked of Him" (1 John 5:14-15).

Again in 1 John 3:22, the apostle offers this nugget of wisdom: "And whatever we ask we receive from Him, because we keep His commandments and do those things that are pleasing in His sight." If we're surrendered, we're keeping His commandments. And one more Scripture for good measure. "Now we know that God does not hear sinners; but if anyone is a worshiper of God and does His will, He hears him" (John 9:31).

— *Prayer* —

Father, in the name of Jesus, I surrender to Your will, Your ways, and Your heart. Father, put Your desires in my heart so I can pray what You want me to pray and see Your will, not mine alone, come to pass through my intercession.

APRIL 17

The Intimate Intercessor

"One thing have I asked of the Lord, that will I seek, inquire for, and [insistently] require: that I may dwell in the house of the Lord [in His presence] all the days of my life, to behold and gaze upon the beauty [the sweet attractiveness and the delightful loveliness] of the Lord and to meditate, consider, and inquire in His temple" (Psalm 27:4, AMPC).

When you realize God is not mad at you—that He likes you and takes delight in even your weakest prayers—it changes your perspective of intercession. Instead of begging and pleading with a faint hope that He might hear you, you are confident He not only hears you but will answer you (see 1 John 5:14-15).

Cultivating the oil of intimacy is critical for the modern-day intercessor. See, I came from a spiritual warfare church background where intimacy was never taught or modeled. When I left that church, I learned how David—who slew Goliath and many other Philistines—also worshipped in deep intimacy. He was a worshipping warrior. The same David that never lost a battle wrote these words in Psalm 63:1-5:

"O God, You are my God; Early will I seek You; My soul thirsts for You; My flesh longs for You in a dry and thirsty land where there is no water. So I have looked for You in the sanctuary, to see Your power and Your glory. Because Your lovingkindness is better than life, my lips shall praise You. Thus I will bless You while I live; I will lift up my hands in Your name. My soul shall be satisfied as with marrow and fatness, and my mouth shall praise You with joyful lips."

Intercessor, make intimacy with God your priority. Don't get so busy doing the work of intercession that you forsake the all-important time with Christ, the Intercessor and the Holy Spirit who helps you pray when you are at a loss for words. Intimacy will add a fire to your intercession that you can't spark any other way. Cultivate the oil of intimacy. It will sustain you in the dry seasons of prayer.

— Prayer —

Father, in the name of Jesus, help me make intimacy a priority over intercession, knowing that intimacy will inform and inspire my intercession. Never let me lose sight of Christ the Intercessor with me as I pray.

Praying Against Prayerlessness

"Watch therefore, and pray always that you may be counted worthy to escape all these things that will come to pass, and to stand before the Son of Man" (Luke 21:36).

Speaking to the church at Thessalonica, Paul said, "Pray without ceasing" (Thess. 5:17). Every church leader and intercessor needs to take that command seriously in this hour as the enemy is roaming and violence is raging.

Over and over again, Scripture admonishes us to pray. That makes prayerlessness pure rebellion. Indeed, I believe prayerlessness is among the greatest sins in the church—and unfortunately some leaders are propagating this sin and discouraging those with true prayer burdens from cooperating with the Spirit of God to bring His will to the earth. It grieves the Holy Spirit.

I've seen for years how prayer is lacking in many churches. Even churches that do have prayer meetings often relegate intercessors to the back rooms, lest their effectual fervent prayer offend the lukewarm saints. Thankfully, I'm seeing more church leaders repent of prayerlessness in this hour.

E.M. Bounds, a 19th Century Methodist who wrote nine important volumes on prayer, said this: "Prayerless praying has no burden, because no sense of need; no ardency, because none of the vision, strength, or glow of faith. No mighty pressure to prayer, no holding on to God with the deathless, despairing grasp, 'I will not let Thee go except Thou bless me.' No utter self-abandon, lost in the throes of a desperate, pertinacious, and consuming plea: 'Yet now if Thou wilt forgive their sin—if not, blot me, I pray Thee, out of Thy book.'"

Intercessors, cast the vision of the necessity of prayer to your Christian friends and family. Don't condemn your church or any other church for prayerlessness. Pray for them and help them see the value of constant prayer. When they see prayer results, they will realign with this heavenly principle and fewer will fall into temptation.

— *Prayer* —

Father, in the name of Jesus, help me to steer clear of prayerlessness. Help me be part of the solution to inspire other Christians to engage in intercession, knowing You delight in the prayers of the righteous.

APRIL 19

Deliverance Intercessors

"These special powerful works will be done by those who have put their trust in Me. In My name they will put out demons. They will speak with languages they have never learned. They will pick up snakes. If they drink any poison, it will not hurt them. They will put their hands on the sick and they will be healed" (Mark 16:17-18).

Deliverance ministry is sorely needed in the Body of Christ. It seems there are not enough deliverance ministers to meet the demand. But along with deliverance ministers, there's another vital need: deliverance intercessors. As the name suggests, deliverance intercessors engage in the work of deliverance ministry—but they are not always the ones commanding demons to "come out." There are several aspects to this worth exploring.

Some deliverance intercessors, for example, are assigned to pray for the lost so they can find deliverance from evil and secure salvation. They are praying to the Lord of the harvest that He would send laborers into the harvest (see Matt. 9:37-38) and asking God to break blinders off their minds.

Other deliverance intercessors are praying for the persecuted church. They are praying for their deliverance, endurance and faith. Still other deliverance intercessors are working with deliverance ministers as part of a team to cast out devils. I want to concentrate on this latter aspect.

Intercessor, deliverance ministers need you to cover them and the one they are praying for during a freedom session. They need intercessors to stand in the gap for the freedom of the one seeking God's mighty hand of deliverance. And they need your prayers against retaliation afterward.

As I write in my book, *Deliverance Protocols & Ethics,* "During the deliverance session, the intercessors should cover the deliverance team and the client in prayer, pushing back darkness, binding devils, praying in the Spirit, pleading the blood of Jesus, binding retaliation, and praying as led."

Just as Jesus has given deliverance ministers power over unclean spirits, to cast them out, He's given you power in prayer to back up the ones standing on the front lines wrestling with demon powers to bring freedom to those in bondage.

— *Prayer* —

Father, in the name of Jesus, give me revelation of my authority and power in prayer to set the captives free. Use me to help break chains off people stuck in enemy bondage through my cooperation with deliverance ministries.

A Pathway to a Greater Prayer Anointing

"The humble in spirit will retain honor" (Proverbs 29:23).

Daniel Nash began his ministry as a preacher in upstate New York. He saw revival twice in his pastorate, yet he laid it all down to pray for the prince of preachers, Charles Finney. Finney saw mass salvations in his revival meetings. What if Nash had been bent on making a name for himself instead of helping Finney succeed in God's work?

Nash demonstrated the type of humility every intercessor should walk in. Like John the Baptist nearly two thousand years before him, Nash's mindset was, "I must decrease so that Christ can increase" (John 3:30). His humility empowered him to pray without ceasing. And in Nash's humility, he left an intercessory prayer legacy.

Someone asked Finney what kind of man Father Nash was. "We never see him. He doesn't enter into any of the meetings." Finney replied, "Like anybody who does a lot of praying, Father Nash is a very quiet person. Show me a person who is always talking, and I'll show you a Christian who never does much praying."

If you want to tap into exponential grace to intercede, humility is a key. James 4:6 makes it plain, "God gives grace to the humble." When Jesus said, "Apart from me, you can do nothing" (John 15:5) He meant nothing. That includes intercession.

That's easy enough to understand, isn't it? But the Bible also says "the just shall live by faith" (see Heb. 10:38). That means we must focus on living our daily lives with the same dependence on Christ that we displayed when we received our salvation. Utter dependence.

Only when we truly understand that apart from Him we can do nothing can He trust us to do the greater works through intercession. Those who know their God shall be strong and do mighty exploits (see Dan. 11:32). Stay humble.

— *Prayer* —

Father, in the name of Jesus, would You give me the grace of humility? Help me understand that apart from You, my intercession is ineffective. But when I pray in You and lean on You, I can drive increase in Your Kingdom.

Praying With Holy Spirit Wisdom

"Jesus answered and said to him, 'Blessed are you, Simon Bar-Jonah, for flesh and blood has not revealed this to you, but My Father who is in heaven'" (Matthew 16:17).

When the Holy Spirit inspired Paul to write the words, "We do not know what God wants us to pray for" (Rom. 8:26, NLT), he meant it. We don't know what we don't know. Sometimes we think we know how to pray concerning an issue, but if we want to be accurate in the spirit and effective in our intercession we need to get the mind of Christ, the Chief Intercessor, on the matter.

That means we need the Holy Spirit's help. Thank God, the Holy Spirit can illuminate the mind of Christ to us. 1 Corinthians 2:10-12 read, "But God has revealed them to us through His Spirit. For the Spirit searches all things, yes, the deep things of God. For what man knows the things of a man except the spirit of the man which is in him? Even so no one knows the things of God except the Spirit of God. Now we have received, not the spirit of the world, but the Spirit who is from God, that we might know the things that have been freely given to us by God."

Paul goes on to write about how we don't speak words that come from human wisdom but words given to us by the Spirit, using the Spirit's words to explain spiritual truths (see 1 Cor. 2:13). In the same way, we don't want to pray words that come from our human wisdom, per say, but prayers inspired by the Holy Spirit.

Thank God for prayer revelation. Jesus said, "It has been given to you to know the mysteries of the kingdom of heaven, but to them it has not been given'" (Matt. 13:11). God wants to share prayer revelation with us. He wants us to know the mysteries of the prayer realm so we can pray more effectively. Jesus wants to say this of you, intercessor: "Blessed are your eyes for they see, and your ears for they hear" (Matt. 13:16).

— *Prayer* —

Father, in the name of Jesus, give me revelation about what to pray. Give me
revelation while I pray. Would You help me to pray accurately in the Spirit
according to Your will and not my will? Bless my eyes and ears to see and hear
what You want me to know.

Making Divine Declarations

"Let them sacrifice the sacrifices of thanksgiving, and declare His works with rejoicing"
(Psalm 1107:22).

You can make divine prophetic declarations with authority over your life, family, ministry, business, or anything else God speaks to you about—and you should. Divine declarations are part of the intercessor's prayer arsenal.

Of course, a declaration is different than a decree. You can make a decree privately, but declarations are public by nature. Here's one way to put it: a decree is an order and a declaration is the announcement of the order.

Merriam-Webster's dictionary defines declare as "to make known formally, officially, or explicitly." And a declaration is "the act of declaring: announcement; the first pleading in a common-law action; a statement made by a party to a legal transaction usually not under oath; something that is declared; a document containing such a declaration."

Intercessors are called to declare the works of the Lord (see Ps. 118:17). His name shall be declared throughout all the earth (see Ex. 9:16), as well as "His glory among the nations, His wonders among the peoples" (1 Chron. 16:24). Moses declared laws (see Deut. 1:5). The Israelites declared peace (see Jud. 21:13). Once, the Lord declared disaster over the wicked king Ahab (see 2 Chron. 18:22).

We can declare the written Word of God or the prophetic word of God. When Peter declared Jesus was the Son of God, the Lord said that flesh and blood did not reveal that declaration (see Matt. 16:13–17). Father God in heaven downloaded that revelation into Peter's spirit.

A prophetic declaration may be a rhema word from Scripture—a verse from the Bible that God illuminates in your spirit—or it could be a direct revelation from the Spirit about a specific situation. It could be a word of wisdom, a word of knowledge, or a prophecy on which you base your declaration in the context of prayer.

— Prayer —

Father, in the name of Jesus, help me to release divine declarations that announce
Your will to the host of heaven and the hordes of hell. Put Your prophetic
declarations in my mouth so the earth lines up with heaven's agenda. Give me
boldness to declare with authority.

APRIL 23

Purposeful Prophetic Proclamations

"Proclaim this among the nations: 'Prepare for war! Wake up the mighty men, let all the men of war draw near, let them come up'" (Joel 3:9).

Prophetic proclamations are similar in nature to declarations. But proclamations go a wee bit further. Proclaim means, "to say or state (something) in a public, official, or definite away: to declare or announce (something); to show (something) clearly," according to *Merriam-Webster's* dictionary. That something, of course, is the will of God.

Another definition of proclamation reads, "the act of saying something in a public, official, or definite way: the act of proclaiming something; an official statement or announcement made by a person in power or by a government." You are authorized to make these official statements in prayer as one who has delegated authority from the government of God.

Jesus gave us authority over serpents and scorpions and all the power of the enemy (see Luke 10:19-20). As I wrote in my book *Waging Prophetic Warfare*, He expects you to make proclamations to establish His Kingdom on earth. We are first and foremost to proclaim the name of the Lord (see Deut. 32:3). In other words, we're called to make His name known.

In Old Testament times, the Israelites proclaimed a Jubilee every fifty years (see Lev. 25:10). It was a supernatural debt cancellation and the setting free of captives. That's the kind of proclamation I love to hear! Samuel had the sad task of proclaiming judgment in Israel, as did many other Old Testament prophets.

When we proclaim, decree, and declare God's Word over a situation, you had better believe it's going to accomplish what it was sent to do. It might not look like it's accomplishing much immediately, but it's dynamic in its power and it will push back darkness.

When we proclaim, decree, and declare God's Word—written or prophetic—we can be sure something is happening in the spirit realm. It may not happen as quickly as we like—or it may happen immediately. I prefer the immediately scenario, but I've learned to endure.

— Prayer —

Father, in the name of Jesus, lead me when it is right and proper to proclaim Your will as my intercessory prayer strategy. Amplify my proclamation so the principalities and powers are put on notice that You reign.

Signing Your Petitions

"For this child I prayed, and the Lord has granted me my petition which I asked of Him"
(1 Samuel 1:27).

When I was in high school, student government leaders would pass around petitions for this or for that. There was always some new petition to sign. Intercessors, we should continually send our petitions to the throne room, signed in the name of Jesus.

What's a petition? In natural terms, a petition is a formal written request made to an authority or organized body (such as a court), according to *Merriam-Webster's* dictionary. It's a call for change. It's an earnest request.

In spiritual terms, you write that request with your mouth, not your hands. The Hebrew word for petition is mish'aiah. According to *The KJV Old Testament Hebrew Lexicon*, it means request, petition or desire. Paul put it this way, "Do not be anxious or worried about anything, but in everything [every circumstance and situation] by prayer and petition with thanksgiving, continue to make your [specific] requests known to God" (Phil. 4:6, AMP).

A petition is a type of prayer that carries an urgent persistence. Ephesians 6:8 (*Berean Study Bible*) reads, "Pray in the Spirit at all times, with every kind of prayer and petition. To this end, stay alert with all perseverance in your prayers for all the saints."

The Greek word for petition in this verse is deesis. It translates as "need, indigence, want, privation, penury; a seeking, asking, entreating." Some of those words are foreign, but you could put it this way: A petition to God is a need or want that comes out of poverty of spirit in response to a real hardship, deprivation or suffering.

A petition to God in this manner is when the burden is too great; when the comforts of life are wholly lacking; when the temptation is too much to bear; when great lack is all around; when the oppression is too extreme. That's when you pull out the petition, like Hannah did when she was desperate for a child.

— *Prayer* —

Father, in the name of Jesus, help me remember the purpose of a petition in prayer. Help me petition Your heart in a way that moves You to come to my rescue. Help me petition in faith that You hear me and will answer me.

APRIL 25

Intercession That Opens and Closes Doors

"The key of the house of David I will lay on his shoulder; So he shall open, and no one shall shut; And he shall shut, and no one shall open" (Isaiah 22:22).

Jesus gave us the keys to the Kingdom, and whatever we bind on earth shall be bound in heaven and whatever we loose on earth shall be loosed in heaven (see Matt. 16:19). As intercessors, many of us have become experts at binding and loosing.

But there's another key that believers can use to open doors that no one can shut and shut doors that no one can open. The Word of God reveals this prophetic key in both the Old and New Testaments. It's the key of David.

Some call it the "Isaiah 22:22 key" but you could also call it the "Revelation 3:7 key" because the prophetic Scripture is mentioned in both books. Isaiah 22:22 reads, "The key of the house of David I will lay on his shoulder. Then he shall open, and no one shall shut. And he shall shut, and no one shall open."

Of course, the "He" in this verse is Jesus. Jesus has the key and can open and shut as He wills. When Jesus opens the door, no man can shut it and when Jesus shuts the door, no man can open it. Our job as prophetic people is to discern His will and Kingdom purpose so we can exercise our authority in His name to open what He wants to open and shut what He wants to shut.

Again, the key is discerning His will. Jesus has not called us to be reckless with the key of David, nor will the Isaiah 22:22 key work if we try to turn it in a direction opposite His will. But when we hear from the Lord, we can turn that key with confidence and decree and declare that doors will open or close. It's a powerful prophetic act that breaks down barriers.

— Prayer —

Father, in the name of Jesus, help me discern when to use the Isaiah 22:22 key in prayer. Teach me how to cooperate with Your Spirit in heaven to open doors You want open and shut doors You want shut through intercession.

APRIL 26

Worshipping Intercessors

"Come before His presence with singing. Know that the Lord, He is God" (Psalm 100:2-3).

We might be quick to think about prayer as spiritual warfare. Not all prayer is spiritual warfare, but spiritual warfare involves prayer. Much the same way, not all prayer is worship but worship and prayer often collide in the heart of the intimate intercessor.

Any way you look at it, one way we demonstrate our worship of God is through our humble prayer. Hebrews 13:15 tells us, for example, "Therefore by Him let us continually offer the sacrifice of praise to God, that is, the fruit of our lips, giving thanks to His name."

Worship is releasing our adoration towards God. Prayer is communicating with God. But, again, worship and prayer often cross over. When we verbally praise God for His character, we are walking in the command of Psalm 100:4-5 and launching into worship and prayer simultaneously:

"Enter into His gates with thanksgiving, and into His courts with praise. Be thankful to Him, and bless His name. For the Lord is good; His mercy is everlasting, and His truth endures to all generations."

When we come confessing our sins so that He hears our prayers, we are expressing humility and thanksgiving for cleansing us from all unrighteousness so He will delight in our prayers. This is a form of worship, acknowledging that He alone can forgive us and help us.

We see worship joined with prayer in Scripture over and over again. Consider Psalm 18:1-3, "I will love You, O Lord, my strength. The Lord is my rock and my fortress and my deliverer; My God, my strength, in whom I will trust; My shield and the horn of my salvation, my stronghold. I will call upon the Lord, who is worthy to be praised; So shall I be saved from my enemies." Amen.

— *Prayer* —

Father, in the name of Jesus, help me maintain a heart of worship as I lift up my voice to petition at Your throne. Would You help me express my praise and worship through prayers that don't cease to adore and glorify Your name?

APRIL 27

The Hur Prayer Anointing

"And Aaron and Hur supported his hands, one on one side, and the other on the other side; and his hands were steady until the going down of the sun" (Exodus 17:12).

You're not always going to be the "Moses" in an intercessory prayer campaign. Sometimes you'll be like Hur. In fact, we need more Hurs. Hur isn't looking to take the lead in every prayer campaign but is content in being a role player, supporting the one God chooses to lead the charge. We find Hur's handwork in Exodus 17:8-13:

"Now Amalek came and fought with Israel in Rephidim. And Moses said to Joshua, 'Choose us some men and go out, fight with Amalek. Tomorrow I will stand on the top of the hill with the rod of God in my hand.'

"So Joshua did as Moses said to him, and fought with Amalek. And Moses, Aaron, and Hur went up to the top of the hill. And so it was, when Moses held up his hand, that Israel prevailed; and when he let down his hand, Amalek prevailed. But Moses' hands became heavy; so they took a stone and put it under him, and he sat on it.

"And Aaron and Hur supported his hands, one on one side, and the other on the other side; and his hands were steady until the going down of the sun. So Joshua defeated Amalek and his people with the edge of the sword."

Hur supported Moses' hands, and thereby supported Joshua's victory. Hur wasn't trying to make a name for himself among the Israelites. He was in it to win it no matter how he was asked to serve. Hur was an intercessory prayer team player. We could all take a lesson from Hur's humble playbook.

Noteworthy is the fact that the name Hur means "noble man." Noble means possessing outstanding qualities, according to *Merriam-Webster*'s dictionary. It means illustrious, notable, and of exalted rank. Hur may have stood in a support role in the battle Joshua was fighting but from heaven's perspective he was walking in a noble rank.

— *Prayer* —

Father, in the name of Jesus, help me walk in humility like Hur. Would You help me walk with a mindset that seeks to serve, not to be served? Would You teach me to be a team player for the sake of Your plans and purposes?

Could Your Next Prayer Meeting be Historic?

"Jesus Christ is the same yesterday, today, and forever" (Hebrews 3:8).

The first historic prayer meeting in the church was on the day of Pentecost, recorded in Acts 2. The believers were gathered on one accord when suddenly the Holy Spirit came in like a mighty rushing wind. Something like tongues of fire rested up on them. But over the last two thousand years the church has seen many more historic prayer meetings.

Take the "Haystack Prayer Meeting." A group of young men were heard under a haystack making this declaration, "We can do it; and we will." Many credit the birth of the American missionary movement to those young men's prayers and declarations. Then there was George Mueller's "Cottage Prayer Meeting." His ministry was birthed there just like Paul and Barnabas' mission was birthed while believers ministered to the Lord in Acts 13.

Let's not forget the "Roof Prayer Meeting" in London where a student knelt down and cried out to God to help him care for orphans. This was the birth of Bernardo Homes that saw over one hundred thousand orphans housed, fed and clothed. John and Charles Wesley gathered at the Holy Club with a college friend to pray, and essentially birthed a revival that birthed Methodism.

And what about Evan Roberts? Before the Azusa Street revival in 1906 was the Welsh Revival in 1904. As history tells it, over 100,000 souls came to Jesus in Wales over the course of nine months. Hundreds of thousands more would come to know the Lord over the next couple of years—and it all started in Moriah Chapel in Loughor, South Wales where Roberts gathered with a few youth and began to pray, "Bend us! Bend us!" and eventually "Bend me! Bend me!"

What if your next prayer meeting was historic? You just never know. Keep praying.

— *Prayer* —

Father, in the name of Jesus, would You help me gain perspective that my prayer meetings can spark a moment in time that makes history? Would You inspire me to pray with a fervor and earnestness that my prayers really can change the course of history?

APRIL 29

Reminding God

"Put Me in remembrance; Let us contend together; State your case, that you may be acquitted" (Isaiah 43:26).

God never forgets a thing—not a thing. He knows all things and remembers everything that ever was. And since He's not bound to our timeline—since He's the God of yesterday, today and forever and the God who was and is and is to come——He knows what's going to happen before it happens. This truth can be mindboggling.

Still, He gives us this truth in Isaiah 43:26, "Put Me in remembrance; Let us contend together; State your case, that you may be acquitted." The enemy tempts us to back down from the promises of God, which are yes and amen. Sometimes, during seasons of intense trial, we forget what belongs to us, the benefits of the covenant, or the prophetic promise God spoke to our hearts.

God hasn't forgotten, but Isaiah 43:26 invites us to put Him in remembrance, I believe, for our sake. It's an invitation to pray in faith. The Hebrew word "remembrance" in that verse is zakar. According to *The KJV Old Testament Hebrew Lexicon*, it means, "to remember, recall, call to mind, be brought to mind, to mention."

When we put God in remembrance, we're mentioning the promise to Him. We're coming to Him with child-like faith saying, "God, I remember what You said in Your Word. I remember the promise. I forgot in the heat of the moment, but now I am choosing stand on what You said to me. You promised healing and wholeness. You promised to defend me and vindicate me. You promised to help me and comfort me. I believe You."

When you repeat the promise to God, faith rises up in your heart. The prayer of faith reaches His heart. Then, suddenly, the prayer answer is in motion. It's just a matter of time. Again, it's not for His sake. He never forgot. He will never break His Word. Putting God in remembrance of what He said is for Your sake. When you forget, He remembers.

— *Prayer* —

Father, in the name of Jesus, help me remember Your Word. I know You never forget your yes-and-amen promises. But sometimes I do. Would you remind me so we can contend together for Your perfect will to come?

The Samuel Chadwick Prayer Anointing

"Seek the Lord and His strength; Seek His face evermore!" (1 Chronicles 16:11)

Samuel Chadwick was a Wesleyan Methodist Minister, a Spirit-filled preacher, author, revivalist—and a man who understood realms of prayer. He started pastoring at 21.

As the story goes, one night his eyes were opened to his pride and reliance on self—and God wrestled with him until he repented. He took all his sermons and threw them into a blazing fire. With that, Jesus baptized him with the Holy Spirit and fire and he was never the same. In his book, *Path of Prayer*, he wrote:

"When the Church is run on the same lines as a circus, there may be crowds, but there is no Shekinah. That is why prayer is the test of faith and the secret of power. The Spirit of God travails in the prayer-life of the soul. Miracles are the direct work of His power, and without miracles the Church cannot live.

"The carnal can argue, but it is the Spirit of God that convicts. Education can civilize, but it is being born of the Spirit that saves. The energy of the flesh can run bazaars, organize amusements, and raise millions; but it is the presence of the Holy Spirit that makes a Temple of the Living God.

"The root-trouble of the present distress is that the Church has more faith in the world and in the flesh than in the Holy Ghost, and things will get no better till we get back to His realized presence and power. The breath of the four winds would turn death into life and dry bones into mighty armies, but it only comes by prayer."

Doubtless, he wrote from what he experienced. He pursued God in prayer and the outcome was an outpouring of anointing, power, glory, fire and more. As he said, "it only comes by prayer."

— *Prayer* —

Father, in the name of Jesus, would You root out of me anything that hinders
Your power from manifesting in my prayer life? Would You help me lay aside the
methods of man and press into Your prayer furnace?

MAY

"Again I say to you that if two of you agree on earth concerning anything that they ask, it will be done for them by My Father in heaven. For where two or three are gathered together in My name, I am there in the midst of them" (Matthew 18:19-20).

There's Transformation in Your Mouth

"By faith we understand that the worlds were framed by the word of God, so that the things which are seen were not made of things which are visible" (Hebrews 11:3).

I heard the Lord say, "I am putting transformation in your mouth. When you speak forth what I tell you to speak, it's going to bring change. It's going to shake up some things in the spirit. It's going to move some things that need to be moved. It's going to bring down some things from heaven, from glory, that need to be established in the earth and even in your life. It's going to shake. It's going to move!"

Your prayers—the words of intercession that come out of your mouth—bring life where death is working to encroach on God's promises. Your prayers—the words of intercession that come out of your mouth—shake the enemy loose from people, situations, and circumstances. Your prayers—the words of intercession that come out of your mouth—bring transformation.

When your prayers are based on the Word of God, you can be sure those words carry transforming power. What is transformation? Transformation is a full sail change—it's a metamorphosis, a reconstruction, a revolution. God wants to use you as a change agent in the earth, cooperating with the Holy Spirit to release intercession that drives the results He wants to see. That transformation is in your mouth. Isaiah 55:10-11 reminds:

"For as the rain comes down, and the snow from heaven, and do not return there, but water the earth, and make it bring forth and bud, that it may give seed to the sower and bread to the eater, so shall My word be that goes forth from My mouth; It shall not return to Me void, but it shall accomplish what I please, and it shall prosper in the thing for which I sent it."

When you release God's Word out of your mouth, know that it will not return void. God's Word changes things. It drives transformation of spirits, souls, bodies, places and things. When you get the revelation that there's transformation in your mouth, it will take your intercession to a new level.

— *Prayer* —

Father, in the name of Jesus, would You help me see the transformational results of my intercession? Would You help me keep in mind that there's transformation in my mouth when the resistance to my intercession comes heavy? Empower as an agent of transformation through prayer.

Offering Identificational Repentance

"We have sinned and committed iniquity, we have done wickedly and rebelled, even by departing from Your precepts and Your judgments" (Daniel 9:5).

Have you ever heard the terminology "identificational repentance"? Intercessors that are sent to lands or people groups often enter into this type of intercession. It's heavy.

John Dawson, author of *Healing America's Wounds*, coined the term the 1990s. Simply stated, identificational repentance is repentance that identifies with and confesses the sins of a nation, city, people group, church, or family before God. Until Dawson's book dusted off this ancient revelation, fewer practiced this intercessory prayer strategy.

We should always go into intercession with repentance, praise, and thanksgiving to our God. But identificational repentance is more than just asking God to cleanse you from all unrighteousness before you pray. Let's look at some definitions so we can thoroughly understand this concept.

Oxford Dictionary defines "identificational" as "relating to or involving identification." Identification is "the action or process of identifying someone or something or the fact of being identified." Repentance is "sorrow for any thing done or said; the pain or grief which a person experiences in consequence of the injury or inconvenience produced by his own conduct," according to *Noah Webster's 1828 Dictionary.*

The late C. Peter Wagner called identificational repentance the power to heal the past. We see Daniel entered into identificational repentance in Daniel 9:3: "Then I set my face toward the Lord God to make request by prayer and supplications, with fasting, sackcloth, and ashes."

Daniel goes on to pray things like "we have sinned and committed iniquity, we have done wickedly and rebelled, even by departing from Your precepts and Your judgments. Neither have we heeded Your servants the prophets, who spoke in Your name to our kings and our princes, to our fathers and all the people of the land" (Dan. 9:5-6). This touched God's heart.

— *Prayer* —

Father, in the name of Jesus, help me identify with the sin of peoples and nations that do not know You. Will You help me stand in the gap with a heart of repentance for a people You want to reach with the power of forgiveness?

Let Your Tears Do the Talking

"My tears have been my food day and night, while they continually say to me, 'Where is your God?'" (Psalm 42:3)

I've cried myself to sleep more than once in the midst of desperate or painful situations. Maybe you can relate. There are times when the need is so great and words escape us. We can't find the right language with which to petition God in the midst of our grief. The good news is your tears of desperation can move God's heart with compassion.

Yes, God hears your tears and, at times, your tears become your prayers. Your tears become your intercession. Corey Russell, a former IHOPKC staffer, once preached a message on tears in which he described this emotional state as one that occurs when you come face to face with your human inability to change anything yourself. In reality, God brings you to that place.

King David was a warrior, but he was also man of tears. David was so distraught at times he could only express his prayer through tears. David cried out for deliverance. David cried out for mercy. David cried when his cruel spiritual father Saul died. He cried when his best friend Johnathan died. He cried when his son Absalom died. David wept at the grave of Abner. In Psalm 6:6 he wrote, "I am weary with my groaning; All night I make my bed swim; I drench my couch with my tears."

God collects our tears in a bottle (see Ps. 56:8). Many have recounted the story of a Salvation Army field worker who wrote to the group's founder, Major William Booth asking, "Sir, we tried every method; what shall we do?" Booth replied, "Try tears."

You can't just "decide" to try tears in the sense that you make yourself cry to manipulate God. But you can yield to the tears when they come. Over and over again, David let his tears do the talking. At one point, he admitted his tears were his food day and night as his enemies mocked his faith in God (see Ps. 42:3). Try tears.

— *Prayer* —

Father, in the name of Jesus, help me to understand the value of my tears. Help me to remember that my heartfelt tears move Your heart of compassion. Help me to not hold back this expression in Your presence.

Praying the Prodigals Back Home

"And he arose and came to his father. But when he was still a great way off, his father saw him and had compassion, and ran and fell on his neck and kissed him" (Luke 20:20).

I wasn't always saved. In fact, you might say I ran from God for years. I didn't grow up in a Christian home. Sure, if you had asked me if I believed Jesus was the Son of God I would have offered a "yes" in mental ascent. But I didn't really know Him. I certainly wasn't living for Him. Quite the opposite.

In college, I met a young man who was a missionary for another religion. When the relationship went sour many years later, it left a bad taste in my mouth for religion. I decided I'd live however I wanted and when I was finished "having fun" I would surrender my life to God. He had other plans.

God interrupted my plans through the power of a praying great grandmother and a praying grandmother. The prayers they prayed over me when I was just a little girl bore fruit. Never underestimate the power of your prayers and declarations over your children.

Isaiah 55:11 (AMPC) says, "So shall My word be that goes forth out of My mouth: it shall not return to Me void [without producing any effect, useless], but it shall accomplish that which I please and purpose, and it shall prosper in the thing for which I sent it." Never underestimate the seeds you've sown into your child's life. Proverbs 22:6 assures us, "Train up a child in the way he should go, and when he is old he will not depart from it."

If you are dealing with a prodigal child, a prodigal husband, a prodigal friend or some other prodigal, ask the Holy Spirit for a specific strategy to pray them back in—and then be on the lookout in faith like the father with the lost son in Luke 15. When the prodigal returns, receive them with joy and don't talk about the past. Rejoice!

— *Prayer* —

Father, in the name of Jesus, would You help me stand in faith, releasing Your battle plan for the soul of the prodigal on my heart? Would You help me not to grow weary in praying for their return to Your heart?

Renouncing 'Religious' Prayers

"And when you pray, do not use vain repetitions as the heathen do. For they think that they will be heard for their many words. Therefore, do not be like them" (Matthew 6:7-8).

You've heard it said, "Jesus didn't die so we could have a religion. He died so we could have a relationship." That's true. It's also true that He doesn't like "religious" prayers. What are religious prayers? Prayers that come out of a heart that's petitioning based on rules rather than relationship.

Religious prayers trust in self—vain repetitions supposing God must respond because we used the right formula. Religious prayers presume on God. Religious prayers find their power in eloquence of speech rather than a surrendered heart. Religious prayers come from a heart of pride. Jesus offers a parable in Luke 18:10-14:

"Two men went up to the temple to pray, one a Pharisee and the other a tax collector. The Pharisee stood and prayed thus with himself, 'God, I thank You that I am not like other men—extortioners, unjust, adulterers, or even as this tax collector. I fast twice a week; I give tithes of all that I possess.'

"And the tax collector, standing afar off, would not so much as raise his eyes to heaven, but beat his breast, saying, 'God, be merciful to me a sinner!' I tell you, this man went down to his house justified rather than the other; for everyone who exalts himself will be humbled, and he who humbles himself will be exalted."

Religion likes to put on a show. Prayers that come from a "religious" rather than a relational heart are often performance-based—too loud, too long or too spectacular—for the sake of those watching. That's why Jesus said in Matthew 6:6-8, "But you, when you pray, go into your room, and when you have shut your door, pray to your Father who is in the secret place; and your Father who sees in secret will reward you openly."

— Prayer —

Father, in the name of Jesus, would You help me root out any religious attitudes in my prayer life? I want to pray to an audience of One. I need You to hear and answer my prayers. Help me pray with humility and sincerity.

Top Secret Prayers

"But when you pray, go into your room and shut the door and pray to your Father who is in secret. And your Father who sees in secret will reward you" (Matthew 6:6, ESV).

Some prayers are best released in secret. I am not talking about in the secret place. That's a different concept. While you can pray secret prayers from the secret place, I'm talking about the secret prayers you pray in private.

While there are times to enlist intercessory prayer support in your endeavors, there are some things that need to remain between you and God. I implore you to hear my words. Even some of your closest friends don't need immediate insight into certain issues of your heart. Jesus is the friend who sticks closer than a brother.

Elliot's Commentary puts it this way: "The principle thus clothed in paradox is, of course, that personal prayer should be strictly personal and private." Understand the meaning of a prayer closet in the *King James Version* of Matthew 6:6, "enter thy closet." In the days Jesus walked the earth and spoke those words, Jewish households had a place for secret devotion.

"Over the porch, or entrance of the house, there was frequently a small room of the size of the porch, raised a story above the rest of the house, expressly appropriated for the place of retirement," *Barnes' Notes on the Bible* offers.

"Here, in secrecy and solitude, the pious Jew might offer his prayers, unseen by any but the Searcher of hearts. To this place, or to some similar place, our Saviour directed his disciples to repair when they wished to hold communion with God. This is the place commonly mentioned in the New Testament as the 'upper room,' or the place for secret prayer."

When you don't know who you can trust with the secret desires of your heart, you can always trust God. God is good at keeping secrets. And keeping secrets from Him is impossible. He knows everything anyway. When you share your secrets with God, you can unburden yourself and find great rewards of divine counsel and intervention.

— *Prayer* —

Father, in the name of Jesus, would You help me to keep the desires of my heart tucked away from the wagging tongues? Help me remember that I don't need to tell everybody my prayer needs, but I can always tell You.

The Brother Roger Prayer Anointing

"Lord, I have loved the habitation of Your house, And the place where Your glory dwells" (Psalm 26:8).

Many intercessors have never heard of Brother Roger. His name was actually Roger Schütz. Brother Roger was twenty-five years old when he entered into World War II. He later founded the Taize Community of modern monks and served there until he was murdered in an evening prayer service in 2005. The community still welcomes thousands of pilgrims every week.

Brother Roger said profound things like, "Sometimes you say to yourself: the fire in me is going out. But you were not the one who lit that fire. Your faith does not create God, and your doubts cannot banish Him to nothingness." He said, "For whoever knows how to love, for whoever knows how to suffer, life is filled with serene beauty."

The youngest child of a Protestant pastor from Bachs in Switzerland, he was a leader in the Swiss Student Christian Movement, which is part of the World Student Christian Federation. Tuberculosis drove him to a monastic life and prayer became a cornerstone.

A friend of Mother Theresa, Brother Roger wrote many books on prayer and reflection. One of his prayers was: "When my inner being experiences an emptiness, the thirst for Your presence remains within me. And when I am unable to pray, You Yourself are my prayer. Jesus, light of our hearts, since Your resurrection, You always come to us. Whatever point we may be at, You are always waiting for us."

Brother Roger is a model of an intercessor who doesn't simply ask but just seeks to be. He certainly prayed for the Jewish refugees he helped escape Nazi persecution in World War II. He certainly prayed for many people and things, but that intercession came out of a place of serenity until he graduated to heaven when he was stabbed to death in the midst of prayer.

— *Prayer* —

Father, in the name of Jesus, help me pray from a place of peace and serenity. Help me pray from a place of oneness with Your heart, knowing with childlike faith that You hear me and delight in my prayers.

Times and Seasons Intercessors

"And of the children of Issachar, which were men that had understanding of the times, to know what Israel ought to do" (1 Chronicles 12:32).

Times and seasons intercessors are critical role players. They pray in both God's now and far-away promises. While "times and seasons" terminology is often relegated to prophets with an Issachar anointing, intercessors are part and parcel to seeing God's times and seasons.

Put another way, just as God anointed one tribe of Israel to see prophetically into times and seasons God is anointing tribes of intercessors today to see into times and seasons. It's crucial that intercessors discern times and seasons as God is a God of times and seasons—and we need to be in His rhythm if we want to see timely prayer answers.

Let's explore times and seasons. Let's look first at times. God doesn't move through time the way we move through time. In the temporal realm, time is linear. In the eternal realm, God can step into and out of time at will. God is moving in the spirit realm rather than the earth realm, where He has set the times and seasons.

A season includes a time. *Merriam-Webster*'s dictionary defines season as, "a time characterized by a particular circumstance or feature." Another definition of season is "a suitable or natural time or occasion." There was a season for David to sit on the throne. Ecclesiastes 3:1 tells us, "To everything there is a season, a time for every purpose under heaven…"

The word "season" in this verse comes from the Hebrew word zeman. It means "a set time, appointed time, time," according to *The KJV Old Testament Hebrew Lexicon.* Daniel 2:21 tells us, "And He changes the times and the seasons…" God changes our times and seasons. God helps us pray into the next season and discern the right time. Ask God for prayer strategies for times and seasons.

— *Prayer* —

Father, in the name of Jesus, would You help me discern the times and seasons by Your Spirit? I want to pray and prepare myself, my family, my church and my city for what You have in store. I want to push back the darkness.

MAY 9

The Children's Bread

"It is not good to take the children's bread and throw it to the little dogs" (Matthew 15:26).

Intercessors, it's no shame to need deliverance. Rather, it would be a shame to need deliverance and not pursue it. Deliverance is essentially breaking enemy bondages off your mind and body.

Jesus came to set the captives free, but just as you are not automatically healed of every disease the moment you get saved you are not necessarily delivered from every demon when you surrender to God. And demons can still enter Christians who have open doors.

Jesus said deliverance is the children's bread (see Matt. 15:26). You are a child of God and if you need deliverance Jesus wants to deliver you by the power of the Holy Spirit. But, how would you know if you need deliverance? I teach more on this in my School of Deliverance as well as my book, *Deliver Yourself from Evil.* But here are a few signs:

You keep hitting a wall. It seems like you get to a certain point in God and can go no further. Something is holding you back and you don't know what it is. You feel like you go around the same mountain over and over again and can never break through. You watch others pass you up in the spirit even though you are as gifted and work as hard as they do. You're frustrated and upset and you've done everything you know to do but you're not growing in God.

Another sign is you are practicing sin and can't seem to stop. It may be a sin everybody sees or a sin nobody but you and God see. If you are practicing sin and you keep trying to stop but can't, you could need deliverance. Of course, if you sin once you aren't going to get a demon. But if you keep practicing sin and refuse to wage war on your sin, you open the door to demons and ultimately to bondage. Something seems to come over you and you can't stop. Pursue deliverance.

— *Prayer* —

Father, in the name of Jesus, if I need deliverance—if I am oppressed by demon powers—would You show me? Jesus, deliver me from evil by the power of Your Holy Spirit. Set me free from every tie that binds.

Intercessors of Adoration

"Oh come, let us worship and bow down; Let us kneel before the Lord our Maker"
(Psalm 5:6).

Intercessors of adoration know how to touch God's heart. That's because before they ever utter a word in prayer, they utter words of praise and worship. They utter words of adoration. Adoration is simply a feeling or demonstration of great affection and devotion. God adores you. How much more should we adore Him in His perfect holiness?

Intercessors of adoration release prayers of adoration. Consider 1 Chronicles 29:11: "Yours, O Lord, is the greatness, the power and the glory, the victory and the majesty; For all that is in heaven and in earth is Yours; Yours is the kingdom, O Lord, and You are exalted as head over all."

David was often found releasing prayers of adoration as he started his psalms. Psalm 29:1-2 says, "Give unto the Lord, O you mighty ones, give unto the Lord glory and strength. Give unto the Lord the glory due to His name; Worship the Lord in the beauty of holiness."

Maybe he got the idea from Moses, who cried out: "Who is like You, O Lord, among the gods? Who is like You, glorious in holiness, fearful in praises, doing wonders? You stretched out Your right hand; The earth swallowed them. You in Your mercy have led forth the people whom You have redeemed; You have guided them in Your strength to Your holy habitation" (Ex. 15:11-13).

The entirety of Psalm 8 is a prayer of adoration: Here are the first two verses: "O Lord, our Lord, how excellent is Your name in all the earth, who have set Your glory above the heavens! Out of the mouth of babes and nursing infants You have ordained strength, because of Your enemies, that You may silence the enemy and the avenger."

Especially if you have been interceding for a long while and are growing weary, the prayer of adoration is one you want to adopt and add to your repertoire. He is worthy of our adoration.

— *Prayer* —

Father, in the name of Jesus, make me an intercessor of adoration. I do adore You. Remind me of Your splendor and majesty when I am weary. Remind me of Your perfect beauty while I war. I will yet praise Your name!

Celebrate Your Prayer Wins

"Let the saints be joyful in glory; Let them sing aloud on their beds" (Psalm 149:5).

When you get prayer answers, do you celebrate? You need to celebrate for persevering to the point of breakthrough. You may have felt like giving up many times, but in your selflessness you kept pressing through for someone else's sake.

I can only imagine how many days and nights the father of the prodigal son spent praying for his boy to return home. He expected his son to return, and we know this because the father saw him coming from far away. He was watching and praying in faith. What did the father do when the son came home? He celebrated. Imagine the scene in Luke 15:20-24:

"And he arose and came to his father. But when he was still a great way off, his father saw him and had compassion, and ran and fell on his neck and kissed him. And the son said to him, 'Father, I have sinned against heaven and in your sight, and am no longer worthy to be called your son.'

"But the father said to his servants, 'Bring out the best robe and put it on him, and put a ring on his hand and sandals on his feet. And bring the fatted calf here and kill it, and let us eat and be merry; for this my son was dead and is alive again; he was lost and is found.' And they began to be merry.'"

Please don't get me wrong I'm not suggesting that the victory is yours alone. Jesus is our victory banner. He gets all the glory. But when He uses you to enforce His will in the earth through intercession, it's worth celebrating the breakthrough.

We, of course, should also celebrate Jesus. He is the Breaker (see Mal. 2:13). Apart from Him, we can do nothing (see John 15:5). But with Him you can release intercession that makes the impossible possible. And when you do, that's reason to celebrate.

— Prayer —

Father, in the name of Jesus, would You help me stop long enough to celebrate the prayer wins? Help me to savor Your goodness, kindness, power and love when the breakthrough comes.

The Andrew Murray Prayer Anointing

"I have been crucified with Christ; it is no longer I who live, but Christ lives in me"
(Galatians 2:20).

Andrew Murray, the South African writer, teacher and pastor whose ministry spanned the 19th and 20th centuries, wrote over two hundred books and tracts over sixty years of ministry. His materials still help Christians everywhere grow up in Christ. Murray was a man of deep prayer.

His personal prayer: "May not a single moment of my life be spent outside the light, love, and joy of God's presence. And not a moment without the entire surrender of myself as a vessel for him to fill full of his Spirit and his love."

Murray had a lot to say about prayer and intercession. For example, in his book, *The Ministry of Intercession: A Plea for More Prayer*, he wrote: "If once believers were to awake to the glory of the work of intercession, and to see that in it, and the definite pleading for definite gifts on definite spheres and persons, lie our highest fellowship with our glorified Lord, and our only real power to bless men, it would be seen that there can be no truer fellowship with God than these definite petitions and their answers, by which we become the channel of His grace and life to men."

Intercessors, we need to take on this mindset. Murray was known for his surrender to God, his abiding in God, his obedience to God—and wrote books along those lines with convicting truths that help draw us into deeper fellowship with God. Murray taught prayer was the means by which God rules the world. He wrote:

"The power of the church truly to bless, rests on intercession—asking and receiving heavenly gifts to carry to other men. Because this is so, it is no wonder that where—owing to lack of teaching or spiritual insight, trust in our own diligence and effort, the influence of the world and the flesh, and that we work more than we pray—the presence and power of God are not seen in our work as we would wish."

— Prayer —

Father, in the name of Jesus, would You give me an intercessory prayer anointing like what you imparted to Andrew Murray? Drive me deeper into holiness, surrender, abiding and intercession that influences the earth for the sake of Your glorious Kingdom.

What If You Had the Breakthrough Now?

"And so it was that as they went, they were cleansed" (Luke 7:14).

It seems intercessors are always after one breakthrough or another in the spirit. We prize prayer answers because it glorifies our King and Chief Intercessor. But some breakthrough prayer answers take longer than others. Indeed, some take decades.

Paul warned us not to grow weary in well doing. Prayer is one manner of well doing. Consider his words from Galatians 6:9 in the Amplified translation: "Let us not grow weary or become discouraged in doing good, for at the proper time we will reap, if we do not give in."

One way we can avoid weariness is to act as if we already have the breakthrough. I learned this lesson from one of my mentors many years ago. She was riddled with cancer and wasn't expected to live another six months. God instructed her to go on a dry fast for a period of time—and she did. Initially, she did not see any change. That's when God gave her a strategy in the form of a question.

God asked her, "How would you be acting if you had the healing now?" That changed her thinking and her behavior. She decided to think, talk and walk like she was healed—like she had the breakthrough prayer answer right that moment. As she did, she saw her healing manifest little by little and then all at once.

That reminds me of the ten lepers in Scripture. Jesus passed through Samaria on His way to Jerusalem and ten men with leprosy where there in a village. Luke 17:13-14: "And they lifted up their voices and said, 'Jesus, Master, have mercy on us!' So when He saw them, He said to them, 'Go, show yourselves to the priests.' And so it was that as they went, they were cleansed."

Jesus told the leper who returned that His faith made him well. Walk in faith as if you have the answer before you see it. That heart attitude will ward off weariness.

— *Prayer* —

Father, in the name of Jesus, would You inspire my heart to walk by faith and not by sight? Would You give me grace to walk as if I am in the breakthrough so I don't get weary waiting for the breakthrough?

Legislating in the Spirit

"Of the increase of His government and peace there will be no end, upon the throne of David and over His kingdom, to order it and establish it with judgment and justice from that time forward, even forever" (Isaiah 9:7).

We talk a lot about the promises of God, but in reality those promises are spiritual laws. When the promises of God manifest in your life or the lives of those for whom you intercede, it's not a coincidence. It's God enforcing a spiritual law because you legislated an issue in the spirit.

We legislate matters in the earth through prayer. In his classic book *The Power of Positive Praying*, John Bisagno writes, "A glass of water chilled to thirty-two degrees becomes ice. When God enacts a situation, it is more than a divine promise. It is a spiritual law. He is not simply saying, 'If you lower the temperature to thirty-two degrees, as a reward I will give you ice. He's saying, 'There will be ice.'"

Looking at prayer as legislating in the spirit gives you a new perspective on intercession. Prayer answers aren't a reward for a job well done. They are a response from heaven to our activating the laws of the Kingdom. When you see "if-thens" in Scripture, these are often invitations to legislation through prayer and intercession.

One example is found in 2 Chronicles 7:14, "If My people who are called by My name will humble themselves, and pray and seek My face, and turn from their wicked ways, then I will hear from heaven, and will forgive their sin and heal their land."

Of course, Kingdom laws can also work against you in intercession. Jesus said, "And whenever you stand praying, if you have anything against anyone, forgive him, that your Father in heaven may also forgive you your trespasses. But if you do not forgive, neither will your Father in heaven forgive your trespasses" (Mark 11:25-26).

We need to know God's promises inside and out, and we need to understand they are more than promises. They are laws with which we legislate on the earth to bring forth His will.

— *Prayer* —

Father, in the name of Jesus, thank You for giving me authority in the earth to legislate in intercession. Thank You for this revelation that You've given me more than a promise to hope for. You've given me laws to stand on.

MAY 15

The George Muller Prayer Anointing

"Then He took the five loaves and the two fish, and looking up to heaven, He blessed and broke them, and gave them to the disciples to set before the multitude" (Luke 9:16).

George Mueller was a Christian evangelist and the director of an orphanage in England. He had over ten thousand orphans under his care. He wasn't big on fundraising but he was big on intercession. In fact, he credits believing prayer for his ability to provide for the children year after year. Mueller once said:

"I have joyfully dedicated my whole life to the object of exemplifying how much may be accomplished by prayer and faith. It is useless; we have already prayed so long that it is useless to continue.

"This is just what Satan would have us say; but let us persevere and go on steadily praying, and be assured that God is both able and willing to do it for us; and that it is the very joy and delight of His heart, for Christ's sake, to give to us all things which are for the glory of His name, and our good and profit. If we do so, He will give us our desire. As assuredly as we are the children of God, if we pray perseveringly, and in faith, the prayer will be answered."

Many people pray and they aren't sure if God even hears them. Intercessors like Mueller release believing prayer. Believing prayer expects answers because believing prayer is founded on pure faith in God.

Mueller tells the story of running out of food at the orphanage. Indeed, they had neither food nor money. The children were waiting on their breakfast but only empty plates awaited them at the table. Mueller said a simple prayer that went something like this: "Father, thank You for what You are going to give us to eat."

Immediately, there was a knock at the door. It was a local baker who felt the children had no bread. He provided it. Just after that, the milkman came the door. His milk cart stalled out right in front of the orphanage and he gave Mueller's kids the milk. God provided milk and bread. In the 1800s, revival broke out in the orphanage. Ask God for the George Mueller prayer anointing.

— *Prayer* —

Father, in the name of Jesus, would You help me rest in You as I labor in intercession? Would You help me pray with childlike faith over seemingly impossible issues? Give me a prayer anointing like George Mueller's.

Intercessors on Fire

"Epaphras, who is one of you, a bondservant of Christ, greets you, always laboring fervently for you in prayers..." (Colossians 4:12).

Intercessor, if you are on fire for God, you will have fire in your belly. You will be fervent in prayer like Epaphras. But what does it mean to be fervent in prayer? How to we pray like Epaphras?

Merriam-Webster's dictionary defines the word "fervent" as very hot or glowing. When something is fervent, it is "exhibiting or marked by a great intensity or feeling." Let's drill down a little deeper to the roots of the word. The English word "fervency" comes from the Greek word "zeo." It literally means "to boil."

As I write in my book *Fervent Faith*, "Can you imagine? Have you ever watched water boil? It bubbles up with utter intensity—and sometimes it even escapes the confines of the pot. Boiling water can't hide its expression. In fact, if you come too close to a pot of boiling water, the steam alone will get your attention. A fervent spirit is on fire for God. A fervent spirit is a passionate spirit. A fervent spirit is a zealous spirit. God likes fervency. Again, He expects us to be fervent in spirit."

Daniel Nash was fervent in prayer. Nash was an intercessor for Charles Finney, a great revivalist in the Second Great Awakening. He once said:

"In the revival at Gouverneur (in which the great majority of the inhabitants, Finney believed, were converted), Nash rose very early and went into a forest to pray. 'It was one of those clear mornings,' said Finney, 'on which it is possible to hear sounds at a great distance.' Nearly a mile away lived an unsaved man who suddenly heard Nash's voice raised in prayer, and no matter how hard he tried, he couldn't shake the reality of his urgent need for a Saviour. In fact, he experienced no relief until he found it in Christ."

It was Elijah's fervent prayer that called down fire from heaven to consume the offering and expose the false prophets of Baal and Jezebel. It was his fervent prayer that called down rain to end the drought in Israel. Ask God to make you fervent.

— Prayer —

Father, in the name of Jesus, would You set me on fire? Give me a fervent spirit determined to burn up every plan of the enemy. Help me to maintain a fervency that is not dependent on what I see with my natural eyes.

MAY 17

Consider Your Ways

"Let us search out and examine our ways, and turn back to the Lord" (Lamentations 3:40).

We know sometimes we have not because we ask not. In other words, we don't have prayer answers because we don't release prayer petitions. But we also know we can pray amiss. For example, we can pray to obtain an idol (something we want more than God's will). If we're really deceived, we may even think it is God's will.

We need to live a lifestyle of self-awareness. That means examining our hearts to make sure there's no waywardness in us. We know the heart is deceitful above all things (see Jer. 17:9). In other words, we can want something so bad we deceive ourselves into believing God gave us those desires. It's dangerous!

Jeremiah also wrote, "Let us search out and examine our ways, and turn back to the Lord; Let us lift our hearts and hands to God in heaven" (Lam. 3:40-41). Of course, you'll need the Holy Spirit's help. If you have already convinced yourself something is God's will when it's not, you'll need the Holy Spirit to convict you of righteousness so you can get your heart back in line with His will.

Along these lines, the psalmist cried out, "Search me, O God, and know my heart; Try me, and know my anxieties; And see if there is any wicked way in me, and lead me in the way everlasting" (Ps. 139:23-24). David prayed, "Who can understand his errors? Cleanse me from secret faults. Keep back Your servant also from presumptuous sins; Let them not have dominion over me" (Ps. 19:12-13).

And again, "Examine me, O Lord, and prove me; Try my mind and my heart" (Ps. 26:2). When we don't know what's in our hearts, the Lord knows. When we ask Him to examine our hearts, He's faithful to show us what we need to see. He will lead us on the path to life—and prayer answers.

— *Prayer* —

Father, in the name of Jesus, would You test my heart? I don't know what I don't know. I want what You want. Try my mind. Reveal any wicked way in me. Convict me of unrighteousness and presumption. Help me.

Interceding in the Face of Judgment

"Therefore He said that He would destroy them, had not Moses His chosen one stood before Him in the breach, to turn away His wrath, lest He destroy them" (Psalm 106:23).

Many nations, including America, are seeing the judgment of God. That's a scary proposition and one that elicits a lot of emotion. Let me tell you what judgment means to me.

My definition of judgment: We are reaping what we've sown and God isn't intervening. We're seeing the consequences of rebellion. The hedges of protection are eaten away and gaps are created by our sinful defiance. God is still the God of judgment. He just hasn't flooded the earth, rained down fire and brimstone, or made nations servants to other nations like He did in the Old Testament. But He is still the Judge.

When Israel sinned, God wanted to wipe her off the map and start all over with Moses. It may have sounded like a nice offer to Moses, given the Israelites' grumbling and complaining. But time and time again, Moses interceded for the people from a heart of mercy. That needs to be our heart as intercessors. Listen in to Exodus 32:9-13 (NLT):

"Then the Lord said, 'I have seen how stubborn and rebellious these people are. Now leave me alone so my fierce anger can blaze against them, and I will destroy them. Then I will make you, Moses, into a great nation.'

"But Moses tried to pacify the Lord his God. 'O Lord!' he said. 'Why are you so angry with your own people whom you brought from the land of Egypt with such great power and such a strong hand? Why let the Egyptians say, 'Their God rescued them with the evil intention of slaughtering them in the mountains and wiping them from the face of the earth'? Turn away from your fierce anger. Change your mind about this terrible disaster you have threatened against your people! Remember your servants Abraham, Isaac, and Jacob.'"

Would you show such mercy to a people who made your life so difficult? Be like God, in judgment, remember mercy (see Hab. 3:2).

— *Prayer* —

Father, in the name of Jesus, help me walk in mercy towards people who have given me a hard time. Would You help me lay down my biases and pray without ceasing for nations that I may find evil? I want to be like Moses.

MAY 19

When the Bowls Tip Over

"Now when He had taken the scroll, the four living creatures and the twenty-four elders fell down before the Lamb, each having a harp, and golden bowls full of incense, which are the prayers of the saints" (Revelation 5:8).

One day in worship at my Ft. Lauderdale church, Awakening House of Prayer, I saw the prayer bowls in heaven tipping over. Unless you've read Revelation 5:8, that might be a foreign concept to you. Let's look at what happens to those prayers in the context of the end times in Revelation 8:3-5:

"Then another angel, having a golden censer, came and stood at the altar. He was given much incense, that he should offer it with the prayers of all the saints upon the golden altar which was before the throne. And the smoke of the incense, with the prayers of the saints, ascended before God from the angel's hand. Then the angel took the censer, filled it with fire from the altar, and threw it to the earth. And there were noises, thunderings, lightnings, and an earthquake."

Our prayers on earth change things. When the bowls are full, they tip over. Maybe you've been praying and praying and praying for the same thing for years and don't see anything changing. Sometimes, it seems like the more we pray the worse it gets. That's what the enemy wants us to think. He wants us to stop praying before we fill the bowls.

Don't give up. Know that with every prayer you pray, the bowl is filling up. Eventually, in God's timing, the bowl will fill up and tip over and prayer answers will overflow into your situation. Don't stop fighting now, you could be on the brink of an overflow. Angels could be preparing to deliver the prayer answer even now.

If you still have a prayer burden, don't stop making intercession. God hears your prayers, which are like a sweet-smelling incense (see Ps. 141:2). Keep releasing your petitions. Keep warring. Keep making supplication. Keep standing in the gap. You may not see the answer just yet, but the golden bowls are filing.

— *Prayer* —

Father, in the name of Jesus, help me remember that the bowls will tip over when they get full. Help me see the bowl as half full and not half empty when I feel like giving up. Help me keep the incense of my prayer rising.

A Sudden Good Break

"And she was in bitterness of soul, and prayed to the Lord and wept in anguish"
(1 Samuel 1:10).

Hannah was desperate and then she was bitter. Intercessors, if we're not careful our desperation combined with a lack of prayer answers can make us bitter, too. Why was she bitter? Hannah was barren and her husband's other wife was taunting her.

1 Samuel 1:6 says, "And her rival also provoked her severely, to make her miserable, because the Lord had closed her womb. So it was, year by year, when she went up to the house of the Lord, that she provoked her; therefore she wept and did not eat."

Her husband just didn't understand, but he wasn't the one being taunted. When the family went to the tabernacle to worship and sacrifice, Hannah took the opportunity to pour out her heart to the Lord.

We read this in 1 Samuel 10:10-11: "And she was in bitterness of soul, and prayed to the Lord and wept in anguish. Then she made a vow and said, 'O Lord of hosts, if You will indeed look on the affliction of Your maidservant and remember me, and not forget Your maidservant, but will give Your maidservant a male child, then I will give him to the Lord all the days of his life, and no razor shall come upon his head.'"

Eli thought Hannah was drunk and rebuked her. She responded: "No, my lord, I am a woman of sorrowful spirit. I have drunk neither wine nor intoxicating drink, but have poured out my soul before the Lord. Do not consider your maidservant a wicked woman, for out of the abundance of my complaint and grief I have spoken until now."

Hannah could have become more bitter but chose humility and saw breakthrough. Eli prayed. She birthed Samuel, and with it a new prophetic movement. When you are tempted to be bitter, remember Proverbs 13:12, "Unrelenting disappointment leaves you heartsick, but a sudden good break can turn life around."

— *Prayer* —

Father, in the name of Jesus, help me discern the voice of bitterness that may rise up against me, to deceive me, in seasons of desperation. When I am waiting on the miracle, help me to stay in faith knowing Your timing is perfect. Help me wait for the sudden good break.

The Political Snare

"The beginning of strife is like releasing water; Therefore stop contention before a quarrel starts"
(Proverbs 17:4).

We need governmental intercessors, but if we're not careful our passion to pray for nations, governments, politicians, elections and other officials will lean too far in the world's direction. Put another way, if we put our faith in who is going to be president or prime minister instead of putting our faith in the Prince of Peace whose government never ends we can step into a snare.

That snare is what I call a political spirit. We've seen it through the ages and it's predominant in this era. Indeed, the political spirit is dividing intercessory prayer groups among party lines, denominational lines and theological lines. The enemy knows a house divided cannot stand (see Mark 3:25). He also knows where there is unity God commands a blessing (see Ps. 133).

The enemy strategically uses politics to breed strife among intercessors—and the Bible offers plenty of warnings about strife. Indeed, while intercession comes through the spirit of prayer, strife comes from works of the flesh (see 1 Cor. 3:3). Proverbs 20:3 tells us, "It is honorable for a man to stop striving, since any fool can start a quarrel." And Proverbs 13:10 says, "By pride comes nothing but strife, but with the well-advised is wisdom."

There are too many biblical warnings about strife to share here. One of the sternest warnings, though, is found in James 3:16: "For where envy and self-seeking exist, confusion and every evil thing are there." How can we expect God to hear our prayers when we're in strife, which He forbids? I urge you, intercessor, not to allow the political spirit or any other strife in your life.

Proverbs 15:8 warns, "A wrathful man stirs up strife, but he who is slow to anger allays contention." Politics can get heated, but the only fire in the intercessor's heart should be the fire of God. Beware the political spirit. It will sully your intercession.

— *Prayer* —

Father, in the name of Jesus, I reject and renounce strife in all its forms. I reject and renounce the political spirit. Shelter me from the strife of tongues. Help me not to be quarrelsome or to contend for political gain.

The Militant Intercessor

"And from the days of John the Baptist until now the kingdom of heaven suffers violence, and the violent take it by force" (Matthew 11:12).

When we got saved, we essentially enlisted as soldiers in the army of God. We are called to be militant. What does militant mean? Militant means engaged in warfare or combat, fighting, and aggressively active.

Here's my definition: Militant intercession is a mode of prayer that aggressively pushes back powers of darkness, combats enemy interference, and contends for the will of God in a matter. Militant intercession is offensive, aggressive and relentless in possessing the gates of the enemy.

Militant intercession relies on what Jesus said in Matthew 11:12, "And from the days of John the Baptist until now the kingdom of heaven suffers violence, and the violent take it by force." *The Amplified Classic* translation puts it a little stronger: "And from the days of John the Baptist until the present time, the kingdom of heaven has endured violent assault, and violent men seize it by force [as a precious prize—a share in the heavenly kingdom is sought with most ardent zeal and intense exertion]."

In her classic book *Possessing the Gates of Your Enemy*, Cindy Jacobs also points to Matthew 11:12 and says this: "Lest I scare you by using that Bible verse, let me tell you I am speaking of spiritual violence ... Militant intercession breaks down strongholds in heaven that release heaven to earth. It is also done onsite and makes a statement on earth. This type of prayer sees that God's Kingdom does indeed come, and His will shall be done on earth as it is in heaven (see Matthew 6:10)."

Militant intercession is one way we take dominion in the earth, according to Genesis 1:16. After all, Jesus told us to occupy until He comes (see Luke 9:13). Jesus came to destroy the works of the devil (see 1 John 3:8). And Jesus is coming back to judge and make war (see Rev. 19:11). Until then, we stand in militant intercession.

— *Prayer* —

Father, in the name of Jesus, give me a militant spirit in the realm of intercession. Make me strong and courageous as I stand in prayer for Your will to be done and Your Kingdom to come in my family, my church, my city and my nation.

Saving the Sick

"And the prayer of faith will save the sick, and the Lord will raise him up. And if he has committed sins, he will be forgiven" (James 5:15).

Anyone can extend their faith to lay hands on the sick and see them recover. But the laying on of hands is not always possible due to distance. That's where healing intercessors come in. A healing intercessor is, as it sounds, an intercessor who presses in for God's healing power to touch people they may not have access to or may never see.

Even if your family or friends live in another city, you can still release your faith in prayer for healing. Even if you can't get into the hospital room, you can still release your faith in prayer for healing. There is no distance in the spirit. Don't let lack of proximity push you into unbelief.

Of course, healing intercessors can also lay hands on the sick or pray for someone in their presence. That's what Moses did when Miriam came against him and she got leprosy. When Aaron saw it, he cried out to Moses and Moses, in turn, cried out to God. If people know you are a healing intercessor, many will cry out to you so you can cry out to God on their behalf. Listen in to Numbers 12:9-13:

"So the anger of the Lord was aroused against them, and He departed. And when the cloud departed from above the tabernacle, suddenly Miriam became leprous, as white as snow. Then Aaron turned toward Miriam, and there she was, a leper.

"So Aaron said to Moses, 'Oh, my lord! Please do not lay this sin on us, in which we have done foolishly and in which we have sinned. Please do not let her be as one dead, whose flesh is half consumed when he comes out of his mother's womb!' So Moses cried out to the Lord, saying, 'Please heal her, O God, I pray!'"

Of course, the Lord healed her. If you are a healing intercessor, know that you have an anointing that travels beyond your proximity. God wants to use you to extend His healing power to those in need, even if it was their fault.

— Prayer —

Father, in the name of Jesus, I am ready, willing and able to stand in the gap as a healing intercessor. I don't need to be seen by people. I just need to be heard by You. Use me to release Your healing power for the wellbeing of Your people and for the glory of Your Son.

The Potency One-Word Prayers

"Do not be rash with your mouth, and let not your heart utter anything hastily before God. For God is in heaven, and you on earth; Therefore let your words be few" (Ecclesiastes 5:2).

When I first got saved, I didn't know how to pray. My prayer life consisted of short prayers, such as "Help" and "Thanks." It wasn't until many years later that I understood how powerful those one-word prayers really are. Sometimes, we need to release long petitions but many times we go on and on when a simple one-word prayer would do.

There is power in the one-word prayer that we sometimes overlook. The power of life is in your tongue, and you don't need lengthy or flowery prayers to touch the heart of your heavenly Father. He bows down His ear to hear your heartfelt prayers (see Ps. 86:1-7).

Indeed, one-word prayers are biblical. Sometimes, saying the name of Jesus itself is a prayer. Once my car was spinning out of control in a bad storm. I was just born again when it happened. Without even thinking, I cried out "Jesus!" and my car suddenly turned itself straight. You can just say "God" and He knows what you need.

When you cry out with sincerity because you don't know what else to say or how to pray, He will answer. He already knows what we need before we need it. Many times, prayer is simply acknowledging our helplessness and His power and willingness to come to our rescue.

"Thanks" was another one of my early prayers, as well as "help." In fact, in Psalm 107 there are four instances in which the praying people uttered the single word "help."

But there are others, such as "Come," which invites the Holy Spirit to help you. Another way to say come is "Maranatha," which is an Aramaic word used in Revelation 22:20 for "Our Lord, come!" Then there's "Hallelujah," a one-word prayer of praise, and "Amen," which is a one-word prayer of agreement with His will.

— Prayer —

Father, in the name of Jesus, remind me that one-word is enough to touch Your heart. When I can't find words to say or pray because of the shock, the grief or the pain, inspire my mouth to cry for help knowing You will hear me and answer me because You love me.

Prayerless Prayer

"Stay alert and be persistent in your prayers for all believers everywhere" (Ephesians 6:18).

Have you ever wondered why prayerlessness is a sin? The great man of prayer E.M. Bounds offers an explanation:

"If prayer puts God to work on earth, then, by the same token, prayerlessness rules God out of the world's affairs, and prevents Him from working. In reality, the denial of prayer is a denial of God Himself, for God and prayer are so inseparable that they can never be divorced."

It's too easy for our corporate prayer—or prayer with a friend—to turn prayerless. We dialogue with each other rather than dialoguing with God. It's too common for intercessors to get distracted with personal trials and cease the intercession that was once unceasing. It's too easy for our prayers to turn into complaints containing no prayer at all.

"One of the greatest sins we commit against ourselves and those around us is the sin of not praying," said Hope MacDonald, author of books like *Discovering How to Pray*. "Our prayerless lives are the sin that keeps the world from knowing Jesus! They are the sin that keeps us from knowing Him!"

Here's the problem: If you sow prayerlessness, you reap powerlessness. Edwin Harvey, author of such books as the *How They Prayed* series, put it this way: "A day without prayer is a day without blessing, and a life without prayer is a life without power." And 19th Century social reformer Sir Thomas Buxton urged, "You know the value of prayer: it is precious beyond all price. Never, never neglect it."

It's easy to neglect prayer—to use our prayer time to catch up on reading or to pray mindless words, rote prayers, or prayerless prayers. We need a revelation of what we lose when we substitute other activities for prayer or let distractions seep into our prayer life or when we pray amiss. D.L. Moody gave us words to ponder: "Next to the wonder of seeing my Saviour will be, I think, the wonder that I made so little use of the power of prayer."

— *Prayer* —

Father, in the name of Jesus, help me never to live in a state of prayerlessness. Wake me up if a slumbering spirit lulls me to sleep during my watch. Open my eyes to the spirit of distraction at work. I don't want to be a prayerless intercessor.

Wilderness Prayers

"So He Himself often withdrew into the wilderness and prayed" (Luke 5:16).

Nobody seems to like the idea of spending a season in the wilderness. The wilderness is a place of solitude. It's an empty region seemingly devoid of opportunity. It's uninhabited and uncultivated. It's a both a place of growth and temptation.

Interestingly, the Holy Spirit drove Jesus into the wilderness—but even after He emerged, He kept going back. Mark 1:12 tells us, "Immediately the Spirit drove Him into the wilderness. And He was there in the wilderness forty days, tempted by Satan, and was with the wild beasts; and the angels ministered to Him."

If the Holy Spirit is driving you into the wilderness, don't resist the experience. Use the time to pray wilderness prayers. What are wilderness prayers? Pray for God to prepare you for your next level of authority. Pray for God to work out of you anything the enemy can use to tempt you out of His will. Pray *The Lord's Prayer.*

When you are in the wilderness, pray God would prime you for your purpose and ready you for your highest calling. Pray that He would inspire your heart to pray without ceasing for His will to come in your life and in the earth. Pray for the winds of refreshing to fill you with new vigor for intercession.

When you are in the wilderness, pray the Holy Spirit would show you things to come. Pray He would share with you strategies for the next season and the next battle. Pray God would teach you how to surrender more fully to Him, to walk in His Spirit and to abide in Him.

When you are in the wilderness, pray God would deliver you of anything that will hinder His ministry of intercession in your life. Pray He would break you free from every tie that binds, all disappointment, frustration or impatience. Pray that He would fill you to overflowing with His Holy Spirit. Just pray.

— *Prayer* —

Father, in the name of Jesus, help me use my wilderness time wisely instead of resisting the experience. Have Your way in me in the wilderness and ready me for my next assignment as I co-labor with Christ in prayer.

MAY 27

Enter Through the Prayer Gate

"Yes, while I was speaking in prayer, the man Gabriel, whom I had seen in the vision at the beginning, being caused to fly swiftly, reached me about the time of the evening offering" (Daniel 9:21).

Prayer is a gateway to encounters. When we go boldly to the throne of grace, we can expect something to shift—if not around us then in us. When we approach our heavenly Father in prayer, He can send answers in dramatic ways.

We see this in the Book of Daniel in the context of the Seventy-Weeks Prophecy. We won't get into the prophecy, but we will look at Daniel's prayer encounter with the angel Gabriel. Imagine pouring out your heart in repentance at length and being interrupted by an angel in the midst of your session. We read this in Daniel 9:20-23:

"Now while I was speaking, praying, and confessing my sin and the sin of my people Israel, and presenting my supplication before the Lord my God for the holy mountain of my God, yes, while I was speaking in prayer, the man Gabriel, whom I had seen in the vision at the beginning, being caused to fly swiftly, reached me about the time of the evening offering.

"And he informed me, and talked with me, and said, 'O Daniel, I have now come forth to give you skill to understand. At the beginning of your supplications the command went out, and I have come to tell you, for you are greatly beloved; therefore consider the matter, and understand the vision.'"

Gabriel goes on to share the meaning of the vision, which is an end-times vision. But here's my point: Be open to God encountering you in prayer in fresh ways. Go into your prayer closet expecting to receive revelation, visions or even angelic visitations that inform your intercession if God chooses.

Remember, you're not seeking an encounter, per se, you are seeing to see God's will done and His Kingdom come in the earth. But know this: God can choose bring you into a trance and show you a vision, like Peter when he was on the rooftop before lunch praying. Indeed, when you seek Him, you may find Him in unusual ways. Still, always test the spirits to see if it is God.

— *Prayer* —

Father, in the name of Jesus, help me stay curious and open to the ways You reveal Yourself or Your messages or Your will while I'm in prayer. Help me walk into my prayer closet with an expectation of encountering Your heart.

Pray for Spiteful Abusers

"But I say to you, love your enemies, bless those who curse you, do good to those who hate you, and pray for those who spitefully use you and persecute you" (Matthew 5:44).

This is a task! The more mature we are in Christ, the easier it is to make intercession for those who spitefully use you and persecute you. What are we to pray, pray tell?

Pray that God would forgive them. Although it's vital that you forgive your persecutors, we are acting like Jesus when we pray for God to also forgive our enemies. Both Jesus and Stephen, while they were being persecuted by enemies of the Gospel, prayed, "Father, forgive them, for they know not what they do" (Luke 23:34; Acts 7:60).

Pray for God to give them a spirit of wisdom and revelation in the knowledge of Jesus. Obviously, your persecutors need a greater revelation of Jesus. The more people truly know Christ, the less they will allow the devil to influence our thoughts, words and deeds.

Pray for God to root them and ground them in love. We know that love is kind (see 1 Cor. 13:4) but whoever slanders is a fool (see Prov. 10:18). The Bible doesn't have anything good to say about fools, but God still loves them—and if they were rooted and grounded in the love of God, they would not gossip, slander or persecute people.

Pray for God's love to abound in them. You can't walk out the Beatitudes without abounding in love. Pray for God to show them His will. Once your persecutor is rooted and grounded in love and understands God's will, they will be more likely to repent.

Beyond that, intercede as the Holy Spirit leads you until you feel a release in your spirit. And remember, Paul admonishes us to "bless those who persecute you; bless and do not curse" (see Rom. 12:14). Move in the opposite spirit. If you respond God's way, you'll be blessed.

— Prayer —

Father, in the name of Jesus, would You give me the grace to make intercession for those who accuse, abuse, and misuse me? Help me forgive and extend mercy to them, the way You have extended mercy to me.

Don't Pray Like the Hypocrites

"And when you pray, you shall not be like the hypocrites. For they love to pray standing in the synagogues and on the corners of the streets, that they may be seen by men. Assuredly, I say to you, they have their reward" (Matthew 6:5).

In Bible times, hypocrite was a Greek word for an actor or stage player. The Greeks did love their plays! Greek actors wore masks to designate the character they were playing. Today, the English word hypocrite takes on a related but more severe meaning.

Merriam-Webster's dictionary defines hypocrite as "a person who puts on a false appearance of virtue or religion." It's sad that the word has been so closely associated with religion, isn't it? A second definition of hypocrite is "a person who acts in contradiction to his or her stated beliefs or feelings."

A hypocritical intercessor is an intercessor who displays showmanship. Showmanship means "the producer of a play or a theatrical show" and "a notably spectacular, dramatic, or effective performer." Hypocrisy and showmanship go hand in hand. And that's the larger part of what Jesus was addressing in this Scripture.

The Pharisees made a show out of prayer. They wanted people to see how pious they were. They wanted to appear spiritually superior. They wanted people to take note of them. That public recognition, unfortunately, was the only reward they would get. They may have looked important in the eyes of man but Jesus called them hypocrites. They were playing the part of intercessors but their heart wasn't in the prayer. Jesus explained in Luke 18:11-14:

"The Pharisee stood and prayed thus with himself, 'God, I thank You that I am not like other men—extortioners, unjust, adulterers, or even as this tax collector. I fast twice a week; I give tithes of all that I possess.' And the tax collector, standing afar off, would not so much as raise his eyes to heaven, but beat his breast, saying, 'God, be merciful to me a sinner!' I tell you, this man went down to his house justified rather than the other; for everyone who exalts himself will be humbled, and he who humbles himself will be exalted."

— *Prayer* —

Father, in the name of Jesus, would You root out of me any and all hypocrisy? I don't want to make a show out of prayer. I don't want to be a Pharisaical intercessor. Help me pray as if You are the only one listening.

The 'Hosos' Prayer

"And whatever things you ask in prayer, believing, you will receive" (Matthew 21:22).

This is a bit of a mystery. Jesus said whatever things you ask in prayer, you'll receive them if you pray believing prayers. What does "whatever" mean? Technically, it doesn't mean you can just ask for anything you fancy in the moment. We know that because James says sometimes we don't get prayer answers because we pray amiss.

So, then, what does "whatever" mean? The Greek word for whatever in that verse is "hosos." It means, "as great as, as far as, how much, how many, whoever," according to *The KJV New Testament Greek Lexicon*. What this really means is whatever you ask according to God's will, you will receive it if you believe.

We have to focus on the believing part here because, in this context, Jesus mentioned faith and doubt. He was contrasting the doubting heart with the believing heart in the context of receiving prayer answers despite opposition. No matter how many obstacles we have, the hosos prayer will position us to overcome. This is the victory that overcomes the world, even our faith (see 1 John 5:4).

Let's look at hosos prayer in context: "So Jesus answered and said to them, 'Assuredly, I say to you, if you have faith and do not doubt, you will not only do what was done to the fig tree, but also if you say to this mountain, 'Be removed and be cast into the sea,' it will be done. And whatever things you ask in prayer, believing, you will receive,'" (Matt. 21:21-22).

Can you see it? Faith in God's Word gives you authority to curse a fig tree and move a mountain. In the same way, faith in God's Word positions you to receive what eye has not seen, nor ear heard, nor even entered into your heart (see 1 Cor. 2:9). Faith leads you into the promises.

— *Prayer* —

Father, in the name of Jesus, help me renew my mind to Your great and precious promises so I can release prayers that are full of faith. I want to release hosos prayers that bring Your will into the earth. I choose to believe.

The Teaching Intercessor

"Now it came to pass, as He was praying in a certain place, when He ceased, that one of His disciples said to Him, 'Lord, teach us to pray, as John also taught his disciples'" (Luke 11:1).

Some people insist you don't need to be taught how to pray. That's a lie from the enemy. The Word of God teaches us plenty about prayer, and we would do well to let the Holy Spirit teach us through the Scripture He inspired. But we would also be wise to submit to teachers who have seen prayer work—people who have experience navigating realms of prayer.

Yes, John 2:27 says, "But the anointing which you have received from Him abides in you, and you do not need that anyone teach you; but as the same anointing teaches you concerning all things, and is true, and is not a lie, and just as it has taught you, you will abide in Him." But that doesn't mean the Body of Christ doesn't need teachers.

Ephesians 4:11-12 shows the need for teachers: "And He Himself gave some to be apostles, some prophets, some evangelists, and some pastors and teachers, for the equipping of the saints for the work of ministry, for the edifying of the body of Christ..." Yes, we even need teachers to teach us to pray, war and make intercession.

John the Baptist and Jesus both taught their disciples to pray. As you mature in the office of intercessor, you should look for those to whom you can teach what you've learned. You should set out to teach your disciples to pray. What do you teach them?

Teach them how to stand in faith in the face of opposition. Teach them how to pray the Word. Teach them how to wage warfare with prophetic words, according to 1 Timothy 1:18. Teach them about the gift of repentance. Teach them how to hear the voice of God and release prophetic intercession. Teach them from the Word and from your personal experience with the God who answers prayer. Teach them.

— Prayer —

Father, in the name of Jesus, would You give me a grace to teach others what You've taught me and what I have learned from seasoned intercessors You have put in my path? I want to share the secrets of intercession with others.

JUNE

"Then you will call upon Me and go and pray to Me, and I will listen to you"
(Jeremiah 29:12).

JUNE 1

The Gift of Empathy

"And if one member suffers, all the members suffer with it; or if one member is honored, all the members rejoice with it" (1 Corinthians 12:26).

It's one thing to have sympathy. Sympathy is admirable as we try to understand another's pain, but our perspective is limited unless we've experienced the same suffering. We cannot identify with the pain of losing a child, for example, if we've never lost a child.

Empathy is deeper. Empathy is the ability to put yourself in someone's shoes to better understand why someone feels the way they do. An empathetic intercessor may share the feelings of the one who is suffering—praying with a keen understanding of another person's emotions with a mind to alleviate that suffering.

The empathetic intercessor is gifted and allowed to feel what another is feeling for the sake of releasing the Holy Spirit's comfort in prayer. Empathetic intercessors are co-laboring with Christ, who empathizes with our weakness because He experienced tremendous pain and suffering when He walked the earth (see Heb. 4:15).

Paul admonishes us to "put on tender mercies, kindness, humility, meekness, longsuffering; bearing with one another, and forgiving one another" (Col. 3:12-13). Sometimes that goes beyond intercession and into action. Paul also told us to, "Rejoice with those who rejoice, and weep with those who weep" (Rom. 12:15).

Job was an empathetic intercessor even before he experienced his trauma in the first chapter of the book that bears his name. He said, "Have I not wept for him who was in trouble? Has not my soul grieved for the poor?" (Job 30:25). The writer of Hebrews urges us to enter empathetic intercession beyond prayer: "Remember the prisoners as if chained with them—those who are mistreated—since you yourselves are in the body also" (Heb. 13:3).

When we're empathetic toward people, when we clothe people, visit them in prison or on the sick bed, it's as if we're empathizing with Jesus. In Matthew 25:40 Jesus said, "Assuredly, I say to you, inasmuch as you did it to one of the least of these My brethren, you did it to Me."

— Prayer —

Father, in the name of Jesus, would You help me to empathize with the ones for whom You've called me to intercede in their times of trouble? Help me to go beyond my own ability and perspective of someone's pain into empathy.

Your Prayer Assignment

"We, however, will not boast beyond measure, but within the limits of the sphere which God appointed us—a sphere which especially includes you" (2 Corinthians 10:13).

In 2021, when Cubans revolved on the Caribbean island and violence was simultaneously rising in South Africa, I knew it was my prayer assignment. I stopped everything I was doing, created prayer points to guide me and others, and entered into immediate intercession.

It wasn't convenient. I had other items on my agenda that morning, even major deadlines. But when God gives you a prayer assignment, you don't shrug Him off. You don't wait until a convenient time. You step into that kairos moment knowing that God will use your prayers to impact the situation for which He is calling you to intercede.

Here's the thing. You should be praying for something but you can't pray for everything. You should be praying for somebody but you can't pray for everybody. There's not grace to stand in a place of prayer God hasn't called you to occupy.

Don't get me wrong. God's not upset with you for praying. That's not the point. The point is you can wear yourself out doing a good thing that's not a God thing. Again, you won't be most effective in an assignment God has not called you to.

James 5:16 tells us, "The effective, fervent prayer of a righteous man avails much." It's not as effective when God doesn't assign it. More than that, you are missing the real assignment where you would be most effective. You are missing an opportunity to bring heaven to earth by standing in the place God called you to pray.

Maybe you can relate. Maybe, like me, people come to you all the time asking you to "keep them lifted." Again, praying is never wrong, but I know you want to be as effective as possible for the Kingdom. You want to redeem your prayer time. Stick to your assignment.

— Prayer —

Father, in the name of Jesus, I want to stay in tune with Your assignment for me. I want to redeem my prayer time because the days are evil. There are so many needs in the earth. Would You make my prayer assignment plain to me?

The Inner Witness

"But there is a spirit in man, and the breath of the Almighty gives him understanding"
(Job 32:8).

Intercessors who cultivate sensitivity to the Holy Spirit can rely on the inner witness to help discern for whom, for what and when to pray. Spirit-sensitive intercessors pick up on His emotions and follow the unction to pray—and discern when breakthrough has come.

Proverbs 20:27 says, "The spirit of man is the candle of the Lord." *The Amplified Classic* translates the word rendered candle as "lamp." This means that God will enlighten us through our spirit.

Have you ever heard someone say, "Well, you've been on my heart." That's the inner witness that spurs an intercessor to pray.

The inner witness may manifest as a check in your spirit about something, and a strong knowing that you need to pray. Maybe something just strikes you and you can't seem to shake the thought. That's the inner witness. Or maybe you have a strong impression something is wrong with someone. That's the inner witness of the Holy Spirit speaking to your conscience through your spirit.

Paul explained, "I am speaking the truth in Christ. I am not lying; my conscience [enlightened and prompted] by the Holy Spirit bearing witness with me…" (Romans 9:1, AMP). The Holy Spirit bears witness with your spirit through enlightenment to your conscience. And He may prompt you over and over until you get the message.

Wesley Duewel, an author and missionary to India for nearly 25 years, wrote these wise words in *Let God Guide You Daily*, "One of my prayer lists names fifty-four persons who are imprisoned for Christ. I try to name each one briefly before the Lord daily. At times as I awakened in the morning, one of those names was instantly on my heart; it was God's special assignment for that day. Sometimes God may bring to your mind someone you have not thought of for months; accept that one as your prayer assignment that day."

— Prayer —

Father, in the name of Jesus, would You make me more sensitive to Your heart?
Would You help me discern the inner witness and how to apply what I am sensing
to the prayer assignment You are giving me?

Silent Prayers

"Hannah was speaking in her heart; only her lips moved, and her voice was not heard"
(1 Samuel 1:13, ESV).

There are times to cry aloud, and there are times to release what I call silent prayers. Silent prayers are prayers that are not spoken out loud. It's just between you and God. It's so deeply personal that you won't share the needs of your heart with anyone else but Him because He's the only one you can trust, the only one who understands and the only one who can help.

Hannah prayed a silent prayer in 1 Samuel 1:12-13, "And it happened, as she continued praying before the Lord, that Eli watched her mouth. Now Hannah spoke in her heart; only her lips moved, but her voice was not heard." The Amplified version says she was speaking in her heart (mind).

Abraham's servant released a silent prayer to God after he made an oath to his leader to find a wife for Isaac. His prayer was extremely specific in Genesis 24:43-45:

"And this day I came to the well and said, 'Please give me a little water from your pitcher to drink,' and she says to me, 'Drink, and I will draw for your camels also,'—let her be the woman whom the Lord has appointed for my master's son.' But before I had finished speaking in my heart, there was Rebekah, coming out with her pitcher on her shoulder; and she went down to the well and drew water. And I said to her, 'Please let me drink.'"

Beyond not knowing who else you can trust to agree with you in prayer other than God Himself, silent prayer has another advantage: the enemy can't hear the petition. The enemy can't read your mind. He doesn't know what you are thinking unless your words or behaviors tip him off. Many times, the enemy stands against the prayers we pray, and it's better to keep it between you and God. Silent prayers can be extremely effective prayers.

— *Prayer* —

Father, in the name of Jesus, would You help me remember that sometimes my petitions are best kept between us because people won't understand—or because the enemy will meddle? Help me see the value of silent prayers.

JUNE 5

The Consecrated Intercessor

"He went a little farther, and falling on His face, He prayed, 'O My Father, if it is possible, let this cup pass from Me. Nevertheless, not as I will, but as You will'" (Matthew 26:39).

Many people pray the prayer of consecration, "If it be thy will, Lord," when they should be praying the prayer of faith. You don't pray the prayer of consecration when you know the will of the Lord. The Word of the Lord is the will of the Lord. So if the Bible makes you a promise, even a conditional promise, you don't have to pray, "If it's thy will."

For example, we know it's God's will to heal and deliver. We don't have to pray, "Heal them, Lord, if it's your will." Of course it's His will. The Bible says by His stripes we are healed (see 1 Pet. 2:21-25). But there is a prayer of consecration. You could also call this the prayer of submission.

You pray the prayer of consecration when don't know what the Lord's will is but you are willing to submit to whatever He wants. You may pray the prayer of consecration over a marriage, a job, a move or any big decision for which there is not a clear principle in Scripture to apply or when you just sincerely don't know what to do.

The prayer of consecration and dedication is also suitable when you have two (or more) godly alternatives from which to choose. The Bible speaks of the good, perfect and acceptable will of the Lord. Sometime the will of the Lord is wide enough to grace more than one decision. I don't know about you, but I want to be smack dab in the middle of God's perfect will, not just on the fringes with what's good and acceptable.

In the prayer of consecration and dedication you may also find yourself putting everything on the altar and asking God to give you back what He wants you to have. The bottom line with the prayer of consecration is You want His will more than your will or anyone else's will.

— *Prayer* —

Father, in the name of Jesus, help me discern when I need to pray the prayer of consecration. Help me to pray boldly when I know Your will but to submit my will to Yours when I just need to trust Your sovereignty.

The Bolette Hinderli Prayer Anointing

"'Whom shall I send, and who will go for Us?' Then I said, 'Here am I! Send me'"
(Isaiah 6:8).

There was once a girl named Bolette Hinderli. She was faithful to watch and pray and God rewarded her with a vision and an intercessory assignment that will encourage the heart of every lover of Christ the Intercessor.

Hinderli was praying when she had a supernatural vision of a man in a prison cell. She had a clear view of his face in the vision. As the account goes, she heard a voice in her spirit that said, "This man will share the same fate as other criminals if no one takes up the work of praying for him. Pray for him and I will send him out to proclaim my praises among the heathen."

Hinderli took the assignment seriously and began to pray and pray and pray some more for this man in the vision. She prayed for his salvation, even though she didn't have a name to lift up. She never gave up on him in prayer. This ordinary country girl was constant, like the persistent widow. She was devoted to her assignment.

Hinderli didn't just pray. She expected to see the answer. She expected to see breakthrough for this nameless man in the prophetic vision. Time passed, but the day of fulfillment came when she was visiting Stavanger, Norway. She heard an ex-convict got saved and was going to preach at one of the churches that night. Lo and behold it was the man in her vision. His name was Lars Olsen Skrefsrud.

In his classic book *Prayer*, Ole Hallsby wrote: "As far as I am able to understand the Word of God, and as far as I can learn from the history of the Kingdom of God, no prayer-task is more important than this. If the right man gets into the right place, there is almost no end to what he can do. Think of men like Martin Luther, Hans Nielsen Hauge, Lars Olsen Skrefsrud, Hans Peter Borresen, William Carey, Hudson Taylor."

— *Prayer* —

Father, in the name of Jesus, give me dreams and visions of the souls for whom You want me to pray. Inspire me not to give up on the prayer burdens You assign me but to pray without ceasing like Bolette?

JUNE 7

Where Are Your Manners?

"Were there not any found who returned to give glory to God except this foreigner?"
(Luke 17:18)

It's easy to take intercessory prayer breakthroughs for granted. Perhaps too easy. When we get the breakthrough, we need to stop and give the glory to God. We need to acknowledge His power, His wisdom and His goodness. We need to return to Him with expressions of love and thanksgiving. He didn't have to do it, but He did.

We see this illustrated in the account of Jesus cleansing ten lepers, a lifechanging experience for these me who were absolute outcasts in society. Luke 17:11-19 reads:

"Now it happened as He went to Jerusalem that He passed through the midst of Samaria and Galilee. Then as He entered a certain village, there met Him ten men who were lepers, who stood afar off. And they lifted up their voices and said, Jesus, Master, have mercy on us!'

"So when He saw them, He said to them, 'Go, show yourselves to the priests.' And so it was that as they went, they were cleansed. And one of them, when he saw that he was healed, returned, and with a loud voice glorified God, and fell down on his face at His feet, giving Him thanks. And he was a Samaritan.

"So Jesus answered and said, 'Were there not ten cleansed? But where are the nine? Were there not any found who returned to give glory to God except this foreigner?' And He said to him, 'Arise, go your way. Your faith has made you well.'"

Jesus pointed out the improper heart attitude. It's poor manners—it's rude—not to give glory to God. It would be many times worse than not thanking someone who took you out for dinner. Get in the habit of stopping to celebrate the victory with the Lord. Praise Him and worship Him just like you did when you were pursuing the breakthrough. You'll need another one.

— *Prayer* —

Father, in the name of Jesus, help me not to walk in an attitude of ingratitude. Help me to remember to stop in between intercessory prayer assignments and give You all the glory. You are worthy to be thanked.

Who Are You Agreeing With?

"Therefore He is also able to save to the uttermost those who come to God through Him, since He always lives to make intercession for them" (Hebrews 7:25).

Did you know Jesus is still praying for you? Speaking by the Holy Spirit, Paul said in no uncertain terms that Jesus is at the right hand of God making intercession for us. That's good news, since Jesus always gets His prayers answered. This should encourage your heart.

Now, let's take it a step further. Intercessors, will you please agree with His intercession for you? Get into agreement with the High Priest of your confession (see Heb. 3:1). The Greek word for confession in this verse is homologia, which means "to say the same thing as." Understanding this, one could say we should pray the same thing over our lives that Jesus is praying. After all, how can two walk together if they are not agreed? (see Amos 3:3)

So, what is Jesus praying for us? We may never know everything Jesus is praying for us. But we do know that He's advocating for us with the Father when we sin. 1 John 2:1 (AMP) tells us plainly:

"My little children (believers, dear ones), I am writing you these things so that you will not sin and violate God's law. And if anyone sins, we have an Advocate [who will intercede for us] with the Father: Jesus Christ the righteous [the upright, the just One, who conforms to the Father's will in every way—purpose, thought, and action]."

I believe when the enemy comes to sift us like wheat, He prays our faith does not fail (see Luke 22:32). I believe He's praying to protect us from the evil one (see John 17:15). I believe He prays that we will walk in love with one another as a demonstration of who He is. After all, Jesus said in John 13:35, "By this all will know that you are My disciples, if you have love for one another."

— *Prayer* —

Father, in the name of Jesus, help me come into agreement with Christ's intercession over me. Help me pray along the lines of what He prayed for His disciples when He walked the earth. I agree with You.

Prayer Fruit That Remains

"By this My Father is glorified, that you bear much fruit" (John 15:8).

As intercessors, we can be busy or fruitful. We can busy ourselves with prayer all day and night and see little fruit. Indeed, busyness and fruitfulness can, at times, be polar opposites. We want to be about our Father's business in prayer, not busily praying amiss.

Busy means you are engaged in activities, but busy can also mean "full of distracting detail." By contrast, fruitful means "yielding or producing fruit, conducive to an abundant yield, abundantly productive," according to *Merriam-Webster's* dictionary. The Bible clearly tells us to be fruitful.

Jesus said in John 15:5-8: "I am the vine, you are the branches. He who abides in Me, and I in him, bears much fruit; for without Me you can do nothing. If anyone does not abide in Me, he is cast out as a branch and is withered; and they gather them and throw them into the fire, and they are burned. If you abide in Me, and My words abide in you, you will ask what you desire, and it shall be done for you. By this My Father is glorified, that you bear much fruit; so you will be My disciples."

Our heavenly Father wants to see fruit that remains. In direct correlation to prayer, Jesus said in John 15:16, "You did not choose Me, but I chose you and appointed you that you should go and bear fruit, and that your fruit should remain, that whatever you ask the Father in My name He may give you."

Jesus wants to us bear fruit in all things, including and especially prayer. In fact, prayer is one of the ways we bear fruit in other areas of our lives because, as He said, apart from Him we can do nothing. So, consider your ways in intercession. Are you fruitful in the Father's business or just busy in prayer that never sees results? Ask God to help you bear prayer fruit that remains.

— *Prayer* —

Father, in the name of Jesus, I don't want to be busy and distracted by many things in prayer. I don't want to be unfocused. I want to bear uber fruitful. Would You help me pray with pinpoint accuracy about the Father's business?

When God Prunes Your Prayer Group

"Every branch in Me that does not bear fruit He takes away; and every branch that bears fruit
He prunes, that it may bear more fruit" (John 15:2).

It can be hard to lose an intercessor in your prayer group. Sometimes, people move away and other times they move on. Sometimes people get overwhelmed and other times they get offended. Sometimes the enemy takes them out and sometimes God moves them on.

Indeed, pruning is never fun, but it is inevitable. Jesus said in John 15:1-8, "I am the true vine, and My Father is the vinedresser. Every branch in Me that does not bear fruit He takes away; and every branch that bears fruit He prunes, that it may bear more fruit. You are already clean because of the word which I have spoken to you. Abide in Me, and I in you. As the branch cannot bear fruit of itself, unless it abides in the vine, neither can you, unless you abide in Me.

"I am the vine, you are the branches. He who abides in Me, and I in him, bears much fruit; for without Me you can do nothing. If anyone does not abide in Me, he is cast out as a branch and is withered; and they gather them and throw them into the fire, and they are burned. If you abide in Me, and My words abide in you, you will ask what you desire, and it shall be done for you. By this My Father is glorified, that you bear much fruit; so you will be My disciples."

Pruning almost always hurts, but it will ultimately lead to greater depths, purer faith and greater prayer answers. Pruning is part of God's process, and we have to trust Him in it and through it. Believe me, you'd rather have Gideon's army than intercessors with wrong agendas, or who are fearful or in strife. One can put a thousand to flight and two can put ten thousand to flight, but the wrong ones can pollute your prayer meeting.

— *Prayer* —

Father, in the name of Jesus, thank You for helping me discern the pruning
process, which can seem sudden and often be disturbing. Thank You that You are
the Master Gardener and You know just what to prune.

JUNE 11

Becoming a Friend of Christ the Intercessor

"Could you not watch with Me one hour?" (Matthew 26:40)

The hour was almost at hand. Judas was about to betray Jesus and He knew it. The disciples were clueless. Jesus celebrated the Passover with the apostles and instituted the Lord's Supper, what we call communion. Jesus predicted Peter's denial. Then the celebration ended and the stage was set for crucifixion.

Jesus took Peter, James and John to the garden to pray. He was looking for his closest friends to agree with Him in prayer. Look at the scene in Matthew 26:36-46:

"Then Jesus came with them to a place called Gethsemane, and said to the disciples, 'Sit here while I go and pray over there.' And He took with Him Peter and the two sons of Zebedee, and He began to be sorrowful and deeply distressed. Then He said to them, 'My soul is exceedingly sorrowful, even to death. Stay here and watch with Me.'

"He went a little farther and fell on His face, and prayed, saying, 'O My Father, if it is possible, let this cup pass from Me; nevertheless, not as I will, but as You will.'

"Then He came to the disciples and found them sleeping, and said to Peter, 'What! Could you not watch with Me one hour? Watch and pray, lest you enter into temptation. The spirit indeed is willing, but the flesh is weak.'

"Again, a second time, He went away and prayed, saying, 'O My Father, if this cup cannot pass away from Me unless I drink it, Your will be done.' And He came and found them asleep again, for their eyes were heavy.

"So He left them, went away again, and prayed the third time, saying the same words. Then He came to His disciples and said to them, 'Are you still sleeping and resting? Behold, the hour is at hand, and the Son of Man is being betrayed into the hands of sinners. Rise, let us be going. See, My betrayer is at hand.'"

Jesus calls us friends when we do what He commands (see John 15:14). As intercessors, our chief command is to pray. Let's not fall asleep on the job.

— *Prayer* —

Father, in the name of Jesus, would You help me be a friend to Christ? I don't want to fall asleep when He wants me to collaborate with Him in prayer, or agree with His heart in intercession. Help me stay steady.

The Jabez Prayer Anointing

"Oh, that You would bless me indeed, and enlarge my territory, that Your hand would be with
me, and that You would keep me from evil, that I may not cause pain!"
(1 Chronicles 4:10)

His mother called his name Jabez because of her pain in childbirth. This marked his life because in Israel's culture your name is especially significant.

Think about it: God changed Abram's name to Abraham, which means father of many nations. Every time someone called Abraham's name, they were declaring he was the father of many nations. They were declaring God's promise over him.

Jabez was a son of Judah—He was a son of praise. But when he was born he was named for the pain he caused. Every time someone called Jabez's name, they were declaring how much sorrow he caused. He was reminded every day of his life about the pain he inflicted. He had to overcome this stigma of causing pain even though the pain technically wasn't his fault.

Nevertheless, Jabez had a revelation of the goodness of God. Let's look at the rest of his story in 1 Chronicles 4:9, "Now Jabez was more honorable than his brothers, and his mother called his name Jabez, saying, 'Because I bore him in pain'." Despite his disadvantages in life, he was more honorable than his brothers—and God honored him for it.

Jabez just wanted God's blessing, and he wasn't shy about asking for it. Scripture singles him out amid a laundry list of the descendants of Judah: "He was the one who prayed to the God of Israel, 'Oh, that you would bless me and expand my territory! Please be with me in all that I do, and keep me from all trouble and pain!'" (1 Chron. 4:10).

Bless me indeed. In some ways, this was an urgent cry for justice. You have to understand that word "indeed." It means without any question, undeniably and in a matter that causes surprise or disbelief. God's blessing on your life will be an indeed blessing. It will surprise people, shock people… How did God answer Jabez's prayer? "God granted his request" (1 Chron. 4:10).

— *Prayer* —

Father, in the name of Jesus, help me take a page out of Jabez's playbook. Help me to walk in honor when it seems the world is against me, knowing that You see me. Help me to boldly pray for Your blessings. Bless me, indeed.

Praying With God's Emotions

"Now as He drew near, He saw the city and wept over it, saying, 'If you had known, even you, especially in this your day, the things that make for your peace! But now they are hidden from your eyes'" (Luke 19:41-42).

Praying with—or through—God's emotions is a powerful form of intercession. Travail is one example, but it goes well beyond travail. God has many emotions, and He can let us feel what He feels about someone or something so we can pray with His heart.

See, when the Bible says David was a man after God's own heart, it meant more than seeking to obey God. David was a student of God's emotions. He wanted to know what God felt about things. He wanted to know God's heart.

God revealed His emotions to Moses. Exodus 34:6-7: "And the Lord passed before him and proclaimed, 'The Lord, the Lord God, merciful and gracious, longsuffering, and abounding in goodness and truth, keeping mercy for thousands...'"

The Holy Spirit has many emotions. Ephesians 4:30 tells us not to grieve the Holy Spirit. He can be grieved just like you can be grieved. We need to know what grieves Him. When you study His emotions through fellowship and reading the Word, you will be able to discern whether it's you or Him that's grieved.

The Holy Spirit has joy. 1 Thessalonians 1:6 speaks of the joy of the Holy Ghost. We need to know what brings Him joy. The Holy Spirit can be vexed, according to Psalm 78:41. Vexation is a feeling of irritation or annoyance. The Holy Spirit is God. God laughs at His enemies. God gets angry. Who do you think inspired Jesus to make a whip?

God mourns. Remember, Jesus wept. God hates. We're supposed to love what God loves and hate what God hates. The Lord rejoices. The Lord can be pleased or displeased. The Lord is compassionate. When we study God's emotions, we will open ourselves up to feel what He feels. When we open ourselves up to feel what He feels, we can pray with His heart.

— Prayer —

Father, in the name of Jesus, would You help me feel what You feel? Would You make me more sensitive to Your emotions? I want to be closer to Your heart so I can pray with Your heart for people, cities and nations.

Prisoners of Hope

"Return to the stronghold, you prisoners of hope. Even today I declare that I will restore double to you" (Zechariah 9:12).

If I am going to be a prisoner, I want to be a prisoner of hope. Intercessors, it's critical that you guard your hope because faith is the substance of things hoped for (see Heb. 11:1). If the enemy can steal your hope, he can steal your faith.

God says, "Come back to the place of safety, all you prisoners who still have hope! I promise this very day that I will repay two blessings for each of your troubles" (Zech. 9:12, NLT). The Amplified translation puts it this way: "Return to the stronghold [of security and prosperity], O prisoners who have the hope; Even today I am declaring that I will restore double [your former prosperity] to you [as firstborn among nations]."

The word hope in these verses is not like the world's hope. The world's hope is a wish.

Bible hope is an expectation. When you expect something, you wait for it. You look or it. You anticipate it. You don't give up on it because you know it's coming.

Bill Johnson, senior leader at Bethel, once said: "Any areas of our life where there is no hope is under the influence of a lie." There is no situation you could face that you are not prepared for or that God doesn't have an answer for. Just think about what He's already brought you through!

As you stand in intercession, you have to do what Moses did when he led the Israelites out of Egypt by way of the Red Sea: hope. You may have to stand like Nehemiah did when there was tremendous opposition to rebuilding the wall around Jerusalem: hope. You may have to pray like Esther when she was trying to save the Jewish people from wicked Haman: hope.

Be like Abraham, hope against hope. Look through the eyes of hope while you're waiting for the prayer answer. Be a prisoner of hope.

— Prayer —

Father, in the name of Jesus, deliver me from the voices of doubt and unbelief. I want to be a prisoner of hope. I will hope against hope because I know all those who put their hope in You will never be put to shame.

The Nikolaus Zinzendorf Prayer Anointing

"A fire shall always be burning on the altar; it shall never go out" (Leviticus 6:13).

Nikolaus Ludwig von Zinzendorf was born in 1700, about two hundred years before the modern-day Pentecostal movement. He goes down in church history as a religious and social reformer in the German Pietist movement. He was also the leader of the Moravian Church.

Many intercessors know Moravian Falls in the North Carolina mountains well. This was one of the many settlements the Moravians established. They landed in the Piedmont of North Carolina in 1753. The Moravians purchased nearly 100,000 acres there. Historian A. J. Lewis writes, "For over a hundred years the members of the Moravian Church all shared in the 'hourly intercession.' At home and abroad, on land and sea, this prayer watch ascended unceasingly to the Lord."

The Scripture they were standing on? Leviticus 6:13, "A fire shall always be burning on the altar; it shall never go out."

What's remarkable is the prayer anointing on Zinzendorf birthed a prayer meeting that lasted for over one hundred years. It didn't start in Moravian falls. It started in the Moravian community of Herrnhut in Saxony in 1727. The around-the-clock prayer watch continued for decades until the Moravians sent three hundred missionaries around the world sixty-five years later in 1791. Besides America, the Moravians traveled to places like Turkey, Lapland and the West Indies.

Zinzendorf once said, "I have but one passion: It is He, it is He alone. The world is the field and the field is the world; and henceforth that country shall be my home where I can be most used in winning souls for Christ... I am destined to proclaim the message, unmindful of personal consequences to myself."

The Zinzendorf prayer anointing is an anointing for unceasing prayer and effective evangelism unto revival. You can still sense the spirit of prayer in Moravian Falls today. Ask God for the Zinzendorf prayer anointing.

— *Prayer* —

Father, in the name of Jesus, would You give me a heart for prayer and evangelism? Would You help me establish prayer in my community with a thrust toward reaching souls? Give me a passion for souls.

Pray for the Spirit of Prayer

"In the same way the Spirit [comes to us and] helps us in our weakness. We do not know what prayer to offer or how to offer it as we should, but the Spirit Himself [knows our need and at the right time] intercedes on our behalf with sighs and groanings too deep for words"
(Romans 8:26, AMPC).

The Holy Spirit is the spirit of prayer. Charles Finney, a preacher and intercessor, understood this all too well. He once wrote, "If people know not the spirit of prayer, they are very apt to be unbelieving in regard to the results of prayer. They do not see what takes place, or do not see the connection, or do not see the evidence. They are not expecting spiritual blessings."

The spirit of prayer is an anointing that helps us pray effectively and without ceasing. We may start out in the flesh but when we repent of our sins and lift up the name of Jesus, we attract the Holy Helper into our intercession. He begins to work with us to release perfect petitions. We need a deeper revelation of our need for the spirit of prayer so we won't release vain repetitions.

"We see from this subject the absurdity of using forms of prayer. The very idea of using a form rejects, of course, the leadings of the Spirit," Finney contended. "Nothing is more calculated to destroy the spirit of prayer, and entirely to darken and confuse the mind, as to what constitutes prayer, than to use forms. Forms of prayer are not only absurd in themselves, but they are the very device of the devil to destroy the spirit and break the power of prayer."

When we pray apart from a spirit of payer, we are praying in our own strength. Jesus made it clear that apart from Him we can do nothing. The Holy Spirit made it clear that we need His help to make intercession. We would do well, as we set out praying, to let one of our first prayers be, "Lord, let Your spirit of prayer descend upon me."

— Prayer —

Father, in the name of Jesus, let Your spirit of prayer rest upon me. I acknowledge that I don't know how to pray as I ought. Holy Helper, help me make intercession. Help me release the perfect petitions for Your glory.

JUNE 17

The Dreaming Intercessor

"In the first year of Belshazzar king of Babylon, Daniel had a dream and visions of his head while on his bed. Then he wrote down the dream, telling the main facts" (Daniel 7:1).

Daniel was a dreaming intercessor. He had intense dreams that drove him to prayer. Maybe you are the same way. Did you know God will give you dreams just for the sake of intercession?

Throughout the pages of Scripture, we see God sharing prophetic intelligence through dreams. Have you ever wondered why? Why does God choose to speak to us while we are in a deep sleep? We may never know all the reasons why but it may be because we're not hearing His instructions through other communication modes.

Dreaming intercessors need patience, at times, to understand the interpretation. Like Daniel's dreams, we may not always be sure of the entire meaning at first. God sent angels at times to help him with the interpretation. God may do the same for the dreaming intercessor. Until then, just keep praying and meditating on the symbols, colors, numbers, events and people in your dream.

If you are not a dreaming intercessor, pray about that, too! You can't push your way into the dream realm but you can ask Him to open it up to you. As I wrote in my book, *Decoding Your Dreams*:

"If you ask God to open your dream life, expect Him to answer. He may not give you a dream the first night. You may have to ask more than once. And it's possible that you are doing something to hinder receiving or remembering your dreams."

If you don't speak dream language, get equipped. God may not be giving you dreams because He knows you wouldn't have a clue what He is trying to tell you. It's also possible you are not remembering your dreams. The Holy Spirit can remind you. Ask Him.

— *Prayer* —

Father, in the name of Jesus, would You open up my dream life? Would You help me understand what You are showing me? Would You help me remember my dreams and pray accurately through them? Make me a dreaming intercessor.

The Visionary Intercessor

"And it shall come to pass in the last days, says God, that I will pour out of My Spirit on all flesh; Your sons and your daughters shall prophesy, your young men shall see visions, your old men shall dream dreams" (Acts 2:17).

More and more, intercessors are getting prayer assignments in visions. According to *The Seer's Dictionary*, the Greek word for vision is horasis, which means "the act of seeing, a vision, appearance," according to the *NAS Exhaustive Concordance*. *Thayer's Greek Lexicon* defines vision as "the act of seeing; the sense of sight; appearance, visible form, a vision, i.e., an appearance divinely granted in an ecstasy."

Receiving prayer assignments in a vision is biblical. Ananias received a prayer assignment to pray for Paul in Acts 9:10-18:

"Now there was a believer in Damascus named Ananias. The Lord spoke to him in a vision, calling, 'Ananias!' 'Yes, Lord!' he replied. The Lord said, 'Go over to Straight Street, to the house of Judas. When you get there, ask for a man from Tarsus named Saul. He is praying to me right now. I have shown him a vision of a man named Ananias coming in and laying hands on him so he can see again.'

"'But Lord,' exclaimed Ananias, 'I've heard many people talk about the terrible things this man has done to the believers in Jerusalem! And he is authorized by the leading priests to arrest everyone who calls upon your name.'

"But the Lord said, 'Go, for Saul is my chosen instrument to take my message to the Gentiles and to kings, as well as to the people of Israel. And I will show him how much he must suffer for my name's sake.'

"So Ananias went and found Saul. He laid his hands on him and said, 'Brother Saul, the Lord Jesus, who appeared to you on the road, has sent me so that you might regain your sight and be filled with the Holy Spirit.' Instantly something like scales fell from Saul's eyes, and he regained his sight. Then he got up and was baptized."

Believe God to receive prayer assignments in visions. Then be sure to follow through in intercession.

— Prayer —

Father, in the name of Jesus, would You open my seer eyes and help me see the visions You are trying to show me? I don't want to miss a prophetic prayer assignment. Help me discern Your prayer assignments through prophetic visions so I can stand for Your will in the earth.

JUNE 19

It Will Be Just as God Said

"Therefore take heart, men, for I believe God that it will be just as it was told me"
(Acts 27:25).

Are you convinced, utterly convinced, that it will be just as God told you it would be? Whether you see a promise in the Word or an angel visits you with a message from heaven, you need to be utterly convinced of God's will before you release your intercession. This is insurance against doubt creeping in to pollute your faith.

Consider this account in Acts 27. Paul appealed to Caesar and was on a ship with criminals to Rome. A great north wind came and was tossing the ship to and fro. It got worse each and every day. But Paul had a word—and he believed that word. Look at Acts 27:18-25:

"And because we were exceedingly tempest-tossed, the next day they lightened the ship. On the third day we threw the ship's tackle overboard with our own hands. Now when neither sun nor stars appeared for many days, and no small tempest beat on us, all hope that we would be saved was finally given up.

"But after long abstinence from food, then Paul stood in the midst of them and said, 'Men, you should have listened to me, and not have sailed from Crete and incurred this disaster and loss. And now I urge you to take heart, for there will be no loss of life among you, but only of the ship.'

"'For there stood by me this night an angel of the God to whom I belong and whom I serve, saying, 'Do not be afraid, Paul; you must be brought before Caesar; and indeed God has granted you all those who sail with you.' Therefore take heart, men, for I believe God that it will be just as it was told me.'"

Convince yourself God's Word is true—and true for you—before you set out to pray. Sometimes, of course, that means seeking His specific will before you release a prayer. Paul wasn't offering wishful thinking. We don't want to release wishful praying.

— *Prayer* —

Father, in the name of Jesus, would You help me to search out Your will as I set out to pray? Help me find the right Word to pray and the right petitions to release. Convince me of Your agenda and convict me if I stray from it.

The Israel Prayer Mandate

"Pray for the peace of Jerusalem: 'May they prosper who love you. Peace be within your walls, prosperity within your palaces'" (Psalm 122:6-7).

Throughout Scripture, we see people making intercession for Israel. So should we.

Nehemiah cried out for God to forgive Israel (see Neh. 1:4-11). Solomon released a petition for God to forgive Israel even into the future (see 1 Kings 8:46-53). Joel cried out to God to spare Israel (Joel 2:12-17).

Moses plead with the Lord when He wanted to wipe them off the map and start over: "Turn from Your fierce wrath, and relent from this harm to Your people. Remember Abraham, Isaac, and Israel, Your servants, to whom You swore by Your own self, and said to them, 'I will multiply your descendants as the stars of heaven; and all this land that I have spoken of I give to your descendants, and they shall inherit it forever'" (Exodus 32:11).

Isaiah declared, "For Zion's sake I will not hold My peace, and for Jerusalem's sake I will not rest, until her righteousness goes forth as brightness, and her salvation as a lamp that burns" (Is. 6:1). Jeremiah wept day and night (see Jer. 9:1). In Lamentations 3:49-50, he wrote: "My eyes flow and do not cease, without interruption, till the Lord from heaven looks down and sees."

Throughout the Psalms, we see people crying out to God for the sake of Israel. The entirety of Psalm 74 is Asaph's prayer for God to deliver Israel from her oppressors. Psalm 85 is passionate plea for God's mercy on Israel. And listen in to the heartfelt cry in Psalm 123:2-4:

"As the eyes of a maid to the hand of her mistress, so our eyes look to the Lord our God, until He has mercy on us. Have mercy on us, O Lord, have mercy on us! For we are exceedingly filled with contempt. Our soul is exceedingly filled with the scorn of those who are at ease, with the contempt of the proud."

— *Prayer* —

Father, in the name of Jesus, would You show me Your heart for Your people Israel? Will You give me the grace to stand in the gap for Your chosen people, crying out for mercy, blessings, grace and peace in the Holy Land?

The Intercessor's Dignity

"Show yourself in all respects to be a model of good works, and in your teaching show integrity, dignity, and sound speech that cannot be condemned, so that an opponent may be put to shame, having nothing evil to say about us" (Titus 2:7-8).

Intercessors are often sorely unappreciated—and even sorely misunderstood. But I believe the Holy Spirit is restoring dignity to the office of the intercessor. Dignity is "the quality or state of being worthy, honored or esteemed; a high rank, office or position, a legal title of nobility or honor," according to *Merriam-Webster's* dictionary.

Realize this: You are never more like Jesus than when you are making intercession. There is a dignity to the office of the intercessor. Even if people don't esteem you, God esteems you when You stand in the authority of Christ, stand in the gap, stand and withstand in the evil day—and keep standing when you've done all you can do.

Of course, if you want to see dignity restored you must walk worthy of that dignity. You must honor leaders, respect others, walk worthy of your calling and otherwise have an excellent spirit. You must watch your words even when you are not watching and praying.

In *Helps to Intercession* author Andrew Murray offers this keen insight: "Pray Without Ceasing. Does that refer to prayer for ourselves or others? To both. It is because many confine it to themselves that they fail so in practicing it. It is only when the branch gives itself to bear fruit, more fruit, much fruit, that it can live a healthy life, and expect a rich inflow of sap.

"The death of Christ brought Him to the place of everlasting intercession. Your death with Him to sin and self sets you free from the care of self, and elevates you to the dignity of intercessor—one who can get life and blessing from God for others. Know your calling; begin this your work. Give yourself wholly to it, and before you know it you will be finding something of this 'Praying always' within you."

— *Prayer* —

Father, in the name of Jesus, would You help me walk in dignity rather than expecting other to treat me with dignity? Help me walk in honor and integrity even when others don't appreciate Your gifts in me.

Strategic Prayer Evangelism

"Rain down, you heavens, from above, and let the skies pour down righteousness. Let the earth open wide, let salvation spring up, let righteousness flourish with it; I, the Lord, have created it"
(Isaiah 45:8).

We can battle against principalities and powers over dark nations all day long, but without prayer evangelism we will only have a partial victory. Yes, principalities and powers keep people blinded to the Gospel. Antichrist spirits abound in nations where false gods are exalted.

Dick Eastman, Chief Prayer Officer at Every Home for Christ, taught me a five-point prayer strategy that shifts nations through the power of the Gospel. Yes, there is power in the Gospel.

Paul said, "For I am not ashamed of the gospel of Christ, for it is the power of God to salvation for everyone who believes, for the Jew first and also for the Greek" (Rom. 1:6). And again, "For the message of the cross is foolishness to those who are perishing, but to us who are being saved it is the power of God" (1 Cor. 1:18).

Here's the strategy. Ask for open hands to minister the Gospel. Proverbs 3:27-29 tells us, "Do not withhold good from those to whom it is due, when it is in the power of your hand to do so. Do not say to your neighbor, 'Go, and come back, and tomorrow I will give it,' When you have it with you. Do not devise evil against your neighbor, for he dwells by you for safety's sake."

Ask for open doors to spread the Gospel, according to Colossians 4:2-3, "Continue earnestly in prayer, being vigilant in it with thanksgiving; meanwhile praying also for us, that God would open to us a door for the word, to speak the mystery of Christ, for which I am also in chains..."

Ask for open minds to receive the Gospel, according to Acts 26:17-18. Ask for open hearts to embrace the Gospel, according to 2 Corinthians 4:6. And ask for open heavens that the Gospel will transform nations, according to Isaiah 45:8. God wants to transform nations, and that means transforming souls.

— *Prayer* —

Father, in the name of Jesus, would You help me incorporate prayer evangelism into my intercession so I can be an agent of transformation in the nations? Give me the grace to make prayer evangelism a priority.

JUNE 23

Don't Stop Striking Now

"And he said to the king of Israel, 'Strike the ground'; so he struck three times, and stopped" (2 Kings 13:18).

I had a vision of an arrow being put into a quiver. The Lord told me that our prayer calls—calls in which we were praying out many prophecies that had been declared over the State of Florida—were an arrow in our quiver. Then He took me to 2 Kings 13 to show me how that worked.

Elijah was sick with the illness from which he would die. Jehoash, the king of Israel, went to meet him, weeping. Elisha showed no emotion, but gave him a strategy 2 Kings 13:15-17:

"And Elisha said to him, 'Take a bow and some arrows.' So he took himself a bow and some arrows. Then he said to the king of Israel, 'Put your hand on the bow.' So he put his hand on it, and Elisha put his hands on the king's hands. And he said, 'Open the east window'; and he opened it. Then Elisha said, 'Shoot'; and he shot. And he said, 'The arrow of the Lord's deliverance and the arrow of deliverance from Syria; for you must strike the Syrians at Aphek till you have destroyed them.'"

That wasn't the end of Elisha's instructions to King Jehoash and it's not the end of this prophetic strategy, either. Let's review Elisha's next instruction to the king in 2 Kings 13:18-19:

"Then he said, 'Take the arrows'; so he took them. And he said to the king of Israel, 'Strike the ground'; so he struck three times, and stopped. And the man of God was angry with him, and said, 'You should have struck five or six times; then you would have struck Syria till you had destroyed it! But now you will strike Syria only three times'."

Intercession is not usually a one and done event. Victory often demands consistency and endurance. Keep on striking in faith even if you don't see anything changing.

— *Prayer* —

Father, in the name of Jesus, would You give me a consistency to keep striking the ground until I beat the enemy back from Your yes-and-amen promises? Help me strike and keep on striking.

JUNE 24

In The Courts of Heaven

"For the Lord is our Judge, the Lord is our Lawgiver, the Lord is our King; He will save us"
(Isaiah 33:22).

I'm not one who runs to the courts of heaven for anything and everything. I don't believe it's necessary to do so, any more than it's necessary to run to a natural court of law for every dispute. But there have been a few times I've looked for vindication from the courts of heaven. There have been times when the Holy Spirit led me to plead my case to the eternal Judge who sits on the throne.

You approach God as Judge in a different way than you approach Him as Healer or Deliverer. We have to remember, first, that God is Judge of all (see Heb. 12:23). God sees everything everyone did to you, but He also sees your flaws and shortcomings. If we have unforgiveness and bitterness in our hearts toward the one who wronged us, we won't find vindication from the Judge. We'll find conviction first. And we should welcome it.

So, before you go to the courts of heaven, repent for any unforgiveness, wrong attitudes, or vengeance in your heart at the throne of grace and receive grace and find mercy to help you. Otherwise, your case will be thrown out until you meet the conditions. Confess your sins in Jesus' name and He is faithful and just to forgive your sin and cleanse you from all unrighteousness (see 1 John 1:9).

Approach God in the courts of heaven with reverential fear. Just as in the natural court, lawyers call the judge "Your honor," you must have a heart posture of honor for God and His Word on which you stand for vindication. The one who wronged you was not operating in the fear of the Lord, but you must. Solomon assured us, "In the fear of the Lord there is strong confidence, and His children will have a place of refuge" (Prov. 14:26).

— *Prayer* —

Father, in the name of Jesus, would You give me a leading when You want me to go to the courts of heaven? I don't want to abuse this revelation by going into extremes. But I don't want to neglect this strategy, either. Help me.

The Changing of the Guard

"Moses My servant is dead. Now therefore, arise, go over this Jordan, you and all this people, to the land which I am giving to them—the children of Israel" (Joshua 1:2).

When I was in London the first time, I watched the changing of the guard at Buckingham Palace intently. The ceremony was quite something, with precision drills and music. There was no such fanfare when Joshua took the baton from Moses. Joshua was expected to jump right in after a short period of grief.

"After the death of Moses the servant of the Lord, it came to pass that the Lord spoke to Joshua the son of Nun, Moses' assistant, saying: 'Moses My servant is dead. Now therefore, arise, go over this Jordan, you and all this people, to the land which I am giving to them—the children of Israel. Every place that the sole of your foot will tread upon I have given you, as I said to Moses'" (Josh. 1:1-3).

The changing of the guard, in some respects, is constant as great prayer warriors pass on to glory and release their mantles. But I heard the Lord say:

"There is a changing of the guard and a handing off of the baton. There are too many seats of governing authority that stand vacant. For those who should have risen up to take the seats that generals from seasons gone by and decades gone by and even in eras gone by have not filled those seats.

"There's a void in the spirit. I am calling you even now to begin to pray for that next generation—those who succeed those who came before them—with that revelation and that power and that mantle and that might. There is a changing of the guard in this new era."

Position yourself properly for the changing of the guard. Watch and pray. Serve an elder in the prayer movement. Intercede for them, sow into them, stand with them, learn from them as Joshua learned from Moses.

— *Prayer* —

Father, in the name of Jesus, would You help me prepare myself for the changing of the guard? Would You show me who to raise up and who to serve? Would You help me glean from elder intercessors so I can carry on in the race?

You Have Power of Attorney

"We have an Advocate with the Father, Jesus Christ the righteous" (1 John 4:1).

Jesus is our advocate, and He has given us power of attorney to execute His will on the earth. Power of attorney in the natural is the authority to act for another person in legal or financial matters. Jesus expects us to use our power of attorney—delegated authority—on the earth to bring heaven's will to the fore.

Since God has chosen to work through men and women on the earth, He had to give us power of attorney to legally execute His plan according to His spiritual laws. Keep in mind the benefits of your power of attorney come through the name of Jesus. Without His signature on the operation, it will falter and fail.

The demons are only subject to you, for example, in His name (see Luke 10:17). Authentic healing, signs and wonders are performed through the name of Jesus (see Acts 4:30). Every knee must bow, in heaven and on earth and under the earth, to the name of Jesus (see Phil. 2:10). Whatever we do, in word or deed, should be unto Him and in His name (see Col. 3:17).

Because Joseph served the Lord, God orchestrated circumstances to give him power of attorney over all of Egypt. He was essentially the Prime Minister of the nation and second in command only to Pharoah. In his wisdom, he used his power of attorney to save the world, including the twelve tribes of Israel, from the effects of famine.

Intercessors, this power of attorney comes with a great responsibility. Use it wisely. Jesus gave you this power of attorney to heal the sick, cleanse the lepers, cast out devils, raise the dead, destroy the works of the devil, preach the Gospel and disciple nations. It's ultimately all about the Great Commission. You have a great privilege and an awesome responsibility. I know you'll use your power of attorney wisely.

— *Prayer* —

Father, in the name of Jesus, would You give me a revelation of the power of attorney You have given me in the earth? Just as Jesus is my advocate in heaven, help me to be an advocate here on earth.

JUNE 27

Intercessors of Presence

"In Your presence is fullness of joy; At Your right hand are pleasures forevermore"
(Psalm 16:11).

God is omnipresent—everywhere all the time. But walking as an intercessor of presence is a much deeper experience. An intercessor of presence is one who has the revelation that she is literally walking with God.

Develop a strong awareness that God lives in you by meditating on Scriptures such as 1 Corinthians 6:19, "Don't you realize that your body is the temple of the Holy Spirit, who lives in you and was given to you by God?"

Discerning God's presence around us, or in an atmosphere, is important so you can respond rightly to Him. If you don't know someone is in the room, you won't pay them any attention.

Sometimes the manifestation of God's presence is dramatic. Sometimes you can see glory clouds. Sometimes you can smell the presence of God. You may hear the audible voice of God. If you are especially perceptive, you can sense the weight in the atmosphere. Sometimes there's a holy hush. God can manifest as a bright light. God can manifest in fire.

Most people will discern the manifest presence of God, but the more difficult part is discerning His presence in our everyday life when there is no worship team to lead you. His presence in our everyday life isn't usually as dramatic.

Brother Lawrence, a 17th Century monk who wrote a series of letters that became the book we know as *The Practice of the Presence of God*, once wrote these words:

"I cannot imagine how religious persons can live satisfied without the practice of the presence of God. For my part I keep myself retired with Him in the depth of centre of my soul as much as I can; and while I am so with Him I fear nothing; but the least turning from Him is insupportable."

— *Prayer* —

Father, in the name of Jesus, teach me to discern the presence of Your Holy Spirit.
I know You never leave me or forsake me, but help me to develop a sensitivity to
Your presence that empowers me to walk in with You.

Out-of-the Box Intercession

"And do not be conformed to this world, but be transformed by the renewing of your mind, that you may prove what is that good and acceptable and perfect will of God" (Romans 12:2).

Out-of-the-box intercessors think—and pray—a little differently. They understand God does not live in a box. Since the Ark of the Covenant was broken, He hasn't been in a box—and He doesn't want His intercessors in a box either. Put another way, praying with the Holy Spirit can and should be an adventure.

If we are not careful, we'll get rote in our prayers. We'll pray the same way for the same things at the same time every day without tapping into the mind of Christ. But God is a creative God and He wants us to tap into His creativity to overcome stubborn obstacles to prayer answers. Praying outside the box allows you to get prayer answers outside your normal reach. That's because out-of-the-box prayers stretch you and your faith.

Maybe you need a change of scenery to shift your perspective on the problem about which you are praying. Many times when we change our prayer location we'll shake ourselves out of our box—our routine—just enough to see, hear and pray things differently. Try praying in a park or while driving in your car. Jesus often went to wilderness places to pray.

Turn your intercession into a thanksgiving session. Rather than asking God one more time for one more thing, just thank Him for a straight hour for everything He's done in the past—all the prayer answers He's delivered through your intercessory prayer ministry. Colossians 4:2 tells us "Continue earnestly in prayer, being vigilant in it with thanksgiving."

Sit before the Lord and ask Him to show you different angles on the situation over which you are making intercession. Challenge your assumptions about how you should pray, acknowledging that you don't know how to pray as you ought. Seek counsel from others who may have a more experience or a different understanding. Just get out of the box.

— Prayer —

Father, in the name of Jesus, would You lead me outside the box of self-imposed routines and limited thinking that keep me from seeing the big picture? I want to be a prayer solutionist. Teach me how to pray out of the box prayers. Make me a creative intercessor.

Intercessory Immediatelies

"Moved with compassion, Jesus touched their eyes; and immediately they regained their sight and followed Him" (Matthew 20:34).

You hear a lot of prophecies about suddenlies. But the Lord showed me another dimension of His moving—immediatelies. We see the concept of "immediately" well over 100 times in Scripture—and there's a marked difference between a suddenly and an immediately.

A suddenly is a "happening, coming, made, or done quickly, without warning, or unexpectedly," according to *Dictionary.com*, while an immediately is "without lapse of time; without delay; instantly; at once."

When it comes to moves of God—God's intervention in my life—I'll take either. But I'd prefer an immediately—a miracle. You might say suddenlies are good, but immediatelies are better when you need prayer answers! Consider just one immediately. We find it in the story of blind Bartimaeus in Mark 10:46-52:

"Now they came to Jericho. As He went out of Jericho with His disciples and a great multitude, blind Bartimaeus, the son of Timaeus, sat by the road begging. And when he heard that it was Jesus of Nazareth, he began to cry out and say, 'Jesus, Son of David, have mercy on me!'

"Then many warned him to be quiet; but he cried out all the more, 'Son of David, have mercy on me!' So Jesus stood still and commanded him to be called. Then they called the blind man, saying to him, 'Be of good cheer. Rise, He is calling you.'

"And throwing aside his garment, he rose and came to Jesus. So Jesus answered and said to him, 'What do you want Me to do for you?' The blind man said to Him, 'Rabboni, that I may receive my sight.' Then Jesus said to him, 'Go your way; your faith has made you well.' And immediately he received his sight and followed Jesus on the road."

Let's believe for immediatelies! Of course, there are also demonic immediatelies. There are immediate threats, immediate attacks, immediate floods, and more. We answer those by taking immediate authority over them in prayer.

— *Prayer* —

Father, in the name of Jesus, would You help me build my faith for immediatelies? I know some prayer answers take time to arrive, but desperate times often call for immediatelies. Help me to pray with immediate faith.

Touching God's Heart

"Behold what manner of love the Father has bestowed on us, that we should be called children of God!" (1 John 3:1)

Every time Jesus was moved with compassion in Scripture, we saw miracles. We, too, can see miraculous prayer answers when we touch Gods heart—but to touch His heart we need to know His heart. When we know His heart, we'll know what moves His heart.

David studied God's heart, and therefore knew how to approach Him in an acceptable way. Moses knew how to touch God's heart and saved a nation of Israelites who were destined for doom. Daniel knew how to touch God's heart and the result was angelic assistance to bring an epic prayer answer.

David, Moses and Daniel had some common ground. In their prayers, they often appealed to God to uphold His reputation and His glory. In Exodus 32:12, Moses prayed, "Why should the Egyptians speak, and say, 'He brought them out to harm them, to kill them in the mountains, and to consume them from the face of the earth'? Turn from Your fierce wrath, and relent from this harm to Your people."

Of course, only prayer offered in faith touches God's heart. The writer of Hebrews tells us, "But without faith it is impossible to please Him, for he who comes to God must believe that He is, and that He is a rewarder of those who diligently seek Him" (Heb. 11:6). Faith touches the heart of God because it seeks to please Him and refuses to give up on His promises.

Persistent prayer touches the heart of God, as does prayer offered in humility. David understood, "The Lord is near to those who have a broken heart, and saves such as have a contrite spirit" (Ps. 34:18). Daniel's prayer of humility takes up the better part of Daniel chapter 9. He lingered in prayer, supplications, fasting, sackcloth and ashes. Are you touching God's heart with your intercession?

— *Prayer* —

Father, in the name of Jesus, teach me how to touch Your heart when I pray. I want to move the hand that moves the world in my intercession. Teach me the ways of Your heart and help me release petitions that honor Your Word.

JULY

"Praying always with all prayer and supplication in the Spirit, being watchful to this end with all perseverance and supplication for all the saints" (Ephesians 6:18).

The Contemplative Intercessor

"Be still and know that I am God" (Psalm 46:10).

You won't find the exact words "contemplative prayer" in the Bible but the concept is scriptural. Contemplative prayer is an ancient Christian practice that dates all the way back to the early church and even to the life of King David. The Psalms give proof of David's contemplative prayer life.

If you ask ten leaders what contemplative prayer is, you may get ten different answers. There's no one standard definition. Contemplation means "a concentration of spiritual things as a form of private devotion: a state of mystical awareness of God's being; an act of considering with attention, study; and the act of regarding steadily," according to *Merriam-Webster*'s dictionary.

Contemplative prayer carries the connotation of intentionality and expectancy. It's waiting on the Lord but it's more than that. It's meditating on who He is, and His glory. Contemplative prayer is prayer that focuses on enjoying intimacy with God. We're beholding His glory according to 2 Corinthians 3:18, "But we all, seeing the glory of the Lord with unveiled faces, as in a mirror, are being transformed into the same image from glory to glory by the Spirit of the Lord."

Contemplative prayer is a thoughtful practice where you focus on the Word of God to the point where you drown out other thoughts, feelings and temporal distractions. You are focusing on the Father, Son and Holy Spirit within you rather than the Father, Son and Holy Spirit outside of you. God's voice becomes clearer through this practice.

Psalm 27:4 also backs up the concept of contemplative prayer: "One thing I have asked from the Lord, that will I seek after—for me to dwell in the house of the Lord all the days of my life, to see the beauty of the Lord, and to inquire in His temple."

Contemplative prayer releases the Holy Spirit's supernatural activity in our spirits as we encounter His heart. Through this practice, we enter into enjoyable communion with God that transforms us from the inside out.

— Prayer —

Father, in the name of Jesus, help me to step into the realm of contemplative prayer based on who You are and what Your Word says. I want to get caught up in the Person of Jesus and see His beauty.

Pray-Reading the Word

"This Book of the Law shall not depart from your mouth, but you shall meditate in it day and night, that you may observe to do according to all that is written in it. For then you will make your way prosperous, and then you will have good success" (Joshua 1:8).

Mike Bickle, founder of the International House of Prayer in Kansas City, taught me the concept of pray-reading the Word. Pray-reading the Word is essentially reading the Word while having a conversation with God about what it says. This is a powerful practice for intercessors.

"It is not enough to study the Bible—we must talk to God as we study. Bible study is meant to lead us to conversation with God by giving us the 'conversational material' for our prayer life. It provides the language we use as we talk to Him" Bickle says. "Using the Bible and speaking the Word back to God makes prayer easy and enjoyable. It 'turns up the volume' in our conversation with God."

So how does one pray-read the Word? When we come across a truth that strikes our heart, we thank God. If you read "God is love," you might say, "Thank You, Lord, for Your perfect love for me." We can also ask God for a deeper revelation of the truth we just thanked Him for, such as, "Father, would You give me more understanding of Your love? Would You help me catch You loving me?"

This creates a dialogue with God that transforms your mind and edifies your spirit. Of course, there are also Scriptures that demand obedience. When we read Scriptures about rejoicing in the trial, we should ask God to help us obey the Word we're reading. We can ask God for the grace of obedience to rejoice in the trial or to walk in other commands.

"The anointing of the Spirit in you is your best teacher," Bickle says. "When you pray the Word in spirit and truth, you and the Spirit work together to provide you with a tailor-made teaching in the Word."

— *Prayer* —

Father, in the name of Jesus, help me grab hold of this concept of pray-reading the Word. It's different from how I've approached the Word and prayer in the past but I can see the great fruit to be had by engaging in this.

JULY 3

The Intercessor's Gift Mix

"Now concerning spiritual gifts, brethren, I do not want you to be ignorant"
(1 Corinthians 12:1).

John Wimber, founder of the Vineyard movement, once said, "Without spiritual gifts functioning I am indeed an incomplete and secularized Christian, and as a result, unable to function in power." No intercessor would want that description.

Intercessors, you have a spiritual gift mix. Clearly, you have a gift to pray, but you also have at least one other of the nine spiritual gifts. Let's look at 1 Corinthians 12:1-11 in the Amplified Bible to get a deeper look at Paul's Spirit-inspired words:

"But to each one is given the manifestation of the [Holy] Spirit [the evidence, the spiritual illumination of the Spirit] for good and profit. To one is given in and through the [Holy] Spirit [the power to speak] a message of wisdom, and to another [the power to express] a word of knowledge and understanding according to the same [Holy] Spirit; To another [wonder-working] faith by the same [Holy] Spirit, to another the extraordinary powers of healing by the one Spirit;

"To another the working of miracles, to another prophetic insight (the gift of interpreting the divine will and purpose); to another the ability to discern and distinguish between [the utterances of true] spirits [and false ones], to another various kinds of [unknown] tongues, to another the ability to interpret [such] tongues. All these [gifts, achievements, abilities] are inspired and brought to pass by one and the same [Holy] Spirit, Who apportions to each person individually [exactly] as He chooses."

A foundational key to operating in spiritual gifts is to earnestly desire them. Many times, we have not because we ask not—or we ask amiss (see James 4:3). Our motives in seeking to unlock and operate in spiritual gifts must be pure. Our motive must be to see God's will be done and His Kingdom come in the earth. Your gifts may only manifest in the context of intercession or that gift mix may include other forms of release. But you have a gift-mix. Eagerly desire to operate in your gifts (1 Cor. 14:1).

— *Prayer* —

Father, in the name of Jesus, would You help me identify my gift mix? Would You help me discern when the gifts of Your Spirit are informing my intercession so I can gain confidence in Your Spirit leading me?

Freedom of Prayer Expression

"Now the Lord is the Spirit; and where the Spirit of the Lord is, there is liberty"
(2 Corinthians 3:17).

There are many different types of intercessors. Some pray loud while others pray quietly. Some weep almost every time they pray or go into deep travail with groanings too deep to be uttered.

Yes, there are many different flows of intercession. Some intercessors literally war at the top of their lungs until they are out of breath and breaking a sweat in hand-to-hand combat with wicked spirits. Other stay on their face prostrate for hours at a time in silence. Still others pace the floor or bow down on their knees with hands lifted high.

Likewise, some intercessors seem to ooze power and authority while others pray simple prayers that touch the heart of God with a voice barely above a whisper. Some intercessors are eloquent and dignified and some are desperate in their cries and don't care who knows it.

Do any of these describe you? You never know what is going to happen when the spirit of prayer hits an intercessor. That's why we must not judge someone's expression of intercession but rather give them the liberty to flow with the Spirit of God even if it's different than how we pray.

There are many streams of intercession. As long as they all flow from the Spirit of God in the name of Jesus, we need to give each other liberty to pray the way He inspires us. Many streams make a great river. Some of those streams may be foreign to you. Some of them may seem more than a wee bit odd. Discern but don't judge through man's eyes.

Where the Spirit of the Lord is, there should be liberty. The context of 2 Corinthians 3:17 indicates freedom from bondage, but we could just as easily adopt this Scripture as being free from religious form and legalistic prayer rules. Yes, all things should be done decently and in order but if we want a free flow of intercession we must keep our hearts open.

— *Prayer* —

Father, in the name of Jesus, would You help me to embrace the many streams of intercession and intercessors I may labor with? Help me to discern Your Spirit in the great river of prayer You are releasing in the earth.

JULY 5

Praying When God Can Be Found

"For this cause everyone who is godly shall pray to You in a time when You may be found; Surely in a flood of great waters they shall not come near him" (Psalm 32:6).

What does it mean to pray when God can be found? Isn't He a very present help in time of need? Isn't He everywhere all the time? Yes, He is. Yet, there is a time of finding. Jesus Himself said, "Seek and you shall find" (Matt. 7:7).

Benson Commentary offers some insight into this verse: "The meaning is, in a seasonable time, while God continues to offer grace and mercy to sinners. By this clause the psalmist seems to intimate the difference between the truly penitent or godly, who pray and cry earnestly to God for mercy in its season; and the wicked and impenitent, who will not do so till it be too late, and the season be lost."

Put another way, it's better to pray before the enemy comes in like a flood than to wait until God has to send a clean up crew to work all things together for good. It's better to pray a prayer of repentance for sinful thoughts, words and deeds than it is to give an open door to the enemy—even though God will eventually take what the enemy meant for evil and turn it for your good.

Benson continues, "Those that have God nigh unto them, which all upright, penitent, praying people have, are so guarded, so advanced, that no waters, no, not great waters, no, not floods of them, can come nigh them to hurt them. As the temptations of the wicked one touch them not, 1 John 5:18, so neither do the troubles of this evil world; these fiery darts of both kinds drop short of them."

We can always find God, but isn't it better to seek Him before calamity strikes? Isn't it wiser to press into His presence as a way of life rather than waiting until after the tragedy to start crying out? He will never turn His back on us as repentant intercessors. Neither must we turn our back on Him when He's calling us to intercession.

— *Prayer* —

Father, in the name of Jesus, help me to pray when You can be found. Help me cultivate a lifestyle of seeking Your face and not just Your hand. Help me to pray at all times, building deep intimacy with the lover of my soul.

There's Profit in Prayer Journaling

"Thus speaks the Lord God of Israel, saying: 'Write in a book for yourself all the words that I have spoken to you'" (Jeremiah 30:2).

Journaling is a powerful exercise. In just fifteen minutes a day, you can record your prayer struggles, revelations, breakthroughs and more. But beyond that, prayer journaling can position you to receive more prophetic insight into your intercession.

Journal what happened when you were in your prayer closet. Did you feel like your prayers were hitting the ceiling? Were you distracted? Was there an open heaven? Journaling can help you discern patterns of how God is moving through you or how the enemy is moving against you.

Journal anything the Holy Spirit showed you or said to you while in prayer. You may forget about it later if you don't. The words you pen may not be critically pertinent in the moment but may carry great significance in the next season. Journal any Scriptures the Holy Spirit highlighted as you were praying and meditate on them.

Journaling can help you work through problems you are encountering in intercession, such as feeling dry, bored or ineffective. As you write down your feelings, the Holy Spirit may speak to You or give you "aha" moments. Journaling is proven to help you remember things. You can track the progress and growth of your prayer life.

Of course, journaling also leaves a record of your breakthroughs. And you'll want to refer back to those victories to encourage yourself in the Lord in the midst of future prayer battles. God told Isaiah, "Now go and write down these words. Write them in a book. They will stand until the end of time as a witness" (Is. 30:8).

So, how do you get started? Get a digital journal or a notebook. Try to journal in the morning or right before you go to bed—or right after you get out of your prayer closet. Give it ten or fifteen minutes and just write. You may be surprised at the results.

— *Prayer* —

Father, in the name of Jesus, would You help me install the habit of prayer journaling? I want to have a record of the prayer breakthroughs. I want to write down the revelations You give me. I want to remember everything You've told me.

Developing Your Prayer Values

"For where your treasure is, there your heart will be also" (Matthew 6:21).

What are your prayer values? Prayer values are principles you live by—hills you will die on. Prayer values are what you stand for in intercession and what you prize and prioritize in terms of executing prayer. Prayer values deal with your character as an intercessor. Prayer values are in line with your mission and vision for prayer.

Your prayer values are important because they guide your beliefs, attitudes and behaviors. Your prayer values are helpful when you have to make difficult decisions. Scripture informs our overall values. Your prayer values will be in line with Scripture but may not be chapter and verse.

For example, at Awakening Prayer Hubs we have values. We will not stop praying for awakening and transforming revival in our cities. Praying without ceasing is part of our DNA. We stand together. We have your back. We're a prayer family. When you suffer, we all suffer. We will stand together in prayer for your victory.

We will honor different streams of prayer. There are many ways to pray. As long as we are praying God's will in Jesus' name we can labor together under His banner. We give up things we love for things we love even more. It's an honor to sacrifice our time in prayer for the sake of the Bride and the lost who need to encounter the Bridegroom's love.

We are faith-filled, big-thinking, bet-the-farm risk takers. We'll never insult God with small thinking and safe living. We are standing for a global awakening and the prophesied billion-soul harvest. We will always work for unity without compromise.

A prayer movement without unity is a prayer movement that's powerless. We will always bring our absolute best. We believe a spirit of excellence honors God and inspires people.

What are your prayer values? Your values are what you treasure. If you've never considered your prayer values, take some time out now with the Holy Spirt to discuss.

— *Prayer* —

Father, in the name of Jesus, would You help me see what I should value most in the realms of intercession? Would You, then, give me the grace to walk in those values without compromise? I treasure what You treasure.

The Dynamics of 'Blessing' Prayer

"And all these blessings shall come upon you and overtake you, because you obey the voice of the Lord your God" (Deuteronomy 28:2).

I was in a Nigerian church in London on my way to France. The service went on for hours and hours and hours (and I actually missed my train to Paris). But something unique happened there that's worth noting. I call it the power of blessing prayer.

I had laid hands on about one thousand people and I was exhausted. At the end of the service, the young pastor instructed everyone to hold up their hands in my direction and say, "I bless you. I bless you. I bless you." This went on for several minutes and I literally felt the power of these blessings come over my life and rest on me. I felt like there was a blessing forcefield around me that held the enemy at bay.

To bless essentially means to speak well of. When God first blessed mankind, He did it with words. Genesis 1:28 reads, "Then God blessed them, and God said to them, 'Be fruitful and multiply; fill the earth and subdue it; have dominion over the fish of the sea, over the birds of the air, and over every living thing that moves on the earth.'"

The blessing of the Lord makes a person rich, and He adds no sorrow with it (see Prov. 10:22). Paul revealed by the Holy Spirit that we are blessed with every spiritual blessing in heavenly places (see Eph. 1:3). Jesus said, "Blessed are the peacemakers, for they shall be called sons of God" (Matt. 5:9).

There are certain things we can do to activate God's blessing in our lives, but there are also things we can say to release blessings. The words, "I bless you" are powerful. Bless yourself. Bless the Lord. Bless your city. Bless your school. Bless your employer. Bless your enemies. When you sow blessings, I believe you reap blessings. Be an intercessor of blessing and watch how God moves through your prayers.

— *Prayer* —

Father, in the name of Jesus, I bless You. I bless myself. I bless the work of my hands. Father, would You bless me indeed? Would You bless me with a spirit of prayer. Would You help me to always bless those who curse me?

JULY 9

Interceding With the Mind of Christ

"For 'who has known the mind of the Lord that he may instruct Him?' But we have the mind of Christ" (1 Corinthians 2:16).

Intercessors, it's critical that we tap into the mind of Christ as we pray. After all, He is the Chief Intercessor. We take our cues from Him. He is the Captain of the Hosts. He has the battle plan.

Have you ever wondered what it means to have the mind of Christ? *Barnes Notes on the Bible* defines the mind of Christ as "the views, feelings, and temper of Christ." And, of course, we know Christ has the mind of God.

The Greek word for mind in 1 Corinthians 2:16 is "nouse." According to *The KJV New Testament Greek Lexicon*, it means, "the mind, comprising alike the faculties of perceiving and understanding and those of feeling, judging, determining; the intellectual faculty, the understanding." When we pray, we want to pray with His judgment, His determinations as to how things should be, and with an understanding of His feelings on the matter.

The Greek word for mind also means, "reason in the narrower sense, as the capacity for spiritual truth, the higher powers of the soul, the faculty of perceiving divine things, of recognizing goodness and of hating evil." When we pray, we want to tap into His reasoning, not our own. We want to intercede according to spiritual truth and perceptions of His divine will to pray in the good and push back the evil.

The Greek word for mind also means, "the power of considering and judging soberly, calmly and impartially" and "particular mode of thinking and judging, i.e thoughts, feelings, purposes, desires." When we intercede, we want to have a sober mind no matter how difficult the assignment. We want to leave our opinions out of the mix and press into His purposes and desires in serious intercession.

How do we access the mind of Christ? The Word reveals His will, His emotions, His thoughts and His ways. The Word and the Spirit who inspired the Word will give you access to Christ's mind.

— *Prayer* —

Father, in the name of Jesus, thank You for giving me access to the mind of Christ, the intercessor. You have not left me to figure out things on my own but You have given me Your Word as a lamp to my feet.

The Noisy Intercessor

"Attend to me, and hear me; I am restless in my complaint, and moan noisily"
(Psalm 55:2).

Nineteenth Century American missionary Adoniram Judson once said, "God loves importunate prayer so much that He will not give us much blessing without it." What a thought!

Jesus taught about importunity in prayer. Importune means to press or urge with troublesome persistence or to request urgently. We are importunate intercessors when we ask and keep on asking (see Matt. 7:7-8). We are importunate intercessors when we ask day and night like the widow in Luke 18. We are importunate intercessors when we won't give up. We are importunate intercessors when we act like the man in Luke 11: 5-8:

"Which of you shall have a friend, and go to him at midnight and say to him, 'Friend, lend me three loaves; for a friend of mine has come to me on his journey, and I have nothing to set before him'; and he will answer from within and say, 'Do not trouble me; the door is now shut, and my children are with me in bed; I cannot rise and give to you'? I say to you, though he will not rise and give to him because he is his friend, yet because of his persistence he will rise and give him as many as he needs."

The great man of prayer E.M. Bounds has some poignant thoughts on importunity Jesus described: "What a study in importunity, in earnestness, in persistence, promoted and propelled under conditions which would have disheartened any but a heroic, constant soul," he said.

"[Jesus] teaches that an answer to prayer is conditional upon the amount of faith that goes to the petition. To test this, He delays the answer. The superficial pray-er subsides into silence when the answer is delayed. But the man of prayer hangs on, and on. The Lord recognizes and honors his faith, and gives him a rich and abundant answer to His faith evidencing, importunate prayer."

— *Prayer* —

Father, in the name of Jesus, would You help me catch the revelation in the parables Jesus offered about importune prayer? Would You help me remember the value of consistent, persistent petitions?

Putting a Demand on God's Ability

"No, someone has made a demand on my ability" (Luke 8:46).

God is all powerful, and we access that power through prayer. We put a demand on that ability through intercession. Luke illustrates this point in his Gospel account of the woman with the issue of blood. We find it in Luke 8:43-48:

"Now a woman, having a flow of blood for twelve years, who had spent all her livelihood on physicians and could not be healed by any, came from behind and touched the border of His garment. And immediately her flow of blood stopped. And Jesus said, 'Who touched Me?'

"When all denied it, Peter and those with him said, 'Master, the multitudes throng and press You, and You say, Who touched Me?' But Jesus said, 'Somebody touched Me, for I perceived power going out from Me.'

"Now when the woman saw that she was not hidden, she came trembling; and falling down before Him, she declared to Him in the presence of all the people the reason she had touched Him and how she was healed immediately. And He said to her, 'Daughter, be of good cheer; your faith has made you well. Go in peace.'"

The Twentieth Century Translation says, "No, someone has made a demand on my ability." God's ability is far greater than our ability but nothing is impossible to the one who releases believing prayer. In his book *In Your Presence*, E.W. Kenyon offered insight into this moment:

"There cannot be any touching of the Master without the Master knowing it. When need touches Him, it makes a demand upon His ability to meet that need; and prayer is the way in which we touch Him. Prayer keeps man in close contact with the Father and with the Word. It is a constant communion with the Father and it enriches one spiritually. It illumines the Word, and illumines the mind; and it freshens and heals the body."

— *Prayer* —

Father, in the name of Jesus, would You give me a revelation of how able and willing You are to release Your power into the circumstances about which I am praying? Help me to humbly put a demand on Your ability.

Teaching Children to Pray

"Train up a child in the way he should go, and when he is old he will not depart from it"
(Proverbs 22:6).

Jesus spoke about having child-like faith, and who better to pray with child-like faith than a child who knows Jesus? We can and should teach children to pray—even before they know how to speak. We should include them in our family prayer time. Even if they don't understand yet what is happening in their minds, their spirits can agree.

Adopt the Isaiah 54:13 mentality: "All your children shall be taught by the Lord, and great shall be the peace of your children." Before they can even speak, they can worship and praise. This is the beginning of the prayer education in practice. Read them Bible stories about prayer and prayer answers. Play the Word of God in their room at night while they sleep. All this feeds their spirits.

When they get a little older, teach your children that prayer is talking to God—it's a conversation with a loving heavenly Father they can't see. Teach them how to pray for simple things with a heart of thanksgiving. Teach them to say grace over their meals and to pray God's blessings over the people they love before they go to bed at night. Teach them there's nothing too big or small to bring to God and that He already knows everything even before we tell Him.

Teach them to forgive and to receive the forgiveness of God. Teach them that they can go to God with anything in prayer and He hears them. Teach them that He cares about the things that concern them. Teach them *The Lord's Prayer*. Beyond this, teach them the value of intercession from a young age. Teach them the rewards of selfless prayer, of standing in the gap for others, especially lost souls.

Finally, teach them they can pray anywhere from their heart—that they don't have to wait until bedtime. And teach them that God may answer prayers in ways they don't expect because He knows best. Teach them to look for the prayer answers and to always give Him the glory.

— *Prayer* —

Father, in the name of Jesus, I want to be a good role model for little children,
whether mine or others. Help me be mindful to teach and model prayer and
intercession for another generation of prayer warriors.

JULY 13

Judgy Prayers

"For judgment will be merciless to one who has shown no mercy; mercy triumphs over judgment" (James 2:13).

Intercessors should have the heart of the Chief Intercessor, Jesus Christ. But it's easy enough to slip into a critical spirit and judge those who come to you for prayer, especially when you've counseled them and prayed with them only to see them continuing down the wrong path.

Paul warned, "Who are you to judge another's servant? To his own master he stands or falls. Indeed, he will be made to stand, for God is able to make him stand" (Rom. 14:4). And James said, "If you criticize and judge each other, then you are criticizing and judging God's law. But your job is to obey the law, not to judge whether it applies to you" (James 4:11, NLT).

There may be no worse type of intercession than judgmental intercession because it does not represent the Saviour's heart. Mercy triumphs over judgment (see James 2:13). Judgmental intercessors pray with a critical heart instead of the heart of the Father. Jesus said, "Hypocrite! First remove the plank from your own eye, and then you will see clearly to remove the speck from your brother's eye" (Matt. 7:5).

At times, we've all had to guard our hearts from judging those He's called us to pray for. We may be called to intercede for people groups that have caused our generations great harm or to pray for someone who has accused us and abused us. When God assigns us to such tasks, He's giving us an opportunity to be more like Jesus. Let's lay our judgement aside.

Remember, Jesus said, "Judge not, that you be not judged. For with what judgment you judge, you will be judged; and with the measure you use, it will be measured back to you. And why do you look at the speck in your brother's eye, but do not consider the plank in your own eye?" (Matt. 7:1-4). Let's get the plank of judgment out of our eye before we pray.

— *Prayer* —

Father, in the name of Jesus, would You show me if there is a speck in my eye? Would You help me rid myself of a judgmental spirit? I don't want to move in judgment. I want to move in mercy like my heavenly Father.

Dead-Raising Intercessors

"And he stretched himself out on the child three times, and cried out to the Lord and said, 'O Lord my God, I pray, let this child's soul come back to him'" (1 Kings 17:21).

The Spirit that raised Christ from the dead dwells in us. We have resurrection power in us that we can release through prayer. Jesus said, "And as you go, preach, saying, 'The kingdom of heaven is at hand.' Heal the sick, cleanse the lepers, raise the dead, cast out demons. Freely you have received, freely give" (Matt. 10:7-8).

We see dead raisings over and over in Scripture. Jesus raised the widow of Nain's son from the dead with a few words (see Luke 7:11-17). He also raised Lazarus from the dead and a ruler's daughter from the dead. Peter raised Dorcas from the dead (see Acts 9:32-43). Paul raised a young man from the dead who fell out of a window while he was preaching (Acts 20:7-12).

But the dead raising started before Jesus walked the earth and before the disciples were baptized in the Holy Spirit. Elijah raised a widow's son from the dead (see 2 Kings 4:18-37). Elisha raised the son of the Shunamite woman from the dead (see 2 Kings 13:21). And a dead man came back to life when grave diggers threw him on top of Elisha's bones.

The Holy Spirit that raised Jesus from the dead is still in the dead-raising business. I believe this miracle is not only up to those with the faith to raise the dead that lay before them. I believe it's also up to nameless faceless intercessors who will pray for resurrection power to work through those who have the boldness to raise the dead.

While it's always up to God whether or not He chooses to raise people from the dead, I believe we might see more dead raisings in the earth today if we understood and released resurrection power through our intercession.

— *Prayer* —

Father, in the name of Jesus, would You give me the faith to release dead-raising prayers? Help me stand in fervent intercession for those who are bold enough to believe You can raise the dead like You did in the days of Elijah, Jesus and Paul. You are the same yesterday, today and forever.

The James Fraser Prayer Anointing

"Praying always with all prayer and supplication in the Spirit, being watchful to this end with all perseverance and supplication for all the saints" (Ephesians 6:18).

You may have never heard of James Fraser, but rest assured heaven and hell knows his name. Fraser was a praying missionary to the Lisu People. The Lisu People is an ethnic group that live in mountainous regions of Asia, such as Myanmar, China and Thailand. You may have never heard of the Lisu People, but God knows them well.

Fraser walked the earth from 1886 to 1938 as part of Hudson Taylor's China Inland Mission. You are probably more familiar with the name Hudson Taylor. Taylor was a British missionary who spent 51 years in China. He brought over 800 missionaries into China and started 125 schools.

Taylor's ministry is credited with 18,000 conversions, which may seem like a small number when compared to Reinhard Bonnke's millions in Africa, but if you consider the times and the spiritual climate in China, the number is more than impressive. Like Charles Finney in America years later, Taylor depended on intercessory prayer to back up his evangelistic efforts. Fraser obliged.

According to BDCC, "His letters home increasingly included more and more details of his efforts to spread the Gospel, the results, and the fierce spiritual opposition, including the sin in his own heart and the fierce attacks of Satan. He began to call more and more upon his friends at home to join him in disciplined, fervent intercessory prayer, believing their work was just as necessary as his. This became the main theme of his missionary communications for years to come."

Fraser learned to pray and to war for converts. He discovered quickly how to walk in Ephesians 6:18: "Praying always with all prayer and supplication in the Spirit, being watchful to this end with all perseverance and supplication for all the saints." As BDCC tells it, "He spent hours, and sometimes entire days, on his knees, begging God to deliver the Lisu—and himself—from the deceitful lies of Satan and from the destructive power of evil spirits."

— Prayer —

Father, in the name of Jesus, would You give me an anointing to pray with all prayer and supplication in the Spirit, persevering even to the point of falling to my knees for hours and days to break through the lies of the enemy?

God Won't Do Your Part

"Therefore the Lord will wait, that He may be gracious to you; And therefore He will be exalted, that He may have mercy on you" (Isaiah 30:18).

It's been said we can't do God's part, but God won't do our part. What is our part? Well, if we are to believe the words of John Wesley, founder of the Methodist movement, "God does nothing but in answer to prayer; and even they who have been converted to God without praying for it themselves, (which is exceeding rare) were not without the prayers of others. Every new victory which a soul gains is the effect of a new prayer."

God knows what we need before we ask and, in His sovereignty, has prepared the answer before we ask because He knows we are going to ask. But most of the time, we still must ask. The asking, praying, and knocking are our part. At times, we don't have because we don't ask.

Twentieth Century American missionary Dr. E. Stanley Jones takes this one step further, "In prayer you align yourselves to the purpose and power of God and He is able to do things through you that He couldn't do otherwise. For this is an open universe, where some things are left open, contingent upon our doing them. If we do not do them, they will never be done. For God has left certain things open to prayer—things which will never be done except as we pray."

Imagine what God hasn't done in your life because you did not ask. Again, this aligns with what James, the apostle of practical faith, taught us in his epistle: "You do not have because you do not ask" (James 4:2). *The Contemporary English Version* of this verse puts it this way: "But you still cannot get what you want, and you won't get it by fighting and arguing. You should pray for it."

Although Jesus is seated at the right hand of the Father making intercession for you, you still have to come into agreement with that intercession through prayer. Let's do our part. Let's pray.

— Prayer —

Father, in the name of Jesus, would You give me the grace to lift every need up in prayer, knowing that You are anticipating my cries and You are ready to give me what I need? Every victory comes through prayer.

Your Inner Life

"Behold, You desire truth in the inward parts..." (Psalm 51:6).

Intercessors, you have two lives. You have a life everyone sees and a life no one but you and God sees. Your outer life—how you live, work and pray publicly—is how others see you. Your inner life is how God sees you. We may be able to hide what's on our mind and our emotional state from others, but we can't hide it from God—and we shouldn't try.

The intercessor's inner life is critical to his intercession. If your thoughts are amiss, your prayers may be amiss. If your inner life is restless, you may find it difficult to engage in listening prayer. If you have hidden motives in prayer, your intercession won't move God. God wants truth in the inward parts (see Ps. 51:6).

Paul delighted in the law of God in his inner life, which is one reason his expression of intercession was so powerful (see Rom. 7:22). David put it this way, "Lord, who may abide in Your tabernacle? Who may dwell in Your holy hill? He who walks uprightly, and works righteousness, and speaks the truth in his heart" (Ps. 15:1-2).

Peter wrote these Spirit-inspired words, "Do not let your adornment be merely outward—arranging the hair, wearing gold, or putting on fine apparel—rather let it be the hidden person of the heart, with the incorruptible beauty of a gentle and quiet spirit, which is very precious in the sight of God" (1 Pet. 3:3-4).

So, let me ask you a reflective question: How's your inner life? What goes on in that mind of yours that you wouldn't want anyone to know? Those may be the little foxes that spoil your prayer vine. If we are going to pray with power—if we are going to pray effectively—we need to tend not just to our prayer life but our inner life. Ask God to help you clean up your inner life.

— Prayer —

Father, in the name of Jesus, would You help me clean up my inner life? Would You help me to think about what I am thinking about so I can submit wrong thoughts to Your Word and thereby renew my mind?

The Abraham Prayer Anointing

"Then Abram fell on his face, and God talked with him" (Genesis 17:3).

Abraham was a man of prayer. While his most memorable prayer may be his intercession to save the righteous in wicked Sodom and Gomorrah, we find his prayer life went well beyond that striking encounter. Abraham wasn't called a friend of God for nothing, and you don't become a friend of God without a strong prayer life.

"When we study Abraham's character, we find that after his call to go out into an unknown country, on his journey with his family and his household servants, wherever he tarried by the way for the night or longer, he always erected an altar, and 'called upon the name of the Lord,'" E.M. Bounds wrote in his classic book *Prayer and Praying Men.*

"And this man of faith and prayer was one of the first to erect a family altar, around which to gather his household and offer the sacrifices of worship, of praise and of prayer. These altars built by Abraham were, first of all, essentially altars about which he gathered his household, as distinguished from secret prayer."

At times, Abraham fell on his face and God would talk to him (see Gen. 17:1-3). Abraham prayed for the king who took Sarai into his harem—and his prayer broke the barrenness off the women in the king's camp (see Gen. 20:17). Abraham prayed for Ishmael in Gen. 17:18: "Oh, that Ishmael might live before You!"

Abraham was not a perfect man. Twice he lied about Sarai being his sister. Once he allowed Lot to come with him on a prophetic pilgrimage even though God told him to leave his family behind. But God is not looking for perfect intercessors. He's looking for intercessors who are willing to be perfected. The Abraham prayer anointing is an anointing to talk to God like a man talks to His friend, without compromising the fear of the Lord.

— *Prayer* —

Father, in the name of Jesus, would You teach me how to walk and talk with You the way Abraham walked and talked with You? I want to cultivate that friendship and pray from that place of knowing that I always have Your ear.

JULY 19

The Intercessor's Reward

"For the Son of Man will come in the glory of His Father with His angels, and then He will reward each according to his works" (Matthew 16:27).

I am convinced that some of the greatest rewards in eternity will go to the nameless, faceless intercessors who stand in the gap and weep in their prayer closets over cities and souls. Intercessors see a certain measure of reward in this lifetime through answered prayer, but eternal rewards have an eternal significance.

Scripture speaks of the reality of eternal rewards over and again. James said, "Blessed is the man who endures temptation; for when he has been approved, he will receive the crown of life which the Lord has promised to those who love Him" (James 1:12). Jeremiah understood God will "give everyone according to his ways and according to the fruit of his doings" (Jer. 32:19).

And Jesus Himself spoke of eternal rewards in the Book of Revelation. "And behold, I am coming quickly, and My reward is with Me, to give to every one according to his work. I am the Alpha and the Omega, the Beginning and the End, the First and the Last. Blessed are those who do His commandments, that they may have the right to the tree of life, and may enter through the gates into the city" (Revelation 12:12-14).

So what are these eternal rewards? There's the victor's crown (see 1 Cor. 9:25-27); the crown of rejoicing (see 1Thess. 2:19); the crown of righteousness (see 2 Tim. 4:8); the crown of life (see Rev. 2:10); the crown of glory (see 1 Pet. 5:4).

Then there's access to the tree of life (see Rev. 2:7); hidden manna and a new name (see Rev. 2:17); authority over nations, the morning star and vindication (see Rev. 2:27); God's name written on you (see Rev. 3:12); and a seat on the throne (see Rev. 3:21).

— *Prayer* —

Father, in the name of Jesus, help me keep in mind that my intercession is making an eternal impact on people's lives, and even cities and nations. Help me keep the eternal rewards in mind when I begin to grow weary.

Pray Everywhere

"I desire therefore that the men pray everywhere, lifting up holy hands, without wrath and doubting" (1 Timothy 2:8).

Some may wonder, "Where is the best place to pray? Where is the best place for our prayer closet? Is it in a den? Is it in a literal closet? Is it in the corner of a room set apart for devotional studies and intercession? Is it in the car or at the church? Is it on a mountain top or at the dinner table before meals?"

Paul suggested that we should pray everywhere. Yes, there are times to pray in seclusion with just you and the Holy Spirit. There are times to pray in church under the corporate anointing. But you can pray anywhere and everywhere—and you should. Praying everywhere means praying in every place you find yourself.

I pray in the shower for protection over my day. I pray while cleaning my house for souls and nations. I pray in the grocery store for ripe avocados (that are not too ripe). I pray for my family while I'm exercising. I pray on airplanes for the plans and purposes of God. I pray in hotel rooms over the assignment God has given me. I pray on the phone with friends.

Praying everywhere means praying in every place. When Paul said, "Pray without ceasing" (see 1 Thess. 5:17) that suggests praying anywhere and everywhere about anything and everything as needs arise. It's part of redeeming the time. When Paul said, "praying at all times in the Spirit, with all prayer and supplication" (see Eph. 6:18) it also suggests praying everywhere as you can't pray at all times if you relegate prayer to your secret place only.

Praying everywhere can also connotate praying in any spiritual condition. Pray when you are joyful and pray when you are grieving. Pray when you are on the mountain top and pray when you are in the valley; when you are sick and when you are well; when you are prospering and when you are in lack; when you are at peace and when you are anxious. Pray everywhere.

— Prayer —

Father, in the name of Jesus, remind me to pray everywhere—in every place. Help me to redeem the time by lifting up praise, petitions, supplications, and intercession to You when the need arises no matter where I am.

The Confident Intercessor

"Now this is the confidence that we have in Him, that if we ask anything according to His will, He hears us" (1 John 5:14).

A confident intercessor is an intercessor filled with faith. If you don't have faith that God hears you when you pray, you won't be confident that the answer is on its way.

Confidence is the state of being certain. The Greek word for confidence in 1 John 5:14 is "parrhesia." One definition of parrhesia is "freedom in speaking, unreservedness in speech" and "without ambiguity," according to *The KJV New Testament Greek Lexicon.*

When we make intercession, we should feel free to speak without reservation to our heavenly Father. We don't need to beat around the bush or be ambiguous. God already knows how we feel about the issue, what we need Him to do and how He will answer the prayer. He wants us to have confidence that He hears and answers before we release our intercession.

The Amplified translation of 1 John 5:14 really spells out the deeper meaning of this verse, which should build our faith: "This is the [remarkable degree of] confidence which we [as believers are entitled to] have before Him: that] if we ask anything according to His will, [that is, consistent with His plan and purpose] He hears us" (1 John 5:14, AMP)

Parrhesia also means "free and fearless confidence, cheerful courage, boldness, assurance." When we come to the throne of grace, God invites us to come with confidence in His open-door policy. He wants us to come with cheerful courage knowing that He delights in the prayers of the righteous (see Prov. 5:8). He wants us to come boldly, with assurance that He will receive us.

The writer of Hebrews tells us, "Do not, therefore, fling away your [fearless] confidence, for it has a glorious and great reward" (Heb. 3:10-35). God wants us to be confident when we approach Him to intercede and then, after we've prayed, to remain confident that He is working.

— *Prayer* —

Father, in the name of Jesus, would You help me build confidence in Your
faithfulness, Your goodness, Your mercy, Your power and Your willingness to
hear and answer my prayers?

The People-Group Intercessor

"Then Peter opened his mouth and said: 'In truth I perceive that God shows no partiality'"
(Acts 10:34).

Just as God calls some intercessors to pray for churches or leaders or governments or sectors of society, God calls other intercessors to take on the burden of intercession for specific people groups. You may not have heard that term, but you can quickly grasp the concept.

A people group is a significantly large sociological grouping of individuals who perceive themselves to have a common affinity with one another, according to the Lausanne Movement. Oftentimes people are grouped by language (tongue), or by a cultural affinity (tribe) or nationality (nation). Jesus is after them all (see Rev. 7:9).

Some say there are as many as 24,000 people groups. Some say as few as 13,000. Regardless of what metric you use, there are thousands of people groups and they all need intercession. Of course, you are not called to intercede for them all but if you walk with the Lord long enough He is likely to put a people group on your heart at some point, perhaps in response to a tragedy in the earth.

Everyone——including you——is part of a people group. The Kurds of Turkey, Iran and Iraq are a people group. A people group is a generation, such as Gen Z. People groups can be a language, such as Spanish-speakers, who live all over the world. India is home to many people groups called castes, even if they speak the same language.

Religion divides people into groups, such as Muslims, Mormons, Buddhists, Hindus and the like. Socio-economic status can divine people into people groups, as well as race and ethnicity. People groups, again, aren't always about nationalities but about deeper identities based on many factors.

Prayer evangelism may target people groups. God is not willing that any should perish. God wants us to lift up lost souls in unreached people groups so they will bow a knee to Jesus in this age unto salvation instead of bowing when it's too late in the age to come.

— *Prayer* —

Father, in the name of Jesus, I am willing to stand in the gap for a people group that You want to assign me. I am willing to make intercession that reaches into the darkest corners of the earth. Here I am. Use me.

JULY 23

Praying the Scary Prayers

"There is no fear in love; but perfect love casts out fear, because fear involves torment. But he who fears has not been made perfect in love" (1 John 4:8).

Scary prayers. What in the world are scary prayers? I heard someone talk about praying the "scary prayers" some years ago and I was curious. Soon, I found myself praying in agreement with prayers too many Christians are too scared to pray.

Scary prayers aren't prayers you pray when you are scared. Here's my definition of scary prayers: Prayers that call on God to help us crucify our flesh, mortify the deeds of our body, purify our hearts, work in us patience and produce a soul that seeks to walk in humility. They are scary prayers because we may not be quite sure what we'll have to go through to see the answer. But we know we will have to change.

Here are some examples of the scary prayers: Father, help me deny myself, pick up my cross and follow You (see Matt. 16:24). God, help me discipline my body and mortify my flesh (see 1 Cor. 9:27). Father, help me to die to my own wants and needs and live for Your purposes alone (see Rom. 14:7). Help me present my body as a living sacrifice (see Rom. 12:1).

Are you getting the picture? Are you praying them with me? Let's continue. The scary prayers sound like this: Father, deliver me from my haughty ways and clothe me with humility (see 1 Pet. 5:5). Father, not my will but Yours be done (see Luke 22:24). Father, conform me into the image of Christ (see Rom. 8:29). Father, examine my heart to see if there is any wicked way in me (see Ps. 139:24).

Often, when I am led to pray prayers like this on my *Mornings with the Holy Spirit* broadcast, the next day's prayer broadcast sees major corporate breakthrough. There's something about a surrendered intercessor who is not afraid to abandon themselves to God for the sake of His work in the earth. When you pray scary prayers, He will work through you in astounding ways.

— *Prayer* —

Father, in the name of Jesus, help me get over the fear of praying the scary prayers. Help me understand my need to crucify my flesh so I won't be tempted to put down my cross. Give me the grace to live a fasted lifestyle so I can release holy prayer power.

JULY 24
Breaking Intercessory Intimidation

"For God has not given us a spirit of fear, but of power and of love and of a sound mind"
(2 Timothy 1:7).

Many young intercessors are intimidated by the authority or eloquence of more seasoned intercessors. That intimidation makes them bold in the prayer closet but timid in the corporate prayer meeting. I know what that feels like because I came up in the Lord with intercessors who could pray heaven down.

Rosalind Rinker, author of *Prayer: How to Have a Conversation with God*, can relate. She was afraid to pray publicly when she started out also: "Faster and faster my heart went," she wrote. "The person who had been praying for some time stopped. There was silence. No. No. No! I couldn't break it. Let someone else do it."

So what do you do if you have a prayer block? You may pray the house down in your closet at home, but when called upon to pray with two or three—or more—you hesitate. Something in you pauses. You freeze up on the inside. And then you are disappointed with yourself later because you know the Lord wanted you to make intercession. What do you do?

Rinker got over it and so did I. Today, prayer flows from my spirit like a Holy Ghost river. I might not be as eloquent as others, but the heartfelt supplications and warfare declarations carry power in His name. Yours can, too, when you refuse to be intimidated by another person's gift.

Root fear of man out of your life. Ultimately, this is a fear issue. There are many types of fears and phobias. If you're typically not fearful in most situations, the fear of man is likely at the root of your public prayerlessness.

You may be comparing yourself to others and decide inwardly that you are not as equipped or as powerful. You may be concerned about people judging you as inadequate in intercession. I assure you, most believers are not critiquing your public prayer. Ask the Lord to deliver you from the fear of man, which brings a snare (Prov. 29:25).

— Prayer —

Father, in the name of Jesus, deliver me from the fear of man. I want to pray in faith, not in a cloud of fear or intimidation or comparison. I want to pray corporately, not only alone. I want to voice the intercessions You have put in my heart boldly. Help me to pray like it's just You and me in the room.

JULY 25

Praying With a Priestly Anointing

"We will rejoice in your salvation, and in the name of our God we will set up our banners! May the Lord fulfill all your petitions" (Psalm 20:5).

Jesus is the High Priest of our confession. Of course, He is both King and Priest, but it's an important distinction. When we operate as a priest in prayer, we are making intercession from a different anointing than when we operate as a king in prayer.

A priestly anointing offers petitions to God. A priestly anointing makes requests known to God. A priestly anointing engages in worship to God. A priestly anointing carries great compassion for the ones for whom they are interceding. Consider Hebrews 4:14-16:

"Seeing then that we have a great High Priest who has passed through the heavens, Jesus the Son of God, let us hold fast our confession. For we do not have a High Priest who cannot sympathize with our weaknesses, but was in all points tempted as we are, yet without sin. Let us therefore come boldly to the throne of grace, that we may obtain mercy and find grace to help in time of need."

When we pray with a priestly anointing, we are coming boldly to the throne of grace to find answers to problems, God's power to intervene, wisdom, grace and more. When Paul spoke of praying at all times in the spirit, with all prayer and supplication for all the saints, he was describing the priestly anointing (see Eph. 6:18).

When Daniel prayed three times a day, he was making petitions with a priestly anointing (see Dan. 6:13). A petition is a request made to an authority—it's a call for change, it's an earnest plea, it's a formal and sometimes urgent request to the courts of heaven.

The priestly anointing is critical to intercession, as you are standing in the gap for another person. You are acting like Jesus, the Chief Intercessor and High Priest, in prayer. Jesus is seated at the right hand of the Father even now, making intercession for us (see Rom. 8:34).

— Prayer —

Father, in the name of Jesus, would You help me understand when to step into the priestly anointing in prayer? Would You teach me to stand like Jesus with His compassion for people in intercession?

JULY 26

Reigning In Prayer as a King

"But you are a chosen generation, a royal priesthood, a holy nation, His own special people, that you may proclaim the praises of Him who called you out of darkness into His marvelous light"
(1 Peter 2:9).

Believers have a duality of standing in the role of both kings and priests. Jesus is King of kings—we are the kings. Revelation 1:6 says He has made us "kings and priests to His God and Father."

Paul told us, "For if by one man's trespass death reigned through him, then how much more will those who receive abundance of grace and the gift of righteousness reign in life through the One, Jesus Christ" (Rom. 5:17). And Peter said, "But you are a chosen race, a royal priesthood, a holy nation, a people for God's own possession, so that you may declare the goodness of Him who has called you out of darkness into His marvelous light" (1 Pet. 2:9).

Jesus is the King of kings. Since you are in Him, you are a king and carry authority in the name of the King. Historically, many intercessors have stood in the role of a priest, praying vertically to God for their needs and the needs of others. But there are times when we need to stand in the kindly anointing.

Dutch Sheets once put it this way, "As Holy Spirit reemphasizes these prophetic words and Scriptures to me, I sense that He is calling His ekklesia to step fully into our responsibility for kingly intercession. The Lord is calling us to shift from merely petitioning the Father, to also making decrees (official orders, edicts or decisions), declarations (announcements or formal statements) and proclamations (the process of binding and loosing) as we are prophetically inspired by Holy Spirit to do so."

As King, Jesus has all authority in heaven and on earth (see Matt. 28:18). He carries the name that is above all names (see Phil. 2:9-11). The government rests on the King's shoulders (see Is. 9:6). When we stand as kings in intercession, we are executing the King's will. We are governing in the earth through prayer.

— *Prayer* —

Father, in the name of Jesus, would You give me the revelation of the kingly anointing? Would You teach me how to stand as a king in intercession, using the keys of the Kingdom to bind, loose and execute your will in the earth?

JULY 27

The Breath of Your Spiritual Life

"The Spirit of God has made me, and the breath of the Almighty gives me life"
(Job 33:4).

In the beginning, God formed man from the dust of the earth and breathed into his nostrils the breath of life. Man became a living creature (see Gen. 2:7). But that isn't the last time we see God's breath at work in our lives.

Just as God's breath caused man to come alive, God breathes on us to empower us. God's breath empowers us for prayer and, indeed, some say God sees prayer as the breath of our spiritual life.

"If we think prayer is something we do only in dignified ceremonies or desperate emergencies we have missed its values. We treat prayer as though it was the spice of life but the Bible prescribes it as a vital staple in our diet," David Hubbard, author of *The Practice of Prayer*, wrote.

"We are content with a dash of praise, a pinch of petition, a drop of confession to bring a slight spiritual flavor to our secularity. We sprinkle a shake or two of the supernatural over our basic humanism and call the mixture religion. But God sees prayer as the breath of spiritual life."

Jesus breathed on His disciples and said, "Receive the Holy Spirit," (see John 20:22). The Holy Spirit is the spirit of prayer. The Holy Spirit is the one who helps us pray when don't know how. The Holy Spirit is the one who prays the perfect prayer because He knows the perfect will of the Father.

Prayer is, indeed, the breath of our spiritual life. It is how our souls and our spirits communicate with His heart. The breath of the Almighty helps us understand what we ought to pray (see Job. 32:8). We need more than a dash or a pinch or a drop. We need more than a shake of the supernatural. We need the breath of life continually.

— *Prayer* —

Father, in the name of Jesus, would You breathe on me again, empowering me to pray without ceasing? Would You help me treat prayer like the very breath of my life and breathe prayers that honor Your purposes in the earth?

Are You Listening, Really?

"Listen to counsel and receive instruction, that you may be wise in your latter days"
(Proverbs 19:20).

Listening prayer is counterintuitive to many intercessors. After all, isn't prayer about petitioning God? Indeed, it is but intercession is more than asking, seeking and knocking. Intercession is also about listening.

The problem is, in our fervency sometimes we're not as effective as we could be because we don't stop to listen for His instruction or His response. Sometimes, we don't let God get a word in edgewise. We are not careful how we listen (see Luke 8:18).

Jesus said His sheep know His voice. I believe God is speaking to us more than we are hearing Him. We need to expect Him to speak to us. If we don't expect Him to speak, He may be speaking but we're not alert enough in the spirit to hear Him. Think about it this way. If you are not expecting someone to come to your house, you may not hear them knock on the door. You'll miss the visit. If we don't expect God to speak—to move—we could miss our visitation.

It's one thing to expect God to speak to you and to hear Him. It's another thing to walk in a listening attitude. Sometimes we're not hearing Him—sometimes He's silent—because we're not asking the right questions. Other times we're not hearing Him because we're not really listening.

You may have to wait on the Lord a while before you hear anything, especially if you are tense and distracted. When He speaks, you're going to want to write down what the Lord is saying to you for the sake of memory and accuracy. This is part of "being careful how you listen."

If you want to hear from God more clearly, spend more time with Him and His Word. Knowing the Word guards us from deception and your knowledge of the Word will make your prayer more effective. There are many voices in the realm of the spirit. If you seek voices, the devil will oblige. If you seek God, He will speak.

— *Prayer* —

Father, in the name of Jesus, would You help me tune my ear to Your voice? Help me to pay attention and listen carefully for Your voice. Help me wait on You to speak sound wisdom before I move into or out of intercession.

JULY 29

Writing History With Your Prayers

"Now Esther spoke again to the king, fell down at his feet, and implored him with tears to counteract the evil of Haman the Agagite, and the scheme which he had devised against the Jews" (Esther 8:3).

If you are an intercessor—a believing intercessor—history is in your hands. I know that's hard to believe, but Scripture validates the notion. You may have heard it said, "History belongs to the intercessors."

Although he may not have been the first to say it, I've traced this revelation back to Walter Wink, who wrote the award-winning trilogy: *Naming the Powers*, *Unmasking the Powers*, and *Engaging the Powers*. Wink's statement may have been taken out of context, as he qualified the type of intercessor who holds history in his hands.

"History belongs to the intercessors who believe the future into being. Even a small number of people, firmly committed to the new inevitability on which they have fixed their imaginations, can decisively affect the shape the future takes," he wrote. "These shapers of the future are the intercessors, who call out of the future the longed-for new present. In the New Testament, the name and texture and aura of that future is God's domination-free order, the reign of God."

Wink went on to say that intercession changes the world and it changes what is possible. God is always looking for an intercessor to get into agreement with His plans and purposes in the earth. He looked for man in the midst of Israel's captivity and found Daniel willing to intercede. He looked for a woman to save the Jews from Haman's wicked plot and found Esther willing to intercede.

"We have been commanded to command. We are required by God to haggle with God for the sake of the sick, the obsessed, the weak, and to conform our lives to our intercessions," Wink wrote. "This is a God who invents history in interaction with those 'who hunger and thirst to see right prevail' (Mat. 5:6, REB) … By means of our intercessions we veritably cast fire upon the earth and trumpet the future into being."

— *Prayer* —

Father, in the name of Jesus, would You help me see what a privilege it is to write history with my prayers? Help me see what a responsibility it is to make intercession so You can answer my petition and bring forth Your plans?

Praying for Your Pastor

"Meanwhile praying also for us, that God would open to us a door for the word, to speak the mystery of Christ, for which I am also in chains, that I may make it manifest, as I ought to speak" (Colossians 4:2-4).

Your pastor needs prayer. Many pastors leave the ministry altogether because of the stress and strain of standing in this office. Specifically, according to a survey from Lifeway Research, pastors leave because they feel a change in their calling (37%), because of conflict in the church (26%), because they are a poor fit for the congregation (13%), because of family issues (17%), moral or ethical issues (13%), burnout (10%), personal finances (8%), and illness (5%).

As you can see, pastors need prayer. Paul the apostle asked the churches to whom he wrote his epistles for prayer over and over again. And he was confident their prayers would help him in his mission. He once told the church at Philippi, "I know that through your prayers and the help of the Spirit of Jesus Christ this will turn out for my deliverance" (Phil. 1:19).

So what's the best way to pray for your pastor? Pray for wisdom and discernment. Pray for strength and health. Pray for strong relationships. Pray for the leader's family. Pray God would help the leader walk in the Word and the Spirit, and have the grace to obey Jesus. Pray against the enemy's plans for their life. Pray against discouragement. Pray for revelation and understanding. Pray for the ministry to be financially abounding. Pray for the pastor to know God's perfect will. Pray for boldness in the face of persecution.

Paul had specific prayer requests: "that utterance may be given to me, that I may open my mouth boldly to make known the mystery of the gospel, for which I am an ambassador in chains; that in it I may speak boldly, as I ought to speak" (Eph. 6:19-20). Paul also asked for prayer for deliverance from his enemies (see Rom. 15:30-32) and that God would open doors for him to do His will for his life (see Col. 4:2-4). Pray as led by the Spirit.

— *Prayer* —

Father, in the name of Jesus, would You give me a burden for my pastor? Would You grace me to help him in the natural and in the spirit by watching and praying over him and his family? I want to be a blessing to my leadership.

The Pro-Life Intercessor

"Before I formed you in the womb I knew you; Before you were born I sanctified you"
(Jeremiah 1:5).

Every intercessor should be pro-life because Christ, our Chief Intercessor, is the way, the truth and the life (see John 14:6). But some intercessors are pricked to the heart over pro-life issues, from the womb to the tomb.

The pro-life intercessor finds a continual flow of repentance coming from their hearts. We stand in identificational repentance for allowing abortion—the murder of innocent babies, murder and assisted suicide—to rage in our nations. We ask for forgiveness over complacency concerning these issues.

Because pro-life prayer can be a wearisome task—after all, intercession on the issue has been going forth since Roe v. Wade in 1973, making it an intergenerational campaign—we need to ask God to fill us with His love for the unborn so we can contend for them out of the passion of His heart.

But there's another angle to pro-life prayer. We need to pray the Lord will minister to terrified women who consider abortion because they are overwhelmed. We need to pray He will open the eyes of their hearts and help them see that He will provide for them if they choose life (see Eph. 1:18). We need to pray God will give these women a deep love for their unborn child.

We also need to pray the church will rise up and be willing to help women with unexpected pregnancies find alternatives to abortion, such as adoption (see Prov. 31:31; Is. 66:13). And we need to pray for the conviction of the Holy Spirit to fall upon every abortion doctor, nurse, administrator and others who have a hand in the murder of innocent babies so they can remove their foot from evil (see John 16:8).

Indeed, the pro-life intercessor's work is never done. Many nations are killing babies daily. And, again, pro-life goes beyond abortion. Stay strong.

— *Prayer* —

Father, in the name of Jesus, give me Your heart for the unborn. Help me not to grow weary in this battle, knowing that even if laws are changed women will find another way to find access to abortions.

AUGUST

"Be anxious for nothing, but in everything by prayer and supplication, with thanksgiving, let your requests be made known to God" (Philippians 4:6).

The Billy Graham Prayer Anointing

"For God so loved the world that He gave His only begotten Son, that whoever believes in Him should not perish but have everlasting life" (John 3:16).

Only God really knows how many people Billy Graham reached with the Gospel. But he may have reached even more through the power of prayer. Graham spent more time in the last years of his life making intercession than he did touring the world with the Good News.

James 5:16 (AMPC) tells us, "The earnest (heartfelt, continued) prayer of a righteous man makes tremendous power available [dynamic in its working]." Graham's prayers were heartfelt, continued and powerful. He understood the power of prayer.

Indeed, Cliff Barrows, a long-time musician and program director for Graham's ministry—once said, "When Billy Graham was asked about the most important steps in preparing for an evangelistic outreach, he always answered that there were three things that mattered most: Prayer, prayer and prayer."

Consider what the man of God had to say about prayer I discovered through the Billy Graham Library. "In the morning, prayer is the key that opens to us the treasures of God's mercies and blessings; in the evening, it is the key that shuts us up under His protection and safeguard." And, "True prayer is a way of life, not just for use in cases of emergency. Make it a habit, and when the need arises you will be in practice."

Graham also said, "We are to pray in times of adversity, lest we become faithless and unbelieving. We are to pray in times of prosperity, lest we become boastful and proud. We are to pray in times of danger, lest we become fearful and doubting. We are to pray in times of security, lest we become self-sufficient."

I always loved Graham's heart for prayer—and intercession. He prayed for presidents. He prayed for churches. He prayed for America in times of crisis. His son, Franklin, said he was mentally alert right up to the end. I have to believe he prayed right up to the end.

— *Prayer* —

Father, in the name of Jesus, would You give me an understanding of the power of prayer like You gave Billy Graham? Help me make prayer and intercession a priority for the sake of the Gospel. Help me never to become so self-sufficient that I fail to fall on my knees in prayer.

AUGUST 2

Prayers That Spill Into the Streets

"Peter and John went to the Temple one afternoon to take part in the three o'clock prayer service"
(Acts 3:1, NLT).

It's easy to stay focused on the prayer closet, but God wants your prayers to spill out into the streets. He wants to demonstrate that Jesus is alive. Peter and John were men of prayer—and you see how their prayer manifested in their daily walk. Look at Acts 3:1-10:

"Now Peter and John went up together to the temple at the hour of prayer, the ninth hour. And a certain man lame from his mother's womb was carried, whom they laid daily at the gate of the temple which is called Beautiful, to ask alms from those who entered the temple; who, seeing Peter and John about to go into the temple, asked for alms.

"And fixing his eyes on him, with John, Peter said, 'Look at us.' So he gave them his attention, expecting to receive something from them. Then Peter said, 'Silver and gold I do not have, but what I do have I give you: In the name of Jesus Christ of Nazareth, rise up and walk.' And he took him by the right hand and lifted him up, and immediately his feet and ankle bones received strength.

"So he, leaping up, stood and walked and entered the temple with them—walking, leaping, and praising God. And all the people saw him walking and praising God. Then they knew that it was he who sat begging alms at the Beautiful Gate of the temple; and they were filled with wonder and amazement at what had happened to him."

Notice how the apostles were on their way to a prayer meeting. The prayer power behind the scenes in the early church led to amazing signs and wonders. Peter and John walked in miracle ministries because their time in the prayer closet was a forerunner for signs and wonders. Yours can be too.

— Prayer —

Father, in the name of Jesus, would You give me a revelation of how deeply my private prayer life affects my public walk, talk and ministry? I want to live and move and have my being in Christ the Intercessor, and, like Him, destroy the works of darkness.

AUGUST 3

Doing Business With God

"Do business till I come" (Luke 19:13).

God is not transactional. He's relational. But that doesn't mean we don't do business with God. Prayer is the basis for bringing blessings down from the spiritual realm to the temporal realm. Remember, we got saved through a spiritual transaction that ushered us out of darkness and into Kingdom light (see John 1:12).

In her classic book on prayer, *Mustard*, Virginia Whitman writes, "When you have a desire or need for something, be it commodity or a service, you make contact with a person or firm you presume could give you satisfaction. What follows is termed 'doing business' with them. Prayer is doing business with God, and is every bit as practical as any earthy transaction."

The idea here is not to pray to God like a big Santa in the sky or a genie in a bottle who offers three wishes. The idea, rather, is for the intercessor to comprehend that when prayer goes up, answers come down. Although sometimes He answers us before we call (see Is. 65:24) most often there is no prayer answer without a prayer request.

Yes, He already knows what we need before we ask but for the sake of relationship we must enter into the faith-inspired, promise-based transaction. But now look at the other side of this concept. Only those in right relationship with God can do business with Him. The primary business God does with unbelievers in the realm of prayer is to bring salvation to a lost soul that cries out to Him.

So, we don't want transactional faith. That is, faith that only expresses itself in an emergency or that supposes one has to be perfect before petitioning the throne of grace. But our prayer of faith is doing business with God in the spirit realm and the results of that transaction appear in the natural realm.

— Prayer —

Father, in the name of Jesus, would You help me understand the transactional dynamics of the prayer of faith? Would You help me understand what it means to do business with You? Teach me how to enter into divine transactions that bring Your will to pass.

Concentrated Prayer

"I also devoted myself to working on the wall" (Nehemiah 5:16).

We always move toward what we focus on. A NASCAR driver is trained with this in mind. If his car is spinning out toward a wall, he turns his eyes away from the wall and focuses on where he wants the car to go to avoid crashing.

Too many times in intercession, we are focusing our prayer power on many random issues when we'd do better to offer concentrated prayer over the most important issue. While it's fine and good to intercede over many things, God always has something on His heart that's a priority of His Spirit. When we focus on His priorities for our prayer time, we'll be more effective.

At Awakening Prayer Hubs, we have a prayer focus each month. Any prayer hub leader can pray about many things, but we've all agreed to pray through the prayer focus so that we have concentrated prayer in hundreds of cities at the same time.

So how do you engage in concentrated prayer? Ask the Holy Spirit for His prayer focus. You can only pray so many hours in the day. So what or for whom does He want you to pray today? What is the urgency of His Spirit? Remember, praying in the Spirit is not just praying in tongues. It's also any prayer that's led by and influenced by the Holy Spirit.

Once you've decided on your prayer focus, fight off every thought or temptation to concentrate on something else. The enemy will try to distract you from your prayer focus with random thoughts, vain imaginations, and other devices. Don't let him pull you off course.

Nehemiah applied Himself to the work on the wall around Jerusalem (see Num. 5:16). That was where He concentrated his energy and his prayer. He refused to come down off the wall for anything or anyone no matter what. When you are standing on the wall or in your watchtower, you must develop that same level of concentration. You cannot be moved off your assignment.

— *Prayer* —

Father, in the name of Jesus, would You help me not to be scattered in prayer, but to tune my heart to Your heart so I can focus on Your prayer focus? You have a prayer agenda for me and I want to stick to it.

The Mary Slessor Prayer Anointing

"Now I beg you, brethren, through the Lord Jesus Christ, and through the love of the Spirit, that you strive together with me in prayers to God for me" (Romans 15:30).

Mary Slessor is best known as a missionary to Calabar, West Africa. This 19th Century pioneer spent almost forty years preaching the Gospel there.

"Her life rivals in many particulars that of David Livingstone. She served in Africa under the United Free Church of Scotland from 1876 to 1915. From an unlettered factory girl in the homeland, she advanced into the foremost rank of missionary pathfinders," wrote Dr. Robert H. Glover in his book *The Progress of World-Wide Missions.*

"Her work was that of a pioneer among the most savage tribes of the Calabar hinterland. Practically singlehanded she tamed and transformed three pagan communities in succession. It is a question if the career of any other woman missionary has been marked by so many strange adventures, daring feats, signal providences, and wonderful achievements."

But make no mistake. She didn't succeed in her mission without a strong intercession mantle. She faced plenty of witchcraft on her mission. She said things like: "Prayer is the greatest power God has put into our hands for service—praying is harder than doing, at least I find it so, but the dynamic lies that way to advance the Kingdom."

Writing to one of her intercessors, Slessor said: "I have always said that I have no idea how or why God has carried me over so many funny and hard places, and made these hordes of people submit to me, or why the government should have given me the privilege of a magistrate among them, except in answer to prayer made at home for me. It is all beyond my comprehension. The only way I can explain it is on the ground that I have been prayed for more than most. Pray on, dear one—the power lies that way."

Slessor understood the power of the Gospel, but she also understood the power of intercession in seeing God's will be done and His Kingdom come on earth as it is in heaven.

— *Prayer* —

Father, in the name of Jesus, would You help me rely on the power of prayer to bring Your will into my life, my family, my city and my intercessory ministry? Give me a revelation of the power of intercession to drive miracles in my midst. Give me a prayer anointing like Mary Slessor.

Working the Greater Works

"Most assuredly, I say to you, he who believes in Me, the works that I do he will do also; and greater works than these he will do, because I go to My Father" (John 14:12).

People who quote Jesus' words in John 14:12 are usually talking about signs, wonders and miracles. But intercessors can also claim these words. I call them Greater Works intercessors.

What is a Greater Works intercessor? An intercessor who believes that greater is He who is in us than he who is in the world, and therefore we can win every prayer battle we fight (see 1 John 4:4). A Greater Works intercessor believes prayer undergirds mass salvation, mass healings, mass deliverances, mass miracles and mass discipleship.

Many people believe for greater miracles, greater signs and greater wonders and we should. But we often take Jesus' words out of context. What is the context? Well, none other than believing prayer. Look at John 14:12-14:

"Most assuredly, I say to you, he who believes in Me, the works that I do he will do also; and greater works than these he will do, because I go to My Father. And whatever you ask in My name, that I will do, that the Father may be glorified in the Son. If you ask anything in My name, I will do it."

Catch that: When we ask the Father in Jesus' name for anything He wants to do—anything according to His will—He will do it. Greater Works intercessors release believing prayer. We are believing for greater signs, greater wonders, and greater miracles. We are believing for greater victories in fierce battles. We are believing for greater manifestations of His glory.

Greater Works intercessors don't need the glory. They are praying in Jesus' name for the greater works that will drive unbelievers—and unbelieving believers—to their knees as His goodness and greatness manifest in their midst. I like the *Amplified Classic* translation of John 14:13-14:

"And I will do whatever you ask in My name [as My representative], this I will do, so that the Father may be glorified and celebrated in the Son. If you ask Me anything in My name [as My representative], I will do it." Are you a Greater Works intercessor?

— *Prayer* —

Father, in the name of Jesus, help me be part of the greater works Jesus promised His church would see through prayer. Help me catch the revelation that, many times the greater work is prayer and prayer drives the greater works. Make me a greater works intercessor.

The Utterly Dependent Intercessor

"I depend on God alone; I put my hope in him. He alone protects and saves me; he is my defender, and I shall never be defeated" (Psalm 62:5-6).

As Christians, we are utterly dependent on God in every way. At times, if we're not careful, we can start taking pride in our intercessory prayer skills and forget that apart from Him we can do nothing. Eloquent prayers are not automatically effective prayers.

Intercessors need to connect to the Vine, the Intercessor, the King Jesus. When we live and move and have our being in Him, abiding in Him, pledging allegiance to His mission, surrendering our desires to His and consecrating ourselves to Him, we will see great fruit in our prayer ministries.

Jesus put it this way in John 15:5-7, "I am the vine, you are the branches. He who abides in Me, and I in him, bears much fruit; for without Me you can do nothing. If anyone does not abide in Me, he is cast out as a branch and is withered; and they gather them and throw them into the fire, and they are burned. If you abide in Me, and My words abide in you, you will ask what you desire, and it shall be done for you."

David was a man after God's own heart—and a man utterly dependent on God in the face of every challenge. We read his beautiful confession in Psalm 62:5-8 (GNT):

"I depend on God alone; I put my hope in him. He alone protects and saves me; he is my defender, and I shall never be defeated. My salvation and honor depend on God; he is my strong protector; he is my shelter. Trust in God at all times, my people. Tell him all your troubles, for he is our refuge."

Intercessor, lean and depend on Him and not on your own understanding. We often don't know how to pray as we ought. And even when we find God's will and intercede accordingly, it is still His Spirit that gives us the unction to pray and the grace to stand in the place of prayer with persistence.

— *Prayer* —

Father, in the name of Jesus, help me see how utterly dependent I am on You. I don't want to think more highly of myself than I ought. I want to pray from a place of dependence on the words of life You share with my heart.

Praying 'Exceedingly'

"For what thanks can we render to God for you, for all the joy with which we rejoice for your sake before our God, night and day praying exceedingly that we may see your face and perfect what is lacking in your faith?" (1 Thessalonians 3:9-11)

Paul prayed night and day exceedingly for a thing. You have to really want something to pray exceedingly. For example, Paul had a special place in his heart for the church at Thessalonica. He told them, "But we, brethren, being bereaved of you for a short season, in presence not in heart, endeavored the more exceedingly to see your face with great desire" (1 Thess. 2:17, ASV).

What does Paul mean by exceedingly? And what does it mean to pray "exceedingly" prayers? Exceedingly prayer is earnest prayer. Exceedingly prayer is prayer to an extreme degree. Exceedingly prayer proceeds from an intense spirit and a mind seriously intent on achieving the answer. Exceedingly prayer also speaks to the amount of prayer put forth on a matter.

God is an "exceedingly" God. He told Abram in a vision, "I am your shield, your exceedingly great reward" (Gen. 15:1). God told Abraham He would make him "exceedingly fruitful." Hundreds of years later, God made the Israelites exceedingly mighty in Egypt (see Ex. 1:7). When Moses sent spies into the Promised Land, they reported it was an "exceedingly good land" (Num. 14:7).

Intercessors, it's time to start praying exceedingly prayers to our exceedingly good God. We need to be like David and be exceedingly glad and exceedingly joyful, praising Him for His great and precious promises, which are yes and amen. Yes, Paul prayed exceedingly prayers over and over again and we should too. Paul put it this way in Ephesians 3:20-21:

"Now to Him who is able to do exceedingly abundantly above all that we ask or think, according to the power that works in us, to Him be glory in the church by Christ Jesus to all generations, forever and ever. Amen." Meditate on the exceedingly promises. Pray exceedingly prayers. Make exceedingly intercession. And expect exceedingly answers.

— *Prayer* —

Father, in the name of Jesus, help me set my prayer sites higher. Give me the grace to pray exceedingly prayers intent on seeing Your will come to pass in the earth. Help me keep in mind that You are a God who acts exceedingly.

In the Waiting Room

"Wait on the Lord; Be of good courage, and He shall strengthen your heart; Wait, I say, on the Lord!" (Psalm 27:14)

Pursuing the will of God in prayer can mean a lot of waiting—sometimes what feels like endless waiting. I know you can relate. We've all been in unpleasant waiting room experiences in the natural and sometimes it doesn't feel much different waiting on the promises of God. At times, we feel weary or impatient. We don't feel like we can wait one more day for the breakthrough.

Even reading this you might feel like you can't handle another heartache, another disappointment, another day of waiting on the victory in intercession. But God sent me to tell you this: You are going to break through. Whether it feels like it or not, while you are waiting on God you are moving towards the future and hope He has in store for you—and those who you are praying for.

Remember David's heart posture: "I waited patiently for the Lord; And He inclined to me, and heard my cry" (Ps. 40:1). And again, "I wait for the Lord, my soul waits, and in His word I do hope" (Ps. 130:5).

Understanding this truth, it's time to come out of the place of hiding and hurting even while you are waiting. God sees the end from the beginning, and He sees your weariness and wondering even now. God is using your discomfort to mold you into the image of Christ, the Chief Intercessor. The waiting will be worth it.

David wrote these words in Psalm 37:7-9 that will sustain you in the waiting when the enemy is doing his level best to get you to complain, pull back or even quit: "Rest in the Lord, and wait patiently for Him; Do not fret because of him who prospers in his way, because of the man who brings wicked schemes to pass. Cease from anger, and forsake wrath; Do not fret—it only causes harm. For evildoers shall be cut off; But those who wait on the Lord, they shall inherit the earth."

— *Prayer* —

Father, in the name of Jesus, would You help me stay calm in the waiting room?
Would You give me the grace to wait well, praising You when impatience is
pouncing? Would You remind me of David's heart posture and heartfelt cries
when I feel like I can't wait any longer?

Awakening the Dawn

"My voice You shall hear in the morning, O Lord; In the morning I will direct it to You, and I will look up" (Psalm 5:3).

I get up at 3:45 a.m. most mornings. Why so early? Because the Lord gave me an assignment to awaken the dawn. Believe me, I'd prefer to stay up all night and sleep until noon, but little by little over the years the Lord has given me wake up calls that are earlier and earlier.

Sometimes, I feel like David when he wrote, "Awake, lute and harp! I will awaken the dawn" (Ps. 108:2). There's something about being up with the Lord before daybreak, taking the time with just He and you before the rest of the world wakes up. There's no competition for your time. You can learn of Him without distraction. Isaiah put it this way: "He awakens Me morning by morning, He awakens my ear to hear as the learned" (Isa. 50:4).

I love the words of E.M. Bounds, an author, attorney and great man of prayer who wrote classic books on prayer, once said this: "The men who have done the most for God in this world have been early on their knees. He who fritters away the early morning, its opportunity and freshness, in other pursuits than seeking God will make poor headway seeking Him the rest of the day. If God is not first in our thoughts and efforts in the morning, He will be in the last place the remainder of the day."

Let those words sink into your heart. There's just something about awakening the dawn. Maybe your schedule doesn't permit you to do this every day—or at all. Maybe you work the night shift. But the principle of putting God first through prayer can still work in your life. When you awake, it can be your dawn.

The psalmist wrote, "My soul waits for the Lord More than those who watch for the morning—Yes, more than those who watch for the morning" (Ps. 130:6). Awakening the dawn gives you the time to get filled with the Word, filled with the Spirit, and filled with faith and hope in the promises of God. Try it.

— *Prayer* —

Father, in the name of Jesus, I want to awaken the dawn. I want to rise up without distraction to seek Your face, hear Your heart and pray without ceasing. Would You show me how I can adjust my schedule to awaken the dawn? Help me remember to put You—and prayer to You—first.

AUGUST 11

Order in the Court!

"At the same time, Paul said, 'Let all things be done decently and in order'"
(1 Corinthians 14:40).

Liberty is a must in prayer meetings. We don't want formulas and religiosity to quench the spirit of prayer. After all, where the Spirit of the Lord is there is liberty (see 2 Cor. 3:17). But that doesn't mean the prayer meeting should be a free for all without any governing authority.

Paul taught protocols for the realms of the spirit (which would include prayer) to a loose Corinthian church. One of them is in 1 Corinthians 14:39-40: "Therefore, brothers, eagerly desire to prophesy, and do not forbid speaking in tongues. Let all things be done decently and in order."

God is a God of order. So while some want to criticize protocols, a reckless approach to intercession can do great damage. I can offer you a practical example. A woman who came to Awakening House of Prayer was clearly wounded and in need of prayer but insisted on praying from the mic. She was essentially praying witchcraft. We had to cut off our live stream.

I instructed the stewards not to allow her to pray from the mic again, but someone ignored my instruction when I wasn't there. This wounded woman started cursing nations from the mic and no one stopped her. People were so offended they left and at least one didn't come back. We can't just allow anyone to pray anything they want. There must be order.

Yes, where the Spirit of the Lord is, there is liberty (see 2 Cor. 3:17) but we don't have to throw order out the window in the name of freedom. Freedom and order are not mutually exclusive concepts. It's not an either/or option. Liberty should not violate the law of love. Intercession is a critical ministry in the Body of Christ. We want to represent Jesus well.

— *Prayer* —

Father, in the name of Jesus, thank You that You are a God of liberty and order and we can have both in our prayer meetings. Help me, Lord, to steward my authority well. Help me to help others rise up in proper protocols so Your prayer mission is accomplished.

Your Prayers Never Die

"These all died in faith, not having received the promises, but having seen them afar off were assured of them, embraced them and confessed that they were strangers and pilgrims on the earth" (Hebrews 11:13).

E.M. Bounds, the author of many powerful books on prayer, wrote these profound words: "Prayers are deathless. They outlive the lives of those who uttered them."

This defies the logic of many intercessors who are contending for breakthrough in the here and now. But consider how many intercessors prayed for over half their lives to see the U.S. Supreme Court overturn Roe v. Wade, effectively putting an end to the federal government's blessing on abortion. Indeed, many intercessors passed on to glory without seeing that monumental day. But their prayers didn't die with them. They filled the bowls in heaven until there came a tipping point after they went on to glory.

Much the same, Abraham didn't see all of God's promises to him come to pass in his lifetime but he kept on praying and believing. The promise was too big to fulfill in a single generation, but he kept pressing toward it. Here's a reminder of the promise in Genesis 12:1-3:

"Now the Lord had said to Abram: 'Get out of your country, from your family and from your father's house, to a land that I will show you. I will make you a great nation; I will bless you and make your name great; And you shall be a blessing. I will bless those who bless you, and I will curse him who curses you; And in you all the families of the earth shall be blessed."

This promise was partially fulfilled hundreds of years later when Joshua took the Israelites triumphantly into the Promised Land. Although we all want to see immediate breakthrough, seasoned intercessors understand some of our prayers will manifest in future generations. Some of our digging in intercession is for the benefit of those who will live in the future. Although we may never see the answer in this lifetime, we will find the rewards of intercession in eternity.

— Prayer —

Father, in the name of Jesus, would You help me take on a long-term mindset, understanding that my prayers today may be for the benefit of the generation of tomorrow? Help me understand that my prayers never die.

Don't Make God Wonder

"He saw that there was no man, and wondered that there was no intercessor"
(Isaiah 59:16).

What a curious Scripture indeed! God wondered that there was no intercessor. We should never make God wonder on our watch.

The New International Version uses even stronger language: "He saw that there was no one, he was appalled that there was no one to intervene." *The New Living Translation* brings it home: "He was amazed to see that no one intervened to help the oppressed."

Being an intercessor is not glamorous but is it glorious in that we are standing before the King of Glory. Being an intercessor is hard work, but we must remember we are co-laboring with Christ the Intercessor in our prayer endeavors. Being an intercessor can be inconvenient but the eternal rewards are worth it.

God is always looking for a man or a woman to stand in the gap. When He can't find one, it must grieve His Spirit. When He can't find one, it's appalling to His good nature. When He can't find one, He's amazed. Let's amaze God with our faith in intercession like the Centurion in Luke 7 whose servant was sick and ready to die. He sent his friends to Jesus for help with a message:

"Lord, do not trouble Yourself, for I am not worthy that You should enter under my roof. Therefore I did not even think myself worthy to come to You. But say the word, and my servant will be healed. For I also am a man placed under authority, having soldiers under me. And I say to one, 'Go,' and he goes; and to another, 'Come,' and he comes; and to my servant, 'Do this,' and he does it. When Jesus heard these things, He marveled at him, and turned around and said to the crowd that followed Him, 'I say to you, I have not found such great faith, not even in Israel'!"

— *Prayer* —

Father, in the name of Jesus, I say yes to the call to intercession even when it's hard, even when it brings retaliation and even when it's inconvenient. Help me cultivate faith in Your Word that undergirds my intercession and makes You marvel. I am ready to stand in the gap.

Shaking Things Loose

"And when they had prayed, the place where they were assembled together was shaken; and they were all filled with the Holy Spirit, and they spoke the word of God with boldness" (Acts 4:31).

Intercession shakes things up and shakes things loose. We see this concept over and again in Scripture, and we should let these examples encourage our hearts even when we don't see anything changing before our eyes.

In the Book of Acts, we see the type of prayer that brings a shaking. After Peter and John were arrested and released for healing the man at the Gate Beautiful in Jesus' name, they ran back to their company of believers and prayed in unity Acts 4:29-31 reads:

"Now, Lord, look on their threats, and grant to Your servants that with all boldness they may speak Your word, by stretching out Your hand to heal, and that signs and wonders may be done through the name of Your holy Servant Jesus. And when they had prayed, the place where they were assembled together was shaken; and they were all filled with the Holy Spirit, and they spoke the word of God with boldness."

Likewise, we see Paul and Silas facing persecution for casting a devil out of a girl in Thyatira. At midnight, the dynamic duo was praying and singing hymns to God and the other prisoners were watching. Look what happens next in Acts 16:26-28:

"Suddenly there was a great earthquake, so that the foundations of the prison were shaken; and immediately all the doors were opened and everyone's chains were loosed. And the keeper of the prison, awaking from sleep and seeing the prison doors open, supposing the prisoners had fled, drew his sword and was about to kill himself. But Paul called with a loud voice, saying, 'Do yourself no harm, for we are all here.'"

Prayer shakes things up. You might not see anything literally shaking when you pray, but things are shaking in the spirit. Demons are trembling. Chains are breaking. If you want to see your city shaken for Jesus, addicts shake free from ties that bind, and corruption shaken by exposure, keep praying.

— *Prayer* —

Father, in the name of Jesus, would You help me release prayers that shake things up? Would You lead me to a company of intercessors that know how to make intercession that shakes demonic walls down, shakes cities with the Gospel and shakes people free from bondage?

Honoring Your Prayer Team

"Render therefore to all their due: taxes to whom taxes are due, customs to whom customs, fear to whom fear, honor to whom honor" (Romans 13:7).

I heard the Lord say, "Honor releases My blessing, My anointing and My great rewards. When you walk in honor with all men, you will experience a greater understanding of My Kingdom principles and you will unlock blessings that were once unseen and unknown to you. Choose humility. Choose honor. I promise you it's worth it."

We need to honor those who labor among us in prayer. When you are part of an intercessory prayer group, remember to honor the prayer warriors among you. Honor simply means respect. Honor means to offer expressions of high regard. Ultimately, if we aren't honoring people we aren't honoring God. When honor goes up, blessings come down.

Peter wrote, "Honor all people. Love the brotherhood. Fear God. Honor the king" (1 Pet. 2:17). And Paul wrote, "Be kindly affectionate to one another with brotherly love, in honor giving preference to one another" (Rom. 12:10). Honoring means to appreciate, celebrate, commend and praise. Honor means to compliment, value and esteem.

Remember, behavior that is rewarded is repeated. You want your fellow intercessors to know their hard work in the prayer closet is appreciated. They are investing their time, their blood, sweat and tears, so to speak. They stood with you to put thousands of demons to flight so the mission could be accomplished. Honor them.

God Himself has crowned us with glory and honor (see Heb. 2:7). He set an example for us to honor others. If we want to be honorable intercessors, we need to sow honor into the lives of those who plow the prayer field with us. We need to do our part to create a culture of honor where we demonstrate love and caring concern, and pray for one another. In doing so, we are honoring Christ the Lord in our hearts and by our actions (see 1 Pet. 3:15).

— Prayer —

Father, in the name of Jesus, would You help me establish a culture of honor in my prayer circle? Would You teach me how to outdo others in showing honor? Would You help me to honor those who labor among me in prayer?

Pressing Into Prayer Marches

"And the Lord said to Joshua: 'See! I have given Jericho into your hand, its king, and the mighty men of valor. You shall march around the city, all you men of war'" (Joshua 6:2-3).

God gave Joshua a strategy to enter the Promised Land. It's what some would call today a prayer march. God told him to gather all the men of war and march around the city once a day for six days. On the seventh day, Joshua was to lead the men to march around the city seven times in silence and then, finally, release a shout.

"It shall come to pass, when they make a long blast with the ram's horn, and when you hear the sound of the trumpet, that all the people shall shout with a great shout; then the wall of the city will fall down flat. And the people shall go up every man straight before him" (Josh. 6:5).

The Israelites took hold of Joshua's divinely-inspired strategy and prepared to execute. Those who were armed went in front of the ark of the Lord. Then there was a rear guard that followed after the ark. They obeyed God's instructions to a tee, even walking in silence day after day after day. (I imagine they were praying to God from the inside.) Then, suddenly, the persistence paid off.

"But it came to pass on the seventh day that they rose early, about the dawning of the day, and marched around the city seven times in the same manner. On that day only they marched around the city seven times. And the seventh time it happened, when the priests blew the trumpets, that Joshua said to the people: 'Shout, for the Lord has given you the city! Now the city shall be doomed by the Lord to destruction, it and all who are in it'" (Josh. 6:15-17).

A prayer march is not the appropriate strategy for every prayer assignment. But it is appropriate for some, especially when it has to do with taking your city for God. Marching around the city in silence, praying on the inside, is a keen strategy for intercessors who want to take the land.

— *Prayer* —

Father, in the name of Jesus, would You lead me to prayer marches when it's the right tactic for the battle in my city? Would You show me the issues on Your heart that mandate mobilizing intercessors and warriors to march for a cause? Make me militant like Joshua.

AUGUST 17

Qualifications of a Strategic Prayer Partner

"Can two walk together, unless they are agreed?" (Amos 3:3)

Having a prayer partner carries many benefits. Beyond the power of agreement, a strategic prayer partner may tap into prophetic revelation that helps your situation. A strategic prayer partner can encourage you to keep pressing when you feel you've hit a wall. And, together, you will find greater accountability in intercession.

Of course, it's a two-way street. You must also be a strategic prayer partner in return. A strategic prayer partner becomes a close confidant to you and you to them. You will always have someone to turn to who you can trust when you need have a desperate and private prayer need.

But, let's face it. Not all prayer partners are strategic. Some of them want to complain more than they pray. Others are too self-focused to call it a real partnership. Still others try to turn prayer into a gossip session. The wrong prayer partner can be nothing but a distraction. That's why you have to choose your strategic prayer partner carefully.

So how do you find a strategic prayer partner? First, pray about it. Ask God to show you with whom to begin to build that relationship. Ask God to connect you with someone with whom you can truly agree and who will truly agree with you, knowing that if you really agree God will hear and answer the prayer (see Matt. 18:19-20).

Once God shows you a potential prayer partner, invite them to pray with you. You'll get a better feel for whether it's a divine connection when you pray together. If it feels right, ask the person to pray with you again. If they agree, set regular meeting times—even if it's only for a few minutes. Some prayer of agreement is better than no prayer of agreement.

Be sure that you keep any and all private information your prayer partner shares with you strictly confidential. Privacy and confidentiality are the foundations for a strategic prayer partnership. If you don't build that trust, neither of you will feel comfortable sharing dire needs.

— Prayer —

Father, in the name of Jesus, help me find a strategic prayer partner. Teach me
how to be selfless, preferring others in prayer. Would You connect me with
someone with whom I can really agree and who will agree with me?

Agonizing in Prayer

"Likewise the Spirit also helps in our weaknesses. For we do not know what we should pray for as we ought, but the Spirit Himself makes intercession for us with groanings which cannot be uttered" (Romans 8:26).

Groaning suggests discomfort at best and agony at worst. Groaning means "to utter a deep moan indicative of pain, grief, or annoyance," according to *Merriam-Webster's* dictionary. Intercessors at times groan in the spirit. They agonize in prayer.

Jesus agonized in prayer in Luke 22:39-44: "Coming out, He went to the Mount of Olives, as He was accustomed, and His disciples also followed Him. When He came to the place, He said to them, 'Pray that you may not enter into temptation.'

"And He was withdrawn from them about a stone's throw, and He knelt down and prayed, saying, 'Father, if it is Your will, take this cup away from Me; nevertheless not My will, but Yours, be done.' Then an angel appeared to Him from heaven, strengthening Him. And being in agony, He prayed more earnestly. Then His sweat became like great drops of blood falling down to the ground."

Have you ever agonized in prayer to the point that you sweat blood? None of us have, though it may almost feel that way at times. Agonizing in prayer is intense pain of the mind that sometimes also affects the body. Agonizing in prayer is, at times, a struggle that precedes death to self. Agonizing in prayer, at times, is a violent struggle or contest with the enemy.

"Prayer is not difficult to understand. It is difficult to do. When was the last time your heart so grieved for those you were interceding for that your entire body agonized along with your mind and heart?" asks Henry Blackaby in his *Experiencing God Day-by-Day* devotional.

"We are a generation that avoids pain at all costs. This is why there are so few intercessors. Most Christians operate on the shallowest levels of prayer, but God wants to take us into the deep levels of intercessory prayer that only a few ever experience. Deep, prolonged intercession is painful."

— *Prayer* —

Father, in the name of Jesus, I am willing to agonize in prayer, not just for myself but for the sake of others. I am willing to go to the depths of intercessory prayer that few ever experience. I am willing to feel the pain of prayer. Teach me how to bear the agony of prayer.

A Six-Point Plan to Know God's Will

"Therefore do not be unwise, but understand what the will of the Lord is" (Ephesians 5:17).

George Muller, a Christian evangelist and director of the Ashley Down orphanage in Bristol, England, had a six-point plan to know God's will. Knowing God's will is critical if we are going to pray prayers that get answered. Muller said, "In trivial matters, and in all transactions involving most important issues, I have found this method is always effective." Here's his plan:

First, he said, "I seek to get my heart into such a state that it has no will of its own in a given matter. When you're ready to do the Lord's will, whatever it may be, nine-tenths of the difficulties are overcome." Second, "Having done this, I don't leave the result to feeling or simply impression. If I do so, I leave myself liable to great delusion."

Third, he said, "I seek the will of the Spirit of God through, or in connection with, God's Word. The Spirit and the Word must be combined. If I look to the Spirit alone without the Word, I lay myself open to great delusions also. If the Spirit guides us, He'll do it according to the Scriptures, not contrary to them. Fourth, he continued, "I take into account providential circumstances. These often plainly indicate God's will in connection with His Word and Spirit."

Fifth, he said, "I ask God in prayer to reveal His will to me. Finally, "Thus, through prayer, the study of the Word, and reflection, I come to a deliberate judgment, according to the best of my ability and knowledge."

Muller acquired land for his orphanage this way. In 1846, he went to speak to the landowner but couldn't find him. Muller decided it wasn't God's will to speak with him that day. When he ran into the landowner the next day, he told Muller he was up all night and made up his mind to give him the land at nearly half the asking price.

— *Prayer* —

Father, in the name of Jesus, help me always to discern Your will. Remind me of Mueller's practice so I can press into Your will, not only in my life but in my intercession for others. Thank You, Lord, for revealing Your will.

Abiding Prayer

"If you abide in Me, and My words abide in you, you will ask what you desire, and it shall be done for you" (John 15:7).

Jesus made a mega promise in John 15:7. Of course, like most of the other seven thousands promises we read in the Bible, they are conditional upon us doing our part. John 15:7 is a classic "if-then" scenario.

If we abide in Jesus and if His words abide in us, then we can ask whatever we desire and we'll get it. The reality is if we are truly abiding in Jesus and His Word is abiding in us, we'll pray the right prayers. We'll ask for the right things. We won't pray amiss.

Beyond John 15:7, we see five additional New Testament admonishments to abide in Jesus. Let's look at each one. Meditate on them and let this truth sink into your heart. 1 John 2:28 reads, "And now, little children, abide in Him, that when He appears, we may have confidence and not be ashamed before Him at His coming."

1 John 2:6 tells us, "He who says he abides in Him ought himself also to walk just as He walked." 1 John 3:24 encourages, "Now he who keeps His commandments abides in Him, and He in him. And by this we know that He abides in us, by the Spirit whom He has given us."

Jesus said in John 15:10, "If you keep My commandments, you will abide in My love, just as I have kept My Father's commandments and abide in His love." And He said in John 8:31, "If you abide in My word, you are My disciples indeed."

So, then, how do we tap into abiding prayer? Meditate on the Word. Meditate on the Christ. Wait upon the Lord. Keep your mind set on things above, and not on the things of this earth (see Col. 3:2). Pray in the Spirit. Pray with a revelation of His presence. Pray without ceasing.

— *Prayer* —

Father, in the name of Jesus, would You teach me how to abide in You all day, every day? Would You teach me how to abide in prayer? Help me renew my mind to the reality of Emmanuel, God with us. Help me to keep a listening ear and an open heart.

Tapping Into Prayer Imagination

"For since the beginning of the world Men have not heard nor perceived by the ear, nor has the eye seen any God besides You, Who acts for the one who waits for Him" (Isaiah 64:4).

Imagination in prayer can be a helpful tool, when used the right way. When your spirit was born again, you gained the ability to see all things possible (see Mark 9:23) within the bounds of your sanctified imagination. From the world's perspective, imagination is "the act or power of forming a mental image of something not present to the senses or never before wholly perceived in reality," according to *Merriam Webster's* dictionary.

While the enemy tries to use your imagination against you—launching vain imaginations at your mind—you can cooperate with God to use your imagination for His glory. God has an imagination and our imagination is one of His great gifts to humankind. Every great invention, for example, was first conceived in someone's imagination. Imagination is part of our creative ability. We need to tap into God-given imaginations.

Anne Townsend, author of *Prayer Without Pretending*, once said: "If I can imagine what it must be like for the one for whom I am praying, then I find that I can begin to intercede for that person. My imagination leads me on to want to be more deeply involved with him in his own life. This involvement leads to caring, caring leads to love, and love leads to intercession."

Consider the Spirit-inspired words of Paul the apostle: "But, as it is written, 'What no eye has seen, nor ear heard, nor the heart of man imagined, what God has prepared for those who love him'—these things God has revealed to us through the Spirit. For the Spirit searches everything, even the depths of God" (1 Cor. 2:9-10, ESV).

Imagination in prayer is not just for intercession. You can pray with your imagination for your own needs. In his best-selling book *The Circle Maker: Praying Circles Around Your Biggest Dreams and Greatest Fears*, author Mark Batterson wrote, "Prayer and imagination are directly proportional: the more you pray the bigger your imagination becomes because the Holy Spirit supersizes it with God-sized dreams."

— *Prayer* —

Father, in the name of Jesus, sanctify my imagination. Help me submit my imagination to Your Word. Help me quickly cast down vain imaginations and everything that exalts itself above the knowledge of Your Word.

Will the Real Intercessors Please Stand Up?

"Stand firm in the faith" (1 Corinthians 16:13).

I heard the Lord say, "I've called you for such a time as this, and make no mistake because I've not made a mistake in calling you to the earth in this hour, by putting My Spirit of prayer upon you. I know that I can trust you to stand in the gap. I know that I can trust you to make up the hedge. I don't have to wonder why there's no one to call upon because I know I can call upon you.

"I heard your heart's cry when you said 'yes' to Me—when you said 'yes' to the call, when you said 'yes' to the mission, when you said 'yes' to My heart. I heard you and I'm taking you up on your offer because I know that you meant what you said. I know when you cried out and said 'Use me, Lord. Here I am. Send me, Lord. Here I am' that you meant it and I will make you able to fulfill your 'yes.'

"I will give you an anointing to break through the bronze gates. I will make your teeth like sharp threshing instruments that will gnaw through the enemy's opposition. I will make you stand and withstand in the evil day. So keep praying, My intercessors, keep waging warfare, My intercessors. Keep standing in the gap I have assigned you to, My intercessors, and you will see eternal rewards that are greater than anything you might expect.

"For I value the intercession of the saints. I value the prayer of My warring people on the earth. Occupy till I come with prayer. Stand and withstand in prayer. Push back the darkness in prayer. Release your prayer for souls in the earth through My Spirit. I will help you. I will make a way for you. I will raise up people to pray for you. I will do things for you when you stand for Me in the earth, in the realm of prayer."

— *Prayer* —

Father, in the name of Jesus, here I am, send me in prayer. Inspire and grace me to pray day and night for Your Kingdom to come and Your will be done. Use me as Your battle-axe. Make a way for me to pray more.

AUGUST 23

What if You Had Thirty Minutes to Live?

"Therefore I also, after I heard of your faith in the Lord Jesus and your love for all the saints, do not cease to give thanks for you, making mention of you in my prayers" (Ephesians 1:15-16).

There was once a man named Dr. Azel Bacchus. The first-ever president of Hamilton college was resting on his death bed when his doctor came by the house. Upon examining Bacchus' symptoms, his doctor left the room without uttering a single word. The news was grim.

As the story goes, when the doctor opened the bedroom door to leave he whispered something to one of Bacchus' household attendants. Dr. Bacchus was curious about the conversation and asked the attendant what the doctor said. "He said, sir, that you cannot live to exceed half an hour."

"Is it so?" said the good man, according to an account in the *Biblical Illustrator*. "Then take me out of my bed, and place me upon my knees; let me spend that time in calling upon God for the salvation of the world."

Bacchus' attendant took his request seriously. As *Biblical Illustrator* documents, Bacchus' last moments on the earth were spent in intercession. What was he praying for? The salvation of souls. Just like David Livingstone, Bacchus died on his knees praying. What a way to go into eternity! I believe great rewards were awaiting him.

If you had thirty minutes left to live, who or what would you pray for? Here's my point: We should pray like there's no tomorrow. We should pray for lost souls that may have no tomorrow. There's no telling how many souls were saved thanks to the intercession released through his mouth.

This gives a deeper meaning to Paul's Spirit-inspired words in 1 Timothy 2:8, "I will therefore that men pray everywhere, lifting up holy hands, without wrath and doubting." It gives a deeper meaning to Psalm 63:4, "Thus I will bless You while I live; I will lift up my hands in Your name." Think about it for a minute. His last words were prayers.

— *Prayer* —

Father, in the name of Jesus, would You help me pray until my dying breath? Give me such a deep passion for prayer that I pray daily just as I die daily until You take me on to glory. Let my last words be prayers.

Burning Out for God

"He was the burning and shining lamp, and you were willing for a time to rejoice in his light"
(John 5:3).

"Now let me burn out for God. After all, whatever God may appoint, prayer is the great thing. Oh, that I might be a man of prayer!" This was the prayer of Henry Martyn, an 18th Century missionary to India and Persia. The Englishman surrendered his life to Christ as a young man after the sudden death of his father.

"I almost think that to be prevented going among the heathen as a missionary would break my heart. I feel pressed in spirit to do something for God," he once said. "I have hitherto lived to little purpose, more like a clod than a servant of God; now let me burn out for God. The flesh shrinks at times, but I do not regret having resigned the world. Life is but a short journey, and then if I be faithful unto death, my gracious reward will begin."

There was a spirit of burning on Martyn, who died in his early thirties. It reminds me of the spirit of burning that was on John the Baptist. Jesus said John was a burning and shining lamp. Oh, that intercessors today would carry a spirit of burning like Isaiah described in Isaiah 4:4.

Like David, we could say, "My heart was hot within me; While I was musing, the fire burned. Then I spoke with my tongue" (Ps. 39:3). Like the men who walked with Jesus on the Road to Emmaus, we can say, "Did not our heart burn within us while He talked with us on the road, and while He opened the Scriptures to us?" (Luke 24:32). Like Jeremiah, we can pray with fire in our bones (Jer. 20:9).

Martyn literally burned out for Jesus, but intercessors don't have to get burned out. The oil in our lamps doesn't have to burn out because we can lean on the Holy Spirit for a fresh outpouring of the spirit of prayer.

— *Prayer* —

Father, in the name of Jesus, help me to burn for You in intercession without burning out. Teach me to walk the fine line of extending myself in intercession without forgetting about intimacy with You that refires my intercession. Let the spirit of burning rest upon me.

Kneeling Hearts

"Oh come, let us worship and bow down; Let us kneel before the Lord our Maker" (Ps. 95:6).

Many are the Scriptures that speak of kneeling. Kneeling is a sign of humility. Kneeling is a way to pay homage to another. A leper came to Jesus, kneeling as He prayed for healing (see Mark 1:40-45). Paul knelt in prayer repeatedly in Scripture. We know every knee will bow to Jesus one day, even if they don't believe in Him today (see Rom. 14:11).

American evangelist D. L. Moody once said, "Every great movement of God can be traced to a kneeling figure." That is the truth. But the kneeling is not always done on bended knee. God is not just looking for a bended knee. He's looking for a kneeling heart.

French poet and playwright Victor Hugo, put it this way. "Certain thoughts are prayers. There are moments when, whatever be the attitude of the body, the soul is on its knees." When the soul is on its knees, so to speak, it speaks to a heart posture that realizes it's dependency on God for the answer.

A kneeling heart is a heart of worship. A kneeling heart is a heart that acknowledges God's power, sovereignty, and willingness to move at the sound of one's voice. A kneeling heart attracts God's attention every time. One may kneel on his knees and pray pretentious prayers like the Pharisee in Luke 11. But a kneeling heart God will not deny.

The heart of man reflects the man (see Prov. 27:19). God looks at the heart (see 1 Sam. 16:7). We are told to keep our hearts with all diligence for out of it flow the springs of life (see Prov. 4:23). Out of the abundance of the heart the mouth speaks (see Matt. 12:34). Out of our hearts flow prayer that touches God's heart, moves Him with compassion and births miracles. Pray with a kneeling heart.

— *Prayer* —

Father, help me to always pray with a kneeling heart. Whether I am prostrate before You, or with hands lifted high, or driving in my car—no matter my physical posture when I pray—help me to pray with a kneeling heart.

Discovering His Strength in Your Weakness

"We now have this light shining in our hearts, but we ourselves are like fragile clay jars containing this great treasure. This makes it clear that our great power is from God, not from ourselves" (2 Corinthians 4:7, NLT).

Every intercessor has a handicap. We're all crippled in some way. Paul told us the Holy Spirit helps in our weaknesses (Rom. 8:26). Maybe our handicap is a season of trial. Maybe it's a season of feeling disconnected from God. Maybe it's a wrong image of ourselves or some other insecurity. God still uses crippled intercessors.

Dick Eastman, Chief Prayer Officer at Every Home of Christ, offers some insight into this truth. "The power of prayer is not reserved for any certain class of people. Historians tell us (George) Whitfield took a little crippled man with him to crusades," he wrote in his book, *No Easy Road.*

"His job was not crusade director or chief musician. He prayed! That was the extent of his duty. As Whitefield preached, this handicapped Christian prayed. Now we see more clearly why Whitefield's sermons rocked the hearts of men. The vividness with which he preached seemed supernatural."

Whitefield was perhaps the most known religious figure in the Eighteen Century. He was the primary figure in the first Great Awakening, a revival in the then-British American colonies. Whitefield himself was also a man of prayer. He said, "The true believer can no more live without prayer, than without food day by day."

Whitefield preached in America in 1739-1740, traveling up and down the colonies. Because there was no church facility large enough to hold the crowds, he preached in open fields and gained no small number of converts. Prayer was the foundation of his vivid preaching.

"Set apart this day for humiliation (fasting) and intercession... and found my heart greatly enlarged in that Divine exercise," Whitefield said. "Intercession is a glorious means to sweeten the heart." No matter what your handicap, you can still pray. You can make intercession with and through your handicap. You can stand in the gap with your handicap. Even when you feel crippled, God is able to make you stand in the gap.

— *Prayer* —

Father, in the name of Jesus, would You help me remember that although I am a fragile jar of clay that I have a great treasure in me? Your Holy Spirt dwells within me and helps me overcome every weakness in prayer. When I am weak, You are still strong. Thank You, Lord.

AUGUST 27

Not So Fast...

"If it is possible, as much as depends on you, live peaceably with all men" (Romans 12:18).

In the Sermon on the Mount, Jesus said plainly: "You have heard that it was said to those of old, 'You shall not murder, and whoever murders will be in danger of the judgment.' But I say to you that whoever is angry with his brother without a cause shall be in danger of the judgment.

"And whoever says to his brother, 'Raca!' shall be in danger of the council. But whoever says, 'You fool!' shall be in danger of hell fire. Therefore if you bring your gift to the altar, and there remember that your brother has something against you, leave your gift there before the altar, and go your way. First be reconciled to your brother, and then come and offer your gift" (Matt. 5:21-24).

Have you ever thought about why Jesus would tell us to leave our gift at the altar? Why, in other words, would God stress the importance of interrupting your sacrifice of prayer to reconcile with someone who has something against you? Isn't intercession critical in the earth? Yes, but so is living at peace with all men as far as it depends on you (see Rom. 12:18).

"We ought carefully to preserve Christian love and peace with all our brethren; and if at any time there is a quarrel, we should confess our fault, humble ourselves to our brother, making or offering satisfaction for wrong done in word or deed: and we should do this quickly; because, till this is done, we are unfit for communion with God in holy ordinances," Matthew Henry writes in his commentary.

Even if it's just an offense our brother has with us—even if we haven't done anything wrong—it can lead to a breach in the spirit if we don't obey Scripture to try to make it right. God is concerned about your brother's offended heart. If nothing else, he should be the first one you pray for.

— *Prayer* —

Father, in the name of Jesus, would You help me to take this command seriously? I want to walk in peace with all men as much as it depends on me. Make me a peacemaker. I want to be fit for prayer.

A Key to Exponential Prayer Power

"Again I say to you that if two of you agree on earth concerning anything that they ask, it will be done for them by My Father in heaven. For where two or three are gathered together in My name, I am there in the midst of them" (Matthew 18:19-20).

Just because two or more people pray together, doesn't mean they truly agree. Sure, Jesus is in the midst of the prayer meeting, but that doesn't mean there's agreement.

What is agreement? In this context, it's to be in harmony about the prayer agenda. Agreement means to have the same purpose in intercession. It's to carry the same opinion about what God wants to do in a situation. Unfortunately, sometimes the more people you add to the prayer meeting the less agreement you have. That's why some intercession should be relegated to the two or three who can truly agree.

The Amplified Classic translation of Matthew 18:19-20 reads, "Again I say to you, that if two believers on earth agree [that is, are of one mind, in harmony] about anything that they ask [within the will of God], it will be done for them by My Father in heaven. For where two or three are gathered in My name [meeting together as My followers], I am there among them."

Agreement in prayer attracts the Holy Spirit. When we truly agree in prayer, we tap into a spiritual realm that opens heavens, sends devils fleeing, and brings God's will to the earth as it is in heaven. Just as the Father, Son and Holy Spirit agree, we need to find people of prayer with whom we can agree. If we disagree on an issue, there's no point in joining hands in prayer over the issue.

The Message translation puts it this way: "When two of you get together on anything at all on earth and make a prayer of it, my Father in heaven goes into action. And when two or three of you are together because of me, you can be sure that I'll be there." If you want to multiply the power in your prayer meeting, everyone needs to get into agreement with His will.

— *Prayer* —

Father, in the name of Jesus, would You help me find a people who can truly agree on Your will? If I am in disagreement with the prayer, would You help me to search my heart for Your will so I can agree with You?

AUGUST 29

Stir Up the Gift in You

"Therefore I remind you to stir up the gift of God which is in you through the laying on of my hands" (2 Timothy 1:6).

Paul imparted spiritual gifts to people in the churches he planted. In fact, he explicitly told the Romans he wanted to visit them in order to impart a spiritual gift that would establish them (see Rom. 1:11). Paul also imparted to Timothy. Second Timothy 1:6 reveals we can receive gifts freely through impartation, but it's up to us to stay stirred up.

Some time after the impartation, Paul told Timothy to stir up the gift. Other versions say, "fan into flames the spiritual gift" (NLT). Others say, "kindle afresh the gift of God" (NASB). Still others say, "keep ablaze the gift of God" (HCSB). I like the fire connection because it speaks of being on fire for God and service to God and His people for His glory. Intercessors are not exempt from the need to stay stirred up.

The reality is, we can feel rusty if we don't exercise our gifts. If you are used to interceding frequently and a season of trial comes where you are mostly praying for you, intercession can feel like riding bike you haven't pedaled in years. You feel a bit wobbly when you start. As an intercessor, you can't allow dust or rust to settle on your gift. Even in a difficult personal season, look for ways to stir up the gift—to rekindle the flame.

It's no accident the Holy Spirit is often depicted as a flame. When He rushed into the Upper Room like a mighty wind on the Day of Pentecost, He rested on each disciple in the form of fire. Consider this: The disciples weren't out preaching the Gospel. They weren't casting out devils or working miracles in that Upper Room.

When the Holy Spirit's fire touched them and gifted them, they were waiting with expectation. They were praying in one accord. Fanning into flames the spiritual gift may look like praying in tongues for an hour a day. It may look like sitting in silence in His presence. It may look like intercession. It may look like worship. What does it look like for you? Ask Him.

— Prayer —

Father, in the name of Jesus, help me become a living sacrifice in intercession.
Give me the grace to pray for others at least as much as I pray for myself. I want
to be selfless, preferring others, and sacrificial in intercession.

The Sacrifice of Prayer

"You also, as living stones, are being built up a spiritual house, a holy priesthood, to offer up spiritual sacrifices acceptable to God through Jesus Christ" (1 Peter 2:5).

Through Christ we are supposed to continually offer up a sacrifice of praise to God, the fruit of lips that acknowledge His name (see Heb. 13:15). In the same way, we should continually offer up a sacrifice of prayer to God, in the powerful name of Jesus. Put another way, our sacrifice of praise can pave the way for the sacrifice of prayer.

What is a sacrifice? An act of offering something precious to God. God delights in the prayers of the righteous because You are acknowledging Jesus' sacrifice on the cross to make a way for You to go directly to the Father in His name. You are demonstrating humility and dependence on the sovereign God who hears and answers prayer.

What is a sacrifice? A sacrifice is losing sight of one's own interests in intercession. It's not only picking up your cross and following Him into the realm of prayer, but also bearing others' burdens in intercession. It's a sacrifice of service sowed with faith to see God's will done.

"The praying which makes a prayerful ministry is not a little praying put in as we put flavor to give it a pleasant snack, but the praying must be in the body, and form the blood and bones," the great man of prayer E.M. Bounds wrote in his book, *Power Through Prayer*.

"Prayer is no petty duty, put into a corner; no piecemeal performance made out of the fragments of time which have been snatched from business and other engagements of life; but it means that the best of our time, the heart of our time and strength must be given."

Christ gave Himself up for us, a fragrant offering and sacrifice to God (see Eph. 5:2). When we give ourselves over to intercession, we are giving ourselves up for Christ. We are coming into His agreement for His Bride. We are setting aside our own needs and focusing on His will. In return, He will reward us for our sacrifice of praise and prayer.

— *Prayer* —

Father, in the name of Jesus, would You help offer the sacrifice of intercession? Help me to consider the needs of others and offer my life as a living sacrifice to see Your will done in earth.

AUGUST 31

The Justice Intercessor

"But let justice run down like water, and righteousness like a mighty stream" (Amos 5:24).

As injustice continues to rise in the earth, God is calling forth justice intercessors. I heard the Lord say, "Ask me for justice. Ask me for what is right because I am the God who makes the wrong things right. I am the Judge of all the earth. So keep crying out. Keep shouting out. Keep standing in the evil day of injustice and you will see I will avenge you of your adversaries speedily."

Now, there are times when we pray for justice for ourselves, but justice intercessors are standing in the gap for others. Their adversary, in this case, is the spirit of injustice. If you are a justice intercessor, Jesus gave you a prayer strategy and some encouragement in Luke 18:1-8:

"Then He spoke a parable to them, that men always ought to pray and not lose heart, saying: 'There was in a certain city a judge who did not fear God nor regard man. Now there was a widow in that city; and she came to him, saying, 'Get justice for me from my adversary.' And he would not for a while; but afterward he said within himself, 'Though I do not fear God nor regard man, yet because this widow troubles me I will avenge her, lest by her continual coming she weary me.'

"Then the Lord said, 'Hear what the unjust judge said. And shall God not avenge His own elect who cry out day and night to Him, though He bears long with them? I tell you that He will avenge them speedily. Nevertheless, when the Son of Man comes, will He really find faith on the earth?'"

It's interesting that there's a requirement for speedy vengeance. It's crying out day and night to God. It requires a commitment to see the Judge's will be done and the enemy pushed back. Are you up for it?

— *Prayer* —

Father, in the name of Jesus, I am willing to take a stand in prayer against the injustices in the earth. If You want to use me as a justice intercessor, give me the grace for day and night prayer that battles the enemy. Help me stand.

SEPTEMBER

"Therefore I say to you, whatever things you ask when you pray, believe that you receive them, and you will have them" (Mark 11:24).

Building a Prayer Culture

"But you must continue in the things which you have learned and been assured of, knowing from whom you have learned them" (2 Timothy 3:14).

Awakening House of Prayer has a culture that values prayer, spiritual warfare, worship, the prophetic, and the many supernatural expressions and gifts of the Holy Spirit. Of course, it took time to cultivate that culture. In other words, cultures are not established overnight.

What's the prayer culture of your intercessory ministry? Your prayer culture is your beliefs, your customs, your expressions of worship and prayer, your theology—including your eschatological views. Your customs are based on your values and inform shared attitudes, goals, behaviors and practices that mark your prayer ministry.

So, how do you build a strong culture? As I write in my book, *Birthing a House of Prayer*, "Your culture starts with your vision. So go back and look at the vision God gave you for intercession. It also depends on your personality. God isn't going to call you to cultivate a culture that's completely contrary to who you are and the gifts you carry. If you have a strong prophetic bent, for example, your culture will naturally be more prophetic."

If you are not the leader of a group, you still have your own prayer culture, and the group you are part of has a prayer culture. No matter what prayer culture you are part of, it's important to respect it. Unless the culture is toxic, don't try to change it. You are there to serve within the context of the culture in unity.

"There is a difference between a church that prays and a praying church. One has prayer programs. The other develops a prayer culture," Daniel Henderson, author of *Transforming Prayer*, so eloquently wrote. "Building a prayer culture takes time. . . and relentless pressure over time. I often say that it is much more a crock pot than a microwave."

— *Prayer* —

Father, in the name of Jesus, would You help me develop my own personal prayer culture according to the gifts and talents You have given me? Help me to align in unity with the corporate prayer cultures You've called me to serve?

Destroying Prayer Distractions

"Martha, Martha, you are worried and distracted by many things" (Luke 10:41).

Have you ever noticed how when you sit down to pray or read the Word, there are often many distractions? Suddenly, everybody and their sister is calling or texting you. You have to go to the bathroom. Your ears itch. You remember that you forgot to set an important appointment. And the list goes on…

Sometimes, we have to battle noise in our minds—or noise in our environment—that work to distract us from praying. Barking dogs, crying kids, and delivery services dropping packages off at your door can be distracting. Ambulances and trains passing by can be distracting.

Paul said, "I am saying this for your benefit, not to place restrictions on you. I want you to do whatever will help you serve the Lord best, with as few distractions as possible" (1 Cor. 7:34). Paul spoke those words in the context of singleness, but they apply just as well to the context of intercession.

Think about this: In elementary school, we learn reading, writing, and arithmetic. We are taught to sit up straight and pay attention. But most of us were never taught how to focus. Distractions abound, but if you can learn to focus you can demolish these devilish agendas to stop your prayers. Remember, he wouldn't be trying to stop you if your prayers weren't powerful.

Here are some practical tips for dealing with natural and spiritual distractions that would quench your prayer life. First, identify and eliminate every possible distraction. Some distractions are especially obvious others are more subtle. Pay attention to what distracts you, and remove it if possible.

Your smartphone dinging every five minutes is an obvious distraction. Put your phone in the other room so you won't be tempted to look at it. Shut it completely off if you must. Have a pen and paper next to you so when random thoughts of undone tasks rise up to distract you, you can quickly jot them down and move on. Focus!

— Prayer —

Father, in the name of Jesus, would You help me overcome every distraction to prayer and study of Your Word? Help me see the root of the distractions and lay an axe to it. Help me to focus myself and Your presence in prayer.

SEPTEMBER 3

Preparing for Prayer

"The Lord is near to all who call upon Him, to all who call upon Him in truth"
(Psalm 145:18).

Before you launch out into intercession, you should be prepared for the journey. Yes, some situations demand crisis intercession. There's no time to think. There's no time to plan. There's no time to prepare. You have to respond immediately and with urgency. But most of the time we can prepare ourselves for a meeting with the King.

So how do we prepare for prayer? It starts with an inward preparation. It starts with confessing our sins and finding cleansing from unrighteousness (see 1 John 1:9). It starts with allowing Him to wash us with the water of His Word and build our faith to intercede for His yes and amen promises (see Eph. 5:26). It starts with waiting on Him to inform your intercession before you open your mouth to utter a prayer.

You can prepare for prayer by meditating on who God is. He is all powerful. He can make the wrong things right and the crooked places straight. He is all knowing. He sees the end from the beginning. He is faithful to watch over His Word to perform it. He is good. He works all things together for good to those who love Him and are called according to His purpose (see Rom. 8:28).

Preparing for prayer is stilling our soul (see Ps. 46:10). It's praising and worshipping Him until we are at peace rather than under pressure; until we are in awe rather in than in anxiety; until we are in wonder rather than in worry. It's waiting to release our intercession until we come to a place of faith-filled assurance that we have an invitation to approach God's throne of grace boldly with our petition.

And here's the thing: If you prepare daily, then when the storm comes you'll be ready to step into prevailing prayer with faith.

— *Prayer* —

Father, in the name of Jesus, help me remember not to rush the process of prayer.
Teach me to get ready for intercession so when I engage with the enemy holding
back the promise I am standing in faith that You will move.

The Forerunner Intercessor

"For this is he of whom it is written: 'Behold, I send My messenger before Your face, who will prepare Your way before You'" (Matthew 11:10).

God is raising up forerunner intercessors to prepare the church for major transitions, including the Second Coming of Christ. Perhaps you've never heard of forerunner intercessors. Let me explain.

A forerunner is someone or something that comes before another. A forerunner intercessor can even serve prophetically as a sign of something that is going to happen through their fervent prayer for things to come.

Forerunner intercessors are preparing the way for the Lord to work in someone's life, city or region. They are spiritual pioneers in the realm of intercession, breaking through barriers to make straight the pathway for the Lord's will to be done on the earth. Isaiah prophesied:

"The voice of one crying in the wilderness: 'Prepare the way of the Lord; Make straight in the desert a highway for our God. Every valley shall be exalted and every mountain and hill brought low; The crooked places shall be made straight and the rough places smooth; The glory of the Lord shall be revealed, and all flesh shall see it together; For the mouth of the Lord has spoken'" (Is. 40:3-5).

John the Baptist was a prophet but he was also a forerunner intercessor. (Remember, all prophets are intercessors, but not all intercessors are prophets.) John prepared the world for a great move of God—the first coming of the Lord Jesus Christ. I believe forerunner intercessors in this hour are preparing the world for another great move of God.

Intercessors are generally misunderstood and sometimes otherworldly because they have their hearts set on heaven's manifestation. But forerunner intercessors may be more misunderstood because they are praying about things that much of the rest of the Body of Christ can't even see yet.

If you are praying for things that aren't even on the Body of Christ's radar screen yet, you could be a forerunner intercessor. Embrace the call.

— *Prayer* —

Father, in the name of Jesus, would You grace me with a revelation of the things
You have planned in the earth so I can agree in prayer? Would You give me the
spirit of a forerunner who is willing to go first in realms of prayer to bring heaven's
will down in our very midst?

The S.D. Gordon Prayer Anointing

"Will he delight himself in the Almighty? Will he always call on God?" (Job 27:10)

If you read classic books on prayer, you'll find a lot of people quoting S.D. Gordon. Gordon, who lived in the early 1900s, wrote more than 25 books, leaving plenty of wisdom behind. His first book sold half a million copies.

Late nineteenth- and early-twentieth-century American pastor and author E.W. Kenyon once said, "S.D. Gordon is a sporadic outburst of divine grace. He is unusual, as are all of God's rare tools… he is perfectly balanced in the Word and in the Spirit. He represents that rare but vanishing class of spiritually minded men of the last generation."

Gordon wasn't just an author of books like *Quiet Talks on Prayer*, he was also a missionary. Gordon spent four years on Oriental and European mission fields. And he had a revelation of prayer that inspires intercessors today. Gordon said things like: "You can do more than pray after you have prayed but you cannot do more than pray until you have prayed."

In relation to others, Gordon also points us back to prayer: "The greatest thing anyone can do for God and man is pray. It is not the only thing; but it is the chief thing," he said. "The great people of the earth today are the people who pray. I do not mean those who talk about prayer; not those who can explain about prayer; but I mean those people who take time and pray."

It's easier to talk about prayer, to teach about prayer, or to plan prayer than it is to pray. Make no mistake, the enemy will pull out all the stops to keep a saint from praying. Gordon helped the people who followed his ministry keep the main thing the main thing. The main thing is prayer. Gordon put it this way, "Our prayer is God's opportunity to get into the world that would shut Him out."

— *Prayer* —

Father, in the name of Jesus, would You give me a revelation of how critical my intercession really is? Help me see prayer as a pathway for You to have Your way in a world that increasingly shuts You out.

SEPTEMBER 6

Looking for the Prayer Answer

"So he went up and looked, and said, 'There is nothing.' And seven times, he said, 'Go again'"
(1 Kings 18:43).

When we pray in faith, we'll look for the answer. We'll expect God to move at the sound of our voice when we lift up petitions that align with His will in the name of Jesus.

Elijah prayed a bold prayer at the showdown at Mt. Carmel: "Lord God of Abraham, Isaac, and Israel, let it be known this day that You are God in Israel and I am Your servant, and that I have done all these things at Your word. Hear me, O Lord, hear me, that this people may know that You are the Lord God, and that You have turned their hearts back to You again" (1 Kings 18:36-27). Immediately, God answered by fire and Israel turned back to Him.

But all prayer answers don't come so immediately. Elijah boldly announced to Ahab that he should, "Go up, eat and drink; for there is the sound of abundance of rain." Ahab believed him and went off to eat and drink, but Elijah went to pray down the rain. He bowed low to the ground, put his face between his knees and prayed. Then Elijah told his servant to go look for rain but there was nothing.

Seven times Elijah told his servant to go look. Finally, on the seventh time he reported, "There is a cloud, as small as a man's hand, rising out of the sea!" (1 Kings 18:44). In this case, Elijah knew exactly what he was looking for. He was looking for the rain and he looked with expectation.

By contrast, we don't always know what the prayer answer looks like. Even still, we should look for God's answer with the same expectation Elijah carried. The challenge is that God may answer in a way that seems almost contrary to what we asked because His ways are higher than our ways. And He knows best. Get in the practice of looking for answers to your intercession. When you expect them, you will surely and eventually find them.

— *Prayer* —

Father, in the name of Jesus, would You help me stir myself up in faith to expect the answer, eagerly waiting for the solutions, the divine intervention, the miracles and more? Help me see Your answers in whatever way they manifest. I want to praise You.

Your Hotline to Heaven

"And in that day you will ask Me nothing. Most assuredly, I say to you, whatever you ask the Father in My name He will give you" (John 16:23).

The words of Christ in John 16:23 sound almost too good to be true. Up until John 16, His disciples went to Him for everything. They asked Him spiritual questions about deliverance. They asked Him to explain His parables. They asked Him for help.

But there came a time when Jesus started preparing them for His departure from the earth. He started getting them ready to go directly to their heavenly Father in His name. He said:

"And in that day you will ask Me nothing. Most assuredly, I say to you, whatever you ask the Father in My name He will give you. Until now you have asked nothing in My name. Ask, and you will receive, that your joy may be full" (John 16:23-24).

The Amplified Classic translates it this way: "In that day you will not [need to] ask Me about anything. I assure you and most solemnly say to you, whatever you ask the Father in My name [as My representative], He will give you. Until now you have not asked [the Father] for anything in My name; but now ask and keep on asking and you will receive, so that your joy may be full and complete."

When we go to the Father in prayer, we are representing Jesus on the earth. Just as Jesus represented the Father on earth, we represent Jesus. Jesus said He only did what He saw the Father do (see John 5:19). Jesus told Philip, "He who has seen Me has seen the Father" (John 14:9).

This was a foreign concept to the disciples. It was after this revelation that they asked Jesus to teach them how to pray. We find *The Lord's Prayer* a chapter later in John 17:1-3. Ask God for a revelation of your ambassadorship in the Kingdom and for Christ's will in the earth so you can represent Him rightly in intercession.

— *Prayer* —

Father, in the name of Jesus, help me represent You rightly in intercession. Help me ask for what You want to see in the earth—nothing more or less. Help me keep on asking for Your Kingdom to come and expect Your answer.

Territorial Intercession

"And seek the peace of the city where I have caused you to be carried away captive, and pray to the Lord for it; for in its peace you will have peace" (Jeremiah 29:7).

Blessed is the nation whose God is the Lord (see Ps. 33:12). But in many cities and nations, God is shut out. These are nations that largely forget God (see Ps. 9:17). And even in cities and nations where Christianity is predominant, there is plenty of darkness to expel.

Yet, God says He will be exalted among the nations, and exalted in the earth (see Ps. 46:10). So how will this happen? It happens through intercession. The late and great evangelist Billy Graham once said, "To get nations back on their feet, we must first get down on our knees."

Our heavenly Father made this promise to Jesus, "Ask of Me, and I will give You the nations for Your inheritance, and the ends of the earth for Your possession" (Ps. 2:8). As those who are set on earth to fulfill the Great Commission and occupy until He comes, we can take this promise as our own as we make intercession for cities and nations.

We must remember that even in dark nations such as those in the Middle East, God has a remnant. Jesus said the Gospel would be preached in all the nations before His return. So, yes, we need to get down on our knees. We need to pray for lost souls in nations, for leaders in nations, for economies of nations, for churches in nations.

Nations are made up of many cities, and there are times when the Holy Spirit will have you lean into prayer for a specific city. Just as we are commanded to pray for the peace of Jerusalem (see Ps. 122:6), we should pray for the peace of our city. And when God assigns us to another city we should be just as fervent in prayer as if it were our own city.

If you've lost your passion to pray for your nation or your city, get in your car and drive around. Look at the homeless people, the prostitutes, the drug addicts and others who are suffering because they don't know Jesus. When you hear the cry of your city and your nation, you will be stirred to pray.

— *Prayer* —

Father, in the name of Jesus, would You give me a passion to make intercession for my city, my nation—and any other cities and nations You want to assign me? The world is made up of cities who need to be reached with the Gospel. Grace me to stand and pray.

SEPTEMBER 9

Life-and-Death Intercessors

"Yea, though I walk through the valley of the shadow of death, I will fear no evil; For You are with me; Your rod and Your staff, they comfort me" (Psalm 23:4).

Have you ever heard of life-and-death intercession? I coined the term for prayer sessions that move beyond a crisis and into life and death. After all, not every crisis is life-and-death. But when you are facing a life-and-death situation, it's more than a crisis.

The Israelites needed a life-and-death intercessor more than once. We see this play out in a dramatic way in the Book of Numbers. Imagine the scene. The Israelites got discouraged journeying through the wilderness and began to speak against God and against Moses. God wasn't pleased. Numbers 21:5-8 tells us:

"So the Lord sent fiery serpents among the people, and they bit the people; and many of the people of Israel died. Therefore the people came to Moses, and said, 'We have sinned, for we have spoken against the Lord and against you; pray to the Lord that He take away the serpents from us.' So Moses prayed for the people. Then the Lord said to Moses, 'Make a fiery serpent, and set it on a pole; and it shall be that everyone who is bitten, when he looks at it, shall live.'"

The power of life and death are in the tongue. Therefore, you can use your tongue to decree life. You can use your mouth to come against the spirit of death. You can prophesy that dry bones will live. You can decree that something or someone shall live and not die (see Ps. 118:17).

The Word of God is alive. You can pray prayers of life despite the enemy's plans to steal, kill and destroy (see John 10:10). God sets before us life and death. Instead of agreeing with the enemy's plans, we can choose life. We can choose to release prayers of life. Ask God to put life in your mouth.

— Prayer —

Father, in the name of Jesus, would You help me stand strong in the midst of life-and-death circumstances? Help me not to be moved by what I see but only to be moved by Your Word and by Your Spirit.

SEPTEMBER 10

Morning, Noon and Night Prayers

"Evening and morning and at noon I will pray, and cry aloud, and He shall hear my voice"
(Psalm 55:17).

David was serious about prayer—so serious that he prayed three times a day. That's unusual in today's hustle culture. Many Christians don't even pray daily, much less three times a day. Should we pray three times a day?

Like David, Daniel did—even though he knew it would get him thrown into a lion's den. That's how committed he was to praying thrice daily. You know the story. Some Babylonians were jealous of Daniel because the Israelite prophet had favor with the king. These evil doers manipulated King Darius into signing a decree that commanded anyone who petitioned any god or man for 30 days besides Darius would be a meal for roaring lions.

"Now when Daniel knew that the writing was signed, he went home. And in his upper room, with his windows open toward Jerusalem, he knelt down on his knees three times that day, and prayed and gave thanks before his God, as was his custom since early days" (Dan. 6:10). Outward circumstances didn't change Daniel's inner commitment to pray three times a day. But why?

The Bible doesn't set forth any command to pray three times a day, though it does say we should continue steadfastly in prayer (see Rom. 12:12-13), continue earnestly in prayer (see Col. 4:2), and always pray without losing heart (see Luke 18:1). But while there's no law that dictates praying three times a day—morning, noon and night—know that it is a spiritual discipline that drives great growth.

Prayer helps us keep our minds set on God and empowers us to carry out our callings. Prayer unlocks wisdom, grace, healing and whatever else we need from God. Prayer deepens our relationship with the Lord. Prayer supercharges our spirits and unburdens our souls. Prayer renews our physical strength and brings peace to our hearts. Prayer changes things.

— Prayer —

Father, in the name of Jesus, I recognize the tremendous value of prayer. Would You help me develop a discipline to pray three times a day—morning, noon and night—even if it's only for a few minutes?

SEPTEMBER 11

The Red Alert Intercessor

"The righteous cry out, and the Lord hears, and delivers them out of all their troubles"
(Psalm 34:17).

Are you a crisis intercessor? A crisis intercessor, or red alert intercessor, is like a first-responder to an emergency. Crisis intercessors are usually on the prayer scene first. They either pick it up in the spirit or respond to the news with immediate intercession. Their attitude is not, "I'll pray about it when I get home." They drop everything to pray.

A crisis intercessor carries a sense of urgency in their spirit. In reality, it's the urgency of the Holy Spirit that dwells on the inside of them. A crisis intercessor stands in the gap to prevent a crisis. A crisis intercessor may not know who they are praying for, much like a paramedic that shows up on the scene to find an unidentified victim.

A crisis intercessor carries wisdom and prophetic intelligence into how exactly to pray. A crisis intercessor believes Romans 8:28 and Genesis 50:20—that God will turn everything around for good, including what the enemy meant for harm— as they pray. A crisis intercessor needs empathy, the ability to truly understand and even share the feelings of another.

A crisis intercessor is selfless. A crisis intercessor wants to bring healing to a person or situation. A crisis intercessor responds to what's urgent on God's heart, whether it has manifested in the natural realm or not. You might not see it but God does and He stirs you to pray.

A crisis intercessor may be awakened in the middle of the night with an urgent prayer assignment. A crisis intercessor is energized in the face of crises because of the anointing and grace on their life. A crisis intercessor may be called away at inopportune times by the Holy Spirit to pray for an urgent situation.

Are you a crisis intercessor? Get more training on crisis intercession in my School of Prayer & Intercession. And pray that God will make you more sensitive to His heart.

— Prayer —

Father, in the name of Jesus, I am willing to be a first responder in the spirit. If You can use me in the midst of the crisis, call on me day or night. Give me the spiritual skills I need to succeed in standing in the gap during crisis.

Cultivating a Determined Spirit

"Because the Sovereign Lord helps me, I will not be disgraced. Therefore, I have set my face like stone, determined to do his will" (Isaiah 50:7, NLT).

I'm a determined. I've always said the best thing I have going for me is I refuse to give up. We can be determined as we want to be, but without determined prayer we won't get very far in God's Kingdom. Determined prayer is essential to our breakthrough.

George Mueller, a nineteenth century Christian evangelist known for building orphanages, once said: "It is not enough to begin to pray, nor to pray aright; nor is it enough to continue for a time to pray; but we must pray patiently, believing, continue in prayer until we obtain an answer."

Hannah was determined to see barrenness broken off her life. She was so determined that she didn't waiver when Eli the priest accused her of being drunk in the temple while she was merely pouring her heart out to God in prayer.

So how do you cultivate a determined spirit? It starts with determining the will of God. When you can see the will of the Lord, you can be confident that He hears your prayers and you will pray with a determined purpose in mind.

Since determined prayer is consistent prayer you need to make a quality decision to stay steady in prayer. Often seeing the prayer answer manifest is like chopping down a tree with an axe. It's going to take more than one swing. You can't pray a few days and then stop praying. You have to determine to pray until you see the answer.

Cindy Jacobs wrote this in her excellent book, *The Power of Persistent Prayer*, "And there are days when we will be distracted, tired, sick, bored, or even downright tired of praying. That's normal; we are, after all, only human. But God has the victory—He just wants our heart and our willingness to pray. He will do the rest!"

The enemy is determined to keep you from praying. You must be more determined to pray through. It's a battle of the wills—and your will aligned with God's will is unstoppable.

— *Prayer* —

Father, in the name of Jesus, would You help me cultivate a determined spirit. I don't want to give up on the brink of breakthrough. Help me set my forehead link flint and give me a backbone of steal to stand against the enemy's determined purposes against my prayer.

The Revelation of Your Amen

"And Ezra blessed the Lord, the great God. Then all the people answered, 'Amen, Amen!' while lifting up their hands" (Nehemiah 8:6).

At the end of your intercession is a four-letter word that carries power you might not have considered. It's the word "amen." Jesus ends *The Lord's Prayer* with "amen." Paul the apostle ended his prayers with "amen" over and again.

The psalmist ended his prayer with "amen and amen" (see Ps. 72:19). Notably, the very last line in the very last book of the Bible ends with "amen." Revelation 22:21 reads, "The grace of our Lord Jesus Christ be with you all. Amen."

So what's with the "amen"? Well, all of God's promises are "yes and amen" (see 2 Cor. 1:20). God has already given the amen and now we need to issue our amen. Amen means firm. It means, "so it is, so be it, may it be fulfilled," according to *The KJV New Testament Greek Lexicon.*

Dick Eastman in his book, *The Change the World School of Prayer*, rightly said, "'Amen' actually is to express our confidence that God will honor our petitions just prayed. 'Amen' means 'May it be so.' It's a word of both confirmation and completion. To add 'amen' to one's prayer is like a judge striking his desk with a gavel, proclaiming, 'It is done.' Uniquely, 'Amen' is also a name given to Jesus in Scripture. In this sense we are ending our prayer with a bold declaration that in Christ we have confidence that our prayers have been heard and answers are on the way. Amen!"

Did you catch that? Amen is a name for Jesus in Scripture. Revelation 3:14 reads, "And to the angel of the church of the Laodiceans write, 'These things says the Amen, the Faithful and True Witness, the Beginning of the creation of God.'"

"The best definition I can find of faith is the dependence upon the veracity of another. The Bible definition in the 11th chapter of Hebrews is, 'Faith is the substance of things hoped for, the evidence of things not seen.' In other words, faith says amen to everything that God says," said the great evangelist, teacher and urban ministry pioneer Dwight L. Moody. "Faith takes God without any ifs. If God says it, faith says I believe it; Faith says amen to it."

— *Prayer* —

Father, in the name of Jesus, You've given me Your yes and amen. Help me to give You my yes and amen. Remind me to end my sessions of prayer and intercession with this emphatic statement of certainty that it shall be done and not waiver from my amen.

Taking a Prayer Bath

"Don't worry about anything; instead, pray about everything. Tell God what you need, and thank him for all he has done" (Philippians 4:6, NLT).

Smith Wigglesworth once said, "I don't spend more than half an hour in prayer at one time, but I never go more than half an hour without praying." What a heart posture! That speaks of a man who knew he was totally dependent on God.

You might say Wigglesworth bathed everything in prayer. Think about the concept of bathing. When you bathe you become immersed in water. To Wigglesworth, that water was prayer. It seems he took every concern, every need, and every problem into His prayer closet.

Intercessors, we need to bathe everything in prayer. We need to drown spiritual attacks against us with prayer. We need to bury our cares in prayer. We need to drench our dryness in prayer. We need to soak our problems in prayer. Everything to God in prayer.

S.D. Gordon, a prolific author and minister in the 18th and 19th centuries, had a deep understanding of this concept. He taught that everything we do must be bathed in prayer before we set out to do it. "One should never initiate anything that he cannot saturate with prayer," he wrote. "The real victory in all service is won in secret beforehand by prayer."

Think about how your life—and the lives of those for whom you are making intercession—could change if you bathed the issues of life in prayer. Think about how many prodigals would come home, how many souls would be saved, how many breakthroughs would be wrought if you bathed everything in prayer. Just think about it. It will inspire you.

E.M. Bounds, a great man of prayer who authored many books on the subject, agreed. He wrote, "No ministry can succeed without much praying, and this praying must be fundamental, ever-abiding, ever-increasing. The text, the sermon, should be the result of prayer. The study should be bathed in prayer, all its duties so impregnated with prayer, its whole spirit the spirit of prayer."

— Prayer —

Father, in the name of Jesus, thank You for the opportunity to come boldly to Your throne of grace to make my petitions about anything and everything that concerns me and the people for whom You've assigned me to pray. I will bathe everything in prayer.

SEPTEMBER 15

The Ruth Ward Heflin Prayer Anointing

"To them God willed to make known what are the riches of the glory of this mystery among the Gentiles: which is Christ in you, the hope of glory" (Colossians 1:27).

Ruth Ward Heflin was considered by many to be a matriarch of modern-day Pentecostalism. Throughout her forty years of ministry, she stood in the gap as a general of prayer and intercession with a heart for Israel and to see the glory cover the earth as the waters cover the sea.

Heflin, who went home to be with the Lord in 2000, said things like, "Our spiritual eyes and ears are open to see and hear as Jesus speaks and leads us in our intercession." She said things like, "As you cultivate a relationship with Him, His power and authority for victory will be ignited and made known in your intercession." She said things like, "We must be intentional of pursuing Him so our spiritual walk and intercession becomes His intercession and we see the breakthrough come."

Think about that for a minute. His intercession can become our intercession. This is how Heflin lived and operated in ministry. She gave us a clue. She was known for saying, "Praise until the worship comes. Then worship until the glory comes. Then stand in the glory."

She wrote a series of books on the glory that would be strong additions to every intercessor's library, such as *River Glory, Golden Glory, Revelation Glory, Revival Glory, Harvest Glory,* and *Unifying Glory.* She learned plenty about walking in the glory before she ultimately went on the glory of heaven.

When we stand in the glory consistently, our ears are open to see and hear as Jesus speaks and leads. When we stand in the glory consistently, we get a revelation of His beauty, His power, and His goodness. When we walk in the atmosphere of heaven, we get revelation from heaven. When we stand in the glory long enough, His intercession becomes our intercession because we feel His heartbeat in prayer.

— *Prayer* —

Father, in the name of Jesus, I want to pray and intercede in the glory. Teach me how to enter Your glory and navigate realms of Your glory in prayer and intercession. Make me a glory intercessor.

SEPTEMBER 16

Put Your Determination Where Your Desire Is

"Delight yourself also in the Lord, and He shall give you the desires of your heart"
(Psalm 37:4).

Put your determination where your desire is. The Holy Spirit spoke those seven simple words to me ... and they bear repeating: Put your determination where your desire is. Friends, that's a key to seeing prayer answers.

What's your desire? What desire has God placed in your heart that burns inside your inward parts with a passion? What is that fire that's shut up in your bones; that blaze that can't be quenched by the nastiest naysayers or the most daunting doubters? Simply stated, what is your desperate prayer request?

Whatever your prayer desire is, stop wishing and get determined. See, the difference between hoping and wishing is significant. A wish is a desire for something that seems unattainable. (But nothing is impossible with God.) Hope, by contrast, is desire with an expectation of attainment. Hope expects with confidence. Hope cherishes a desire with anticipation. Hope breeds faith—and faithful determination generates grace.

Put your determination where your desire is. If your desire is for your household to be saved, or for your spouse to abandon some annoying behavior, your determination is bound to prayer. James 5:1 says the effective fervent prayer of a righteous person makes tremendous power available. You can't change people no matter how determined you are. But you can pray for them with a sincere heart and open the door for God to move in their lives—and you should.

You need determination to overcome the resistance to your prayer and intercession. That resistance may serve as confirmation that your desires are in line with God's will. That confirmation should give you joy unspeakable and full of glory. That joy will invigorate you with strength. That strength will fuel your faith and activate God's grace. And that grace will empower you to continue persevering in the face of any opposition. Believe this: God's grace is sufficient to overcome anything that stands between you and His will.

— *Prayer* —

Father, in the name of Jesus, would You give me a determination to press and keep on pressing in prayer and intercession for the desires You have put in my heart? Would You help me set my face like flint to stand against the resistance to my intercession?

SEPTEMBER 17

Precision Prayers

"What do you want Me to do for you?" (Mark 10:51)

When Jesus was walking through Jericho, a blind man named Bartimaeus cried out to Him. He was crying for mercy. The crowd told him to shut up, but he cried all the more. That desperate cry caused Jesus to stop dead in His tracks and the Messiah called the blind man over to meet Him. What happens next is a lesson in the need to release specific prayers.

"And throwing aside his garment, he rose and came to Jesus. So Jesus answered and said to him, 'What do you want Me to do for you?' The blind man said to Him, 'Rabboni, that I may receive my sight.' Then Jesus said to him, 'Go your way; your faith has made you well.' And immediately he received his sight and followed Jesus on the road" (Mark 10:50-52).

Bartimaeus released a general request for mercy, but Jesus wanted the blind man to be more specific. He wanted the blind man to extend his faith for something distinct and definite. Jesus knew what Bartimaeus wanted. It was clear to everyone he was blind. Nevertheless, Jesus asked him to be more specific. Why? Because when a detailed request is made, there's no denying the answer.

Paul put it this way in Philippians 4:6-7 (AMP), "Do not be anxious or worried about anything, but in everything [every circumstance and situation] by prayer and petition with thanksgiving, continue to make your [specific] requests known to God. And the peace of God [that peace which reassures the heart, that peace] which transcends all understanding, [that peace which] stands guard over your hearts and your minds in Christ Jesus [is yours]."

Think about it. Bartimaeus had faith that Jesus could heal him, but Jesus wanted him to express that faith in detail. Mercy could have meant money to the blind beggar. His specific prayer got him something money couldn't buy: his eyesight.

— Prayer —

Father, in the name of Jesus, would You remind me to be specific and pray with details of what I am hoping and praying for? Help me not to pray in such general terms that I can't discern the answer. I want to be able to give You the glory You deserve when the prayer answer comes.

SEPTEMBER 18

Supercharging Your Prayer Life

"I ate no pleasant food, no meat or wine came into my mouth, nor did I anoint myself at all, till three whole weeks were fulfilled" (Daniel 10:3).

Andrew Murray said, "Prayer is reaching out after the unseen; fasting is letting go of all that is seen and temporal. Fasting helps express, deepen, confirm the resolution that we are ready to sacrifice anything, even ourselves to attain what we seek for the Kingdom of God."

Fasting is abstaining from food or some activity to focus on God. But it's just as much what you do instead of activities as it is the fast itself. If you fast and sit on the couch and watch TV all day, you are merely going on a glorified diet. You will get some of the benefits of fasting but you are missing the spiritual point. Fasting is not a diet. It's a spiritual discipline.

Jesus didn't say "if" you fast, He said, "when you fast." And He said it more than once. Look at Matthew 6:16-18: "Moreover, when you fast, do not be like the hypocrites, with a sad countenance. For they disfigure their faces that they may appear to men to be fasting. Assuredly, I say to you, they have their reward. But you, when you fast, anoint your head and wash your face, so that you do not appear to men to be fasting, but to your Father who is in the secret place; and your Father who sees in secret will reward you openly."

Fasting supercharges your prayer life. Fasting crucifies the flesh. As your flesh decreases, your spiritual sensitivity increases. It's easier to hear from God and pray His heart. Fasting gives you supernatural power over demonic oppression. Fasting can produce emotional breakthrough, spiritual breakthrough, or breakthrough in bad habits that plague our prayer lives. Those breakthroughs ripple down and lead to breakthrough in other areas of your life, such as your finances and relationships.

— Prayer —

Father, in the name of Jesus, would You lead me and guide me into fasting? Give me the grace to fast, whether it's food or media or even people who are distracting me from Your heart. I want to supercharge my prayers. I want to decrease so You can increase.

285

SEPTEMBER 19

Singing Your Prayers

"But at midnight Paul and Silas were praying and singing hymns to God, and the prisoners were listening to them" (Acts 16:25).

When Paul and Silas were in prison, they were essentially singing their prayers. You can too. Perhaps you don't consider yourself a singer, but your prayer song sounds like a sweet melody in God's ears. It's a joyful noise to Him (see Ps. 95:1).

Just as Paul tells us to address one another in psalms and hymns and spiritual songs, singing and making melody to the Lord with your heart, we can address the Lord with spiritual songs that make our petitions melodic prayers (see Eph. 5:19). Often this is spontaneous, but you can also just decide to sing your prayers.

Paul once said, "I will pray with the spirit, and I will also pray with the understanding. I will sing with the spirit, and I will also sing with the understanding" (1 Cor. 14:15). We can pray in tongues in song. We can praise in tongues. We can worship in tongues. And we should. Psalm 47:7 tells us, "For God is the King of all the earth; Sing praises with understanding." The psalmist said, "I will sing to the Lord as long as I live; I will sing praise to my God while I have my being" (Ps. 104:33).

You can also play classic hymns like "It is Well with My Soul," which are essentially prayers. Consider the lyrics and you'll see the prayer confession in it:

"When peace like a river attendeth my way, when sorrows like sea billows roll; Whatever my lot Thou hast taught me to say, 'It is well, it is well with my soul!' It is well with my soul! It is well, it is well with my soul! Though Satan should buffet, though trials should come, let this blest assurance control, that Christ hath regarded my helpless estate, and hath shed His own blood for my soul." Singing your prayers can stir up your intercession. Try it.

— *Prayer* —

Father, in the name of Jesus, would You inspire me to sing my prayers. Would you give me a new song in prayer? Just as You sing songs of deliverance over me, would You teach me to share what's on my heart with Your heart through song? I will make a joyful noise.

Open Heaven Intercession

"Now it came about in the thirtieth year, on the fifth day of the fourth month, while I was by the river Chebar among the exiles, the heavens were opened and I saw visions of God"
(Ezekiel 1:1).

Since Ezekiel didn't write anything before Ezekiel 1:1, we don't know for sure what caused the heavens to open up before his very eyes. But if I had to settle on an explanation, I'd settle on prayer and intercession.

Ezekiel was a priest who lived among the Jewish captives carried away to Babylon. God later called him as a watchman and a prophet. He straddled three anointings, all of which depended on prayer and intercession to operate as he did.

Ezekiel's name means "strengthened by God." How do we find strength in God? Through prayer. Indeed, Ezekiel was a man of intercession. It was to him God said, "So I sought for a man among them who would make a wall, and stand in the gap before Me on behalf of the land, that I should not destroy it; but I found no one" (Ez. 22:30). But God did find one in Ezekiel.

Open heaven intercession is intercession that opens the heavens and the subsequent ease in prayer. God alone can open the heavens, but He does so in response to prayer. We see God respond with an open heaven and the Holy Spirit descend like a dove when Jesus prayed (see Luke 3:21-22). Likewise, we see Peter praying before heaven opened up with the vision of the animals in the sheet (see Acts 10:11).

So, what kind of prayer causes God to open the heavens and give us glimpses of the unseen realm, open our eyes to visions, or pour out His Spirit? We can find such a prayer when Elisha prayed for his servant in the face of warfare: "'Lord, I pray, open his eyes that he may see.' Then the Lord opened the eyes of the young man, and he saw. And behold, the mountain was full of horses and chariots of fire all around Elisha."

As you stand in intercession, ask God to open the eyes of your heart.

— *Prayer* —

Father, in the name of Jesus, I want to see what You want to show me in the Spirit. I want to receive supernatural sight so I can pray more effectively about the issues on Your heart. Would You open the eyes of my heart?

SEPTEMBER 21

God Quits When Man Quits

"I have fought the good fight, I have finished the race, I have kept the faith" (2 Timothy 4:7).

James Goll taught me, "God quits when man quits." What a statement! God is not a quitter. He is long-suffering, but many times we give up in intercession before we break through the resistance to seeing God's will come to pass. We allow a fainting spirit to discourage our hearts.

Daniel 7:25 warns us that the enemy comes to wear out the saints. But Paul gives us a Spirit-inspired exhortation in Galatians 6:9, "And let us not grow weary while doing good, for in due season we shall reap if we do not lose heart." *The Message Translation* puts it this way, "So let's not allow ourselves to get fatigued doing good. At the right time we will harvest a good crop if we don't give up, or quit."

We have to guard our hearts from the fainting spirit that wants us to give up and give in before we see the prayer answer. We never know if our next prayer is going to tip over the bowls in heaven or empower an angel in the battle to bring the prayer answer. God quits when man quits.

There is an appointed time for the intercessory breakthrough. God is working behind the scenes, answering your prayers and arranging circumstances to bring the promises to pass. He is taking what the enemy meant for harm and turning it for good. He really is. But if we look with our natural eyes instead of our spiritual eyes, our soul may want to quit. God quits when man quits.

Intercessors, be steadfast in your supplications. Be immovable in your intercession. Abound in the work of warfare. Do this with a heart full of faith knowing in the Lord your labor is not in vain (see 1 Cor. 15:18). Lay aside the weight of weariness. Lay aside the sin of unbelief. Know that there is a great cloud of witnesses cheering you on (see Heb. 12:1).

— Prayer —

Father, in the name of Jesus, would You give me the grace to stand and keep standing when I've poured my guts out in intercession and still see nothing changing? Would You help me tap into Your all-sufficient grace to keep pressing until I cross the finish line?

The Kathryn Kuhlman Prayer Anointing

"And the glory which You gave Me I have given them, that they may be one just as We are one"
(John 17:22).

When people think of Kathryn Kuhlman, a woman who saw many miracles in her ministry, they think of the incredible words of knowledge and healings. Fewer consider her prayer life. But her prayer life was the secret to the miracles. Kathryn once said:

"I pray all the time because if I limited the Holy Spirit to a certain number of hours a day, I would be in danger of using Him for my own purpose. If, for instance, I spent one hour a day in prayer, I would expect the Holy Spirit to reward me for that hour. I would begin to feel that it was that hour in prayer that caused the 'anointing' in the meeting. No, I cannot use the Holy Spirit in that way. I must practice His presence all of the time."

What an attitude to take on! This is the essence of what Paul meant when he said, "pray without ceasing" (see 1 Thess. 5:16). She knew all too well that she had no power in and of herself to heal anyone. She said, "All I can do is point you to the way—I can lead you to the Great Physician and I can pray; but the rest is left with you and God."

Because of her prayer life—because she was a woman of prayer—she shifted atmospheres everywhere she went. She prayed and emptied herself of herself before she stepped onto the platform. She cried out to God because she knew the power came only from His Spirit.

Oral Roberts, the Voice of Healing evangelist and founder of Oral Roberts University, knew Kathryn well and witnessed her prayer life in action. Doing his best to describe what he saw, he said, "It was like they were talking back and forth to each other, and you couldn't tell where Kathryn started and the Holy Spirit left off. It was a oneness."

— *Prayer* —

Father, in the name of Jesus, would You give me the revelation You gave Kathryn Kuhlman? Help me walk as one with You. Help me pray as one with You. Help me lean into You with utter dependance on Your willingness and ability to answer my heart.

SEPTEMBER 23

Inspecting Your Prayer Life

"You can pray for anything, and if you have faith, you will receive it" (Matthew 21:22).

How's your prayer life? Consider this notion: Your personal life—how you live day to day, how you treat others, how you conduct yourself when no one is looking, and so on—affects your prayer life. Whatever is not of faith is sin (see Rom. 14:23).

John Lavendar, author of *Why Prayers Are Unanswered*, once wrote, "The first thing that should concern you in your conversation with God is personal cleansing. Before you pray for a change of circumstances, you should pray for a change in character." Charles Spurgeon, a 19th Century Englishman known as the prince of preachers, agreed, adding, "For a successful season of prayer the best beginning is confession."

Thankfully, if we confess our sin He is faithful and just to forgive us of our sin and cleanse us (see 1 John 1:9). But beyond sins of commission are sins of omission. Inconsistent prayer will not birth consistent results. We all go through seasons where it's hard to keep the intercessory fire burning. That's when we need to discipline ourselves to stay consistent and to stay in faith when the answer seems far off.

"A person's prayer life is obviously only as strong as that person's faith is in God," Dick Eastman, Chief Prayer Officer at Every Home for Christ, wrote in his book, *Change the World School of Prayer*. He adds, "faith is essential to the only kind of prayer God answers—believing prayer."

So we're back to our daily life. Faith works by love (see Gal. 5:6). So if we are not walking in love we are walking in sin. The more we walk in the fruit of the Spirit, the more fruit we'll see in our prayer life. Paul put it this way: "Though I have all faith, so that I could remove mountains, but have not love, I am nothing" (1 Cor. 13:2).

— *Prayer* —

Father, in the name of Jesus, I don't want to hinder my prayer life by my thoughts, moods and attitudes outside the prayer closet. Help me walk in love. Help me walk in Your Spirit. Help me to cultivate the fruit of the Spirit. Help me inspect my prayer life and let You show me where I need to change.

290

Yielding to Impromptu Intercession

"So it was, when I heard these words, that I sat down and wept, and mourned for many days"
(Nehemiah 1:4).

Impromptu intercession. You can't plan it. No, not if it's truly impromptu. Impromptu intercession is an unction from the Holy Spirit to co-labor with Him prayer. It comes about suddenly and often ends just as suddenly. It can last seconds, minutes or hours.

What is impromptu intercession? Intercession that bubbles up from within you without notice. It's unplanned intercession. It's spur of the moment intercession. It's impromptu, automatic, instinctive, improvised intercession. It is often reserved for those who are sensitive enough to the Holy Spirit to partner with Him in prayer. But, believe me, He knows how to get your attention.

I remember a time when I was on a magazine deadline. If I missed the deadline, it would cost $10,000 a day. God was leading me to pray, but I reminded Him of the deadline. He didn't care about the deadline and led me into impromptu intercession for over an hour. I still met the deadline.

Nehemiah can probably relate. He entered into impromptu intercession when he got bad news. Bad news, by the way, often elicits impromptu prayer and intercession. It's a Spirit-inspired knee-jerk reaction to what the enemy is plotting and planning—or what he has already done.

"And they said to me, 'The survivors who are left from the captivity in the province are there in great distress and reproach. The wall of Jerusalem is also broken down, and its gates are burned with fire.' So it was, when I heard these words, that I sat down and wept, and mourned for many days; I was fasting and praying before the God of heaven" (Neh. 1:3-4).

Job 35:9-15 (*The Message*) tells how God pours impromptu songs in our hearts. If you run in prophetic circles, you are used to impromptu songs so impromptu intercession shouldn't be foreign to you. Impromptu intercession can catch you completely off guard. It can take you to new realms of prayer in the spirit. It can open up prophetic rivers. Yield to it.

— *Prayer* —

Father, in the name of Jesus, would You help me discern Your tug into impromptu intercession? Would You give me a heart that turns first to prayer and intercession in the face of bad news?

SEPTEMBER 25

The Jacob Knapp Prayer Anointing

"And my speech and my preaching were not with persuasive words of human wisdom, but in demonstration of the Spirit and of power" (1 Corinthians 2:4).

Though he was a well-known evangelist in his day, you have probably never heard of Jacob Knapp. But make no mistake: heaven and hell know his name well. Knapp was born in 1799 and worked for the Lord until 1874. No one could count all the souls saved through his ministry.

Knapp was known for spiritual power, but his efficacy in evangelism and his ability to release the power of the Gospel came through prayer. After his mother passed away when he was just a teenager, he turned to prayer and Bible study. It was prayer to a Saviour he didn't really know that led him later to pray for souls that didn't know his Saviour.

"I often repaired to the barn or grove in the silent hours of the night, and poured out my soul in prayer to God. At length, one Lord's Day morning, I took my Bible and hymn-book, and repaired to the woods, with a determination never to return without relief to my soul," he said. "I went some distance from human sight or hearing, laid myself down on a grassy knoll, and prayed and read, and read and prayed."

After grieving his mother's loss and finding God, he started organizing prayer meetings in his neighborhood. These prayer meetings drew people to salvation in Christ.

When Knapp prayed for an outpouring of the Spirit, God answered. In relation to a Boston meeting in 1841, he said, "The very atmosphere seemed impregnated with the divine influence. No one could come into the room where we were without recognizing the presence of God. At times it seemed as if I was overwhelmed with the gracious fulness of God, and that my poor and limited faculties could bear no more."

Thousands came to Christ through his ministry. His Gospel presentation was so power-packed it was once said that wherever Knapp went, "infidelity turned pale, and Universalism gave up the ghost."

— *Prayer* —

Father, in the name of Jesus, would You inspire me to read and pray until Your
Word and Spirit within me burst forth with demonstrations that Jesus is alive?
Give me prayer power that births revival in my city for the sake of souls? Give me
an anointing to pray like Knapp prayed.

Steering Clear of Spiritual Kryptonite

"Jesus said to him, 'If you can believe, all things are possible to him who believes.' Immediately the father of the child cried out and said with tears, 'Lord, I believe; help my unbelief!'"
(Mark 9:23-24)

Unbelief makes the intercessor a skeptic. God cannot truly use an intercessor who is bound by unbelief. Unbelief demonstrates a distrust for God, essentially rejecting the truth of His Word in any given prayer matter. God won't do anything through a heart of unbelief.

As odd as it sounds, it's possible to pray in unbelief. Consider the ministry of Christ, who was empowered by the all-powerful Holy Spirit Himself during His earthly ministry. Jesus decided to visit His hometown to bless them, but few got blessed because they couldn't believe He was who He said He was.

"Now He could do no mighty work there, except that He laid His hands on a few sick people and healed them. And He marveled because of their unbelief. Then He went about the villages in a circuit, teaching" (Mark 6:5-6).

At times, even His own disciples didn't believe. Jesus rose from the dead just like He prophesied He would, but they could scarcely believe it. Jesus took issue with that in Mark 16:14-15: "Later He appeared to the eleven as they sat at the table; and He rebuked their unbelief and hardness of heart, because they did not believe those who had seen Him after He had risen."

Catch that. Unbelief is related to a hard heart. What makes our heart hard? Many things, including sin, pride, setbacks, and disappointments, to name a few. Maybe you didn't receive the miracle prayer answers you hoped for in the last season and hope deferred made your heart sick (see Prov. 13:12). Maybe you listened to the voice of doubt so long, the enemy talked you out of believing.

If you have unbelief in your heart, the good news is it's easy to get rid of it. The strategy is called repentance. Ask the Lord to forgive you for having a hard heart of unbelief. Ask Him, "Help my unbelief."

— Prayer —

Father, in the name of Jesus, I realize it's possible to unknowingly have unbelief in my heart. Would You root out any hidden unbelief in my heart so I can pray more effectively? Lord, I believe. Help my unbelief.

Reading Your Prayer History

"I went out after it and struck it, and delivered the lamb from its mouth; and when it arose against me, I caught it by its beard, and struck and killed it" (1 Samuel 17:35).

When you stand in the gap long enough, you have a prayer history that will sustain you when you come under enemy fire. When you have a history in intercession, you have a history of breakthroughs with which to encourage yourself when prayer answers seem to evade you.

Think about it. David was beside himself when he returned to his base in Ziklag. While on the run from Saul, he made his home there only to find it in ashes. His wives and children, and those of his warring men, were captured. His loyal mighty men suddenly wanted to stone him.

This could have been the end of David, but he had a prayer history with God. 1 Samuel 30:6 (KJV) says, "And David was greatly distressed; for the people spake of stoning him, because the soul of all the people was grieved, every man for his sons and for his daughters: but David encouraged himself in the Lord his God."

Some translations say, "strengthened himself." How did David strengthen and encourage himself? I believe he kept his past victories in mind. Before he defeated Goliath at the Valley of Elah, he told the Israelites, "Your servant has killed both lion and bear; and this uncircumcised Philistine will be like one of them, seeing he has defied the armies of the living God" (1 Sam. 17:36).

Years has passed since the lion and the bear—and the giant. David had even more history with God showing Himself strong. David had even more prayer answers. At this point in his life, he could say, "I killed the lion, the bear, the giant and hundreds of Philistines. God came through for me then, and He will come through again."

Focus on the progress you've made in intercession rather than the challenges alone. Focus on the wins rather than the losses. Focus on God rather than the enemy.

— Prayer —

Father, in the name of Jesus, remind me of my prayer victories when the enemy tries to hinder my hope and fight my faith. Help me remember all the times You answered me, came to the rescue, and gave me the victory in intercession so I can stay encouraged.

Intercession Discretion

"Keep sound wisdom and discretion" (Proverbs 3:21).

As intercessors, we need to master the art of discretion. God may show you things about people that He doesn't want repeated to anyone. He just wants you to stand in the gap and agree in prayer for His will in their life. Likewise, people may share intimate details of their struggles with you, hoping you will pray. You need to keep it confidential.

Discretion is showing discernment and good judgment. Discretion is the ability to make responsible decisions. Discretion is the art of being discreet. A discreet intercessor is capable of preserving prudent silence. A discreet intercessor is like a vault, holding secrets of God and people for the purpose of intercession.

Solomon, the wisest man on the face of the earth, understood discretion. He offers some sound advice on the matter in the Book of Proverbs the Holy Spirit inspired him to pen. Proverbs 11:22 paints a vivid picture: "As a ring of gold in a swine's snout, so is a lovely woman who lacks discretion."

Again, Solomon wrote, "My son, let them not depart from your eyes—Keep sound wisdom and discretion; So they will be life to your soul and grace to your neck." Notice here how wisdom, grace and life are connected to discretion (Prov. 3:21-22).

By contrast, if you break your confidentiality agreement with God or someone who requests prayer, you may bring harm to the person God wants you to help through intercession. Think of the pain of betrayal when someone finds out you shared their secret need with another. This amounts to gossip, even if it wasn't your intent. Always remember, a gossiping intercessor is a compromised intercessor.

Again, Solomon wrote, "My son, pay attention to my wisdom; Lend your ear to my understanding, that you may preserve discretion, and your lips may keep knowledge" (Prov. 5:1). As an intercessor, God is giving you some keen wisdom: preserve confidentiality. Keep the secrets. Pray without ceasing.

— Prayer —

Father, in the name of Jesus, make me discreet. Deliver me from the temptation to tell others what I see in a person who just needs prayer coverage. Help me not to use my discernment to judge but to plead for Your will in their lives. Help me keep Your secrets.

SEPTEMBER 29

Serious Supplication

"Give ear to my prayer, O God, and do not hide Yourself from my supplication" (Psalm 55:1).

When Esther learned of Haman's plot to extinguish the Jews, she didn't just make a request of the king. No, she made supplication. When a need is urgent, you need to make supplication.

What is supplication? The Greek word for supplication is "deesis." It means, "need, indigence, want, privation, penury" and infers a seeking, asking, and entreating God. The Hebrew word for supplication means supplication. Supplication is a humble entreaty. It's an acknowledgment of one's helplessness to change a situation or meet a need.

Paul understood this, and wrote, "Be anxious for nothing, but in everything by prayer and supplication, with thanksgiving, let your requests be made known to God (see Phil. 4:6). When we're anxious over something, supplication is the right prayer strategy.

Jesus made supplication to the Father: "Who, in the days of His flesh, when He had offered up prayers and supplications, with vehement cries and tears to Him who was able to save Him from death, and was heard because of His godly fear" (Heb. 5:7). Both Jeremiah 3:21 and Jeremiah 31:9 connect weeping with supplication.

We see supplication throughout the book of 1 Kings and 2 Chronicles. David found himself in dire straits again and again. He asked the Lord to hear the voice of his supplication and was confident that God did hear him (see Ps. 6:9; Ps. 28:2). In fact, David made supplication over and over again throughout the psalms, solidifying this as a key prayer strategy for one who understands their helplessness in the face of a trial.

Daniel was known to set his face toward God and make supplication (see Dan. 9:3). And God promised to pour on the house of David and on the inhabitants of Jerusalem the spirit of grace and supplication (see Zech. 12:10). When you are in an urgent situation, ask God for the spirit of grace and supplication.

— *Prayer* —

Father, in the name of Jesus, lead me into supplication when I am at the end of myself. Give me the spirit of grace and supplication when I am in crisis. Like David in the wilderness, help me recognize my need for the Holy Helper.

Heavenly Authorization

"Behold, I give you the authority to trample on serpents and scorpions, and over all the power of the enemy, and nothing shall by any means hurt you" (Luke 10:19).

Intercessor, you have authority. Until you get a revelation of that authority, your prayer power will be limited. I heard the Lord say:

"I've authorized you. You carry an authority that defies every enemy plan in your life. I've given you keys to My Kingdom—and the authority to turn the lock on the door that is holding you back from breakthrough.

"Understand and know that when I call you to do something, I've given you everything you need to carry out the assignment. Your authorization gives you the right to use My name, to plead My blood, to bind, to loose, to decree, to declare, to prophesy, and to occupy until I come.

"You are authorized to walk in divine health, to walk in divine wealth, and to walk in the fullness of My Spirit. You are authorized to speak My Word and I will confirm it with signs following. You are authorized to command the enemy to bow before the Christ in you. There is no greater authority on the earth than the name of Jesus. I have marked you with that name. You are authorized. Act like it."

In Luke 10:19, Jesus told His disciples, "Behold, I give you the authority to trample on serpents and scorpions, and over all the power of the enemy, and nothing shall by any means hurt you." In the world, authority means power of influence to command a thought, opinion, or behavior. But the Greek word for authority in the Bible is exousia, which means "authorization."

This Greek word also means "physical and mental power; the ability or strength with which one is endued, which he either possesses or exercises." When God authorized you, He gave you the physical and mental power, the ability and strength to make intercession. Jesus authorized you to intercede effectively when He delegated His very own authority to you. Know that!

— *Prayer* —

Father, in the name of Jesus, thank You for authorizing me for my prayer assignment. Thank You for giving me authority over all the power of the devil. Open my eyes to the magnitude of the authority I carry in the name of Jesus. I stand as one authorized for victory!

OCTOBER

"The heartfelt and persistent prayer of a righteous man (believer) can accomplish much [when put into action and made effective by God—it is dynamic and can have tremendous power]" (James 5:16, AMP).

OCTOBER 1

When You Feel Your Prayers Aren't Working

"And let us not grow weary while doing good, for in due season we shall reap if we do not lose heart" (Galatians 6:9, NLT).

When I recently heard Christians suggesting that a prayer initiative for America was useless I was struck to the core with the realization that the Body of Christ is far from unified. I mean, if we can't unify around prayer, what can we unify around?

For all the impactful prayer movements in the Body, I still run into some believers who seem embittered by the efforts. They throw up their arms and ask, "Why even bother praying anymore?" because they don't see the fruit of their supplications. Yet faith is the evidence of things not seen (see Heb. 11:1). I shudder to think what would happen if we stopped praying for our cities and nations.

Here's the deal: With rights come responsibilities—and both apply to prayer. We have the right to come boldly to the throne of grace for anything we need— but we also have a responsibility to pray. Jesus said, "When you pray," not "If you pray" (see Matt. 6:6). Jesus wouldn't have told us to pray if it was a useless endeavor.

Indeed, the Bible commands us to pray instead of getting anxious (see Phil. 4:6). We are charged to pray for those who persecute us (see Matt. 5:44). We are supposed to pray for those in authority (see 1 Tim. 2:1-4). God's prayer list is quite specific. When we pray His Word in faith, He hears us. And we know if He hears us, He answers us.

Although our prayers are not solely results-focused, the results will eventually become visible if we remain faithful to believe God's Word doesn't return to Him void. Let us not become weary or faint in praying for God's will. We will reap a harvest from our faithful prayers if we do not give up (see Gal. 6:9). And reaping a harvest of prayer results can sure light a fire in the heart of a believer who wants to see God's Kingdom manifest. As that fire spreads, so does God's will across the earth.

— Prayer —

Father, in the name of Jesus, help me pray with faith that sees the answer before it manifests. Help me not to grow weary in my intercession but to hopefully wait for the harvest of prayer answers.

The Happy Intercessor

"If I say, 'I will forget my complaint, I will put off my sad face and wear a smile'" (Job 9:27).

Beni Johnson, the late wife of Bethel's Bill Johnson, wrote a book called *The Happy Intercessor*. Her aim with the book was to help intercessors catch the heartbeat of heaven. She wanted to fire up even the weariest prayer warriors with her revelations.

The book is rooted in Zephaniah 3:17, "The Lord your God is in your midst, a victorious warrior. He will rejoice over you with joy, He will be quiet in His love, He will rejoice over you with shouts of joy." *The New Living Translation* puts it this way: "For the Lord your God is living among you. He is a mighty saviour. He will take delight in you with gladness. With his love, he will calm all your fears. He will rejoice over you with joyful songs."

Johnson also offered the *The Amplified Classic* version: "The Lord your God is in your midst, a Warrior who saves. He will rejoice over you with joy; He will be quiet in His love [making no mention of your past sins], He will rejoice over you with shouts of joy."

When you meditate on Zephaniah 3:17 in any translation, well, it makes you happy. As she rightly notes, Jesus is our example of joy. I like to say He's the glorious, victorious, warrior God who has never lost a battle. She teaches how to pray from His heart. I like to say we need to get out of our heads and into His heart when we intercede.

Intercession can bring us into weeping. Intercession can cause us to feel deeply grieved by what grieves the Holy Spirit. But intercession should also be a happy place for the prayer warrior. That's because when we make intercession, we are in His presence where there is fullness of joy.

— *Prayer* —

Father, in the name of Jesus, make me a happy intercessor. I know intercession is serious work, but help me to feel Your pleasure in my prayer so that I can lean into Your joy, which is my strength. Teach me to intercede from a place of knowing You will move.

OCTOBER 3

Playing to Your Prayer Strengths

"They go from strength to strength; Each one appears before God in Zion" (Psalm 84:7).

We all have natural and spiritual gifts and talents. Intercessors, you have strengths and weaknesses in your prayer life. It can be tempting to focus on your weaknesses, especially when you see someone who is strong in an area where you don't have much experience in prayer. Instead, play to your prayer strengths.

You'll be a more effective intercessor if you play to your strengths. You'll be more confident in your intercession if you play to your strengths. You'll strengthen your strengths when you play to your strengths. You'll be more satisfied with your prayer when you play to your strengths.

So what are your intercessory prayer strengths? Are you like Anna who prayed day and night and had great prayer stamina? Are you strong in listening prayer, so that you hear the intercessory prayer strategy clearly and execute it fully with confidence? Do you have a heart of worship with an anointing to praise and sing your prayers?

Maybe you have been a student of the Word for decades and the Word oozes out of you in intercession. Or maybe you can pray in tongues for hours on end, releasing the perfect prayers. Still maybe you have a prophetic spirit and you prophesy in prayer, or you are a prayer warrior with a mantle to bust demons.

Although God wants us to grow in prayer and diversify our prayer life, the reality is we are all different. Every intercessor is unique and your prayer strengths are gifts God has given you to match the prayer assignments He offers you.

Don't take pride in your strengths or beat yourself up for your weaknesses. God gave you your strengths. He is your refuge and your strength (see Ps. 46:1). He is your strength and shield (see Ps. 28:7). Like David said, "It is God who arms me with strength, and makes my way perfect" (Ps. 18:32).

— *Prayer* —

Father, in the name of Jesus, would You help me to see my intercessory prayer strengths—the strengths You have gifted me with—so I can make the most effective, confident intercession possible? Help me play to my strengths.

OCTOBER 4

Conquering Your Prayer Weaknesses

"And He said to me, 'My grace is sufficient for you, for My strength is made perfect in weakness.' Therefore most gladly I will rather boast in my infirmities, that the power of Christ may rest upon me" (2 Corinthians 12:9).

Just as every intercessor has prayer strengths, we also have prayer weaknesses. You can improve on those weaknesses over time, but you shouldn't dwell on them in the meantime.

For example, if you are a new Christian you won't have much of the Word in you. You shouldn't let that stop you from making intercession. If you are not yet baptized in the Holy Spirit, you can't pray in tongues. Don't let that stop your intercession. If you haven't been equipped in spiritual warfare you won't understand the rules of engagement. But you can still petition God without confronting demons.

The enemy would like nothing more than to stop you from praying. He wants to discourage your heart by pointing out your weaknesses. Don't let him. You will grow out of some of those weaknesses as you mature in Christ. You will gain wisdom, revelation and understanding that will make you more effective in the future than you are now. You will grow in knowledge of God and His ways.

Jesus sympathizes with our weaknesses (see Heb. 4:15). Paul had the audacity to say that he is content with his weaknesses, "for when I am weak He is strong" (see 2 Cor. 12:10). Sometimes, we just have to be content with our weakness, knowing that God can work through us despite what we don't know or don't have.

If you feel a weakness is holding you back in your prayer life, ask the Holy Spirit to help you overcome it. And remember, it may not be a spiritual weakness. It could be weakness in discipline, or a weakness in time management or some other natural weakness that hinders your intercession.

And remember Paul's words in Philippians 4:13, "I can do all things through Him who strengthens me." If God gave you a prayer assignment, He will strengthen you to complete it. He really will.

— *Prayer* —

Father, in the name of Jesus, would You help me not to let my weaknesses worry me? Help me overcome the weaknesses I can tackle, and help me realize that what is beyond my control doesn't limit Your work through me.

OCTOBER 5

Don't Poison Your Prayers

"Whenever you stand praying, if you have anything against anyone, forgive him [drop the issue, let it go], so that your Father who is in heaven will also forgive you your transgressions and wrongdoings [against Him and others]" (Mark 11:25, AMP).

Unforgiveness to the intercessor is like an oil spill to ocean life. Such pollution harms the soul of the intercessor and grieves the Holy Spirit within him. The problem is, unforgiveness can be as sly as the snake in the Garden of Eden. Few want to admit they are walking in unforgiveness. We tend to shove it below the surface of our emotions as if it won't seep out in other areas of our intercessory ministry.

Unforgiveness is a major hindrance to your prayer life. Jesus said in Mark 11:25, "And whenever you stand praying, forgive, if you have anything against anyone, so that your Father also who is in heaven may forgive you your trespasses."

Think about it for a minute. If your Father doesn't forgive your trespasses, your lifeline to God is kinked. Have you ever tried to water the garden with a hose that has a kink in it? No water comes out. You have to unkink the hose to restore the flow. Forgiveness hinders your flow.

You may still pray with eloquence and what seems like power. But eloquence from an unforgiving soul doesn't move God's heart. He's not hearing your prayers. In fact, Jesus said in Mark 6:14, "For if you forgive men their trespasses, your heavenly Father will also forgive you." The inverse of that is if you don't forgive, your Father won't forgive you. That's a scary proposition for the intercessor battling darkness.

Ask the Holy Spirit to show you if there is anyone in your life you need to forgive—even if it's yourself. Some intercessors are even mad at God because a prayer answer didn't come in a life-or-death situation. It's never God's fault. Choose to forgive. Your emotions may not immediately change but your heart will.

— *Prayer* —

Father, in the name of Jesus, show me if there is anyone I need to forgive. I do not want the poison of unforgiveness in my soul. I do not want my intercession to be ineffective. I do not want to grieve Your heart. I choose to forgive anybody and everybody who has wronged me.

Pivot Prayers

"David said to Abigail, 'Blessed be the Lord, God of Israel, who sent you this day to meet me. And blessed is your discretion, and blessed are you who have kept me this day from coming to shed blood and from avenging myself with my own hand'" (1 Sam. 25:32-33).

God uses turning point intercessors at strategic times in history—or in the lives of individuals at critical moments of transition. Esther was a turning point, or hinge, intercessor. Her intercession made a massive impact on history. Haman wanted to kill all the Jews. Mordecai discovered the wicked plot and got a message to Queen Esther. All intercessors need to have this mindset of self-sacrifice Esther carried.

Even now, turning point intercessors are stationing themselves at the crossroads of history, standing in the gap and positioning a person, place or nation for great change. Of course, you can't decide to be a turning point intercessor or any other type of intercessor. God gifts you and places you in the role and assignment He chooses. Although you may engage in many types of intercession in your prayer career, hinge intercessors are alert and activated for key moments to make the right petition at a critical time.

Abigail was a turning point intercessor. Nabal offended David, refusing to help him and his army in time of need. David decided to war against Nabal. Word got back to Nabal's wife, Abigail. In 1 Samuel 25, she rushes to meet him on his way. 1 Samuel 25:23-27 reads:

"When Abigail saw David, she hurriedly got down from the donkey and fell before David upon her face. And she bowed herself to the ground. So she fell at his feet and said, 'Against me alone, my lord, is the guilt. Please let your handmaid speak in your ears, and hear the words of your handmaid. Please do not let my lord set his heart against this worthless man, against Nabal. For as his name is, so is he. Nabal is his name and folly is with him. But I, your handmaid, did not see the young men of my lord, whom you sent.'"

David was grateful for her act of intercession. Are you a turning point intercessor? Stand by to release pivot prayers.

— *Prayer* —

Father, in the name of Jesus, I'm willing to be used as a hinge intercessor. I'm willing to stand in the gap at critical junctions of transition and turning points for people, cities and nations. Teach me and use me for Your glory.

OCTOBER 7

Don't Curse Your Prayer

"He shall have whatsoever he saith" (Mark 11:23).

The enemy of your prayer is strategic. He hates it when you pray so he will try to get you to curse your prayer before it has a chance to come to pass. Cursing your prayer is speaking death over the prayer you just released in faith.

Let's say you are praying for someone's healing. You are standing in faith believing in that moment for a monumental breakthrough. Then, suddenly, you get a call from someone who tells you that the condition of your friend has worsened instead of improving. The temptation will be to come in agreement with the bad report and speak death instead of life.

The power of death and life are in your tongue. You can choose to water your prayer with words of faith despite the circumstances, or you can yield to the enemy's pressure on your tongue to reverse your intercession—and essentially call in the enemy's plans and purposes instead of God's will.

Jesus said, "For assuredly, I say to you, whoever says to this mountain, 'Be removed and be cast into the sea,' and does not doubt in his heart, but believes that those things he says will be done, he will have whatever he says" (Mark 11:23). Don't pray for healing and confess sickness. Don't pray for prosperity and confess poverty. Don't pray for the prodigal to come home and then criticize them for backsliding in the next breath.

Jesus also said, "If you abide in Me, and My words abide in you, you will ask what you desire, and it shall be done for you" (John 15:17). His words may abide in you—and come through your mouth—in intercession but a key to moving stubborn mountains is to let His words abide in you—and in all your conversation about the mountain. You might not get what you pray if you're not careful what you say.

— *Prayer* —

Father, in the name of Jesus, help me not to curse my prayers. Let my tongue cleave to the roof of my mouth if I am tempted to say anything that is not edifying to myself and others, or that doesn't glorify Your Son.

Midnight Intercession

"But at midnight Paul and Silas were praying and singing hymns to God, and the prisoners were listening to them" (Acts 16:25).

You've heard it said it's always darkest before the dawn. You've also heard it said that God is never late. He always shows up on time. Indeed, many times God shows up at the midnight hour. Knowing this, some prayer warriors engage in what I call midnight intercession.

Midnight intercession might be at midnight, but when I speak of midnight intercession I am talking about the point at which everything is coming to a head. It's intercession in a moment where if God doesn't show up, all hope is lost. It's intercession that defies the circumstances and prays without ceasing in faith that He won't be late.

Paul and Silas engaged in midnight intercession. They were ministering in Thyatira when they encountered a young girl with a spirit of divination. Paul was troubled by the demon in the girl and, after a few days, cast it out. That put the city in an uproar and Paul and Silas landed in jail. They were in the inner prison and their feet were in stocks.

Acts 16:25-26 relates the rest of the story: "But at midnight Paul and Silas were praying and singing hymns to God, and the prisoners were listening to them. Suddenly there was a great earthquake, so that the foundations of the prison were shaken; and immediately all the doors were opened and everyone's chains were loosed."

The psalmist understood this concept, writing "The cords of the wicked have bound me, but I have not forgotten Your law. At midnight I will rise to give thanks to You, because of Your righteous judgments. I am a companion of all who fear You, and of those who keep Your precepts" (Ps. 119:52-63).

Midnight intercession breaks chains. Midnight intercession breaks the enemy's grip. Midnight intercession sets the captives free from affliction and addiction. Know when it's time to enter midnight intercession.

— *Prayer* —

Father, in the name of Jesus, lead me and guide me into times of midnight intercession. Remind me You will show up to break chains and open doors. Increase my faith to engage in intercession when reality defies Your promises.

OCTOBER 9

Your Electric Company

"And being let go, they went to their own company, and reported all that the chief priests and elders had said unto them" (Acts 4:23).

Just as there are companies of prophets in the Bible, there are companies of intercessors rising up today. What is a company of intercessors? It's group of intercessors who share like precious faith (see 2 Pet. 1:1).

A company is an association, a network, a fellowship, a group, an organization, or a unit of intercessors. But why do we need them? Why can't we hole up in our prayer closets alone? First, your prayer anointing accomplishes more when you are with the right prayer company. One can put a thousand to flight and two can put ten thousand to flight (see Deut. 32:30). You unlock more prayer power in a company of unified intercessors.

Look what happened to Peter and John in the early days of the church. They were sorely persecuted by the Pharisees for healing the man at the Beautiful Gate. Acts 4:23 says, "And being let go, they went to their own company, and reported all that the chief priests and elders had said unto them."

This wasn't just any group of Christians. I believe many who were part of this company had been in the Upper Room the day the Holy Spirit came in like a mighty rushing wind, filled the room and released the baptism that left them speaking in other tongues.

Acts 4 reveals the immediate response to the apostles' report of persecution wasn't fear or complaining. It was prayer. What did they pray for? They prayed for God's determined purposes to be done. They prayed that the Lord would hear the threats of the Pharisees. They prayed to receive boldness to preach the Word, with healing, signs and wonders manifesting in the name of Jesus. This prayer company prayed in unity and got a swift answer.

"And when they had prayed, the place where they were assembled together was shaken; and they were all filled with the Holy Spirit, and they spoke the word of God with boldness" (Acts 4:31). When you are in right prayer company, it shakes up enemy plans.

— Prayer —

Father, in the name of Jesus, help me find the right prayer company. Lead me and guide me to those of like precious faith who will not cower in fear when opposition comes but will double up in prayer to glorify Your name.

OCTOBER 10

Preparing for Promotion

"The king then presented Daniel with a lot of gifts; he promoted him to governor of Babylon
Province and put him in charge of the other wise men" (Daniel 2:48).

God is going to raise up humble intercessors who give Him glory for the breakthrough. Doors are going to open. Authority is going to increase. And demons are going to tremble. I heard the Lord say:

"I am promoting My faithful ones in this season to positions in My Spirit and in the natural that defy human reasoning. My faithful ones have prayed and sought My face and walked in My will with the little things, and I am making them ruler over more in My Kingdom.

"Those faithless ones will be demoted while my faithful ones are raised up in this hour. Those walking in pride will be brought low. Those walking in arrogance will not stand in My special places in this season. But those who have walked in the low places with Me, I will exalt and raise up and send out with an anointing to stand and withstand in this hour."

How do prepare yourself for a promotion? Don't try to make it happen. No man on earth and no devil in hell can stop what God wants to do in your life—but you can make a big mess trying to make it happen. Remember, whatever you do to get somewhere, you'll have to keep doing to stay there.

Don't be jealous of another intercessor's promotion. God won't promote a jealous heart. Jealousy is a work of the flesh (see Gal. 5:20). Trust God with the timing. Ecclesiastes 3 declares, "To everything there is a season." Work on your character. If you were ready to handle the promotion now, God would give it to you now.

Many times, we need to develop the character that will keep us where the anointing will take us. Practice humility. Humility has no rights. Finally, once God exalts you, stay humble. Pride comes before a demotion.

— Prayer —

Father, in the name of Jesus, would You help me prepare myself for the promotion You have prepared for me? I want to step into greater anointings and authority in intercession so I can make a bigger impact for Your Kingdom. Help me get ready.

OCTOBER 11

Eliminating Entitlement Mindsets

"Create in me a clean heart, O God, and renew a steadfast spirit within me" (Psalm 51:10).

Heart posture is everything in prayer and intercession. We can pray in the name of Jesus all day but if our heart is not properly postured toward Him, we will not see the results we're hoping for. The name of Jesus is not an appendage we attach to the end of our prayer in conclusion. Jesus Himself offers a parable in Luke 17:7-10:

"And which of you, having a servant plowing or tending sheep, will say to him when he has come in from the field, 'Come at once and sit down to eat'? But will he not rather say to him, 'Prepare something for my supper, and gird yourself and serve me till I have eaten and drunk, and afterward you will eat and drink'?

"Does he thank that servant because he did the things that were commanded him? I think not. So likewise you, when you have done all those things which you are commanded, say, 'We are unprofitable servants. We have done what was our duty to do.'"

Jesus doesn't owe us anything. We don't deserve anything. We are here to serve His plans and purposes in the earth. However, He is gracious and wants to bless us and our intercession for others. He wants to demonstrate His goodness and glory. But it's not the posture of our physical body—standing, kneeling, laying prostrate—that concerns God most. It's the posture of our heart. Everything flows out of the heart (see Prov. 4:23).

"Praying in Jesus' name is not a mechanical password, which, if used faithfully, guarantees automatic acceptance of all prayer," said William McBirnie, author of *The Search for the Twelve Apostles*. "Instead, it should come from our deeply felt sense of our own unworthiness and Christ's worthiness. God will answer a prayer for Jesus' sake when He will not answer it for our sake."

— *Prayer* —

Father, in the name of Jesus, before I come to You in the name of Your glorious Son, help me posture my heart to lean on the only worth One. Help me posture my heart in a way that delights to pray Your will.

When Job Prayed for His Friends

"And the Lord restored Job's losses when he prayed for his friends. Indeed the Lord gave Job twice as much as he had before" (Job 42:10).

When you are under attack, people around you will be tempted to tell you what you've done to open the door to the enemy in your life. Many times, they will act like Job's friends. You know what I mean.

Eliphaz comes over to your house to tell you how it's all your fault because you have some hidden sin in your life (see Job 4:7-8). After he leaves, Bildad calls to confirm Eliphaz's poor prophecies (see Job 8:20). Finally, Zophar acts as a third witness to condemn you in the battle (see Job 11:14-17).

Job persevered, according to James 5:11. But he didn't get the breakthrough until he blessed those who were essentially cursing him—questioning his character. Intercessors, people will misunderstand you and accuse you at times. The quicker you can pray for them, the quicker you can get double for your trouble. Look at Job 42:10-13:

"And the Lord restored Job's losses when he prayed for his friends. Indeed the Lord gave Job twice as much as he had before. Then all his brothers, all his sisters, and all those who had been his acquaintances before, came to him and ate food with him in his house; and they consoled him and comforted him for all the adversity that the Lord had brought upon him. Each one gave him a piece of silver and each a ring of gold.

"Now the Lord blessed the latter days of Job more than his beginning; for he had fourteen thousand sheep, six thousand camels, one thousand yoke of oxen, and one thousand female donkeys. He also had seven sons and three daughters. After this Job lived one hundred and forty years, and saw his children and grandchildren for four generations. So Job died, old and full of days."

Again, know that you will be misunderstood. And that misunderstanding may be painful. You may be accused, rejected, and shunned. Pray for those who hurt you and position yourself for the payback.

— *Prayer* —

Father, in the name of Jesus, help me to remember to pray for those who judge my heart and my motives. Help me to bless those who misunderstand me and accuse me when I am down. I want double for my trouble.

The Pinnacle of Prayer

"For all the law is fulfilled in one word, even in this: 'You shall love your neighbor as yourself'" (Galatians 5:14).

Kenneth Hagin, founder of the Word of Faith movement, once opined that much of what we pray with our understanding is selfish. Too often, he said, our prayers sound like the old farmer who always prayed, "God, bless me and my wife, my son John and his wife—us four and no more." While we would never outwardly utter those words, if we're not careful our prayer life can grow selfish.

"True prayer never stops with petition for one's self. It reaches out to others. The very word intercession implies a reaching out for someone else. It is standing as a go-between, a mutual friend, between God and someone who is either out of touch with Him, or is needing special help," wrote S.D. Gordon, an author and lay minister from the latter part of the 19th and early part of the 20th century.

"Intercession is the climax of prayer. It is the outward drive of prayer. It is the effective end of prayer outward," he continued. "Communion and petition are upward and downward. Intercession rests upon these two as its foundation. Communion and petition store the life with the power of God; intercession lets it out on behalf of others."

Indeed, intercession is the pinnacle of prayer. The climax, or pinnacle, is the highest point. The climax marks a turning point in the action of the spiritual battle. It's the peak, the capstone, the apex. There is no higher service than intercession. It's the crowning point, the zenith, the crest of our prayer lives. So, how do we get there?

"The climax of prayer exists when people disregard petty whims and think first of those less fortunate," Dick Eastman, Chief Prayer Officer at Every Home for Christ, wrote in the *Change the World School of Prayer.* "An intercessor must bid farewell to self and welcome the burdens of humanity. In truth, the climax of prayer is intercession."

— *Prayer* —

Father, in the name of Jesus, warn me if I adopt an "us for and no more" prayer strategy. Make me selfless in prayer, willing to lay my life down for the cause of Christ the way Christ laid His life down for the church.

OCTOBER 14

Praying for the Persecuted Church

"Blessed are those who are persecuted for righteousness' sake, for theirs is the kingdom of heaven"
(Matthew 5:10).

If you are reading this devotional, you probably have more freedom than our brothers and sisters in the persecuted church. The persecuted church is the Body of Christ in nations where believers suffer persistently cruel treatment because of their faith in Jesus. Believers are often hidden "underground" in such nations and may be imprisoned or killed for their faith.

We need to pray for the persecuted church, which numbers over 300 million by some counts. But how do we pray effectively for these believers? Pray that as persecuted believers share in Christ's suffering they can maintain a rejoicing heart because of their hope in God (see 1 Pet. 4:12-14). Pray that God would protect them and keep them from the evil one (see Matt. 26:39).

But don't stop there. Pray God would grant persecuted believers boldness to continue to share the Gospel with unbelievers in their nations (see Eph. 6:20). Pray that, in their suffering, persecuted believers would feel the presence and grace of God (see John 15:19-20). Pray that persecuted believers would find provision for all their needs in Christ (see 2 John 2).

But don't stop there. Pray persecuted believers would stay faithful in their surrender and service to Jesus despite the hardships (see Rev. 2:10-11). Pray God would give them the right words to say when they face trial or interrogation (see Luke 12:12). Pray persecuted believers would have discernment and wisdom in their plight (see Matt. 10:16-18).

But don't stop there. Pray persecuted believers would learn to lean on God for anything and everything (see 2 Cor. 1:7-9). Pray signs and wonders would flow from them, convincing even the hardest hearts that Jesus is alive (see Acts 4:30). Pray God would deliver them from evil (see Psalm 91:5). Please, keep praying for the persecuted church.

— Prayer —

Father, in the name of Jesus, would You give me a burden for the persecuted church? Help me remember how blessed I am and how there but by the grace of God go I. Help me to pray without ceasing for my brothers and sisters who are suffering for the faith.

OCTOBER 15

The Moses Prayer Anointing

"Then Moses said, 'If you don't personally go with us, don't make us leave this place'"
(Exodus 33:15, NLT).

Moses had one of the most powerful revelations of prayer of anyone in the Bible. He was a man of presence, power, purpose and petition. It all started with the presence. One of Moses' prayers was, "Please, show me your glory!" (Ex. 33:18).

His stance was, "If your Presence does not go with us, do not bring us from here" (Exodus 33:15). That was the foundation of his power and guided his purposeful prayer life. From that place of presence, Moses lifted up powerful petitions to see God's purposes fulfilled in the earth.

Beyond stopping the plagues through powerful petitions, Moses saw the Red Sea parted through presence-based prayer. This was not only a real event, but a prophetic picture of the power of prayer to overcome the impossible. Moses cried out to God in the face of sure doom and God gave him a strategy (see Ex. 14:15-18).

Beyond the Red Sea victory, Moses' presence-based prayer life released petitions that brought miraculous provision to the Israelites more than once. When there was no water, "Moses cried out to the Lord, saying, 'What shall I do with this people? They are almost ready to stone me!'" (Ex. 17:4). It wasn't a lengthy prayer. It was just a cry from his heart. God gave Moses the strategy to strike the rock and water came forth.

While David wrote most of the psalms, Psalm 90 is fully a prayer of Moses. You can almost hear the presence-driven words of the prophet in the seventeen verses, beginning with: "Lord, You have been our dwelling place in all generations. Before the mountains were brought forth, or ever You had formed the earth and the world, even from everlasting to everlasting, You are God."

Moses was an intercessor of presence. Over and over again, we saw Him touch God's heart because He prayed not to a God who was far off but a God with whom He spoke to as a friend face to face. Ask God for prayer anointing Moses carried.

— *Prayer* —

Father, in the name of Jesus, would You give me a prayer anointing like Moses'? I want to pray from a place of presence. I want to cry out to the God who is a very present help in time of need, knowing that in Your nearness You will hear me and I will hear You.

Escaping the Comparison Trap

"According to the eternal purpose which He accomplished in Christ Jesus our Lord, in whom we have boldness and access with confidence through faith in Him" (Ephesians 3:11-12).

Since the enemy hates prayer, he'll do just about anything he can to shut you down. One keen strategy against younger intercessors is to entice them into the comparison trap. This happened to me when I was first saved. I heard seasoned intercessors crying out to God with such fervor and power that it made me feel "less than." I didn't feel like I could or should pray in the group because, after all, what did I have to offer?

That strategy stunted my prayer life, as we grow in prayer not just through study but through praying. Put another way, you can learn a lot through studying prayer just like you can learn a lot about cooking by reading recipe books. But if you don't actually put prayer into practice you have no prayer answers, no growth, no experience.

Comparison works to shut your mouth because you don't feel strong enough, powerful enough or anointed enough—or whatever enough—to stand in the gap. This is a subtle lie of the enemy that we need to discern and cast down. Believe me, seasoned intercessors are not judging you when you pray from a pure heart of devotion. Quite the contrary, they will cheer you on.

When we compare our prayer power, anointing, or style with others, we are in danger of breaking agreement in intercession. We may look at others as the competition and begin striving instead of flowing with the Spirit in prayer. We may start moving in jealousy or envy and break the unity in the spirit or even release strife into the meeting.

When we compare our prayer life with someone else's, it can cause us to feel insecure, it can steal our joy, it can stall our progress in intercession. When we compare our prayer life with someone else's, we are in danger of trying to become someone God has not called us to be. You have a unique prayer gift, talent, skill and anointing. Be you.

— *Prayer* —

Father, in the name of Jesus, help me avoid the temptation to compare my prayer life with others. Help me instead posture my heart to learn from those who are more experienced than me so we can all rise together.

Marketplace Intercession

"So he called ten of his servants, delivered to them ten minas, and said to them, 'Do business till I come'" (Luke 19:13).

Marketplace intercessors are rising. A marketplace intercessor is one who is specifically anointed to pray for businesses. They may or may not have any background in business other than the Father's business.

A marketplace intercessor prays for the success of the company to which they are assigned. They may pray for the leadership and the employees, or for witty inventions and favor to secure customers and contracts. They may pray against enemy attacks. While many businesses are purposefully connecting with marketplace intercessors and offering specific prayer requests, other intercessors are completely Spirit-led.

"I am convinced that the lack of intercessors is one of the major missing ingredients in the business world. Marketplace intercessors must respond," said James Goll, founder of God Encounters Ministries and author of many books on prayer. "Prayer shields must be put in place for these struggling businesses."

Beyond prayer, marketplace intercessors may also offer spiritual insights to business leaders they receive during listening prayer. Because wisdom, revelation and understanding often come in the context of prayer, marketplace intercessors may receive prophetic intelligence that's helpful to business owners or executives. And that gives them an edge in the marketplace.

"We have prophetically called forth these new 'Josephs' into being, be we must now become proactive with the global prayer movement," Goll continued. "Prayer warriors must assist their brothers and sisters in their endeavors. We must partner together both in the office and in our prayer closets."

Are you a marketplace intercessor? If you are, you may feel a draw toward current events, the stock market, the economy, or specific businesses. You may find yourself praying for a friend's business or random businesses in your community.

— *Prayer* —

Father, in the name of Jesus, if You want me to step into marketplace intercession, highlight the company for which You want me to pray. Give me keen insights and strategies, like You gave Joseph, to help them succeed.

The Martin Luther Prayer Anointing

"But that no one is justified by the law in the sight of God is evident, for 'the just shall live by faith'" (Galatians 3:11).

A German theologian in the 15th Century, Martin Luther led the Protestant Reformation that changed the face of Christianity. The Catholic priest had more than a monumental task trying to convince the church that "the just shall live by faith" (see Rom. 1:17).

Prayer was Luther's lifeline amid the massive resistance to his divine revelation. Because he understood the power of prayer he continued fighting the good fight of faith. Luther's work was spiritual and natural. He once said, "Work, work, from early until late. In fact, I have so much to do that I shall spend the first three hours in prayer."

Luther insisted he could not neglect prayer for a single day. He understood that God wants us to pray, and He listens not because we are worthy but because He is merciful. Luther noticed the less he prayed, the harder things were and the more he prayed the better it went. This is true in all our lives, whether we realize it or not.

"No one can believe how powerful prayer is and what it can effect, except those who have learned it by experience," Luther said. "Whenever I have prayed earnestly, I have been heard and have obtained more than I prayed for. God sometimes delays, but He always comes."

History tells us Luther died at just 62 years old and was buried in front of the pulpit of the Castle Church in Wittenburg where he had posted his famed *95 Thesis* containing his world changing revelation just ten years before. He went on to glory as a hero to Protestants, though the Catholic church considered him an agent of Satan.

But Luther goes down in prayer history as a man who understood realms of prayer that many do not. He said, "If I should neglect prayer but a single day, I should lose a great deal of the fire of faith." And, "The fewer the words, the better the prayer."

— *Prayer* —

Father, in the name of Jesus, would You teach me how to pray like Luther? Help me understand that the more I pray, the better things go—that the more I pray the more effective I can be for Your Kingdom in my generation. Make me an agent of reformation through prayer.

OCTOBER 19

The Theology of Prayer

"All Scripture is given by inspiration of God, and is profitable for doctrine, for reproof, for correction, for instruction in righteousness, that the man of God may be complete, thoroughly equipped for every good work" (2 Timothy 3:16-17).

You don't have to be a theologian to be an intercessor, but you should nevertheless understand the theology of prayer. That's because when you understand the theology of prayer you will pray more accurately and effectively—and therefore see more prayer answers.

The most effective intercessors embrace theology—which is the study of God. They are students of the character, nature, ways and emotions of God. In his classic book, *The Cycle of Prayer*, Ralph Herring offers this profound insight:

"Prayer is that which makes it possible for God to seemingly at least change His mind without being inconsistent. It is His favorite method of reigning in difficult and distressing situations. Only a sovereign God could inspire prayer and only a sovereign God can answer it. A man's concept of God, therefore, determines the depth of his prayer life. Real prayer begins and ends with God enthroned."

Ponder that thought. A man's concept of God determines the depth of his prayer life. If you see God as punitive you will find yourself battling guilt, which sullies your faith. If you see God as anything other than all powerful, you may doubt His ability.

David was a man with solid theology. Consider the diversity of David's prayers, which were based on that theology. When he sinned, he prayed, "Have mercy upon me, O God, according to Your lovingkindness; According to the multitude of Your tender mercies, blot out my transgressions. Wash me thoroughly from my iniquity, and cleanse me from my sin" (Ps. 51:1-2).

When he was in danger, he cried out, "Deliver me from my enemies, O my God. Defend me from those who rise up against me" (Ps. 59:1). When he needed wisdom he pled, "Show me Your ways, O Lord; Teach me Your paths. Lead me in Your truth and teach me, for You are the God of my salvation; On You I wait all the day" (Ps. 25:4-5). Be a prayer theologian.

— Prayer —

Father, in the name of Jesus, I want to have a prayer life based on sound theology like David. I want to know the God to whom I am praying intimately. Would You teach me about Your heart? Give me a hunger to learn of You. Would You make me a prayer theologian?

The Intercessor's DNA

"When I call to remembrance the genuine faith that is in you, which dwelt first in your grandmother Lois and your mother Eunice, and I am persuaded is in you also" (2 Timothy 1:5).

When you think of DNA you may think of natural characteristics. But there's also spiritual DNA. God created you as a unique spirit and breathed the breath of life into you. But He also uses people to shape our lives.

We can receive spiritual mantles from our parents or ancestors. Have you ever noticed many ministers have children who follow their footsteps into ministry? That's because they may carry the same—or similar—gift mixes.

Your natural lineage can inform your intercessory prayer anointing. Consider Ruth Ward Heflin, a woman who understood the realms of intercession and glory. Many people do not know that Heflin was a descendent of the 18th Century revivalist Jonathan Edwards. Surely, she was inspired by stories of Edwards' prayer life.

But you can also inherit spiritual DNA, of sorts, from those who inspire you to press into prayer. You can catch the spirit of prayer that is on them. Many people hear how Edwards prayed for many hours a day and read his Bible on horseback as he traveled from meeting to meeting to preach.

"Edwards was so devoted to prayer that it is hard to find a daily routine for him that wasn't permeated with it," wrote Donald Whitney in his book *Pursuing A Passion for God Through Spiritual Disciples: Learning from Jonathan Edwards.* "He prayed over his studies, and he prayed as he walked in the evening. Prayer was both a discipline and a part of his leisure."

But many don't know that Edwards was inspired by David Brainerd, a missionary who died at age twenty-nine due his deep devotion to evangelism and prayer. Brainerd died of tuberculosis in Edwards' home. Edwards saw it as God's providence.

Of his last days on earth, Edwards said, "Brainerd's prayers in the family were stunning. Even his prayers returning thanks for food were awe inspiring." Appreciate your natural and spiritual DNA.

— *Prayer* —

Father, in the name of Jesus, would You show me my spiritual lineage in prayer and intercession? And would You help me appreciate those whose prayer life has inspired me, those who taught me to pray, and those who prayed for me as I learned to stand in the gap?

OCTOBER 21

To Repeat or Not Repeat Your Prayer?

"Now we know that God does not hear sinners; but if anyone is a worshiper of God and does His will, He hears him" (John 9:31).

To repeat the same prayer over again, or not the repeat? That is the question on the minds of some intercessors. As legend has it, Smith Wigglesworth rebuked people who came up to his prayer line for the same healing petition more than once.

Jesus also rebuked the Pharisees for repetitive prayers. We read these words in Matthew 6:7, "And when you pray, do not use vain repetitions as the heathen do. For they think that they will be heard for their many words."

The Message translation puts it this way, "The world is full of so-called prayer warriors who are prayer-ignorant. They're full of formulas and programs and advice, peddling techniques for getting what you want from God. Don't fall for that nonsense. This is your Father you are dealing with, and he knows better than you what you need."

But look at the definition of vain. The Greek word for vain means "to stammer; to repeat the same things over and over, to use may idle words, to babble, prate." So Jesus wasn't saying we can't pray for the same thing more than once. Quite the contrary. In the Parable of the Persistent Widow, a woman cried repeatedly to the unjust judge, "Avenge me of my adversary" (see Luke 18:3).

Dick Eastman, Chief Prayer Officer at Every Home for Christ puts it this way: "At no time did He say we cannot repeat a petition. He was merely addressing the 'worthless' praying the Pharisees offered primary for show. Indeed, even Jesus Himself repeated a prayer."

Yes, Jesus Himself prayed the same prayer three times in one night as He suffered in the Garden of Gethsemane, saying, "Father, if it is Your will, take this cup away from Me; nevertheless not My will, but Yours, be done" (Luke 22:42). You can repeat a prayer when you pray with sincere heart. God hears your prayers. And some prayers need to be repeated to push back darkness.

— Prayer —

Father, in the name of Jesus, please help me not to pray in vain. But help me pray prayers of faith over and again, thanking You every step of the way, knowing the answer is on the way. I stand in awe of the God who hears me.

The Dark Night of the Soul

"Because narrow is the gate and difficult is the way which leads to life, and there are few who find it" (Matthew 7:14).

When you travel down the narrow path that leads to life, you will eventually encounter a place many call the dark night of the soul. Intercessors who seek to go deep into secret realms of prayer will have to learn to a live a life of faith and trust in the One who hears and answers prayer. But, let's face it, the dark night of the soul be scary.

Know this: You are not alone. You are with the Chief Intercessor and even though you can't feel Him or hear Him or see Him moving at the sound of your voice, He has a message for you. Indeed, Oswald Chambers, author of *My Utmost for His Highest*, once said, "When you are in the dark, listen, and God will give you a very precious message."

John of the Cross, a 16th Century Spanish Carmelite monk who wrote *The Dark Night of the Soul*, put it this way: "The reason why the soul not only travels securely when it thus travels in the dark, but makes even greater progress, is this: In general the soul makes greater progress when it least thinks so, yea, most frequently when it imagines that it is losing.

He continues, "Having never before experienced the present novelty which dazzles it, and disturbs its former habits, it considers itself as losing, rather than as gaining ground, when it sees itself lost in a place it once knew, and in which it delighted, traveling by a road it knows not, and in which it has no pleasure.

"As a traveller into strange countries goes by ways strange and untried, relying on information derived from others, and not upon any knowledge of his own—it is clear that he will never reach a new country but by new ways which he knows not, and by abandoning those he knew—so in the same way the soul makes the greater progress when it travels in the dark, not knowing the way."

— *Prayer* —

Father, in the name of Jesus, help me discern what is really happening inside me when I find myself in a dark night of the soul. Help me to stay the course, to keep my eyes on You, knowing that Your eyes are always on me.

OCTOBER 23

Hearts Knitted in Intercession

"That their hearts might be comforted, being knit together in love" (Colossians 2:2).

You've heard it said, "The family that prays together stays together." That is true, and it's not just natural families but spiritual families.

Charles Finney, a great revivalist in the Second Great Awakening, put it this way: "Nothing tends more to cement the hearts of Christians than praying together. Never do they love one another so well as when they witness the outpouring of each other's hearts in prayer."

Consider the disciples praying in the Upper Room preceding Pentecost. They were, as Jesus commanded, waiting there in Jerusalem for the empowerment of the Holy Spirit. They didn't fully know what to expect, but they were expecting. After the Holy Spirit came in like a mighty rushing wind and something like tongues of fire fell upon each one of them, it forever changed them.

That is what's called a shared spiritual experience. First, they shared their hearts in prayer. Then they saw a prayer answer that defied anything they could have imagined. Those shared spiritual experiences led to a knitting together of their hearts in love that birthed a church marked by signs, wonders and miracles. Look at Acts 4:32-35:

"Now the multitude of those who believed were of one heart and one soul; neither did anyone say that any of the things he possessed was his own, but they had all things in common. And with great power the apostles gave witness to the resurrection of the Lord Jesus.

"And great grace was upon them all. Nor was there anyone among them who lacked; for all who were possessors of lands or houses sold them, and brought the proceeds of the things that were sold, and laid them at the apostles' feet; and they distributed to each as anyone had need."

This is how the church should be. And notice how it all started when they prayed together. The family that prays together, stays together.

— Prayer —

Father, in the name of Jesus, teach me how to pray in such a way that it comforts and strengthens all who hear my heart's cry. Set me among a group of intercessors with clean hands and pure hearts so we can ascend together.

OCTOBER 24

The Law of Prayer

"But this I say: He who sows sparingly will also reap sparingly, and he who sows bountifully will also reap bountifully" (2 Corinthians 9:6).

Just as there are spiritual laws that govern prayer—such as faith and patience paving the way for inheriting the promises of God and the law of blessings and curses—there are laws of prayer.

"The law of prayer is the law of the harvest," said Leonard Ravenhill. "Sow sparingly in prayer, reap sparingly; sow bountifully in prayer reap bountifully. The trouble is we are trying to get from our efforts what we never put into them."

The law of the harvest says you can only reap what you sow—and you reap the same kinds of seeds you sow. It doesn't take an agricultural expert to understand that we reap a specific harvest based on the specific seeds we've sown. If you sow apple seeds, you'll see a harvest of apple trees—not watermelons. If you sow corn seeds, you'll reap ears of corn—not grapes. That's why we need to be specific in our prayer.

Sometimes we get what seems to be an immediate harvest from a seed we've sown—for better or worse. I've heard many stories of people sowing their last penny believing God for a financial breakthrough and getting an unexpected check in the mail three days later. But much of the time we reap in a future season. We reap in the due season.

The law of the harvest says you reap exponentially on what you sow. Every farmer understands this principle—or they would never sow. The reality is if you sow an apple seed, it yields an apple tree with countless apples and countless more seeds. Although the apple seed is tiny, when it is planted and watered a tree grows that feeds many. There's a multiplication effect of sowing seed into the ground.

Every time you pray according to God's will, you are sowing seeds against which you will one day reap an exponential harvest. God is not just adding to—He's multiplying. Jesus said in the Parable of the Sower: "Other seeds fell into good ground and produced grain: a hundred, sixty, or thirty times as much" (Matt. 13:8).

— Prayer —

Father, in the name of Jesus, help this revelation sink into my head and into my heart. I want to reap a bountiful harvest of prayer answers. So help me to sow prayer abundantly. Help me to make effective, accurate intercession in Your will.

OCTOBER 25

Eloquence vs. Power

"And I, brethren, when I came to you, did not come with excellence of speech or of wisdom declaring to you the testimony of God" (1 Corinthians 2:1-5).

Some intercessors are eloquent. Some are powerful. Some are both. But if I had to choose, I'd pick power over eloquence every day of the week.

Eloquent prayer is poetic prayer. Eloquent prayer is persuasive expressiveness. But we don't really need to persuade God to do His will. He is ready, willing, and able to answer every prayer released that agrees with His plans and purposes.

Moses missed the point when God first called him, saying to God, "O my Lord, I am not eloquent, neither before nor since You have spoken to Your servant; but I am slow of speech and slow of tongue" (Ex. 4:10). Moses would soon find out he didn't need eloquence. He just needed the power of God.

Power is the ability to produce an effect. Power is the legal or official authority, capacity or right. Power is to move with great speed or force. Hannah Moore, author of the classic book *Practical Piety*, put it this way: "Prayer is not eloquence, but earnestness; not the definition of helplessness, but the feeling of it; not figures of speech, but earnestness of soul."

Paul the apostle may have learned from Moses' mistake—a mistake that eventually angered God. Paul was a man of prayer and he was also a man of power. Paul communicated his preference for power over eloquence in his first letter to the Corinthian church:

"And I, brethren, when I came to you, did not come with excellence of speech or of wisdom declaring to you the testimony of God. For I determined not to know anything among you except Jesus Christ and Him crucified. I was with you in weakness, in fear, and in much trembling. And my speech and my preaching were not with persuasive words of human wisdom, but in demonstration of the Spirit and of power, that your faith should not be in the wisdom of men but in the power of God" (1 Cor. 2:1-5).

— *Prayer* —

Father, in the name of Jesus, help me not to be conscious of how I pray but to focus on praying Your will and releasing Your power into circumstances that defy Your plans. I want to operate in high levels of prayer power.

Discerning the Winning Prayer Strategy

"If any of you lacks wisdom, let him ask of God, who gives to all liberally and without reproach, and it will be given to him" (James 1:5).

Paul gave us a heads up: We don't what God wants us to pray for (see Rom. 8:26, NLT). If we're not careful, we'll get rote in our prayer. We'll use the same three types of prayer for every intercession session. The reality is, we need to discern what type of prayer to release in every situation. Thank God, the Holy Spirit helps us discern.

There are entryway prayers, such as prayers of confession, adoration, and thanksgiving that we should always include in our intercession sessions. There are prayers of dedication, consecration and contemplation that are helpful in our devotional life. But in intercession, we need to discern the right tool from the prayer toolbox.

Maybe that's praying in the Spirit. Maybe it's prophetic prayer, wherein the Holy Spirit informs your prayer. He may give you a Scripture to pray, show you a picture, or just lead you to pray boldly in your native language. Maybe the Holy Spirit will lead you into travail. Maybe someone is sick and you need to release the prayer of faith (see James 5:15).

Perhaps you discern you need more firepower—that you need to join with one or two others in the prayer of agreement or corporate prayer. Maybe you need to engage in all out spiritual warfare prayer, binding and loosing, pushing back darkness and so on.

Sometimes we have a prophetic word or Scripture to stand on as we set out into our intercession session, and sometimes we just don't even know where to begin. How do you know what type of prayer to pray? Well, again, the Holy Spirit can inform you. Or you may just start praying and He will graciously lead you into a specific type of prayer as you set out in intercession.

When you know that you don't know how to pray as you ought, ask the Holy Spirit to help you discern the prayer strategy. Ask for prayer wisdom. He is faithful to pour it out.

— *Prayer* —

Father, in the name of Jesus, teach me how to flow with the Holy Spirit as I make intercession. Teach me how to lean on His wisdom as I make intercession with faith that He knows all things and even the perfect way to pray. I want to pray Your way.

When Your Prayer Life is Under Attack

"Therefore, my beloved brethren, be steadfast, immovable, always abounding in the work of the Lord, knowing that your labor is not in vain in the Lord" (1 Corinthians 15:58).

"Satan dreads nothing but prayer. His one concern is to keep the saints from praying. He fears nothing from prayerless studies, prayerless work, prayerless religion. He laughs at our toil, he mocks our wisdom, but he trembles when we pray." So said Samuel Chadwick, a Wesleyan Methodist minister in the 19th and 20th centuries.

Chadwick couldn't speak truer words. Satan hates when you pray. He will attack your prayer life at strategic times—often at the times when you most need to be praying. What more opportune time could he find than when you are in dire straits and the only way out is answered prayer? We must not be ignorant of the enemy's devices (see 2 Cor. 2:11).

So how do you discern when your prayer life is under attack? There are too many symptoms to list here. I want to focus on just this one: lacking a passion for prayer. Usually, a strong urge to throw in the towel on your assignment accompanies that lack of passion.

I've seen this too many times in intercessory prayer groups over the years, including our Awakening Prayer Hubs movement. People often join prayer ministries with fire and passion. They pray, war, petition and the like until the enemy swats back at them in retaliation. Sometimes that's because they stepped into realms of prayer they shouldn't've and stirred up unnecessary warfare against themselves. Whatever the reason, they grow weary in well doing, and Paul warned us against letting that happen (see Gal. 6:9).

When you are under spiritual attack, your knee-jerk reaction is often to quit—to forfeit. Maybe he's tried that tactic on you with your personal prayer life or your prayer group. Quitting while you are overwhelmed or feeling defeated is not the way the Lord leads. We must discern the devil and his tactics. Certainly, one of them is to attack relentlessly so you will quit. Know this: When you refuse to quit, he'll eventually back off.

— Prayer —

Father, in the name of Jesus, would You help me discern when my prayer life is under attack so I don't fall for the temptation to step out of my prayer assignment? Help me resolve in my heart that quitting is not an option.

Living to Pray

"Night and day she served God in the temple by praying and often going without eating"
(Luke 2:37).

Some intercessors have a prayer life. Others live to pray. There's a vast difference between these two realms and it can take us time to catch the revelation that escorts us from a simple prayer life to a life immersed in prayer and intercession.

E.M. Bounds is an example of a man who lived to pray. W.H. Hodge, the man who put many of the great man of prayer E.M. Bounds' works into print, described him as a man hidden away with God. He wrote:

"I have been among many ministers and slept in the same room with them for several years. They prayed, but I was never impressed with any special praying among them until one day a small man with gray hair and an eye like an eagle came along.

"We had a ten-day convention. We had some fine preachers around the home, and one of them was assigned to my room. I was surprised early next morning to see a man bathing himself before day and then see him get down and begin to pray. I said to myself, 'He will not disturb us, but will soon finish.' He kept on softly for hours, interceding and weeping softly, for me and my indifference, and for all the ministers of God.

"He spoke the next day on prayer. I became interested, for I was young in the ministry, and had often desired to meet with a man of God that prayed like the saints of the apostolic age. Next morning, he was up praying again and for ten days he was up early praying for hours. I became intensely interested and thanked God for sending him. 'At last,' I said, 'I have found a man that really prays. I shall never let him go.' He drew me to him with hooks of steel."

E.M. Bounds lived to pray. Anna the prophetess lived to pray? Do you?

— *Prayer* —

Father, in the name of Jesus, would You give me a revelation that spurs in me a passionate desire to pray day and night? I don't want to just pray to live. I want to live to pray. Teach me how to pray without ceasing.

OCTOBER 29

When God Says No

"And it came to pass on the seventh day, that the child died" (2 Samuel 12:18).

David's prophet Nathan had a hard word for the king. Because David took another man's wife, got her pregnant and had her husband murdered, the prophet said, his child would surely die. Although the child survived birth, Scripture tells us the Lord struck the boy with sickness. But Nathan's prophetic word didn't stop David from praying.

"David therefore pleaded with God for the child, and David fasted and went in and lay all night on the ground. So the elders of his house arose and went to him, to raise him up from the ground. But he would not, nor did he eat food with them. Then on the seventh day it came to pass that the child died," (2 Sam. 12:16-18).

When the child died, David did something that seemed unusual. He got up, washed and anointed himself, and changed his clothes. Then he went into the house of the Lord and worshipped. That's not the typical reaction of one who prayed for someone to live and didn't get the prayer answer over which they wept.

"Then his servants said to him, 'What is this that you have done? You fasted and wept for the child while he was alive, but when the child died, you arose and ate food.' And he said, 'While the child was alive, I fasted and wept; for I said, 'Who can tell whether the Lord will be gracious to me, that the child may live?' But now he is dead; why should I fast? Can I bring him back again? I shall go to him, but he shall not return to me" (2 Samuel 12:21-23).

Marshall Dods, a Scottish minister from the 1800s, once wrote, "An answered prayer is not always a blessing, sometimes it is a doom." When we get a "no" from God, we have to stand in faith that a "yes" may have ended up in misery even when we're miserable in our present condition.

— *Prayer* —

Father, in the name of Jesus, help me to trust You completely to give me the right answer to my intercession. Help me not to grow discouraged with delays or denials. I trust that You, Father, know best.

Don't Quench the Spirit of Prayer

"Do not quench the Spirit" (1 Thessalonians 5:19).

Paul said these Spirit-inspired words emphatically: Do not quench the Spirit. Other translations urge, "Do not stifle the Holy Spirit (NLT)" or "Do not extinguish the Spirit" (Berean) or "Do not quench [subdue, or be unresponsive to the working and guidance of] the [Holy] Spirit" (AMP).

Still other versions of 1 Thessalonians 5:19 plead, "Do not restrain the Holy Spirt" (GNT) and "Don't put out the Spirit's fire" (ISV). And "Don't turn away God's Spirit" (CEV). *The Passion Translation* puts it this way: "Never restrain or put out the fire of the Holy Spirit."

It's hard to imagine why we would dare to quench the Holy Spirit for any reason, especially as intercessors. But He can be quenched. So how do we quench the Holy Spirit?

We quench the Spirit when we don't acknowledge Him in our daily life. We stifle the Holy Spirit when He stirs us to pray but we ignore the stirring. We subdue the Holy Spirit when we don't submit to His leadership. We restrain the Holy Spirit when we don't yield our tongue to His utterance.

We put out the Spirit's fire when we disobey the Word of God. We turn away from God's Spirit when we set our eyes on worthless things. We quench the Holy Spirit when we ignore His still small voice in our lives. We put out His fire when we are in unbelief.

Indeed, there are many ways we can quench the work of the Holy Spirit in our lives. And we may not realize just how often we do it. It's not just our actions. It's the doubt and unbelief of those for whom or with whom we are interceding. If we find ourselves in an atmosphere of doubt, we may be better of praying alone.

Jesus faced this issue in His hometown. Because the people did not respect the Holy Spirit in Him, He couldn't do many mighty works there (see Mark 6:5). Let's be careful not to quench the Spirit.

— *Prayer* —

Father, in the name of Jesus, help me never to quench the working of Your generous Spirit in my life. Please warn me before I think, say, do or pray something that quenches Your fire. Please, Lord, make me more sensitive to Your holy heart.

OCTOBER 31

The Harp and the Bowl

"Now when He had taken the scroll, the four living creatures and the twenty-four elders fell down before the Lamb, each having a harp, and golden bowls full of incense, which are the prayers of the saints" (Revelation 5:8).

Prayer ministries like the International House of Prayer in Kansas City made the harp and bowl model popular on the earth in our generation. But it has always been popular in heaven. You may have wondered what harp and bowl means in the realm of prayer.

The harp represents worship. The bowl filled with the incense of the saints represents prayer. There's a power unleashed when you combine prayer and worship in this way. In the harp and bowl model, intercessors release prayer and often the worship leaders sing the prayers. The worship brings everyone's attention to the Lord in unity. The prayer releases a heart's cry for His will to be done and His Kingdom to come to earth as it is in heaven.

"Worship and intercession must go together; the one is impossible without the other," said Oswald Chambers, a Scottish Baptist evangelist who wrote *My Utmost for His Highest*. "Intercession means that we rouse ourselves up to get the mind of Christ about the one for whom we pray."

Mike Bickle, founder of IHOPKC, explains it this way: "The prayer leader's main job is to keep the isolated phrase obvious to the prophetic singers. In other words, to give the singers a big target at which to aim. The prayer leader's second job is to watch the involvement of the room. The goal is to see the room in one accord. They watch to see if the antiphonal singing is inspiring the room to engage with God. If the antiphonal singing goes too long the room disengages."

So how does this work if you are praying solo? You can still worship and pray. You can still engage in worship and intercession. Worship first and then let your intercession flow out of that worship. When you run out of prayer, go back into worship. It's an ebb and flow that will make your intercession more intimate.

— *Prayer* —

Father, in the name of Jesus, help me grasp this harp and bowl model that we see in heaven. Help me to worship prayerfully and pray with a heart of praise and worship. Teach me to ride the wave of worship into intercession and back again.

NOVEMBER

"Watch and pray, lest you enter into temptation. The spirit indeed is willing, but the flesh is weak" (Matthew 26:41).

Making Intercession for Leaders

"Therefore I exhort first of all that supplications, prayers, intercessions, and giving of thanks be made for all men, for kings and all who are in authority, that we may lead a quiet and peaceable life in all godliness and reverence" (1 Timothy 2:1-2).

Believers have a Spirit-inspired biblical mandate to pray for leaders. Always remember, most leaders want and need your prayers. Think of Paul. The apostle asked the churches to whom he wrote his epistles for prayer over and over again. And he was confident their prayers would help him in his mission:

"Strive together with me in your prayers to God on my behalf (Rom. 15:30). "I know that through your prayers and the help of the Spirit of Jesus Christ this will turn out for my deliverance" (Phil. 1:19).

Of course, there's a right way and a wrong way to pray for leaders—spiritual and secular. The wrong way is praying your opinions the affairs of their lives. The wrong way is praying your will or desire for the leader. The wrong way is to pray presumptuous prayers. So, what is the right way?

Effective prayer for leaders is earnest prayer. If your heart is not in it, it's not effective. Effective prayer for leaders is continued prayer. Leaders need prayer consistently, not every once in a while. Effective prayer for a leader is sincere prayer that wants to see the leader succeed. Effective prayer for a leader is prayer based on the Word of God. Effective prayer for a leader could be praying in the spirit for them.

In Romans 8:26 (AMP), Paul wrote, "In the same way the Spirit [comes to us and] helps us in our weakness. We do not know what prayer to offer or how to offer it as we should, but the Spirit Himself [knows our need and at the right time] intercedes on our behalf with sighs and groanings too deep for words."

There are many appropriate prayers for leaders. The best prayers are those informed by the Word of God and inspired by the Spirit of God. Lean into the Holy Spirit as you pray for leaders and those in authority in the church, cities and nations. There's a blessing in obedience.

— *Prayer* —

Father, in the name of Jesus, help me obey Your command to pray for kings and those in authority, whether I like them or agree with them. Help me stand as an agent of blessing through prayer and not cursing through my opinions about how leaders operate and the decisions that they make.

The Governmental Intercessor

"Of the increase of His government and peace there will be no end, upon the throne of David and over His kingdom, to order it and establish it with judgment and justice from that time forward, even forever. The zeal of the Lord of hosts will perform this" (Isaiah 9:7).

I heard the Lord say, "I am looking for governmental intercessors in this region that will rise up in My Spirit and legislate the territory with My Word. I am seeking those who understand how the courts of heaven operate and will explore what the enemy has said and is saying over your city. I am looking for prayer warriors who understand how to tap into My plans ... and co-labor with My Spirit to bring My Kingdom down. I am looking."

Webster's dictionary defines govern as "to direct and control; to regulate by authority; to influence; to direct; to restrain; to steer or to regulate the course of; to exercise authority to maintain the superiority." Put another way, governing is exercising authority.

Now let's bring that into the realm of intercession. The simplest way to explain governmental intercession is praying with authority. A governmental intercessor prays with authority into governments, whether church governments, local, state, national or international governments.

Think about it this way: Governments are organizations through which politicians exercise authority and distribute power. There is no higher government than the government of God. Governing intercessors have delegated authority in Christ to decree God's will to be done and His Kingdom to come on earth—and in governments.

Having authority alone is not enough. You can have a bank account full of money and still go hungry if you don't withdraw funds to buy food. The enemy will continue attacking us if we don't exercise our authority. 1 Peter 5:8-9 tells us, "Be sober and watchful, because your adversary the devil walks around as a roaring lion, seeking whom he may devour. Resist him firmly in the faith, knowing that the same afflictions are experienced by your brotherhood throughout the world."

— *Prayer* —

Father, in the name of Jesus, would You help me understand my authority to govern affairs in the earth? Would You give me a deeper revelation of the authority Christ delegated to me?

NOVEMBER 3

Keys to Prayer Productivity

"See then that you walk circumspectly, not as fools but as wise, redeeming the time, because the days are evil" (Ephesians 5:15).

The business world loves to talk about productivity hacks. After all, who doesn't want to do more with less? Who doesn't want to work smarter instead of harder? Likewise, if I am going to pray, I want my prayer to be productive. And I know you do, too. The good news is there are principles for productive prayer that you can employ today.

Productive prayer is prayer that aligns with God's will. Therefore, before I set out to pray for a matter, I need to understand what God wants in the situation. If we are going to pray for God's will to be done and God's Kingdom to come, we need to know what His will is before we pray. Otherwise, we'll be fruitless. Many times, it's easy to see with your plain eyes how to intercede. Other times, we need to pray for a revelation of God's will before we pray over the problem.

Productive prayer is undistracted prayer. If you are going to set out on an intercessory prayer agenda, you need to be undisturbed. That's why Jesus spoke of going into your prayer closet alone. Just as a cubicle worker in an office can be easily distracted by the music or conversation of co-workers around him, the intercessor can be easily distracted by the goings on around them. Aside from corporate prayer, get in quiet place.

Productive prayer is believing prayer. You need to build your faith up to pray for the need at hand before launching out into intercession. If you are making intercession for someone's healing, for example, consider meditating on the healing Scriptures first so your prayers are filled with faith that brings results. Taking the time to prep yourself before the prayer session will pay dividends in the form of prayer answers. What are your keys to productive prayer?

— *Prayer* —

Father, in the name of Jesus, would You help me find ways to be more productive
in prayer? Would You show me my inefficiencies? I want to bear much fruit
through my intercession. Teach me what I don't know.

When You Have to Pray Alone

"Then Jesus came with them to a place called Gethsemane, and said to the disciples, 'Sit here while I go and pray over there'" (Matthew 26:36).

In 2012, I was sitting in a prayer room searching and seeking the will of the Lord. He truly is a rewarder of those who diligently seek Him (see Heb. 11:6). After some time seeking, I got a clear answer. He said, "Make prayer your life's work."

Honestly, I had no idea what that meant at the time. So, I prayed on it for thirty days. I didn't share it publicly because I didn't want man's opinion. I wanted God's revelation. At the end of the thirty days, I determined God wanted me to start a house of prayer. So, I did.

We launched with a bang. We had a facility and a decent core group that was praying six days a week. But, pretty soon, the excitement wore off and I was standing there alone every Saturday at 4 p.m. It was like sitting in an empty movie theatre—but it wasn't empty. The God who told me to make prayer my life's work was there.

Still, after months of this I grew a wee bit weary. Nevertheless, with resolve I prayed, "Lord, I will stand here and pray by myself until Jesus comes back if that's what it takes to make prayer my life's work." At one point, I thought He was going to take me up on that offer. Months went by and nary a soul darkened the door.

The reality is, sometimes you do have to pray alone. It's powerful to have prayer partners and corporate prayer groups. But sometimes, you have to pray alone. Sometimes, the Holy Spirit wants to teach us lessons in perseverance. Sometimes, He wants to guard us from people with wrong motives.

If you have to pray alone for a season, so be it. Jesus prayed alone quite often, even in the Garden of Gethsemane. Remember, you are not really alone.

— *Prayer* —

Father, in the name of Jesus, would You help me to enjoy the power of praying alone? Would You help me not to despise having to stand in the gap all by myself? Would You help me remember that I'm never really alone because Your Holy Spirit is with me?

The Lifestyle of an Effective Intercessor

"And that you put on the new man which was created according to God, in true righteousness and holiness" (Ephesians 4:24).

We can learn plenty about the lifestyle of an intercessor by looking at heroes of intercession in the Bible, like Daniel or Moses. It seems all the great intercessors from Scripture had lifestyle factors in common. Faith is the foundation, of course, as an intercessor without faith isn't much of an intercessor at all.

The lifestyle of an intercessor demands we clothe ourselves with the Lord Jesus Christ, the Chief Intercessor (see Rom. 13:14). He is our model intercessor, and we should live as Christ lived (see 1 John 2:6). That means living a lifestyle of holiness.

An unknown author once said, "All hindrance to prayer arises from ignorance of the teaching of God's Holy Word on the life of holiness He has planned for all His children, or from an unwillingness to consecrate ourselves fully to Him." The lifestyle of an effective intercessor, then, lays aside every weight and sin that would hinder prayer (see Heb. 12:1).

If we want to pray in the promises of God, we need to strive for holiness, without which no one shall see the Lord (see Heb. 12:14). Paul put it this way: "Therefore, having these promises, beloved, let us cleanse ourselves from all filthiness of the flesh and spirit, perfecting holiness in the fear of God" (see 2 Cor. 7:1-2).

Intercessor, you were saved with a holy calling, not according to your works, but according to His own purpose and grace that was given to you in Christ Jesus before time began (see 2 Tim. 1:9). You are a chosen race, a royal priesthood, a holy nation, a people for His own possession (see 1 Pet. 2:9).

Intercessor, God has called you to present yourself as a living sacrifice in prayer, holy and acceptable to God, which is your spiritual worship (see Rom. 12:1). That doesn't mean you are perfect. No, there is no perfect one but Jesus. But it means you seek first the Kingdom of God and His righteousness (see Matt. 6:33). God will give you the grace of holiness.

— *Prayer* —

Father, in the name of Jesus, make me holy even as You are holy. Give me the grace to attain new levels of holiness. Perfect me in Your love. I want to live a lifestyle that is worthy of Your high calling for my life. I clothe myself with Christ and choose to walk in the Spirit.

Overcoming a Stagnant Prayer Life

"Wherefore I put thee in remembrance that thou stir up the gift of God, which is in thee by the putting on of my hands" (2 Timothy 1:6).

It can happen to anyone. Suddenly, a fiery prayer life can become stagnant. Instead of releasing rivers of intercession or streams of prayer you feel like there's a kink in the works. You feel like you are not advancing in prayer. And it's frustrating.

The first step to overcoming a stagnant prayer life is to diagnose the issue. So, what causes a stagnant prayer life? It could be any number of things, such as being distracted from His Word or His presence, enemy interference, physical exhaustion, natural distractions, unconfessed sin, known disobedience and the like.

When we discern our prayer life is stagnating, we need to examine our hearts. We need to see if we've grieved the Lord. We need to hear from Him because He knows the answer to the problem. Instead of just trying to press through it in frustration, which will only make matters worse, take some time out to pray and listen.

It could be something as simple as shaking up your prayer routine. Maybe you need to find a new place to pray, or some new people to pray with. Maybe you need a prayer partner who carries their share of the weight. Maybe the grace has lifted for the assignment you've been pressing into. Maybe you need to find something about which you are passionate—a new prayer assignment.

Maybe (and this will sound counterintuitive) you need to take a break from intercession for a few days or a few weeks to get refilled, refreshed, and refired. Maybe you're dealing with intercessory prayer burnout. Maybe you need to discern the root of the spiritual warfare that's trying to stop you from praying.

Maybe you need to look back at the prayer breakthroughs you've seen in your ministry and encourage yourself in the Lord to keep going. Maybe you need to remember why you stepped into the ministry of intercession to begin with. Maybe you need some new revelation on the power of prayer that you're lacking. God will help you get to the root of it. He will fire you up. Ask Him.

— *Prayer* —

Father, in the name of Jesus, would You help me to get still before You and take counsel from You about this issue of stagnation? I want to flow with Your all-knowing Spirit in intercession. Help me break through the stagnation and stay on fire for You in prayer.

The Intercessor's Resilience

"For a righteous man may fall seven times and rise again, but the wicked shall fall by calamity" (Proverbs 24:16).

How resilient are you, intercessor? Do you faint in the midst of a long prayer battle, or does the resistance invigorate you? Resilience is simply the ability to recover from or adjust easily to something bad happening or to an unexpected change.

Paul the apostle was as resilient as they come. He kept going when the going got tough. We see this mindset manifesting in his words: "We are hard-pressed on every side, yet not crushed; we are perplexed, but not in despair; persecuted, but not forsaken; struck down, but not destroyed—always carrying about in the body the dying of the Lord Jesus, that the life of Jesus also may be manifested in our body" (2 Cor. 4:8-10).

Paul went through a lot—and never stopped praying. He endured to the end. He completed his race. He finished his course. He raised up others to carry the Gospel in the same spirit. He wrote, "Who shall separate us from the love of Christ? Shall tribulation, or distress, or persecution, or famine, or nakedness, or peril, or sword? As it is written: 'For Your sake we are killed all day long; We are accounted as sheep for the slaughter.' Yet in all these things we are more than conquerors through Him who loved us" (Romans 8:35-37).

Intercessor, the road isn't always easy. But you can choose to be resilient. Micah put it this way: "Do not rejoice over me, my enemy; When I fall, I will arise; When I sit in darkness, the Lord will be a light to me" (Micah 7:8).

It's not about never faltering, never wavering, or never falling down. It's about getting back up again and again, running back to the prayer closest again and again, and standing in faith again and again. You can do this! Ask the Lord to give you a resilient spirit and keep your eyes on Him.

— Prayer —

Father, in the name of Jesus, would You make me resilient? Would You give me apostolic grit like Paul had when he wrestled the beast at Ephesus and met with all manner of obstacles? Help me keep standing in prayer.

Praying to Escape Temptation

"Watch and pray, lest you enter into temptation. The spirit indeed is willing, but the flesh is weak" (Matthew 26:41, KJV).

Just as the enemy tempted Jesus in the wilderness, the enemy loves to tempt intercessors into all manner of sin. That's because he knows what James 5:16 says, "The effective, fervent prayer of a righteous man avails much." When we are not in right standing with God—when we are walking in unconfessed sin—our prayers will not be effective.

Intercessor, the enemy is going to tempt you in many ways. He will tempt you into prayerlessness, into pride, into gossip and many other sins. He especially likes to tempt intercessors with sins of the mouth in attempts to defile your holy tongue. When the temptation comes, remember what Paul said in 1 Corinthians 10:13:

"No temptation has overtaken you except such as is common to man; but God is faithful, who will not allow you to be tempted beyond what you are able, but with the temptation will also make the way of escape, that you may be able to bear it."

When you feel tempted to say something you shouldn't say or do something you shouldn't do, take a deep breath. Stand up and walk away. God's grace is sufficient to escape the temptation.

Remember these words from the writer of Hebrews, "For in that He Himself has suffered, being tempted, He is able to aid those who are tempted." And again Hebrews 4:15-16 tells us, "For we do not have a High Priest who cannot sympathize with our weaknesses, but was in all points tempted as we are, yet without sin."

When you are being tempted, you are in a time of need. God has already anticipated the temptation. Our way of escape is to do what the Word says. Give no place to the devil (see Eph. 4:27). Turn to Jesus, Your High Priest. Run to the throne of grace. and "Submit to God. Resist the devil and he will flee from you" (James 4:7).

— *Prayer* —

Father, in the name of Jesus, would You help me remember to run to You immediately, without delay, when I'm tempted. Help me to resist every enemy temptation and to continually submit myself to You.

The Johann Ludwig Prayer Anointing

"The Lord opened her heart to heed the things spoken by Paul" (Acts 16:14).

"Like Dr Livingstone, he died on his knees at prayer on November 26, 1881," a statement on the pillar reads. That statement is speaking of Johann Ludwig Krapf. Krapf lived and died in the 19th Century. He was a German missionary to East Africa and an explorer.

Krapf was a pioneer in East Africa as one of the first Europeans to see Mount Kenya. The Anglican Church of Kenya counts him as its founding father. Despite his long-term success, Krapf didn't immediately succeed in his missions. His tenacity in prayer broke him through.

Speaking of the people of Tigre, whose ruler had forbidden Europeans from entering the territory and thereby shutting out evangelists, Krapf did not lose heart. That's because eight thousand copies of Scriptures found their way in first. He knew the Word and prayer works.

In a letter home he wrote, "Meanwhile we will not cease to pray for that unfortunate land, especially commending to the Lord the many copies of His precious Word, that He would bless them and make them witnesses of His truth."

Krapf understood that although we need evangelists in the fields, prayer can drive salvation through miraculous means. He once wrote, "Though every mission should disappear in a single day and leave not a trace behind, I would still cleave to mission work with my prayers, my labors, my gifts, with my body and soul; for there is the command of the Lord Jesus Christ, and where that is there is also His promise and His final victory."

What a revelation of the power of prayer he had! Indeed, Krapf was known to get off his camel while the caravan went ahead, find a bush and kneel behind it to pray that the Gospel would find open hearts in the African peoples when they got there to preach it. He preached and prayed until the day he passed into glory, on his knees.

— *Prayer* —

Father, in the name of Jesus, would You give me a determination to pray without ceasing for lost souls in Africa and beyond? Give me a revelation that my prayers can go where no person has been to drive salvation.

The Intercessor's Sin Against the Lord

"Moreover, as for me, far be it from me that I should sin against the Lord in ceasing to pray for you; but I will teach you the good and the right way" (1 Samuel 2:23).

If we're honest, sometimes we don't feel like praying for stiff-necked, stubborn people. If we're honest, sometimes it seems like it's not doing one bit of good—and it can be wearisome. But if the Lord is calling you to pray for a person, people group or nation, it would be a sin not to obey His instructions.

Samuel found himself in this position. When Israel wanted a king just like other nations, the prophet warned them it would not go well for them. He explained the price they would pay for rejecting God's rulership. But they didn't listen. Some chapters later in the nation's timeline, Samuel reminded the Israelites that if they walked in God's statutes He would be with them—but if they rebelled the hand of the Lord would be against them.

Next, Samuel called on the Lord to send thunder and rain as a sign to them that their request for any king other than the King of all the earth was sinful. That's when the spirit of the fear of the Lord fell upon them and they asked for prayer. Look at 1 Samuel 12:23-25:

"And all the people said to Samuel, 'Pray for your servants to the Lord your God, that we may not die; for we have added to all our sins the evil of asking a king for ourselves.'

"Then Samuel said to the people, 'Moreover, as for me, far be it from me that I should sin against the Lord in ceasing to pray for you; but I will teach you the good and the right way. Only fear the Lord, and serve Him in truth with all your heart; for consider what great things He has done for you. But if you still do wickedly, you shall be swept away, both you and your king.'"

Ask the Lord to give you a grace for people who defy God's wisdom. Ask Him to help you refrain from the sin of prayerlessness.

— Prayer —

Father, in the name of Jesus, would You help me to remember that I am on assignment for You in intercession, no matter who You should send me to? Would You help me not to sin against You by not praying?

Interceding for Iniquities

"The soul who sins shall die. The son shall not bear the guilt of the father, nor the father bear the guilt of the son. The righteousness of the righteous shall be upon himself, and the wickedness of the wicked shall be upon himself" (Exodus 18:20).

Intercessors don't talk much about iniquity, but we should. Part of the reason why we don't talk much about it could be because we don't understand the power in prayer to intercede for iniquities.

Iniquity is the consequence or punishment for sin. It's not the sin that passes on from one generation to the next. It's the iniquity resulting from unforgiven sin. God is willing to forgive iniquity. Consider His words through Jeremiah 31:34: "No more shall every man teach his neighbor, and every man his brother, saying, 'Know the Lord,' for they all shall know Me, from the least of them to the greatest of them, says the Lord. For I will forgive their iniquity, and their sin I will remember no more."

God is merciful. His justice does not do away with His mercy. Sometimes He's just looking for an intercessor to pray over a people group. He's looking for someone to stand in the gap to avert the ongoing consequence and devastating punishment for sin. Moses was an intercessor for iniquities.

Listen in to Numbers 14:17-20: "And now, I pray, let the power of my Lord be great, just as You have spoken, saying, 'The Lord is longsuffering and abundant in mercy, forgiving iniquity and transgression; but He by no means clears the guilty, visiting the iniquity of the fathers on the children to the third and fourth generation.'

"Pardon the iniquity of this people, I pray, according to the greatness of Your mercy, just as You have forgiven this people, from Egypt even until now.' Then the Lord said: "I have pardoned, according to your word."

God wants to show mercy. God will pardon iniquities under the right conditions. Pardon means to excuse an offense without exacting a penalty, according to *Merriam-Webster*'s dictionary. Pardon means to forgive a fault. God is a God of forgiveness. Be an intercessor for those with iniquities.

— *Prayer* —

Father, in the name of Jesus, make me willing to stand in the gap for those who are suffering from iniquities, whether their own or as the result of a generational curse. Give me compassion for those in the bonds of iniquity.

Throne Room Prayers

"Immediately I was in the Spirit; and behold, a throne set in heaven, and One sat on the throne"
(Revelation 4:2).

God invites us to the throne room to release our prayers. Specifically, He says, "Therefore let us draw near with confidence to the throne of grace, so that we may receive mercy and find grace to help in time of need" (Heb. 4:16). We can receive, of course, much more than mercy and grace when we release throne room prayers.

Throne room prayers are prayers we pray with a revelation that we are seated in heavenly places with Christ Jesus even now (see Eph. 2:6). Throne rooms prayers are prayers we release from an ascended place, a place of confidence in our right to stand before Him as sons and daughters, priests and kings called to rule and reign on the earth (see 1 Pet. 2:9).

If you have a condemnation mindset, you won't have confidence to approach the throne room. In order to pray throne room prayers, we need to understand there is no condemnation for those who are in Christ Jesus, who walk according to the spirit and not according to the flesh (see Rom. 8:1). In other words, even when we sin we need to run to the throne room with boldness and faith in the promise of forgiveness.

Hebrews 10:19-23 reads, "Therefore, brethren, having boldness to enter the Holiest by the blood of Jesus, by a new and living way which He consecrated for us, through the veil, that is, His flesh, and having a High Priest over the house of God, let us draw near with a true heart in full assurance of faith, having our hearts sprinkled from an evil conscience and our bodies washed with pure water. Let us hold fast the confession of our hope without wavering, for He who promised is faithful."

Don't hesitate to approach the throne of grace, whether to receive mercy, find grace, make a petition, ask for help or anything else. God has an open-door policy to the throne room. You don't need a special invitation.

— *Prayer* —

Father, in the name of Jesus, help me remember to run to the throne even before I run to the phone to call other intercessors. Jesus, You are the Chief Intercessor and You are always praying. Help me come with a humble boldness to ask for Your help.

NOVEMBER 13

Unraveling Prayer Mysteries

"They must be committed to the mystery of the faith now revealed and must live with a clear conscience" (1 Timothy 3:9).

In many ways, prayer is a mystery. By faith, we petition a God we can't see. We don't know the practical mechanics of how the answers come but our sovereign God does miracles when we pray. Consider Joshua. He was passionately fighting a battle—and routing the enemy. The only problem was the sun was going down.

"Then Joshua spoke to the Lord in the day when the Lord delivered up the Amorites before the children of Israel, and he said in the sight of Israel: 'Sun, stand still over Gibeon; And Moon, in the Valley of Aijalon.' So the sun stood still, and the moon stopped, till the people had revenge upon their enemies" (Joshua 10:12-14). How did this happen? It's a mystery.

The prophet Isaiah prophesied a death sentence to the King Hezekiah. Hezekiah cried out to the Lord for more time and in 2 Kings 20:9-11 we read:

"Then Isaiah said, 'This is the sign to you from the Lord, that the Lord will do the thing which He has spoken: shall the shadow go forward ten degrees or go backward ten degrees?' And Hezekiah answered, 'It is an easy thing for the shadow to go down ten degrees; no, but let the shadow go backward ten degrees.' So Isaiah the prophet cried out to the Lord, and He brought the shadow ten degrees backward, by which it had gone down on the sundial of Ahaz." How did this happen? It's a mystery.

In his book *The Change the World School of Prayer*, Dick Eastman wrote, "Those who give up on praying because they do not understand this 'gift of the bended knee' have failed to recognize that prayer itself is a mystery, something that 'puts us in awe.' Unfortunately, there are some who demand a more complete explanation of a concept before accepting it."

— *Prayer* —

Father, in the name of Jesus, would You help me get out of my head and into Your heart? Help me not to try to figure out how You are going to move, but rather to trust that You will move at the right time in the right way.

344

Faith, Patience and Prayer

"Imitate those who through faith and patience inherit the promises" (Hebrews 6:12).

Some intercessors have more faith than patience. Others have more patience than faith. The reality is, we need both.

Abraham and Sarah didn't start out with both faith and patience. Abraham lied more than once as he wandered through the land. He told rulers that Sarah was his sister for fear they would kill him so they could take her.

Later, the couple had a prophetic word about a son, but Sarah was barren, and they were both beyond childbearing years. Abraham had grown in faith and believed God. Sarah was still playing catch up and laughed. She was also impatient, and in her impatience she encouraged Abraham to sleep with Haggar and birth Ishmael. The family dynamics were beyond dysfunctional.

Intercessors, we must build up our faith. We do that by reading the Word, praying in the Spirit and taking Paul's advice in Romans 12:12, "Rejoice in hope, be patient in tribulation, be constant in prayer." We can rejoice in the hope of the promise we don't yet see, and we must be patient through the trials on the way to our triumph. All the while, we must continue to pray.

The writer of Hebrews put it this way: "And we desire that each one of you show the same diligence to the full assurance of hope until the end, that you do not become sluggish, but imitate those who through faith and patience inherit the promises" (Heb. 6:10-11). And Paul offered, "But if we hope for what we do not see, we wait for it with patience" (Rom. 8:25, ESV).

David understood this concept when he was running from Saul in the wilderness, waiting on God to fulfill the promise of his kingship. He wrote, "I waited patiently for the Lord; he inclined to me and heard my cry" (Ps. 40:1). David waited over twenty years to see the promise. So did Abraham. However long you must wait, wait patiently.

— *Prayer* —

Father, in the name of Jesus, help me wait patiently. I don't want to get out of faith and into my flesh. I don't want to try to help You bring the promise to pass. You don't need my help. You just want my trust. So I will trust You.

The Daniel Prayer Anointing

"Then I set my face toward the Lord God to make request by prayer and supplications, with fasting, sackcloth, and ashes" (Daniel 9:3).

The Daniel prayer anointing sets off a war in the heavens, and perseveres until the angelic hosts win the fight with the principalities and powers resisting the prayer answers. Daniel was a man of excellence. He was a man of integrity. He was consistent and persistent in his intercession—and the world hated him for it.

Daniel made a decision to pray without ceasing—and on schedule. Daniel didn't complain about praying alone—day after day on his knees in front of his window—because he knew he was not alone. He knew God Almighty was with him. Daniel instead was courageous in prayer, defying the edict not to bow to any other god but King Darius. Darius wasn't his God. He prayed on through the persecution.

Daniel was passionate about his purpose in prayer, identifying with the sins of a nation and pleading in repentance for liberation. Daniel prayed the Word of God in humility with faith and great wisdom. Daniel added fasting to his prayers to a covenant-keeping God of grace and mercy who loves His people.

I often wonder if Daniel was in heated intercession when his friends Shadrach, Meshach and Abednego were in the fiery furnace. He was aware of the plight of his Israelite brothers who, like him, determined not to defile their bodies with the food of Babylon but to trust God in all things.

I often wonder if Daniel's intercession led to the eventual repentance of King Nebuchadnezzar. Daniel interpreted a dream and then offered, "Therefore, O king, let my advice be acceptable to you; break off your sins by being righteous, and your iniquities by showing mercy to the poor. Perhaps there may be a lengthening of your prosperity" (Dan. 4:27).

We see Daniel's heart for Israel as a nation, for his friends in trial and even for an evil king who oppressed the nation he loved. Can we do the same?

— *Prayer* —

Father, in the name of Jesus, would You help me to pray like Daniel, knowing that You will send angel armies to deliver the answer if You have to? Would You teach me to pray for all people, my friends and even my enemies, with a dedication to see Your will done?

Climbing the Prayer Stairs

"So Jesus said to them, 'Because of your unbelief; for assuredly, I say to you, if you have faith as a mustard seed, you will say to this mountain, 'Move from here to there,' and it will move; and nothing will be impossible for you" (Matthew 17:20).

Some mountains are more stubborn than others. And sometimes your faith is not as strong as you thought when the opposition to God's promise arises.

At times, we try to cast the mountain into the sea in one fell swoop when we only have the faith to move it an inch. We expect instant breakthrough wrapped in a miracle but we need to build our faith muscle to move the mountain.

"It is too frequently our experience to pray for the conversion of a loved one for years without an answer. That is not because God isn't willing to save the loved one, it's because we are not praying sensibly and with faith," writes Rosalind Rink in her classic book, *Prayer: Conversations with God.*

"It is like trying to take one giant leap from the bottom of the stairs to the top of the stairs. We want to get to the top of the stairs. We talk and talk about going and yet there we stand. The reason being, it is impossible to get from the bottom to the top of a flight of stairs in one step. Stairs were made to be used, but they were made to be used one step at a time," she wrote.

"The prayer of faith is like that. Climbing the steps is what we mean by a faith-sized request. Take one step at a time. Pray only what you believe God can do for a certain person in a definitely situation in a given time period."

That's a powerful illustration. But let's go back to the mountain analogy for a moment. This will set you free. Even if you only move the mountain an inch at a time, you are building faith to move it closer to the sea every time you pray.

— Prayer —

Father, in the name of Jesus, help me to take the stairs one step at a time, according to the faith I've developed in Your Word. Help me not to try to move beyond my faith in intercession, least I get weary and discouraged.

NOVEMBER 17

Intercessory Integrity

"The integrity of the upright will guide them..." (Proverbs 11:13).

We need integrity in prayer. We need integrity in intercession. Integrity is a firm adherence to a code of especially moral or artistic values. It's incorruptibility. It's soundness of mind. It's an undivided heart.

In Psalm 86:11, David cried, "Give me an undivided heart, that I may fear Your name." When we're making intercession, we need a sound mind—not a double mind. We need a heart united to fear His name, not a divided heart. We need right motives or we'll pray amiss.

Proverbs 10:9 declares, "He who walks with integrity walks securely." We must remember that as intercessors, we are often in the line of enemy fire. If we want the full benefits of protection as gap-standers, we need to walk with integrity.

Integrity is more than honesty but includes honesty. Integrity is following God's law even when no one is watching. Integrity is letting your yes be yes and your no be no. Integrity is praying for someone when you tell them you will. Integrity is trustworthiness.

Our trials will expose the integrity or lack of integrity in us. When we are in the fiery furnace, will we maintain our intercession for others? When we're walking through the storm, will we keep releasing our petitions?

When John the Baptist found himself in prison, he started questioning if Jesus was really the Messiah. Keep in mind he was the prophet who baptized Jesus and announced Him as Saviour. Job, by contrast, had integrity even when he was under a severe trial.

"Then his wife said to him, 'Do you still hold fast to your integrity? Curse God and die! But he said to her, 'You speak as one of the foolish women speaks. Shall we indeed accept good from God, and shall we not accept adversity?' In all this Job did not sin with his lips'" (Job 2:9-10). Intercessors, don't sin with your lips.

— *Prayer* —

Father, in the name of Jesus, I want to be an intercessor with integrity. Show me areas of my life where I have a divided heart. Would You show me any areas where I have a double-mind? Would You help me walk in integrity?

NOVEMBER 18

A Heart-to-Heart With God

"Inside the Tent of Meeting, the Lord would speak to Moses face to face, as one speaks to a friend" (Exodus 33:11).

Moses talked to God like a man talks to His friend. In other words, Moses had conversations with God. Abraham had conversations with God. Job had conversations with God. Is your prayer life a diatribe or a conversation? Engaging in conversations with God opens up new dimensions of revelation, wisdom, understanding and prayer answers.

Think about it for a minute. When Jesus walked the earth with His disciples, they had a running conversation. The disciples didn't just sit there and watch Jesus work miracles. They asked Jesus questions—and He answered. They asked Him to explain the parables—and He released revelation. They asked Him to teach them how to pray—and He taught them gladly.

Jesus' disciples asked Him why they couldn't cast a devil out—and He told them. They shared their revelation with Him—and He confirmed it. Sometimes they asked Him the wrong questions—"Can we sit at Your right hand and your left in glory"—and He corrected them. They asked Him about signs of His return—and He broke down the signs of the times in specific detail. Jesus is the same yesterday, today and forever. He still wants to talk to you.

Again, Moses talked to God like a man talks to his friend. God told Aaron and Miriam, "I speak with him face to face, even plainly, and not in dark sayings; And he sees the form of the Lord. Why then were you not afraid to speak against My servant Moses?" (Num. 12:8)

Now remember this, Jesus said, "No longer do I call you servants, for a servant does not know what his master is doing; but I have called you friends, for all things that I heard from My Father I have made known to you" (John 15:15).

Talk to God. He doesn't need all the religious lingo and doesn't care for the pretence. He just wants to have a conversation. Pray to God with reverence, yes, but know that He calls you friend.

— *Prayer* —

Father, in the name of Jesus, help me to get the revelation that prayer is not just making a petition or releasing a decree, but many times prayer is and needs to be a conversation. Help me remember to let You speak.

The Potential of Creative Prayer

"Hear instruction and be wise, and do not disdain it" (Proverbs 8:33).

Creative prayer unlocks the ability or power to create in your life what God wants to create. He is still Creator God, but many times He co-labors with you to create in the earth realm. He will give you precise instructions in prayer and intercession.

Remember when Noah built the ark? This was the fruit of creative prayer: "And God said to Noah, 'The end of all flesh has come before Me, for the earth is filled with violence through them; and behold, I will destroy them with the earth. Make yourself an ark of gopherwood; make rooms in the ark, and cover it inside and outside with pitch'" (Gen. 6:13). The result was the salvation of humanity.

How about when Moses built the ark of the covenant many years later? This was also the fruit of creative prayer. God used that ark to help lead the Israelites through the wilderness. Later, David received the blueprint for the temple that Solomon would later build. Again, this was the fruit of creative prayer. And God didn't just give the order. He gave exacting instructions on how to build.

We all need to enter the realm of creative prayer. Creative prayer is where we find instructions to build our lives, build our ministries, build our families, and build everything else we're called to build according to God's strategic blueprint.

Proverbs 8:32-34 offers some insight into creative prayer: "Now therefore, listen to me, my children, for blessed are those who keep my ways. Hear instruction and be wise, and do not disdain it. Blessed is the man who listens to me, watching daily at my gates, waiting at the posts of my doors."

Creative prayer occurs in the context of fellowshipping with the Holy Spirit. When you have a lifestyle of prayer, God doesn't have to wait for you to ask for instructions. You've demonstrated your heart is open to receiving His creative commands.

— *Prayer* —

Father, in the name of Jesus, help me enter into this dimension of creative prayer. Help me incline my ear to hear Your instructions about what You want to build and give me the grace to carry our Your plans.

Please, Don't Grieve the Holy Spirit

"And do not grieve the Holy Spirit of God, by whom you were sealed for the day of redemption"
(Ephesians 4:20).

Do not grieve the Holy Spirit of God. That was Paul's emphatic plea. *The New Living Translation* says, "And do not bring sorrow to God's Holy Spirit by the way you live."

The Passion Translation puts it this way, "So never grieve the Spirit of God or take for granted his holy influence in your life." *The Contemporary English Version* exhorts, "Don't make God's Spirit sad."

Since the Holy Spirit is the spirit of prayer, when we grieve Him it can be difficult to pray at all, much less pray effectively and fervently to tap into the tremendous power available to us in the name of Jesus. But what does it mean to grieve the Holy Spirit? The word "grieve" in this verse means "to make sorrowful; to affect with sadness, cause grief, to throw into sorrow; to grieve, offend; to make one uneasy; to vex, irritate, offend, insult."

That's a lot to consider. We need to get to know the Holy Spirit, who is the Third Person of the Trinity, and understand what He likes and does not like so that we don't cause Him grief, sorrow, offense, irritation and uneasiness. We need Him to help us pray and do anything and everything else.

"If I knew that the Holy Spirit was grieved, if I knew the Holy Ghost would depart from me, I would never again walk out on this stage. I would never make a pretence of things but in that hour I would be the most ordinary person that ever lived, and nothing would happen," Kathryn Kuhlman said, as recorded in *A Spiritual Biography of God's Miracle Worker*.

"I could say the same words, go through the same form, do the same things, but the secret power is the Holy Ghost. I cannot use the Holy Spirit. I can't do it. The Holy Spirit must use the vessel. Understand something. You can have the greatest talent in the world but it will never accomplish anything for God unless the Holy Ghost uses it."

— *Prayer* —

Father, in the name of Jesus, please, please help me never to grieve the Holy Spirit. Help me to walk with Him in a manner that's worthy of His presence in my life. I don't want to grieve the One who informs my intercession.

Your Burning Bush Moment

"Take off your sandals, for you are standing on holy ground" (Exodus 3:5).

I'll always remember my burning bush moment. Well, actually, the bush was smoking. I was heading into the back door of my condo building when I noticed a bush at the entryway was smoking. I stopped to look because it was more smoke than a cigarette—or even two cigarettes—could muster. I examined the bush carefully and could not see any natural source of smoke.

I must have looked foolish, and that may have been part of the point. God was trying to get my attention. He was also trying to show me something I wasn't seeing. He was trying to tell me something I wasn't hearing. He got my attention at the smoking bush and shared truth with me soon after that helped me break through to the next level.

Moses had an encounter with God at the burning bush and it changed his life. Like me, Moses passed by a burning bush and said, "This is amazing. ...Why isn't that bush burning up? I must go see it" (Exod. 3:3) What the Bible says next is also amazing: "When the Lord saw Moses coming to take a closer look, God called to him from the middle of the bush, 'Moses! Moses!'" (Exod. 3:4).

Think about it for a minute. What if Moses hadn't stopped to look? Burning bushes were not all that uncommon in the desert. But this one caught Moses' attention and he turned aside. If he had kept on walking—if he was not sensitive to the Spirit—he would have walked right past this life-defining encounter.

In that encounter, Moses heard the voice of the God of Abraham, Isaac, and Jacob. He heard the God who created the world. He heard the God who was greater than the gods of Egypt. He heard God call His name and say, "Moses, Moses, I will be with you." Moses was called. He was commissioned. He was promoted. He was sent. Don't miss your burning bush moments.

— Prayer —

Father, in the name of Jesus, make me sensitive to Your heart. I don't want to miss my burning bush moment. I don't want to miss my highest calling or the commissioning to the next level. Help me see You moving.

When You Don't Feel Like Praying

"Whoever has no rule over his own spirit is like a city broken down, without walls"
(Proverbs 25:28).

We've all been there. There are times when we just don't feel like praying. Maybe we're tried. Maybe we're angry. Maybe we're discouraged. Whatever the feeling is that keeps us from praying, we need to rise above it.

We are all emotional beings. As I wrote in my book *101 Tactics for Spiritual Warfare*, God gave us emotions—and God Himself has emotions: "Our emotions can be a great motivator at items and a great enemy at other times. If we pick and choose which emotions we will submit to God and which ones we'll allow free reign in our souls, we will wind up unstable—and wound up. We'll find ourselves holding on tight as the emotional roller coaster turns us upside down and leave us spinning in circles."

Indeed, Watchman Nee, author of such books as *Spiritual Discernment, Secrets to Spiritual Power* and *Let Us Pray,* said emotions are the believer's number one enemy. But J. Hudson Taylor, the great missionary to China, didn't let the enemy use his emotions against him. He defied his emotions and prayed on. He credited "emotionless prayer" with his major impact on the church in China.

The reality is, we don't need to be in the mood to pray. In fact, our mood would likely improve if we did pray. And maybe that needs to be our first prayer, "God, help me to shake off this discouragement, this anger, this anxiety…" Like Hudson, we need to enter into emotionless prayer.

David Hubbard, author of *The Problem With Prayer Is…* put it this way, "When it comes to prayer, feeling is not the most important thing. Feelings are fickle, easily influenced by health, morale, weather and mood. Prayer is too important to put at the mercy of our feelings." Indeed, if we wait to feel like praying chances are we'll seldom pray and often suffer from the resulting of prayerlessness.

— *Prayer* —

Father, in the name of Jesus, help me overcome my fickle feelings. Help me to recognize when my emotions are trying to sabotage my time in the secret place and to choose to let my spirit lead. Teach me how to enter "emotionless prayer" for the sake of those who need divine intervention.

NOVEMBER 23

The Nameless, Faceless Intercessor

"Take heed that you do not do your charitable deeds before men, to be seen by them. Otherwise you have no reward from your Father in heaven" (Matthew 6:1).

There's been a lot said about the nameless, faceless generation. Many of those are nameless, faceless intercessors who stay hidden in their prayer closets impacting lives in the earth and building up eternal rewards.

Let's face it. Intercession is largely a thankless job in this era. Intercessors often aren't admired or applauded in their lifetime, but heaven is cheering you on. Heaven knows your name. Hell knows your name.

"The training in prayer sometimes seems difficult because we are not recognized and appreciated," said the late Donald Demaray, who served as a professor of preaching at Asbury Theological Seminary. "But the work of intercession is largely a private affair: it is usually done in secret where people do not see us, and most will never know the hours of work invested."

When it comes to intercession, our motive must be to see God's will come to earth as it is in heaven. We must adopt a Colossians 3:23 mindset, "Whatever you do, do it heartily, as to the Lord and not to men."

If we hope to gain eternal rewards, we need to be selfless. If we do our good deeds to be seen by people we have no reward from our heavenly Father. We're not supposed to give weight to who knows we've labored long nights in prayer. We're supposed to serve the Lord through our intercession.

"To the selfish person this problem is most serious. Little recognition awaits the man or woman who answers the call to prayer," Dick Eastman writes in *The Change the World School of Prayer.* "Those who become involved in this mission of prayer must come to grips with its 'behind the scenes' nature. Most of our efforts will be expended behind the closed doors of a lonely prayer closet, out of sight from others who labor more publicly in the harvest."

— *Prayer* —

Father, in the name of Jesus, would You help me not to seek attention or recognition for my humble service to You? Seeing Your will done in any assignment is my inspiration and my great reward. Co-laboring with You in selflessness is my heart's cry.

NOVEMBER 24

Give It Up for God

"I have been crucified with Christ; it is no longer I who live, but Christ lives in me; and the life which I now live in the flesh I live by faith in the Son of God, who loved me and gave Himself for me" (Galatians 2:20).

In prayer, we're often looking for what God can do for us—or for the one for whom we're praying. But mature intercessors go beyond "gimme" prayers to sacrificial prayers that ask, "Lord, what can I give up for you?" Yes, we need to ask God to do things for us, with us and through us. But that should not be the extent of our prayer life. The mindful intercessor sincerely wants to decrease that He may increase (see John 3:30).

What does God want you to give up for the sake of intercession? What does He want you to cut out of your life to follow Him more completely? What is He leading you to surrender in order to climb higher in prayer? He may just tell us, but He loves when we ask Him.

Jesus said, "If you want to be perfect, go, sell what you have and give to the poor, and you will have treasure in heaven; and come, follow Me. But when the young man heard that saying, he went away sorrowful, for he had great possessions" (Matt. 19:21-22).

Intercessors, we must understand that our true riches are in Christ and we will see our greatest rewards in eternity. Peter wrote, "For to this you were called, because Christ also suffered for us, leaving us an example, that you should follow His steps" (1 Peter 2:1).

Whatever He asks us to give up for the sake of intercession is worth it. Whatever He wants you to put on the altar is worth the temporary pain of loss you may feel. I promise, it's worth it. And, by the way, there are also rewards in this age. Jesus said, "Then Jesus spoke to them again, saying, 'I am the light of the world. He who follows Me shall not walk in darkness, but have the light of life'" (John 8:12).

— Prayer —

Father, in the name of Jesus, I ask You with all humility and sincerity, what can I give up for You and the sake of the Gospel? What can I lay down so I can pick up Your perfect will? What can I sacrifice for Your Kingdom?

Operation Mobilization

"Consecrate a fast, call a sacred assembly; Gather the elders and all the inhabitants of the land into the house of the Lord your God, and cry out to the Lord" (Joel 1:14).

Cindy Jacobs and Lou Engle have been among the most effective people in our generation in mobilizing intercessors. Mobilizing intercessors is to put them into action. Mobilization is releasing intercessors into an assignment. It's assembling them and making them ready for war duty. It's marshalling God's prayer assets in the earth for a common purpose.

This is what God told the prophet Joel to do in Joel 2:15-17, "Blow the trumpet in Zion, consecrate a fast, call a sacred assembly; Gather the people, sanctify the congregation, assemble the elders, gather the children and nursing babes; Let the bridegroom go out from his chamber, and the bride from her dressing room. Let the priests, who minister to the Lord, weep between the porch and the altar; Let them say, 'Spare Your people, O Lord, and do not give Your heritage to reproach, that the nations should rule over them.'"

Mobilization is also the strategy God gave Esther to save the Jews: "Go, gather all the Jews who are present in Shushan, and fast for me; neither eat nor drink for three days, night or day. My maids and I will fast likewise. And so I will go to the king, which is against the law; and if I perish, I perish!" (Es. 4:16).

We should ask God for a mobilization anointing because there is strength in numbers. W. E. Sangster, a British Methodist preacher who lived from 1900 to 1960 explains, "The gates of hell prevail against us for lack of prayer, the Kingdom is impeded in its coming for the lack of prayer. You could be of service to God, to the nation, and to the world, if you would form, or help form, a prayer cell. It might be the most useful thing you have done in your life."

— *Prayer* —

Father, in the name of Jesus, would You give me an anointing and influence to mobilize intercessors, even if it's just two or three, for Your Kingdom purpose? Give me a gathering anointing to arrange corporate prayer so we can drive out the enemy from our midst.

NOVEMBER 26

The Power of Praying on Your Knees

"And when he had said these things, he knelt down and prayed with them all" (Acts 20:36).

We can pray anywhere at any time and from any position. But I learned a valuable lesson when I first got saved. Nobody taught me this lesson. I hadn't read in Scripture because I hadn't read much Scripture. Intuitively—or more accurate, as led by the Spirit without knowing—I began to pray on my knees.

There's something about praying on your knees. It's a powerful exercise that demonstrates humility. Scripture says every knee will bow to Jesus one day. Praying on your knees is bowing our hearts to Him, acknowledging our helplessness and our heart to obey His commands.

Surely, it's much easier to stand, lay prostrate, sit or lay in your bed and pray than to pray on your knees. Praying this way, especially for long periods, is uncomfortable at best. But John Wesley wore grooves in the wood at his prayer altar—and we know the fruit of his prayer life.

Jesus, at times, prayed on his knees. Luke 22:41 reveals, "And He was withdrawn from them about a stone's throw, and He knelt down and prayed." And we know the fruit of His prayer life. Paul the apostle kneeled before the Father to pray (see Eph. 3:14). And we know the fruit of his prayer life.

Peter knelt down to pray and saw a miracle. Acts 9:40 tells us, "But Peter put them all out, and knelt down and prayed. And turning to the body he said, 'Tabitha, arise.' And she opened her eyes, and when she saw Peter she sat up." We saw the fruit of his prayer life.

Solomon knelt down to pray after the temple was completed and it created an atmosphere few had experienced before: "And so it was, when Solomon had finished praying all this prayer and supplication to the Lord, that he arose from before the altar of the Lord, from kneeling on his knees with his hands spread up to heaven" (1 Kings 8:54). Soon after, the glory filled the place so the priests couldn't even stand up!

All prayer is powerful. But there is something about consistently praying on your knees. It's as if our hearts are bowing before Him in worship as our mouths utter our petitions.

— Prayer —

Father, in the name of Jesus, would You give me a deep revelation concerning the power of praying on my knees? I know I can pray anywhere, but I want to pray with humility. Let my outward expression demonstrate my heart.

NOVEMBER 27

Can You Pray With Me One Minute?

"Redeeming the time, because the days are evil" (Ephesians 5:16).

Did you know it takes about a minute to pray *The Lord's Prayer*? One-minute prayers can be a powerful and strategic way to redeem those few minutes waiting in traffic or in between appointments. Indeed, praying one-minute prayers is a good way to redeem the time (see Eph. 5:16).

Think about it. A minute is only one sixtieth of an hour. It's sixty seconds. It's a brief time period, but you can pack it with prayer power. That minute you pray instead of checking social media could tip over the bowls in heaven and bring a breakthrough. That minute you pray instead of chatting could be the moment someone gets saved, healed or delivered.

A minute is not much of a time investment, but if you prayed just one minute once every waking hour that adds up in a hurry. Over the course of a week that's over two hours of concentrated prayer with very little effort. One-minute payers are a great way to incrementally increase your prayer time and build prayer muscle.

Consider some of the shortest prayers in the Bible and how effective they were. Lord, have mercy on me, a sinner (see Luke 18:13). Have mercy on us, Son of David (see Matt. 20:31). Lord, help me (see Matt. 15:25). Jesus, remember me when You come into Your Kingdom (see Luke 23:39-43).

But it's not just personal prayer. You can release short intercessory prayers. Stephen prayed, "Lord Jesus, receive my spirit... Lord, do not hold this sin against them" (see Acts 7:59-60). In a minute or less, you can pray for someone to have wisdom, or strength, or healing, or peace, or provision or joy. And the list goes on.

One-minute prayers position you to buy up opportunities to see God move. One-minute prayers help us take advantage of dead spots in cars, elevators, and grocery store lines to release the power of God. Always remember, prayers don't have to be long to be powerful.

— *Prayer* —

Father, in the name of Jesus, would You remind me to pray those short prayers as often as I can? Help me breathe prayer like I breathe oxygen. Help me pray about every little thing as it comes up, asking You into the situation, with short prayers.

NOVEMBER 28

Riding the Prayer Wind

"The wind blows where it wishes, and you hear the sound of it, but cannot tell where it comes from and where it goes" (John 3:8).

I love it when the wind of the Spirit is on my intercession. I can sense both His empowerment and His pleasure. I can discern a strong anointing. Sometimes it comes suddenly. My prayer feels dry and anything but supernatural, but then the wind blows.

How does that happen? Riding the prayer wind—or tapping into Holy Spirit power in intercession—comes by aligning ourselves with the heart of the Father and His will and His dreams. It comes from surrendering our tongues to the Holy Spirit's utterance so He can not only pray with us but through us. I heard the Lord say:

"I am releasing a spiritual momentum. I am releasing the wind of God. I am releasing witty inventions and new ideas. But, you must grab a hold of them with your spirit and not with your flesh. I am releasing a spiritual momentum for whosoever will say yes to running with Me.

"If you'll say yes to running with Me, if you'll say yes to walking with Me—really walking with Me—if you'll say yes, the spiritual momentum, you'll catch it. You will walk in it. The favor of God will follow you. It will chase you down. The blessings will overtake you. But you must set aside the childish things. And you must set aside the temptations of the flesh. Set them aside.

"Read My Scriptures. Read the Word. Meditate day and night, therein. Look how Jesus walked and do what He did and you can have what He had. The greater works I've called you to do depends on your self-discipline. It depends not just on giftedness, because these signs follow all those who believe.

"If you believe, these signs can and will follow you. But it's the self-discipline. It's the courage. It's the fearlessness. It's the wherewithal. It's the, 'Yes, Lord; I will be inconvenienced to pray for somebody on the street.'"

— Prayer —

Father, in the name of Jesus, help me to abandon myself totally to Your will in prayer so I can experience the wind of the Spirit at my back, propelling me forward into new realms of intercession that accomplish Your agenda.

The David Brainerd Prayer Anointing

"Certainly every man at his best state is but vapor" (Psalm 39:5).

David Brainerd was an influencer of influencers. Indeed, he influenced the likes of Jonathan Edwards, John Wesley, Charles Spurgeon, William Carey, Jim Elliot and Leonard Ravenhill. He should influence all of us to pray without ceasing.

Brainerd was an American missionary to Native Americans who lived in the 1700s. His parents died early and he was known as a morose character, somewhat obsessed with life as but a vapor. He was also known to seep into depressions followed by encounters with God. He started studying for ministry at Yale College in 1739 but soon came down with tuberculosis, which would eventually end his life.

Despite this infirmity, he was zealous for the Gospel—and he was also zealous in prayer. Brainerd wrote, "This morning about nine I withdrew to the woods for prayer. I was in such anguish that when I arose from my knees I felt extremely weak and overcome. ...I cared not how or where I lived, or what hardships I went through, so that I could but gain souls for Christ."

Brainerd hung his life on prayer, knowing God hears and answers. He had some hard words for those who chose to ignore the power of prayer: "The idea that everything would happen exactly as it does regardless of whether we pray or not is a specter that haunts the minds of many who sincerely profess belief in God. It makes prayer psychologically impossible, replacing it with dead ritual at best."

Brainerd once said, "Give yourself to prayer, to reading and meditation on divine truths: strive to penetrate to the bottom of them and never be content with a superficial knowledge." And again, "When you cease from labor, fill up your time in reading, meditation, and prayer: and while your hands are laboring, let your heart be employed, as much as possible, in divine thoughts."

A secret to his prayer life was urgency. He knew his time was short, and he prayed without ceasing and left a legacy that inspired generations after him.

— *Prayer* —

Father, in the name of Jesus, help cultivate an urgency about intercession. Why pray later when I can pray now? Help me to see what hangs in the balance and spur me to redeem the time in prayer.

Discerning the Signs of the Times

"You know how to discern the face of the sky, but you cannot discern the signs of the times"
(Matthew 16:3).

The signs of the times are all around us—quite literally. We are in the end times and we need to recognize this truth, watching and praying about the signs of the times that are manifesting and accelerating as well as the signs of the times that have yet to appear.

It's important to study the signs of the times and to remain alert in the spirit. Indeed, Jesus expects us to see what's coming by the signs in the earth. He flat out rebuked the Pharisees for not discerning the signs of the times in their day. Look at Jesus' words in Matthew 16:1-3:

"Then the Pharisees and Sadducees came, and testing Him asked that He would show them a sign from heaven. He answered and said to them, 'When it is evening you say, 'It will be fair weather, for the sky is red'; and in the morning, 'It will be foul weather today, for the sky is red and threatening.' Hypocrites! You know how to discern the face of the sky, but you cannot discern the signs of the times."

Jesus, more than any of the apostles, emphasized the need to discern the times. Read Christ's Olivet Discorse in Matthew 24. And check out my book, *The End Times Watchman*, which will give you an in-depth, easy-to-understand look at how to watch and pray in the end times. If you don't recognize the signs of the times, you could try to pray away some end times events and find yourself praying against God's will.

There are about 150 chapters that relate end times events and trends. Paul the apostle spoke of the end times quite a lot in his epistles. He said, "But know this, that in the last days perilous times will come" (2 Tim. 3:1). Some of the signs Paul pointed out in the verse following are manifesting right before our eyes. Intercessor, know the signs of the times.

— Prayer —

Father, in the name of Jesus, would You help me discern the signs of the times? I don't want to be like the Pharisees, who read the Word but couldn't discern the signs all around them. Help me understand Your end times plan.

DECEMBER

"Call to Me, and I will answer you, and show you great and mighty things, which you do not know" (James 33:3).

The Rise of Reese Howells Intercessors

"Not by might nor by power, but by My Spirit,' says the Lord of hosts" (Zechariah 4:6).

I see a new generation of Reese Howells-like intercessors arising in this hour, praying the news and shifting history through crisis intercession.

Reese Howells carried an unusual mantle for prayer marked by uncommon faith. For Howells, intercession went leaps and bounds beyond a prayer assignment. The Holy Spirit led him down rarely-trodden paths to make him who he was.

Reese Howells is perhaps best known for praying the news in the midst of a crisis facing Britain in World War II. But, as I write in my book, *The Making of a Watchman*, God trained Howells for years before the war broke out.

Howells was head of the Bible College of Wales during those dark days, but he fearlessly led prayer watches that contributed to the defeat of an evil Nazi regime. Gloom and doom media headlines did not deter the faith of this watchman intercessor who kept praying the news.

Howells wrote: "There have been so many places bombed in London, even Buckingham Palace has been touched. I was burdened to pray for the King and Queen, and I believe our prayer will be answered. I am just watching how God will take hold of the enemy."

Notice Howells said he was watching how God would take hold of the enemy. He was watching. He was praying. What followed goes down in history as the Miracle at Dunkirk. So, what does this new generation of Reese Howells intercessors look like? Here's a picture of some of the characteristics of this history-making intercessor who laid down his life in prayer for the cause of Christ.

Reese Howells intercessors count the costs, knowing that true intercession is costly but it's worth the reward. Reese Howells intercessors make intercession from a place of abiding in the Lord, letting the Holy Spirit live through them. Reese Howells intercessors wait on God for instructions on how to pray before engaging in intercession. And that's just the beginning. Ask God to give you a heart for intercession like Reese Howells.

— *Prayer* —

Father, in the name of Jesus, help me enter into realms of watching and interceding like Your servant Reese Howells. Teach me how to go beyond myself in prayer to see Your will done in earth as it is in heaven. Give me the grace to wait on Your voice before I release my voice.

The Intercessory Prayer Leader

"But whoever desires to become great among you, let him be your servant. And whoever desires to be first among you, let him be your slave" (Matthew 20:26-27).

You may not be a leader of other intercessors just yet. But you do have leadership over yourself and as you lead yourself well, God may give you leadership in the lives of other intercessors. Prayer leaders need wisdom.

Wise prayer leaders know when to challenge intercessors to come up higher, push a little harder, press a little longer—and when to move on to another assignment. Wisdom knows when the Holy Spirit wants to shift the prayer momentum in a new direction.

Prayer leaders are more than intercessors who lead intercessors. True prayer leaders are intercessors who teach intercessors how to operate smarter, faster and more effectively in the realms of prayer.

Prayer leaders learn quickly that encouragement is a key to longevity. The enemy wants to wear out intercessors, but savvy prayer leaders continue to release sincere, Holy Spirit-inspired encouragement that combats the devil's discouragement.

Sincerity is a hallmark of the greatest prayer leaders. Beyond sincerity in prayer, there's sincerity of praise, sincerity in correction, sincerity in connection and sincerity in listening. Without sincerity, prayer leaders will not succeed for long.

Prayer leaders who do not cultivate trust with their intercessors will not make the impact they hope to see. Just as faith is the currency of the Kingdom, trust is the prayer leader's wealth. Intercessors won't follow a prayer leader they don't trust, no matter how powerfully they can pray.

One of the greatest assets of a prayer leader is consistency. Just as consistency is a key to seeing answered prayer, consistency is a key to leading intercessors into victories in even the hardest-fought spiritual battles.

Prayer leaders have learned the art of asking God to do His will, but the most effective prayer leaders have also learned the art of asking intercessors the right questions. The right questions yield insight into the intercessors' passion, strength and challenges in prayer.

— *Prayer* —

Father, in the name of Jesus, prepare me to be a prayer leader. Give me wisdom in how to lead myself and lead others, through realms of prayer and bumps in the road to character growth. I want to be an effective leader.

DECEMBER 3

The International Intercessor

"Look among the nations and watch—be utterly astounded! For I will work a work in your days which you would not believe, though it were told you" (Habakkuk 1:5).

I heard the Lord say, "I am marking international intercessors who will pray without ceasing for places on the map where their foot has never stepped on to. I am marking international intercessors, those who will cross geopolitical lines in the spirit because of the prayer burden that I place on their hearts.

"I am marking these global transformers who have a history of intercession, who have a future of intercession, who have a presence indicated and marked by intercession.

"I am sending you forth to lands that you may never visit in the natural, but lands that I have put upon your heart to pray for without ceasing until you see the promise of My Spirit for the land far and wide. You have not seen with your eyes but you have heard the cry in the spirit for the people in that land who are hungry for an outpouring.

"I am marking international intercessors who are just as concerned with the foreign land as with their homeland. For I have not called you to merely pray for your own territories. These international intercessors have a call that is far above and far behind and far to the left and far to the right. The circumference and the metron—the territory I have given these ones—goes beyond what they can see. It goes beyond what they even know.

"Begin to learn of cultures and begin to learn about history, you international intercessors. Begin to learn of languages. Begin to learn of past revivals in these lands. For I will use you to be a change agent in the earth in the land that I am appointing to you, the metron that I am assigning to you, the territory that I am causing you to tread upon in the spirit.

"Do not worry and do not fear because you will tread not only on the land but on serpents and scorpions and nothing shall by any means harm you as you go about My business in these nations."

— *Prayer* —

Father, in the name of Jesus, teach me how to watch over nations in the spirit.
Help me see Your plans and purposes in the nations so I can make effective
intercession. Help me discern brewing enemy attacks so I can dismantle demonic
weapons with the power of prayer.

Absolutely No Excuses

"But they all with one accord began to make excuses. The first said to him, 'I have bought a piece of ground, and I must go and see it. I ask you to have me excused'" (Luke 14:18).

It's easy to make excuses for prayerlessness. We all go through seasons where we are too busy or too tired or too overwhelmed or too (fill in the blank) to make intercession. After all, intercession takes time and energy. Intercession can lead, at times, to sleepless nights and great angst.

When our kids' schedules seem too demanding, we can use parenthood as an excuse. When ministry or career gets too demanding, we can use work as an excuse. When our bodies feel sick or hungry, we can use our need for rest as an excuse. But when we understand what's truly at stake we'll find a way to pray. Indeed, we make time for what's most important in our lives.

I was convicted by the prayer determination of Susanna Wesley. You may not have heard of her before now, but you aren't likely to forget her. Susanna was the mother of eleven children, including revivalists John and Charles Wesley. The founder of the Methodist movement, John was known to rise at four o'clock in the morning to pray—and when he had much to do he prayed longer.

Doubtless, his mother modeled that dogged determination and dedication to prayer. Likewise, Charles Spurgeon, the prince of preachers, once said, "I am sure that, in my early youth, no teaching ever made such an impression upon my mind as the instruction of my mother." So, how did Susanna pray without ceasing with eleven children, with all the cooking, cleaning, and more?

This was Susanna's strategy: She pulled her apron over her head when she set out to pray. This was a signal to her children, from the eldest to the youngest, that she was praying. It was the equivalent to a modern-day "do not disturb" sign. Her prayer closet was hidden under an upside-down apron. This kind of commitment should do away with all our excuses.

— *Prayer* —

Father, in the name of Jesus, would You help me never to make an excuse about praying? Help me do away with any and all excuses my carnal nature or my natural circumstances may bring into my path.

DECEMBER 5

The War to Enter the Prayer Closet Door

"Keep away from worldly desires that wage war against your very souls" (1 Peter 2:11).

Many years ago the Holy Spirit told me, "There's a war to enter the door." There is indeed sometimes an all-out war to enter the door of your prayer closet. You may not see it as a war. You may see it as being busy or tired. That's the deception.

There are many enemies of your prayer life—from fleshly to demonic—that can hinder you from engaging in militant intercession. Billy Graham offered: "Satan will contest every hour you spend in Bible reading or prayer."

Paul, who prayed in the spirit more than anyone in his day, put it this way: "The sinful nature wants to do evil, which is just the opposite of what the Spirit wants. And the Spirit gives us desires that are the opposite of what the sinful nature desires. These two forces are constantly fighting each other, so you are not free to carry out your good intentions" (Gal. 5:17).

You can have all the good intentions in the world to pray, but good intentions are not enough. You need determination in your spirit and in your soul to win the war to enter the door because the enemy is determined to hinder you at every turn.

The enemy knows if he can keep you out of the prayer closet, he can keep from receiving insight from your Champion defender in the battle you are facing. The enemy knows if he can keep you out of the prayer closet, he can keep you from tapping into the empowerment you need to succeed.

Indeed, the enemy erects many obstacles and sets up much opposition on the pathway to the intercessor's prayer closet. Some of the enemies of your prayer life are in your own mind, such as disappointment over an apparent loss, which can weaken your faith in the next intercessory prayer campaign. But make no mistake. The enemy is at hand, but you can prevail against him!

— *Prayer* —

Father, in the name of Jesus, give me a grit and a grace to win the war to enter the door—and to stay in the prayer closet until my assignment is complete. Help me discern and overcome the spiritual forces working against me.

Secrets of Intercession

"The secret of the Lord is with those who fear Him, and He will show them His covenant"
(Psalm 25:14).

Everyone—even God—has secrets. Choosing whether to—and to whom—a secret is revealed rests solely in the power of the secret holder. In the secret dimension, God is the revealer of secrets (sees Dan. 2:47).

There are secrets of intercession God wants to reveal to you—but you must be ready to receive them. Jesus said, "I still have many things to say to you, but you cannot bear them now. However, when He, the Spirit of truth, has come, He will guide you into all truth; for He will not speak on His own authority, but whatever He hears He will speak; and He will tell you things to come" (John 16:12-13).

We know God reveals His secrets to two different types of people: His servants the prophets (see Amos 3:7) and those who fear Him (see Ps. 25:14). Deuteronomy 29:29 tells us, "The secret things belong to the Lord our God, but those things which are revealed belong to us and to our children forever, that we may do all the words of this law."

When David revealed the Lord counsels him and his mind instructs him at night (see Ps. 16:7) he was tapping into the secret counsel of God. God spoke to David's spirit and his spirit communicated with his mind.

Remember, one of the names of God is Wonderful Counselor (see Is. 9:6). His secret counsel is wonderful and His counsel stands forever (see Ps. 33:11). The counsel of the Lord always stands (see Prov. 19:21). God often gives us counsel in secret so the enemy is not aware of the wisdom He is imparting to overthrow his wicked plots.

God wants to share secrets of intercession with us. The unfortunate reality is too few will learn the secrets of intercession because they won't pay the price to cultivate a lifestyle that gains them access.

— *Prayer* —

Father, in the name of Jesus, help me position my heart to receive the secrets of intercession that will make me more effective. Would You make me able to bear the secrets of intercession that will inspire me to pray without ceasing?

Warning: Doctrinal Danger

"Don't make rash promises, and don't be hasty in bringing matters before God"
(Ecclesiastes 5:2, NLT).

As in any area of Scripture, there are wrong theologies about prayer and intercession. Sometimes, we've been taught incorrectly so we pray incorrectly. When we do, that's called praying amiss and we won't get answers to our intercession. That can lead us to frustration and even burnout.

What are dangerous prayer doctrines? There are many and some are more dangerous than others. Ecclesiastes 5:1-2 offers a prayer warning: "Walk prudently when you go to the house of God; and draw near to hear rather than to give the sacrifice of fools, for they do not know that they do evil. Do not be rash with your mouth, and let not your heart utter anything hastily before God. For God is in heaven, and you on earth; Therefore let your words be few."

Jesus warned about manipulative and hypocritical prayers in Matthew 6:5-7: "And when you pray, you shall not be like the hypocrites. For they love to pray standing in the synagogues and on the corners of the streets, that they may be seen by men. Assuredly, I say to you, they have their reward.

"But you, when you pray, go into your room, and when you have shut your door, pray to your Father who is in the secret place; and your Father who sees in secret will reward you openly. And when you pray, do not use vain repetitions as the heathen do. For they think that they will be heard for their many words."

Some people pray the prayer of consecration over everything, such as healing or deliverance when it's always God's will to heal. That's a faith-stealing prayer. You only pray the prayer of consecration when you don't know what God's will is. How do you avoid dangerous prayer theology? Paul said, "Be diligent to present yourself approved to God, a worker who does not need to be ashamed, rightly dividing the word of truth" (2 Tim. 2:15).

— *Prayer* —

Father, in the name of Jesus, help me not to pray amiss. Help me never to make intercession that's contrary to Your Word. Give me a hunger to read the Word and grace me to rightly divide it so I don't step into prayer error.

The Making of an Intercessor

"Then I went down to the potter's house, and there he was, making something at the wheel"
(Jeremiah 18:3).

Though intercessors are called from their mothers' wombs, most aren't born filled with the Holy Spirit and prayer wisdom. Indeed, every intercessor goes through a making process. The making process may look different for every intercessor because we all have different experiences, different assignments and different anointings—but the process is real and can be painful.

God is our Maker, and the making process never ends. He is always working to conform us into the image of Christ, the Chief Intercessor who has never stopped praying in the throne room from His position at the right hand of the Father. He is faithful to complete the good work He started in us (see Phil. 1:6). The more "made" we are as intercessors, the more effective is the intercession we make. We want to be intercessors of honor. Paul told Timothy:

"But in a great house there are not only vessels of gold and silver, but also of wood and clay, some for honor and some for dishonor. Therefore if anyone cleanses himself from the latter, he will be a vessel for honor, sanctified and useful for the Master, prepared for every good work" (2 Tim. 2:20-21).

God has prepared you and is preparing you for the good work of intercession. Your job is to yield to the hand of the Maker on the Potter's wheel. Your job is to resist the temptation to resist the hand of the Potter. Your job is to allow Him to remove the impurities from your soul that hinder your prayer life. Your job is to get on a course of study He inspires.

You have your part to play in the making, but God is the Maker. Don't strive with Him. Isaiah prophesied: "Woe to him who strives with his Maker! Let the potsherd strive with the potsherds of the earth! Shall the clay say to him who forms it, 'What are you making?' Or shall your handiwork say, 'He has no hands'?" (Is. 43:9). Let Him decide what kind of intercessor to make you. Father knows best.

— *Prayer* —

Father, in the name of Jesus, make me into the intercessor You've called me to be.
I want to walk worthy of my calling. Help me not to strive with You and resist
Your hand when I can't see what You are doing. Help me stand.

DECEMBER 9

Making 'Mention' in Your Prayer

"For God is my witness, whom I serve with my spirit in the gospel of His Son, that without ceasing I make mention of you always in my prayers" (Romans 1:9).

Paul had a habit of "making mention" of people in his prayers. Have you ever wondered what that means? It's important that we grasp the concept of the mention.

Making mention means to remember someone in your prayers. *The Voice* translation puts it this way, "I am continually speaking to Him on your behalf in my prayers" (Eph. 1:16). Let's look at how Paul operated in this prayer strategy as it is recorded four times in his ministry.

In Ephesians 1:16 he wrote, "Therefore I also, after I heard of your faith in the Lord Jesus and your love for all the saints, do not cease to give thanks for you, making mention of you in my prayers."

In 1 Thessalonians 1:2-3, Paul wrote, "We give thanks to God always for you all, making mention of you in our prayers, remembering without ceasing your work of faith, labor of love, and patience of hope in our Lord Jesus Christ in the sight of our God and Father."

Again in Romans 1:9, Paul wrote, "For God is my witness, whom I serve with my spirit in the gospel of His Son, that without ceasing I make mention of you always in my prayers." And again in Philemon 1:4-5, he wrote, "I thank my God, making mention of you always in my prayers, hearing of your love and faith which you have toward the Lord Jesus and toward all the saints."

When he remembered these people—whether by someone giving him an update or as prompted by the Holy Spirit—he prayed for them by name. Paul wasn't merely releasing a random prayer for all the churches he planted. It was a prayer specific to their needs. He may not have prayed hours for each one, but he purposely prayed for them by name.

— *Prayer* —

Father, in the name of Jesus, would You help me remember the people for whom You want me to pray? Help me make a habit of calling people, companies, cities, and nations out by name with specific petitions rather than blanket prayers alone.

Surviving Satan's Sifting

"And the Lord said, 'Simon, Simon! Indeed, Satan has asked for you, that he may sift you as wheat. But I have prayed for you, that your faith should not fail; and when you have returned to Me, strengthen your brethren" (Luke 22:31-32).

Every intercessor goes through a what the older generation calls a "sifting." Think about what it means to be sifted. Sifting means to put through a sieve. A sieve is a device that you pour something through, such as flour, to separate the finer material from the coarser material. It's how you sort out what's useless or even harmful from what's necessary and valuable.

Job suffered perhaps the most severe sifting we see in Scripture. Indeed, it was so traumatic that his wife suggested he curse God and die. But notice that Satan had to get permission from God to sift Job. We see the account in Job 1:6-12:

"Now there was a day when the sons of God came to present themselves before the Lord, and Satan also came among them. And the Lord said to Satan, 'From where do you come?'

"So Satan answered the Lord and said, 'From going to and fro on the earth, and from walking back and forth on it.' Then the Lord said to Satan, 'Have you considered My servant Job, that there is none like him on the earth, a blameless and upright man, one who fears God and shuns evil?'

"So Satan answered the Lord and said, 'Does Job fear God for nothing? Have You not made a hedge around him, around his household, and around all that he has on every side? You have blessed the work of his hands, and his possessions have increased in the land. But now, stretch out Your hand and touch all that he has, and he will surely curse You to Your face!' And the Lord said to Satan, 'Behold, all that he has is in your power; only do not lay a hand on his person.' So Satan went out from the presence of the Lord."

If you are being sifted, lean into God. He won't let more come upon you than you can bear. And you will come out with double for your trouble.

— Prayer —

Father, in the name of Jesus, would You help me discern my seasons of sifting so I do no faint and lose heart? I don't want to resist a process You are allowing. I want to be purified so I can emerge with greater authority.

DECEMBER 11

Living From the Inside Out

"For it is God who works in you both to will and to do for His good pleasure"
(Philippians 2:13).

All changes starts within our spirits. When we were born again, we became new creatures in Christ. The Holy Spirit, who is the change agent, dwells within our spirit. When we pray in the spirit, with His help, for His will, it doesn't just change the circumstances around us—it changes us.

"I pray because I can't help myself. I pray because I'm helpless. I pray because the need flows out of me all the time, waking and sleeping," C.S. Lewis once said. "It doesn't change God. It changes me."

Edward Bauman, author of *Intercessory Prayer*, says sincere prayer nearly always influences the life of the one who prays. "The intercessor often becomes a nobler and purer person as selfish desires and self-centered anxieties are forgotten. Thoughts, attitudes, and actions are oriented around a new center. The warming influences of altruism spread and become dominant, and a new dimension is added to our spiritual vision because we look upon our fellows with new eyes, aware of being joined with them in a new type of creative fellowship."

Bauman tells of a man named Susurrus. Susurrus was a pious man but had the vice of gossiping about everyone's faults. One day, Susurrus was sharing some juicy gossip with a friend, who suggested he go home and pray for the person about whom he was gossiping. The change in him was reportedly remarkable.

"His heart is so entirely changed by it that he can now no more privately whisper anything to the prejudice of another than he can openly pray to God to do people hurt," Bauman said. "Whisperings and evil-speaking now hurt his ears like oaths and curses, and he has appointed one day in the week to be a day of penance as long as he lives, to humble himself before God in the sorrowful confession of his former guilt."

— *Prayer* —

Father, in the name of Jesus, please change me as I labor in intercession to see situations, circumstances and the hearts of people change. Make me more compassionate. Make me more loving. Make me more merciful.

Reasoning With God

"Come now, and let us reason together,' says the Lord" (Isaiah 1:18).

God is not an unreasonable God, but His reasoning is higher than our reasoning. Put another way, His thoughts are higher than our thoughts (see Is. 55:8).

What does it mean to the intercessor when God says, "Let us reason together"? Some translations say, "Come now, let's settle this." It's an invitation, of sorts, to draw near to the throne of grace to find grace and obtain mercy in a time of need (see Heb. 4:16).

The Authorized Version suggests the thought of a discussion between equals, according to *Elliott's Commentary for English Readers*. But certainly we are not equal to God. Elliot's goes on to explain how Hebrew implies the tone of one who gives an authoritative ultimatum, as from a judge to the accused, who had no defense, or only a sham defense, to offer.

When we're making intercession for the lost, or for a wayward Christian or for cities and nations, often we have to reason with God. *Benson Commentary* says this is like two contending parties arguing a case. We see God allowing man the opportunity to reason with Him several times in Scripture, including Gen. 18:23-32, Ex. 4:1-17, Micah 6:1-2 and Job 23:3-7:

"Oh, that I knew where I might find Him, that I might come to His seat! I would present my case before Him, and fill my mouth with arguments. I would know the words which He would answer me, and understand what He would say to me. Would He contend with me in His great power? No! But He would take note of me. There the upright could reason with Him, and I would be delivered forever from my Judge."

God told Micah, "Arise, plead your case before the mountains, and let the hills hear your voice. Hear, O you mountains, the Lord's complaint, and you strong foundations of the earth; For the Lord has a complaint against His people, and He will contend with Israel" (Micah 6:1-2).

— *Prayer* —

Father, help me reason with You for the sake of others, like Abraham when He pled for the righteous in the wicked city Sodom, or Moses when he pled for the rebellious Israelites. Help me stand as an intercessory reasoner.

DECEMBER 13

The Intercessory Missionary

"We will give ourselves continually to prayer and to the ministry of the word" (Acts 6:4).

Are you an intercessory missionary? Maybe you've never heard the term, so let me explain. An intercessory missionary is an intercessor who takes on prayer as a full-time occupation. Mike Bickle, founder of International House of Prayer in Kansas City, defines an intercessory missionary as, "one who does the work of the Kingdom from the place of prayer and worship, while embracing a missionary lifestyle and focus."

Clearly, not everyone is called to this lifestyle, but God is raising up more intercessory missionaries in this hour. Do we see this in the Bible? Yes, we do. We see it in both the Old Testament and the New Testament and as we move deeper into the end times this concept becomes more vital than ever.

David supported intercessory missionaries during his reign. 1 Chronicles 23:5 tells us, "four thousand praised the Lord with musical instruments, 'which I made,' said David, 'for giving praise.'" 1 Chronicles 25:7 tells us, "So the number of them, with their brethren who were instructed in the songs of the Lord, all who were skillful, was two hundred and eighty-eight."

Indeed, many references to intercessory missionaries come through end times prophecies in the Old Testament that point to New Testament believers. Isaiah prophesied about prayer ministries that would operate 24/7 until Jesus returns. Isaiah 62:6-7 reads, "I have set watchmen on your walls, O Jerusalem; They shall never hold their peace day or night. You who make mention of the Lord, do not keep silent, and give Him no rest till He establishes and till He makes Jerusalem a praise in the earth."

In the New Testament, we see Anna the prophetess who committed most of her life to prayer and watching for the First Coming of Christ. And throughout church history, there have been many who have accepted the call. Consider The Moravians and Count Zinzendorf in the 1700s, who set a 24/7 prayer watch in Germany.

— *Prayer* —

Father, in the name of Jesus, would You show me what my calling is in the
intercessory prayer movement? Would you show me when to watch and pray?
Show me how to do my part in the global chorus of praying saints. I want to be
about the business of prayer.

DECEMBER 14

Prayer is the Prerequisite

"My voice You shall hear in the morning, O Lord; In the morning I will direct it to You, and I will look up" (Psalm 5:33).

When I was in college, I always ran into prerequisites. If I wanted to take a certain class, often there were prerequisites. A prerequisite is something that is necessary to do in order to get where you want to go. It's a step you must take before you can get what you really want.

I've learned that prayer is a prerequisite for everything. And part of praying without ceasing is praying before every little thing we do. When we make prayer a prerequisite, we are setting ourselves up for the successful completion of the task at hand, whether that's getting to work on time or having a successful meeting.

The Kingdom is full of prerequisites. We had to accept Jesus through what is commonly known as "the sinner's prayer" before He would hear any other petition. We know the fear of the Lord is the prerequisite for wisdom (see Ps. 111:10). We know seeking first the Kingdom of God and His righteousness is the prerequisite to seeing everything else we need added to our lives (see Matt. 6:33).

All of God's promises are "yes and amen" in spirit, but there are often prerequisites—or conditions—we must meet before we acquire them. For example, if we want to reap we have to sow (see Gal. 6:7). If you want a liberal dose of wisdom, the prerequisite is asking (see James 1:5). If you want the peace of God that passes all understanding, you must choose not to be anxious for anything and pray instead (see Phil. 4:6).

Now, with that in mind, remember that prayer is the prerequisite—the essential element—in involving God in all the issues of your life. Prayer is the prerequisite—the imperative—for breakthrough. Prayer is the prerequisite—the absolute must—before you engage in crucial conversations, do the job interview, apply for the scholarship, or even step foot out of your house every day. If you'll make prayer the prerequisite, you'll prosper in everything you do.

— *Prayer* —

Father, in the name of Jesus, help me to remember to pray and ask You for Your strength, wisdom and guidance before I set out to do anything. Apart from You, I can do nothing.

The John Knox Prayer Anointing

"For my people, my Jewish brothers and sisters. I would be willing to be forever cursed—cut off from Christ!—if that would save them" (Romans 9:3).

"Give me Scotland or I die!" That was the prayer of John Knox, a man who was willing to perish for his nation. Like Paul almost wished he was cursed and cut off from Christ for the sake of Israel, Knox agonized for the salvation of the Scotts.

Knox was born in Scotland in 1514 during the third year of Luther's Protestant Reformation, a time when it was dangerous to defy the Catholic church. In fact, Knox when into hiding when "Bloody Mary," the Roman Catholic Mary Tudor, became queen and started mass persecution of Protestants in 1553. John Calvin was his mentor.

Knox goes down in history as a leader in the Protestant movement and the founder of Scottish Presbyterianism. But he is perhaps best remembered for his prayer life. Noteworthy is how Mary Queen of Scots reportedly said, "I fear the prayers of John Knox more than all the assembled armies of Europe."

What else did John Knox pray? We don't have much on record, but we do get a glimpse for how he viewed prayer as a necessity for believers. He once wrote, "For if the fire may be without heat, or the burning lamp without light, then true faith may be without fervent prayer." Give me Scotland or I die was a fervent prayer, indeed! God did give Knox Scotland, in a sense. His prayers ushered in a great revival and many were saved.

Like many others, he spent his last moments on earth praying and meditating on God. He would pray, "Come, Lord Jesus. Sweet Jesus into Thy hand I commend my spirit. Be merciful, Lord, to Thy Church, which Thou hast redeemed. Give peace to this afflicted commonwealth. Raise up faithful pastors who will take charge of Thy Church. Grant us, Lord, the perfect hatred of sin, both by evidences of Thy wrath and mercy."

— *Prayer* —

Father, in the name of Jesus, would You give me a passion for souls? Would You give me the grace to fervently pray for the lost in my nation and the nations to which You assign me? Make me fervent in intercession.

Remember This Critical Prayer Assignment

"Jesus spoke these words, lifted up His eyes to heaven, and said: 'Father, the hour has come. Glorify Your Son, that Your Son also may glorify You'" (John 17:1).

Intercessors, you are committed to servant prayer—prayer that serves the interests of others. You have answered the call to lay your life down for the cause of Christ. But here's a friendly warning: Don't forget to pray for yourself.

Indeed, praying for yourself is not selfish unless praying for yourself is all you do. Consider when you are on a plane readying to take flight. The flight attendant goes through a series of instructions, including an admonition in case of emergency: Secure your own oxygen mask before you try to help others secure theirs.

Jesus understood that and prayed for Himself. So did Paul the apostle. David prayed for himself all the time! Jacob prayed for himself. Jonah prayed for himself. Hezekiah prayed for himself. Praying for yourself is critical to your intercessory prayer success. After all, there are times when you and Jesus may be the only ones praying for you.

Prayer is your personal lifeline to God. If you are not praying for you, you may grow weak and weary over time. Praying for yourself builds you up when the enemy is tearing you down. Praying for yourself keeps you strong in the Lord and the power of His might. Praying for yourself helps keep you in the center of His will.

So, what should you pray for yourself? God wants to meet all your spiritual and natural needs, but I defer mostly to praying for what I need in order to accomplish His will. Sometimes that's wisdom. Sometimes that's peace. Sometimes that's resources to forward His plans through my life.

The key, as in everything, is to let the Holy Spirit lead you in praying for yourself. Sometimes we think we know what we need but we don't know how to pray as we ought. Praying for yourself is not selfish. It's strategic.

— *Prayer* —

Father, in the name of Jesus, would You help me remember through the long hours of intercession not to neglect to pray for myself? I know Jesus is praying for me, but I also know I need to make my requests known to You.

DECEMBER 17

Dreaming With God in Prayer

"Eye has not seen, nor ear heard, nor have entered into the heart of man the things which God has prepared for those who love Him" (1 Corinthians 2:9).

Many years ago in the context of prayer, God suddenly began to speak to me. He was making me a new promise, challenging me in my faith, urging me to pray. I heard the Lord say:

"I am marking you with My glory. I am changing you from the inside out. It's time to embark on a new season of chasing Me. You will be more effective. You will be more efficient. You will do more with less. You can't see it. It's hard for you to believe it but I am the Author of it.

"Take the limits off. Take the lid off. I am opening new doors for you. It's not just about favor. I'm shifting you from favor to open heavens. You will not strive but you will not lack. I have gone before you to make a way for you. The divine connections are right around the corner. They are just ahead. You will see them and know them.

"I am indeed giving you double for your trouble. I will put in your hands as much as you can believe Me for. How much can you believe Me for? Dream again. Dream big dreams. Dream wild dreams. Dream with Me, and I will dream with you."

God wants us to dream with Him, and He will give us as much as we can believe Him for. The question really is, how much can we believe Him for? And, it's not enough to believe it, you have to pray and believe so you can receive.

Start with asking God to change you from the inside out. Ask Him to remove the limits from your mind. Ask Him to open new doors of revelation about prayer and teach you how to open the heavens over your life through prayer. Pray for the divine connections. Pray that God would help you to believe for what He wants to give you. Those prayer answers glorify Jesus.

— Prayer —

Father, in the name of Jesus, would You help me expand my capacity to believe and receive? I know You want me to dream with You but doubt and unbelief sometimes limit my prayers. Help me breakthrough to a new measure of faith so I can make an impact in the earth through prayer.

Moving the Hand that Moves the World

"Indeed My hand has laid the foundation of the earth, and My right hand has stretched out the heavens; When I call to them, they stand up together" (Isaiah 48:13).

It's been said, "Prayer moves the hand that moves the world." This line comes out of a poem from John Wallace: "That power is prayer, which soars on high, through Jesus, to the throne, and moves the hand which moves the world, to bring salvation down."

Wallace was part of a prayer meeting that sparked a revival in Ulster over one hundred fifty years ago. He and three other men decided to meet in an old schoolhouse near the village of Kells in the winter. The revival their prayer ignited spread through the United Kingdom and reportedly led to 100,000 converts.

This was a step-by-step process rather than a wildfire. The first person was converted in January 1858. By springtime of 1859, that one prayer meeting multiplied into sixteen prayer meetings and the revival started seeping beyond Ulster into Ahogill and then Ballymena. Later in the movement, there were over one hundred prayer meetings held every week. The more prayer that went forth, the more souls that were saved.

And these weren't celebrity intercessors. *Revival Library* records, "No world-famous name is associated with the revival. Nevertheless, beginning in the prayer meetings and wayside conversations of a few humble work-people, it speedily attained the proportions of a national movement."

Reverend S. Moore testified to the meetings in Ballymena: "From dozens of houses, night and day, you would hear, when passing along, loud cries for mercy from those under conviction, or the voice of prayer by kind visitors, or the sweet, soothing tones of sacred song. Business seemed at a standstill."

Intercessors, as you stand in the gap to pray for revival remember that revival is about driving the church back to prayer and prayer in this context is about bringing lost souls into the Kingdom. Like Wallace wrote in his famed poem, prayer moves the hand that moves the world, to bring salvation down.

— *Prayer* —

Father, in the name of Jesus, would You help me be a fire starter that ignites revival for the sake of souls? I want to see prodigals come home, backsliders find their way, and lost souls come into Your eternal Kingdom.

Prevailing Prayer Martyrs

"I saw the woman, drunk with the blood of the saints and with the blood of the martyrs of Jesus" (Revelation 17:6).

When I was young in the Lord I stumbled upon a copy of *Foxe's Book of Martyrs*. It horrified me. John Foxe chronicled the accounts of Christian persecution in Europe in the 1500s. Many believers were crucified, put to death by the sword or burned alive on a stake to discourage others from confessing faith in Christ. Some of them died for praying. Most of them died praying.

"Quirinus, bishop of Siscia, being carried before Matenius, the governor, was ordered to sacrifice to the pagan deities, agreeably to the edicts of various Roman emperors. The governor, perceiving his constancy, sent him to jail, and ordered him to be heavily ironed; flattering himself, that the hardships of a jail, some occasional tortures and the weight of chains, might overcome his resolution," Foxe writes.

As he was dying, he prayed "It is no new thing, O all-powerful Jesus, for thee to stop the course of rivers, or to cause a man to walk upon the water as thou didst thy servant Peter; the people have already seen the proof of thy power in me; grant me now to lay down my life for thy sake, O my God."

We still see modern-day martyrs—and some of them are intercessors. Dietrich Bonhoeffer, killed by the Nazis, was one of them. Most of the modern-day martyrs are nameless and faceless, people in the persecuted church we'll only meet in heaven.

Even though they are no longer walking the earth, we know the martyrs never stop crying out. Revelation 6:9-10 reads, "When He opened the fifth seal, I saw under the altar the souls of those who had been slain for the word of God and for the testimony which they held. And they cried with a loud voice, saying, 'How long, O Lord, holy and true, until You judge and avenge our blood on those who dwell on the earth?'"

— *Prayer* —

Father, in the name of Jesus, would You give me the courage to lay down my life in prayer? I know I will probably never have to die for the sake of intercession. Nevertheless, let me die to self for the sake of intercession. Help me to die daily so that others don't have to.

The Charles Finney Prayer Anointing

"So the word of the Lord grew mightily and prevailed" (Acts 19:16).

"Unless I had the spirit of prayer, I could do nothing." Such are the words of Charles Finney. Born in 1972 and passing on to glory in 1875, Finney goes down in American history as one of her greatest revivalists—and he relied on prayer and fasting to get results. His intercession was as intense as it gets.

Indeed, the "father of modern revivalism," was as much a student of prayer as he was a preacher. He started out as an attorney until he got saved. As such, he understood how to plead the case for lost souls to the Lord in prayer. And he won many!

Finney once said, "I have a retainer form the Lord Jesus Christ to plead His cause…" Indeed, he pled with men to receive Christ and pled with Christ for the souls of men who didn't yet know Him. He opined, "Effective prayer is prayer that attains what it seeks. It is prayer that moves God, effecting its end."

Finney was a pioneer in that he adopted what he called "New Measures" that allowed women to pray in mixed public meetings—something some denominations still don't allow today. He understood the power of corporate prayer, saying, "Nothing tends more to cement the hearts of Christians than praying together, never do they love one another so well as when they witness the outpouring of each other's hearts in prayer."

The man who wrote books on how to lead revivals and saw the fruit of revival over and again through prayer taught on the concept of the prevailing prayer that he practiced. Said Finney, "Prevailing prayer is that which secures an answer. Saying prayers is not offering prevailing prayer. The prevalence of prayer does not depend so much on quantity as on quality."

— *Prayer* —

Father, in the name of Jesus, give me a revelation of how revival begins with prayer. Give me a persevering spirit to argue the case of lost souls with the Father of Salvation who sent His Son to pave the way to eternity for all men.

The Mightiest Force in the Universe

"That your faith should not be in the wisdom of men but in the power of God"
(1 Corinthians 2:5).

Scientific genius Dr. Cortland once wrote, "Prayer is the mightiest force in the universe." Read that again. Scientists study various aspects of the physical world through experiments that provide answers to problems. But Dr. Cortland knew prayer is the ignition point of power that solves every problem. He understood the power of God was greater than any other power.

Ezra wrote, "Yours, O Lord, is the greatness, the power and the glory, the victory and the majesty; For all that is in heaven and in earth is Yours; Yours is the kingdom, O Lord, and You are exalted as head over all" (1 Chron. 29:11). God is all powerful, but He has granted us access to His power to heal, deliver, and see miracles through prayer. When we release our prayer, He releases His power.

Charles Spurgeon, a 10th Century "prince of preachers," put it this way: "The power of prayer can never be overrated. They who cannot serve God by preaching, need not regret it if they can be mighty in prayer. The true strength of the church lies there. This is the sinew which moves the arm of omnipotence. If a man can but pray, he can do anything. He that knows how to overcome the Lord in prayer, has heaven and earth at his disposal. There is nothing, man, which thou canst not accomplish if thou canst but prevail with God in prayer."

God created the heavens and earth by His great power (see Jer. 32:17). God upholds the universe through the word of His power (see Heb. 1:3). Paul told us of the immeasurable greatness of His power to us who believe (Eph. 1:19). God has given us power over all the power of the enemy (see Matt. 28:18). And that power is released through prayer.

The great man of prayer E.M. Bounds put it this way: "Prayer breaks all bars, dissolves all chains, opens all prisons, and widens all straits by which God's saints have been held."

— *Prayer* —

Father, in the name of Jesus, would You give me a deeper revelation of the power of prayer? I don't want to get into works of the flesh or lean on the arm of flesh. I want to lean on You, and not my own understanding.

Unfolding Your Prayer Map

"Do not move the ancient landmark [at the boundary of the property] Which your fathers have set" (Proverbs 22:8, AMP).

I have maps all over my house. I love to see the nations spread out before me. And I love to pray with maps. It helps me keep my vision for cities and nations in view. In my book, *Decoding the Mysteries of Heavens War Room,* I had a vision that included a map. I'll share part of it here:

"I could not hear every word spoken, but I discerned the intensity of this strategic meeting. The finger of God was pointing to different places on a world map. As He would point to specific nations and cities, those areas of the map would light up with fire and glory. These are hotbeds of spiritual activity in the earth—areas where there is a battle for transforming revival that precedes what is perhaps the final harvest."

Every Home for Christ created the World Prayer Map, which offers a geographical representation of the world, a list of every country, and prayer prompts. With this map, thousands of believers pray every day for the Great Commission to be fulfilled in the nations, as well as for missions-minded ministries and leaders of governments.

Different from spiritual mapping, a prayer map serves as a prompt to pray for cities and nations as God leads. A practical instruction: Look at the map. Sit and wait on the Lord. He can highlight a city or nation to you. You can literally pray your way around the world with a prayer map.

S.D. Gordon, a prolific author of Christian books in the late 19th and early 20th centuries, once said, "It is most difficult to put your finger on a single spot of the world map that is not being torn and uptorn by unrest in one shape or another."

Indeed, the needs are many and the intercessors seem too few. It's remarkable that in just five minutes a day, you can lift up many nations in prayer. If you have a heart for the nations, praying with a map can fuel your intercession.

— *Prayer* —

Father, in the name of Jesus, teach me how to pray with a map in hand and nations on my heart. Help me make accurate intercession for the problems the world faces, knowing that You alone can bring change.

Prayer is Caught and Taught

"Now it came to pass, as He was praying in a certain place, when He ceased, that one of His disciples said to Him, 'Lord, teach us to pray, as John also taught his disciples'" (Luke 11:1).

Prayer is both caught and taught. Let me say that again. Prayer is both caught and taught. Some will tell you that we shouldn't be part of prayer schools, but this is a strategy of the enemy to keep you ignorant to the laws that govern prayer. After all, when Jesus' disciples asked Him to teach them how to pray He did not rebuke them and tell them they should already know. Rather, He taught them. Likewise, John the Baptist taught his disciples to pray.

Beyond what we call *The Lord's Prayer*, Jesus taught plenty about prayer. He taught us to pray for those who persecute us (sees Matt. 5:44). He taught us to shut the door to our prayer closet and pray secretly rather than as a show (see Matt. 6:5-15). He taught us to ask, seek and knock—and to keep on asking until we see the answer (see Matt. 7:7-11).

Jesus taught us to pray in agreement with others (see Matt. 18:19-20). He taught us to pray in faith and not allow doubt to interfere with our intercession (see Matt. 21:21-22). He taught us not to make pretentious prayers (see Mark 12:38-40). Jesus taught us to pray to the Lord of the harvest to send out laborers (see Luke 10:2).

Jesus also taught us to pray through parables, such as the Widow and the Unjust Judge. He taught us to watch and pray (see Luke 21:36). He taught us to pray that we won't fall to temptation (see Luke 22:40). He taught us to pray to the Father in His name (see John 14:12-14).

Yes, Jesus taught us all this and more about prayer. But He also commanded His disciples to wait on the power of the Holy Spirit. The Holy Spirit is the spirit of prayer. We can know everything in the world about the mechanics of prayer and still not know how to pray as we ought. We need to catch the spirit of prayer.

— *Prayer* —

Father, in the name of Jesus, would You give me deep revelation into what Jesus taught about prayer? Instruct me in the laws of prayer. Help me catch the spirit of prayer through elders who know how to tarry.

The John of the Cross Prayer Anointing

"For there is one God and one Mediator between God and men, the Man Christ Jesus"
(1 Timothy 2:5).

St. John of the Cross goes down in history as a teacher of prayer. John of the Cross, a 16th Century Spanish mystic, introduced the concept of the dark night of the soul in a book called *Dark Night of the Soul.*

In it, he writes, "No matter how much individuals do through their own efforts, they cannot actively purify themselves enough to be disposed in the least degree for the divine union of the perfection of love. God must take over and purge them in that fire that is dark for them, as we will explain."

The teachings of John of the Cross made prayer accessible and God approachable to the common man of his day. Intercessory prayer was not relegated to a few super spiritual monks but to every man or woman. Prayer, he taught, drives deeper trust in the God who answers our intercession.

John said things like: "Never give up prayer, and should you find dryness and difficulty, persevere in it for this very reason. God often desires to see what love your soul has, and love is not tried by ease and satisfaction." Therein, he acknowledged the dryness and difficulty at times, but spurs us on to determined intercession.

John also said, "He who avoids prayer is avoiding everything good." And, "Seek in reading and thou shalt find in meditation; knock in prayer and it shall be opened in meditation." And, "He who interrupts the course of his spiritual exercises and prayer is like a man who allows a bird to escape from his hand; he can hardly catch it again."

John of the Cross propagated teachings about the importance and simplicity of prayer. His teachings gave disciples of Christ confidence that God knows what is best for us and will do what is best for us through intimate fellowship and prayer.

— Prayer —

Father, help me enter into the simplicity of prayer, knowing that You hear my heart. Would You help me not to neglect my duty to pray as a spiritual exercise? Would You inspire me to release words that move Your heart?

Christ the Intercessor

"For Christ has not entered the holy places made with hands, which are copies of the true, but into heaven itself, now to appear in the presence of God for us" (Hebrews 9:24).

When I was young in the Lord, I read a book called *Christ the Healer* by F.F. Bosworth. The book offers a revelation of God's healing power based on the premise that Jesus redeemed us from our diseases when He atoned for our sins. Jesus is our Healer. But Jesus is also our Intercessor. When we get a revelation of Christ the Intercessor, it will impassion our prayer life in ways we can't imagine.

Think about it. We are never more like Jesus than when we are making intercession. When Jesus hung on the cross, it was the ultimate act of intercession, which is defined as the action of intervening on behalf of another. Jesus intervened on our behalf. Biblically speaking, He who had no sin became sin for us, so that we could become the righteousness of God in Him (see 2 Cor. 5:21).

Jesus is still making intercession for us. Paul reminds us, "Who is he who condemns? It is Christ who died, and furthermore is also risen, who is even at the right hand of God, who also makes intercession for us" (Rom. 8:34). That has always fascinated me. *The New Living Translation* says he is "pleading for us." *The Message* relates that Jesus is "in the presence of God at this very moment sticking up for us."

If Scripture had pointed this out once, it would have been enough. But Hebrews 7:25 gives us another picture of Christ the Intercessor: "Therefore He is also able to save to the uttermost those who come to God through Him, since He always lives to make intercession for them."

Catch that and personalize it. He always lives to make intercession for you. Thanks be to God we have an advocate with the Father—Christ the Intercessor. Ask your heavenly Father to give you a revelation of Christ the Intercessor.

— Prayer —

Father, in the name of Jesus, I'm so grateful Jesus is making intercession for me. What an awesome thought! Help me to gain a deep revelation of this when I feel like I am standing alone in the prayer closet without support.

Rekindling Your Prayer Fire

"Rejoice in the Lord always. Again I will say, rejoice!" (Philippians 4:4)

The trials of life can't put out your fire. Spiritual warfare can't put out your fire. Sickness and disease can't put out your fire. Betrayal can't put out your fire. And God is certainly not trying to put out your fire.

As intercessors who stand in the gap, you are often under fire. But it's how you respond to the fire that matters. Feeling sorry for yourself puts out your fire. Moaning, grumbling and complaining puts out your fire. Blaming other people for your problems puts out your fire. I humbly submit to you that if you are only on fire for God when everything is going well, you're not really on fire for God.

Consider Peter's words: "Beloved, do not think it strange concerning the fiery trial which is to try you, as though some strange thing happened to you; but rejoice to the extent that you partake of Christ's sufferings, that when His glory is revealed, you may also be glad with exceeding joy" (1 Pet. 4:12-13).

You may be under fire. You may even be in the fire. If you've lost your fire, the pathway to light yourself up again is rejoicing. Eleven verses in the Bible tell us to rejoice. If you want to burn and shine like John the Baptist at the height of this ministry, don't get offended with Jesus when the trial comes like John did when He was in prison. Again, I say rejoice.

Paul wrote, "We can rejoice, too, when we run into problems and trials, for we know that they help us develop endurance" (Rom. 5:3, NLT). Take Isaiah's heart posture in Isaiah 61:10, "I will greatly rejoice in the Lord, my soul shall be joyful in my God." Rejoice in the Lord no matter what comes your way and you'll maintain a passion that drives the devil out.

— *Prayer* —

Father, in the name of Jesus, help me remember to rejoice when the fiery darts come against me. Help me rejoice when the fiery trial comes. Help me rejoice in who You are and what You have done for me. I will rejoice always.

DECEMBER 27

Standing on God's Sovereignty

"The Lord has established His throne in the heavens, and His sovereignty rules over all" (Psalm 103:19).

God chooses to work through praying people on the earth most of the time. But we must also acknowledge the His sovereignty. Sovereign refers to one who has supreme authority. God is Almighty. As the all-wise Creator of the universe, He has the full right and power to do what He chooses without any interference from outside sources.

In my younger years walking with the Lord, I didn't study God's sovereignty. It can be hard to wrap your head around. I came from a camp that insisted we have all authority in the earth and we are the ones who allow the enemy to attack because we don't stand in prayer. That is only partly true. In reality, we know that God gave the enemy permission to attack Job.

When God purposes something, it will be according to His plan. Job put it this way: "I know that You can do everything, and that no purpose of Yours can be withheld from You" (Job 42:2). God already knows everything that's going to happen before it happens. Nothing surprises Him, ever.

Isaiah 46:9-10, tells us, "Remember the former things of old, for I am God, and there is no other; I am God, and there is none like Me, declaring the end from the beginning, and from ancient times things that are not yet done, Saying, 'My counsel shall stand, and I will do all My pleasure.'"

That certainly doesn't mean we shouldn't pray. What it means for the intercessor is that we can pray without ceasing over an issue but God is ultimately going to have His way in His timing. He chooses how or when to answer. People don't always get healed in this lifetime, for example, and we don't know why. We must lean into the revelation of a sovereign God who is good and perfect and knows best.

As intercessors, we must stand on Romans 8:28, "And we know that all things work together for good to those who love God, to those who are the called according to His purpose."

— *Prayer* —

Father, in the name of Jesus, help me understand Your sovereignty in a deep way so that when I don't see results from my prayers, I can trust that You still heard my prayers and are executing Your purposes in the earth.

Don't Touch God's Glory

"I am the Lord, that is My name; And My glory I will not give to another, nor My praise to carved images" (Isaiah 42:8).

Doubtless, you've heard intercessors take the credit for someone's breakthrough. You may have even done this—or been tempted to do it—yourself.

Here's how it happens: You feel led to pray or are asked to pray for someone's concern. They come back to you and tell you about the breakthrough. You can't help it. Before you even realize it, these words are coming out of your mouth: "I prayed for you!" Other times, people want to give you glory for the prayer answer.

Intercessors, we have to be careful not to touch God's glory. We may have released the petition, but He's the One Who has the power to bring the answer to pass. We don't want to grieve the Holy Spirit. We see two incidents of people trying to glorify man in the Book of Acts—and two different responses. First, look at Acts 12:20-23:

"Now Herod had been very angry with the people of Tyre and Sidon; but they came to him with one accord, and having made Blastus, the king's personal aide their friend, they asked for peace, because their country was supplied with food by the king's country.

"So on a set day Herod, arrayed in royal apparel, sat on his throne and gave an oration to them. And the people kept shouting, 'The voice of a god and not of a man!' Then immediately an angel of the Lord struck him, because he did not give glory to God. And he was eaten by worms and died."

God is not going to strike you dead if you touch His glory. But why would we dare to take credit for His works? We need to be like Paul and Barnabas who refused to touch God's glory after the miracle in Lystra. Paul prayed. A man was healed. And the people tried to sacrifice to him and Barnabas as gods. The duo didn't allow it. Neither should we.

— *Prayer* —

Father, in the name of Jesus, help me to never, ever touch Your glory. Help me to point people back to Your generous Spirit when they see breakthrough through my intercession. Help me to stay quiet about my prayer life.

DECEMBER 29

The Knowing Intercessor

"No longer do I call you servants, for a servant does not know what his master is doing; but I have called you friends, for all things that I heard from My Father I have made known to you" (John 15:15).

Have you ever heard someone talk about a sixth sense? In the secular world, they are talking about paranormal phenomenon like Extra Sensory Perception. That's not what we're talking about here. That's witchcraft.

Knowing in the spirit is part of the intercessor's discernment, and it has nothing to do with familiar spirits or the paranormal. It has to do with the supernatural. Interestingly enough, *Merriam-Webster's* dictionary has sixth sense listed. The dictionary's definition is a "power of perception like but not one of the five senses; a keen intuitive power."

So what is our definition of knowing from the intercessor's perspective? It's a way of receiving prophetic revelation or intelligence that is not obvious to the other spiritual senses. It's an awareness in your spirit that translates to knowledge in your mind without any direct communication from God through the five spiritual senses. It's spiritual perception and understanding without explanation as to how you know what you know. (Take my series on Knowing at www.schoolofthespirit.tv/knowing.)

So what's really happening here? Our spirits are being informed by the mind of Christ.

1 Corinthians 2:16 tells us, "For "who has known the mind of the Lord that he may instruct Him?" But we have the mind of Christ." *Barnes Notes on the Bible* defines the mind of Christ as "the views, feelings, and temper of Christ." And, of course, we know Christ has the mind of the Father.

The Holy Spirit makes known to you in your spirit the mind of Christ. 1 Corinthians 2:10-11 assures us, "For the Spirit searches all things, yes, the deep things of God. For what man knows the things of a man except the spirit of the man which is in him? Even so no one knows the things of God except the Spirit of God."

— *Prayer* —

Father, in the name of Jesus, help me tap into knowing—the discernment that offers me insight into Your will in a matter and how I should pray over an issue. Give me Your mind on the matter.

Glory Intercessors

"For behold, the darkness shall cover the earth, and deep darkness the people; But the Lord will arise over you, and His glory will be seen upon you" (Isaiah 60:2).

I want to remind you again of something Ruth Ward Heflin used to say, "Praise until the worship comes. Worship until the glory comes. Then stand in the glory." We should also pray in the glory. God is looking for glory intercessors.

I heard the Lord say, "My glory is not to be taken lightly. My glory is not to be mocked. My glory is to be entered into with reverence, with holy fear and trembling, with awe… For I am indeed pouring out My glory more and more as the darkness begins to rise in the earth.

"I am determined that My people not only taste and see My glory, but walk in My glory to demonstrate to a lost world that I am a living God and a loving God. I am looking for carriers of My glory who will steward My presence and release My gifts without seeking their own glory.

"I am looking for those who will host My presence with Kingdom understanding and look beyond a single meeting to the transformative power of My Spirit in the earth. I am calling on you now to press into My glory, not for your sake but for the sake of the nations. My glory will indeed cover the earth like the waters cover the sea."

Intercessors, it's time for you to step into new realms of glory and to release glory through your intercession. In order to walk in glory realms, you need to understand who you are in Christ and what belongs to you.

Meditate upon Psalm 8:3-6 until it renews your mind: "When I consider Your heavens, the work of Your fingers, the moon and the stars, which You have ordained, what is man that You are mindful of him, and the son of man that You visit him? For You have made him a little lower than the angels, and You have crowned him with glory and honor."

— *Prayer* —

Father, in the name of Jesus, help me see my crown of glory. Help me pray from a place of glory. Help me carry and release Your glory through my intercession. Thank You, Lord, for a deeper revelation of glory prayer.

Interceding for God's New and Next

"Behold, I will do a new thing, now it shall spring forth; Shall you not know it? I will even make a road in the wilderness and rivers in the desert" (Isaiah 43:19).

Even though Ecclesiastes 1:9 states emphatically there is nothing new under the sun, some things are new to you. God has fresh anointings, fresh revelation, fresh perspectives and more. He has new relationships in mind for you, new promotions, new levels of glory and so on. God is always leading us into a new thing.

Isaiah prophesied quite a lot about new things. In Isaiah 43:18-19, he prophesied, "Do not remember the former things, nor consider the things of old. Behold, I will do a new thing, now it shall spring forth; Shall you not know it? I will even make a road in the wilderness and rivers in the desert." That's encouraging because it suggests God makes a way out of no way.

Isaiah also prophesied about new things in Isaiah 48:6, "You have heard; See all this. And will you not declare it? I have made you hear new things from this time, even hidden things, and you did not know them." When we prophesy the new things, we cause what was hidden to an individual to become known——at least in part.

Many believers are stuck in a rut. They can't see the new thing. They want something new, but they are not hearing the voice of the living God sharing His heart and His plans with them. One prophetic word can unveil God's direction for the next season. One prophetic utterance can announce the new thing God wants to do in someone's life. And that can make all the difference.

Pray in the Spirit and ask the Lord to show you the new thing He wants to do, or the next thing God wants to bring you or someone else into. Pray with as much detail as you can, including people, timings and what it will take to step into the new thing God has prepared.

— *Prayer* —

Father, in the name of Jesus, help me see the new thing You want to do in my life as I pray. Help me see the new things You want to do in my family, my city, my nation—and those for whom You've called me to intercede.

ABOUT JENNIFER LECLAIRE

Jennifer LeClaire is senior leader of Awakening House of Prayer in Fort Lauderdale, Florida, founder of the Ignite Network, and founder of the Awakening Prayer Hubs prayer movement. Jennifer formerly served as the first-ever female editor of *Charisma* magazine and is a prolific author of over 50 books. You can find Jennifer online at www.jenniferleclaire.org. Get equipped at School of the Spirit at www.schoolofthespirit.tv.

Visit her South Florida church at www.awakeninghouseofprayer.com.

JOIN THE PRAYER MOVEMENT

Awakening Prayer Hubs is a prayer movement with a heart to see souls saved, and revival and awakening in the nations. We have hundreds of prayer hubs in dozens of nations. Our prayer hub leaders are equipped and resourced to succeed as prayer furnaces in their cities. Launch a hub, join a hub or sponsor a hub at www.awakeningprayerhubs.com.

GET EQUIPPED FOR THE CALL

At School of the Spirit, you'll find an in-depth selection of courses on prayer, spiritual warfare, deliverance and prophetic ministry, creative arts, Christian living and more. There's never been a better time to invest in yourself. Go deeper into the things of God with me and students from all over the world. Get equipped at www.schoolofthespirit.tv.